Orange County—1752-1952

Edited by

HUGH LEFLER AND PAUL WAGER

Authors

George P. Vuchan
Douglas L. Rights
Ruth Blackwelder
Hugh T. Lefler
Hugh F. Rankin
Blackwell Robinson
Elmer L. Puryear
Fletcher M. Green

J. G. de R. Hamilton
Phillips Russell
Edgar W. Knight
Robert B. House
Sylvester Green
Paul W. Wager
L. J. Phipps
Wallace E. Caldwell

William S. Powell

Chapel Hill
1953

This volume was reproduced from
a 1953 edition located in the
Publishers's private library
Greenville, South Carolina

Please direct ALL correspondence and book orders to:
**Southern Historical Press, Inc.
PO Box 1267
375 West Broad Street
Greenville, SC 29602-1267
www.southernhistoricalpress.com**

Originally printed: Chapel Hill, N.C.
Reprinted by: Southern Historical Press, Inc.
                         Greenvill, SC   29601
ISBN 978-0-89308-805-7
Printed in the United States of America

Contents

PREFACE	vii
MAP OF ORANGE COUNTY	xii
CHAPTER I	1
Physical Characteristics	
CHAPTER II	10
The American Indian in Orange County	
CHAPTER III	14
Settlement and Early History	
CHAPTER IV	24
Orange County and the War of the Regulation	
CHAPTER V	41
Orange County in the Era of the American Revolution	
CHAPTER VI	68
The Founding of the University of North Carolina	
CHAPTER VII	83
Orange County Politics, 1789-1860	
CHAPTER VIII	95
Slavery in Orange County	
PICTURE SECTION	Following page 96
CHAPTER IX	107
War and Reconstruction in Orange County	
CHAPTER X	124
Periodicals and Editors in Orange County	
CHAPTER XI	130
Education in Orange County	
CHAPTER XII	147
The University of North Carolina in Chapel Hill	
CHAPTER XIII	157
Orange County's Contributions to Medical Progress	

CHAPTER XIV 166
    History of the County Government

PICTURE SECTION .... Following page 192

CHAPTER XV 228
    Agriculture and Rural Life

CHAPTER XVI 265
    Industry, Past and Present

CHAPTER XVII 288
    The Churches of Orange County

CHAPTER XVIII 318
    Fraternal Orders in Orange County

PICTURE SECTION .... Following page 320

CHAPTER XIX 322
    Dictionary of Orange County Biography

CHAPTER XX 341
    Appendices

PREFACE

To have allowed the two hundredth anniversary of Orange county to pass without a memorial volume would have been unworthy of the citizenry of a county with such an illustrious history. Yet, as the time for the observance of the anniversary drew near, it was recognized that there was no single historian available with time to do the necessary research and write the text. The only alternative was to distribute the work among several people, and that is the course which was followed. All of the persons who were persuaded to write chapters were busy people but they were willing take on an extra assignment to help achieve such a worthy purpose. Each deserves and is hereby accorded our sincere thanks, both for responding so graciously to the appeal and for writing, under pressure of time, a chapter of such high quality. The experience has been a wonderful demonstration of what can be achieved through community spirit and cooperative effort.

It cannot be claimed that this volume is a definitive history of Orange county. Such a history remains to be written, and ought to be written. Indeed, the enterprise should not be too long deferred, for sources become lost or dimmed with the passage of time. When the writing of such a history is undertaken, the present volume should be of great usefulness. Naturally its usefulness for research purposes would be greater were there copious footnotes, particularly those citing sources. But, after reflection, it was decided to write a book for general readers, fully mindful of what was being sacrificed in the way of aid to research. It will be noted, however, that the text itself often gives the source, generally if not minutely.

A further reason for deciding in favor of a popular, rather than a carefully documented, volume was lack of time to verify all the facts and dates given. Many cannot be verified from any known source, though a careful historian, in combing fugitive materials, is likely to stumble upon evidence that fills a gap in a broken record or corroborates an unconfirmed assumption. While all the contributors to this book have been painstaking and have refrained from resorting to inference, they have necessarily introduced many statements of fact based on a single source of evidence. The future historian must therefore be warned not to accept every fact and every date given as absolutely reliable. There are undoubtedly numerous errors, but it is to be hoped that most of them are slight ones. There are also omissions, which we regret, but time did not permit a more comprehensive undertaking.

Admitting its shortcomings, the editors consider the work one of which Orange county citizens may be proud. It brings within the covers of one book a wealth of information and a lot of history. Two hundred years is a long sweep of time, and not all the significant events, nor all the characters who figured prominently in them, have been given adequate treatment. Yet, this "sketch book," written by nearly a score of authors, has succeeded amazingly well, we think, in presenting an unbroken history and in capturing much of the spirit of each period.

While each contributor deserves high praise, personal mention will be made here of only one—and that for the reason that it was his last literary effort. Shortly after finishing the chapter which he, though ill, had generously consented to write for this anniversary volume, death came to Dr. Edgar W. Knight. Providence decreed that the country's greatest educational historian should pen his last article on the history of education in his own county. Present and future citizens of Orange county will be more appreciative of their educational heritage because of his illuminating appraisal of that heritage.

The contributors to this volume are far more numerous than those whose names appear as authors. Each author pressed others into service—gathering facts, verifying dates, or helping in other ways. To attempt to list these willing helpers would almost certainly result in some oversights; hence it seems best to let them, with a very few exceptions, remain anonymous. They were glad to contribute to a civic enterprise, yet they deserve and have our profound gratitude.

Personal mention should be made, however, of a few contributors or cooperators, either because they are not citizens of the county or for other special reasons. Among these are Professor Algie I. Newlin, of Guilford College, who wrote the section dealing with the Quakers in the chapter on churches. Valuable assistance in assembling data for this same chapter was rendered by Jesse T. Nettles, Jr., a student of history at the University. The portion of the chapter on agriculture dealing with the Farmers Home Administration was prepared by Walter T. McPherson, the local representative of this federal agency. The section on public health in the chapter on government was written by Dr. W. P. Richardson.

Much of the material in the chapter on agriculture and some of the material used in other chapters had been assembled by Mr. Wager over a period of years by reason of a grant from the General Education Board. Originally collected for use in a different type of county study, it was decided to make it available for inclusion in this volume. Grateful acknowledgement is hereby made to the General Education Board for the somewhat fortuitous but nonetheless substantial contribution which it has made to this county history. Recognition is also given to the Institute for Research in Social Science at the University of North Carolina for its indirect contribution, several of the authors being or having been on the Institute staff. Miss Blackwelder has specifically requested that it be recorded that her chapter is a direct product of Institute stimulation and support. Special thanks are due to Rev. Samuel T. Habel for the valuable assistance given in preparing the chapter on churches, to Hugh F. Rankin for the great amount of help given in reading proof and in preparing the index, and to Miss Dena Neville for a vast amount of secretarial assistance freely and gladly rendered.

This book was conceived, written and published in a period of about ten months. Such an accomplishment would have been impossible without the fine spirit of cooperation everywhere evidenced. The goal still would not have been attained had not the printer waived every rule of the trade. We were permitted to deliver the chapters as they were completed—even before they were completed—adding to and editing the galley sheets. Half of the book had been printed when the last chapter was handed in. For the patience, forbearance, and untiring aid of Mr. and Mrs. William Pugh of the Orange Printshop, we are supremely indebted.

Preface

We want to extend our thanks to the many people who uncovered and made available to us the many fine illustrations which so enrich the volume. Finally, we would recognize and pay tribute to L. J. Phipps, chairman of the bi-centennial committee, who, more than anyone else, conceived the book, worked assiduously on it, and assumed responsibility for its publication.

It has been a pleasure to help get out this historical record as a part of Orange county's observance of its two hundredth birthday. If it is read and enjoyed by the people of the county and others over the state and nation whose forebears have lived here, all who have participated in its publication will feel amply rewarded.

HUGH T. LEFLER
PAUL W. WAGER

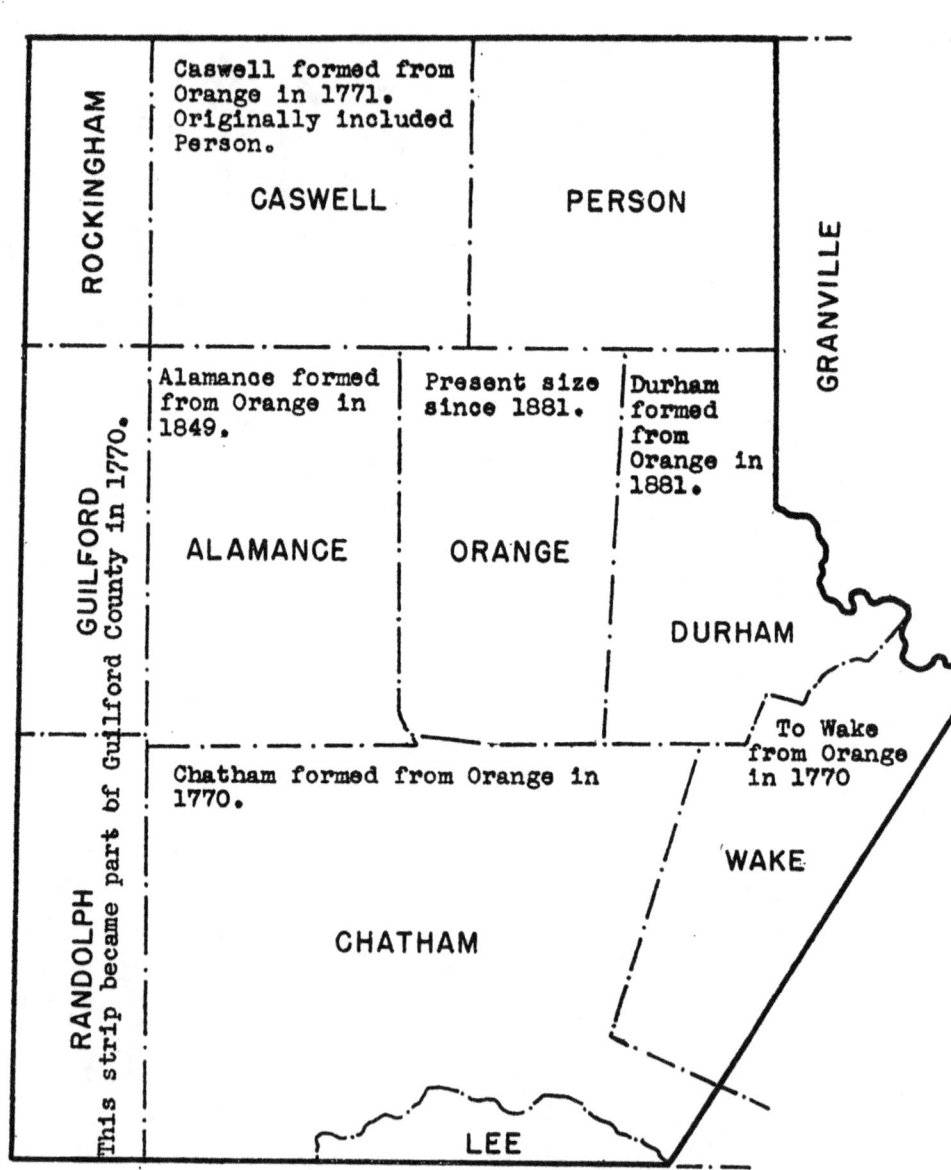

CHAPTER I

PHYSICAL CHARACTERISTICS

By GEORGE P. VUCHAN

Teacher, Thompson Public School, Raleigh, N. C.

[*An adaptation of a chapter from* An Atlas for Orange County, North Carolina. *A Master's thesis in Sociology presented at the University of North Carolina, 1948*]

Orange county today is but a small part of the vast area which it once embraced. Successive partitions have reduced it to about one-tenth of its original size. Its present area is 398 square miles or about 254,720 acres. The county has an average width of 14 miles, the eastern and western boundaries being nearly straight lines, but converging slightly to the south. The length of the county from north to south is 28 miles. The county is crossed by the 36° parallel north latitude and the 70° west meridian.

Topographically, Orange county is typical of the Piedmont. An excellent description is found in the Soil Survey of Orange County, made by E. S. Vanatta in 1918 and published in 1921:

> The prevailing topography is that of a gently rolling upland or peneplain, with an elevation varying from 500 to 600 feet over the greater part of the county where the underlying rocks are hard, and from 250 to 400 feet in the southeastern corner, underlain by the Triassic rocks . . . and its surface slopes from the northwest toward the east and southeast. The county includes three fairly distinct topographic divisions, which conform with the character of the underlying rock formations and the results of stream action, the latter being a powerful factor in producing the uneven surface features. These subdivisions are recognized as follows: (1) a broad belt of gently rolling to strongly rolling country occupying the greater part of the county, and underlain by slate; (2) rolling, broken, and steep areas occurring as belts in the northwestern and southern parts, and in numerous smaller areas throughout the county, representing the areas underlain by granite; and (3) a small area of low-lying, undulating to gently rolling country, underlain by Triassic rocks, occurring in the extreme southeast corner of the county and known as the arm of the sea. . .

> The bottom lands in Orange county are generally narrow and inextensive, especially through the granite and slate belts ... The bottom lands through the Triassic belt in the southeastern corner of the county (the softest and most easily weathered rock material in the county) are moderately extensive, but even these are in many places cut off by dikes of harder rocks.

Though the general elevation of the county varies from 250 to about 600 feet, Couch, Blackwood, Bald, Crawford and Occoneechee Mountains and Mount Collier have a greater altitude. The Occoneechee Mountains, near Hillsboro, which have an elevation of 830 feet above sea level, are the highest in the county. Hillsboro has an elevation of 548 feet.

SOILS

Orange county was fortunate in having had a soil survey made as early as 1918. The United States Department of Agriculture in conjunction with the North Carolina Department of Agriculture completed the survey during the field season of 1918. The greater part of the data herein presented will be from the report of this survey.

Although there are twenty-three soil types listed in Orange county, these all can be included in three major groups: heavy red soils, gray to red, silt or floury-textured soils, and light-colored sandy surface soils. Table I lists all the soils and their relative extent.

From the table it can be seen that approximately two-thirds of the county is included in the first four soil types listed. Due to their predominance, these are, therefore, the chief soils with which the farmers must work.

With twenty-nine per cent of the county covered by Georgeville silt loam it should be described in some detail:

> The Georgeville silt loam consists of a light grayish brown to light reddish brown silt loam underlain at a depth of 6 to 10 inches by a bright-red, compact, friable silty clay to clay. The surface soil dries out in many places to a yellowish-red color. Small fragments of slate rock frequently occur through the soil and over the surface, and occasionally quartz and fragments of basic rocks. In general, the organic content of the soil is low, and it is inclined to pack after the summer rains.

TABLE I
PERCENTAGE OF DIFFERENT SOILS IN ORANGE COUNTY

Soil	Percent
Georgeville silt loam	29.0
Davidson clay loam	21.4
Conowingo silt loam	10.4
Alamance silt loam	5.7
Georgeville stony silt loam	3.6
Wilkes coarse sandy loam	3.2
Durham coarse sandy loam	3.2
Appling sandy loam	3.1
Wilkes sandy loam	3.0
Iredell loam	2.6
Congaree silt loam	2.5
Durham sandy loam	2.5
Cecil sandy loam	1.9
White Stone fine sandy loam	1.5
Georgeville gravelly silt loam	1.5
Durham fine sandy loam	1.1
Appling stony sandy loam	.9
Appling fine sandy loam	.8
Appling coarse sandy loam	.6
Iredell stony loam	.5
Cecil clay loam	.4
Cecil stony loam	.4
Granville fine stony loam	.2

Source: E. S. Vanatta, *Soil Survey of Orange County, North Carolina* (Washington, D. C.: U. S. Department of Agriculture, 1921), p. 19

    This is the most extensive soil type in the county. It is found throughout the slate belt, which covers the central part of the county and occupies approximately 80 per cent of this belt. The topography is undulating along the ridge crests and gently rolling to rolling along the stream slopes. Very little of this type is so rolling or broken as to curtail its adaptation to the clean-cultivated crops when properly terraced, although occasional areas, especially along the larger stream slopes, may be too rough for cultivation. Drainage is everywhere thorough.
    The Georgeville silt loam is an important soil, probably 40 per cent of it being in cultivation. . . .This soil is primarily adapted to grains and grasses . . .It is low in organic matter and washes readily, as is evidenced by the numerous abandoned gullied fields now in cultivation.

The Davidson clay loam soil covers a bit more than a fifth of the county, so it and the Georgeville silt loam together make up 50 per cent of the county. Quoting again from the *Soil Survey*:

> The Davidson clay loam to a depth of 6 to 12 inches consists of a dark brown or reddish-brown to dull red, heavy loam to clay loam, underlain by a dull-red or maroon-red, smooth, friable clay. The deeper, more loamy, and more brownish soil occurs in the wooded areas, while over the cultivated fields, more or less affected by erosion, the surface soil is shallower, heavier and redder. A lack of quartz grains through the subsoil results in a characteristic smooth, velvety feel in this section of the three-foot profile. . . . .
>
> The Davidson clay loam is of considerable agricultural importance, owing to its large extent and its excellent adaptation to the general farm crops of corn, wheat, oats, and the various legumes.
>
> The type occurs through the central part of the county, generally along stream slopes. Its topography varies from gently rolling to rolling. . . . .
>
> The Davidson clay loam is naturally strong and productive and may be easily brought into a highly productive condition.

The soil third in importance because of its quantity is Conowingo silt loam. It is found in a little more than ten per cent of the county, chiefly in the slate belt and in association with Alamance silt loam. It is primarily utilized for grain production. According to Vanatta:

> The Conowingo silt loam consists of a light-gray to almost white, floury silt loam extending to a depth of 5 to 8 inches, where it passes through a pale yellow compact silt loam to silty clay loam slightly streaked with gray. This extends to a depth of 14 to 20 inches below the surface. The subsoil is tough, plastic, yellowish-brown to greenish-brown clay. . . . .Small iron stains and concretions frequently occur throughout the soil section, especially in the larger and more nearly level areas of the type. Small gravel, composed of slate and quartz fragments, frequently occur on the surface and through the soil, though rarely in quantities sufficient to influence the soil character. The organic content of the soil is low, and cultivated fields are likely to pack and bake after rains. . . . .
>
> The topography is level to undulating and in places rolling, and drainage is poor, especially through the more nearly level tracts, where water stands on the surface for some time after rainy periods and leaves the soil in a cold, water-logged condition during the winter and spring months. . . . .Owing to the impervious

character of the subsoil, the surface drainage in the rolling areas is at times excessive, resulting in serious erosion.

The fourth most common type of soil, extending over 5.7 per cent of the county's area, is Alamance silt loam. It is found mostly in the Buckhorn vicinity and in the southwestern part of the county. A high percentage of this soil is in cultivation because of its favorable topography, it being undulating to gently rolling. Concerning the composition we find:

> The surface soil of the Alamance silt loam is a light-gray to almost white, floury silt loam passing at 3 to 5 inches into a pale-yellow silt loam which extends to a depth of 8 or 10 inches. The subsoil is a yellow, compact, friable silty clay frequently mottled with gray in the lower part of the 3-foot section. Small fragments of slate and quartz occasionally occur on the surface and throughout the soil, but rarely in sufficient quantities to affect its handling qualities. . . . .The organic content of the soil is low, and this deficiency, together with its fine texture, causes the soil to pack badly following the summer rains, makes crops liable to damage from drought, and induces destructive erosion on the slopes.

The remaining third of the soil is divided into 19 types, ranging from 3.6 per cent for the Georgeville stony silt loam to .2 per cent for the Granville fine sandy loam. The Georgeville stony silt loam is found on the larger hills and on the rougher stream slopes in the slate region and is not suited for agriculture to any degree. If any one generalization could be applied to the soils of Orange county it would be that they are lacking in organic matter although many of the soils respond to fertilization without difficulty.

The soils of the Durham, Appling, White Stone, and Granville series that have good drainage are almost perfectly adapted to the raising of bright tobacco. The entire series does not quite cover 14 per cent of the soils but, because of its cash crop product, the group is important out of all proportion to its size. This series can be found throughout the county and is scattered, but most commonly the Durham group is found in the northwestern section and the Appling in the southern end, as are the Granville and White Stone soils.

Drainage and Streams

Orange county is drained in a general easterly and southeasterly direction, lying in two river basins: the Cape Fear and the Neuse. In the northeastern section the Eno and the north branch of Little river, with their tributaries, drain that part of the county into the Neuse river. The Eno is the largest stream in the county. New Hope and Morgan creeks drain the eastern and southeastern sections of Orange into the Cape Fear river, while Haw river and Cane (originally Cain) creek drain the western and southwestern area into the Cape Fear, also.

Nowhere in the county can there be found any large upland regions without sufficient natural drainage. In a few places there are flat areas that drain poorly, but the opposite condition of too rapid a flow is more often discernible. Rapid currents are general on the streams and for the most part they have a good fall, enabling them to be utilized for water power.

In recent years many farmers throughout the county have built ponds and small lakes upon their lands, but there are no natural lakes of any consequence in Orange county. University lake, the largest body of water in the county, covers approximately 220 acres and has a capacity of about 600 million gallons. The lake was constructed in 1932 to furnish the municipal water supply for Chapel Hill, Carrboro, and the University of North Carolina. The dam is located two miles southwest of Chapel Hill.

Hogan's lake, covering approximately 17 acres, and Eastwood or "Grandma's" lake, having an approximate surface area of 65 acres, are two other sizable bodies of water. A smaller lake of about 15 acres is located on the Lucas farm, south of Hillsboro. In addition to the lakes mentioned, there are approximately 100 acres in farm ponds throughout the county.

Climate

The climatic conditions of Orange county are not unlike the average conditions for the Piedmont. The cold waves that reach Orange county in the winter months are subdued and modified by the mountains to the west. The greater part of the snow in

Orange is due to the storms along the coasts which are often accompanied by north or northeast winds. And like most of the Piedmont, the greater part of the summer precipitation in Orange county results from late afternoon and evening thunder showers.

Meteorological data for the county have been kept for over forty years and although the records have not been gathered in the center of the county—the station is located at Chapel Hill—there is no great variation within the county. The average temperature for January has been 41.2°F., while for July the average has been 78.8°F. The highest temperature ever recorded was 107°F. and the lowest was -6°F. The average date for the last killing frost in the spring is April 5 and November 1 is the average date for the first frost in the fall, thus giving 210 days in the growing season.

Erosion

Erosion has taken a heavy toll of soils over much of the county. This can be attributed to a number of factors—the undulating to strongly rolling topography, the susceptibility of certain soil types to washing, and the emphasis that has been placed on cotton, corn, tobacco and other row crops. In the course of one hundred and fifty years thousands of acres of worn out land have been abandoned. Left unprotected, such discarded lands are further damaged by erosion until reclaimed by pine trees. As a result many pine lands today are little more than subsoil and disintegrated rock material.

Not all depleted soils have acquired a forest cover. Most upland pasture consists of worn out crop land and, if the erosion has been severe, it is not readily converted into good pasture. The presence, however, of some upland pastures in excellent sod indicate the possibilities of this type of utilization.

Although the strips of alluvial soils are not subject to erosion, many of them have been damaged by a deposit of silt from the uplands. Flooding and silting of the bottomlands has been materially lessened when the run-off from the uplands was retarded by terraces and a vegetative cover.

Other things being equal, the severity and destructiveness of erosion tends to increase with the degree of slope. Most Piedmont soils are erodible if the slope exceeds two per cent, and only 8 per cent of the land in Orange county has a slope as gentle as 2 per cent. In fact the slope on 50 per cent of it exceeds 10 per cent, and many steep fields are in cultivation.

LAND CLASSIFIED BY SLOPE

Degree of Slope	Acres	Per cent of Total
0 to 2 per cent	19,968	8
2 to 7 per cent	66,400	25
7 to 10 per cent	42,432	17
10 to 14 per cent	57,408	23
14 to 25 per cent	52,416	21
Over 25 per cent	14,976	6
	253,600	100

FOREST CONDITION

The Forest Resource Appraisal of North Carolina of 1945, in sampling and describing forest conditions in the Piedmont, provides a reasonably accurate picture of the situation in Orange county. We quote.

> The Piedmont shows an increase in under-sawlog pine. This is a temporary condition. It is apparent that pine is to be succeeded by hardwoods in this region. . .Hardwoods grow up under pines and eventually take over the ground. The climax type is hardwoods; establishment of pine stands is due to happenings which temporarily upset the natural scheme of plant succession. An opening is created by an unnatural disturbance. From scattered pines that have always been present on dry ridges, if nowhere else, winged seeds invade and stock the opening. . . .At least half of the Piedmont forest has been under the plow at one time or another during the last 150 years. High-yielding stands of pine grew up in the fields that were constantly being abandoned. By the time earlier old field stands have been cut one, two, or three times, the oaks, hickories and other hardwoods have taken possession.
> If the agricultural practice of a county still features the cycle of land clearing and abandonment, that county will continue to have stands of pine. . .However, farm leaders are successfully working to end this primitive type of farming. Soil conservation practices will enable good lands to stay productive, so they will

not be abandoned; therefore this time - honored cycle can not be depended upon indefinitely to renew the source of pine timber. Whether foresters can develop practical means of keeping pine in the Piedmont remains to be seen. Probably it can be done if landowners can be persuaded to expend the necessary effort.

Chapter II

THE AMERICAN INDIAN IN ORANGE COUNTY

By Douglas L. Rights

President Wachovia Historical Society
Author, The American Indian in North Carolina

Signs of the American Indian have been noted throughout the area of present Orange county.

Although no deep deposits of camp or village refuse have been found to indicate habitation of the Indians for a long period of time before their history is recorded, the mild climate, numerous streams, and extensive forest land furnished an inviting location that must have attracted early inhabitants.

In the neighborhood of Chapel Hill the Indians left evidence of their occupation. On the Mason Farm, along the Raleigh road just beyond Chapel Hill, 150 whole arrowheads were found one afternoon in a cotton patch. Associated were unfinished arrowheads, stone tools for their manufacure, and flint chips. The Indian arrowheads were donated to the Museum of Geology at the University of North Carolina.

A burial ground was reported along the creek nearby, where former possessions of Indians were found, including white trade beads. Sand from this site was hauled away and used in making mortar for the building of dormitories at the University.

Morgan's creek flowed through outcrops of stone used for making arrowheads, described by Professor Collier Cobb, Sr., as igneous sheared slate.

When the curtain rose for the drama of history to begin, the land that is now Orange county was occupied by small tribes of Siouan origin.

The Great Trading Path from Virginia to the Catawba nation led through the region of present Hillsboro and Mebane to Haw river.

The first description of this famous Indian trail was given by John Lederer, a German doctor, in June, 1670. He told of his visit to the Eno Indians along the Eno river near present Hillsboro. His narrative reads:

> The country here, by the industry of these Indians, is very open and clear of wood. Their town is built round a field, where in their sports they exercise with so much labour and violence, and in so great numbers, that I have seen the ground wet with sweat that dropped from their bodies: their chief recreation is slinging of stones. They are of mean stature and courage, covetous and thievish, industrious to earn a penny; and therefore hire themselves out to their neighbours, who employ them as carryers or porters. They plant abundance of grain, reap three crops in a summer, and out of their granary supply all the adjacent parts. These and the mountain-Indians build not their houses of bark, but of watling and plaister. . . . .Some houses they have of reed or bark; they build them generally round: to each house belongs a little hovel made like an oven, where they lay up their corn and mast, and keep it dry. They parch their nuts and acorns over the fire, to take away their rank oyliness; which afterwards pressed, yield a milky liquor, and the acorns an amber-colour'd oyl. In these, mingled together, they dip their cakes at great entertainments, and so serve them up to their guests as an extraordinary dainty. Their government is democratick; and the sentences of their old men are received as laws, or rather oracles, by them.

More than two centuries later this comment was written:

> Not far from Eno Town the young braves of North Carolina and Duke universities still carry on their ball play with much labour and violence, the government of the country is still Democratic, and the three crops a year are possible for farmers who space their corn plantings properly.

Fourteen miles west-southwest Lederer found the Shackory Indians dwelling upon a rich soil. These seem to tally with the Shakori (Shoccoree), or Saxapahaw, sometimes called Sissipihaw, dwelling on Haw river in the neighborhood of Haw fields.

Another traveler, John Lawson, came along the trading path from the south in 1701. The trail was followed across "three Great Rivers," identified as Little and Big Alamance rivers and Haw river. The Haw river ford, which was crossed "with great Difficulty, (by God's Assistance)," was in the neighborhood of the present village of Swepsonville, and bordered lands which Lawson described as "extraordinary Rich."

As he traveled through Haw Fields, he met a trading caravan of thirty horses led by several horsemen. The leader, a man named Massey, from Leeds in Yorkshire, England, advised Lawson to secure Eno-Will, a faithful Indian guide, who was to be found at one of the villages in the Occoneechee neighborhood. This Indian was a Shakori by birth, whose people had been met by Lederer at Haw river and who had since joined the Eno and another tribe known as Adshusheer.

The Occoneechee Indians had fled from their island home at the confluence of Dan and Staunton rivers and were then in the region of the Eno river, where they left their name in the "Occoneechee Hills," not far from present Hillsboro. An archaeological report of a survey and excavation in this area, conducted under the auspices of the Archaeological Society of North Carolina, is given by Joffre L. Coe in his study, "The Cultural Sequence of the Carolina Piedmont," printed in *Archaeology of Eastern United States*, edited by James B. Griffin, published by the University of Chicago Press, 1952.

The Occoneechee (Occaneechee) Indians provided Lawson with a feast of "good fat Bear, and Venison." The Indians' cabins, or lodges, were festooned with dried bear and deer meat, "a good sort of Tapestry," which caused Lawson to declare that the Indians possessed "the Flower of Carolina; the English enjoying only the Fag-end of that fine Country."

Eno-Will agreed to guide Lawson to eastern Carolina. A halt was made at Eno town, located on a "Pretty Rivulet" fourteen miles east of the Occoneechee, and northwest of the present city of Durham. Here Lawson wrote this character sketch of his Indian friend:

> Our Guide and Landlord, Enoe-Will, was of the best and most agreeable Temper that I ever met with in an Indian, being always ready to serve the English, not out of Gain, but real Affection; which makes him apprehensive of being poisoned by some wicked Indians, and was therefore very earnest with me, to promise him to avenge his Death if it should so happen. He brought some of his chief Men into his Cabin, and two of them having a Drum and Rattle, sung by us as we lay in Bed, and struck up their Music to serenade and welcome us to their Town. And though at last, we fell asleep, yet they continued their Concert till Morning.

Soon after this visit of John Lawson, the Siouan tribes of the Piedmont departed for eastern Carolina. Apparently all of the Indians in the region later included in Orange county had disappeared by the time white settlement of the area began.

CHAPTER III

SETTLEMENT AND EARLY HISTORY

By RUTH BLACKWELDER

Associate Professor of History, Lenoir Rhyne College

Former Research Assistant in the Institute for Research in Social Science, University of North Carolina.

In 1740 only a few white families were scattered along the Hico (Hyco), the Eno, and the Haw rivers in the area that became Orange county. There were not twenty taxables in that region in 1748, but by 1751 Governor Gabriel Johnston reported that settlers were "flocking in," mostly from Pennsylvania. Alexander Mebane, Orange county's first sheriff, returned 1,113 tithables for the years 1752 and 1753, a figure which would indicate a total population of approximately 4,000 when the county was formed in 1752. By 1767 Orange had the largest population of any county in North Carolina.

The great migration from Pennsylvania to Piedmont Carolina came in the middle of the eighteenth century. Scotch-Irish and German immigrants, finding the price of land too high for them in Pennsylvania, journeyed southward along the "Great Wagon Road" through the Shenandoah valley to Carolina. From 1745 to 1760 land was granted along the many creeks and rivers in every part of Orange county. Grants on New Hope creek are recorded for Bladen county as early as 1745 and along Deep river in 1749. According to the records for Granville county there were land grants in northern Orange on the Hico river in 1748 and along the Dan river and the Hogan and County Line creeks in 1751. In central Orange grants on the Eno river were entered for the year 1751.

The Eno community, about seven miles north of Hillsboro, was the most distinctly Scotch-Irish settlement in the county. Scotch-Irish also lived east of the Haw river. One of the largest landowners in that area was Samuel Strudwick, an Englishman, who was granted land in the Haw Fields (Hawfields) to satisfy a debt which Governor George Burrington owed his father. William Blackwood's grant on Buffalo creek was entered in the land grant office in 1752; Gilbert Strayhorn's on Prestwood creek in 1755. Alexander Mebane, the first sheriff of the county, owned land along Cain creek in 1756 and James Hunter on Stinking Quarter and Sandy creeks in 1757. James Stockard's land was in the Back Creek section and William Montgomery's was on the Buckhorn. Marmaduke Kimbrough, who built the first courthouse for Orange county, entered his 640 acres on Pole Cat creek in 1752.

There were Scotch-Irish in eastern Orange—in the Little river and New Hope creek sections. Mark Morgan secured a land grant in the New Hope area as early as 1747, William Craig and Richard Caswell in 1756. Hogans, Blackwoods and Freelands also settled in that area. Charles White located in what is now Chatham county. The Scotch-Irish in what is now Guilford county organized Buffalo Presbyterian church in 1756. Although Cumberland county was the especial home of the Scotch Highlander, Highlanders also built homes in southern Orange, in what is now Chatham county.

Germans held the land west of the Haw river. The pioneers in that group were Lutherans. Ludwig Clapp's grant of 640 acres on the Alamance was recorded in 1752. Michael Holt's large acreage lay along the Great and Little Alamance. John Faust had land on Cain creek and Adam Trolinger on the west bank of the Haw river, near the present railway crossing. Among the pioneer Germans were Christian Faust, Jacob Albright, Peter Sharp, Philip Snotherly and David Ephland (Efland). By 1773 there were so many Germans in western Orange that J. F. D. Smyth, an English traveler, experienced difficulty in finding anyone who understood his language in some areas west of Hillsboro.

There were other distinct settlements in Orange county. English emigrants from Virginia settled in northern Orange along the Hico river and County Line creek. "South Ireland" near Stoney creek, in present Alamance county, indicates the Irish element. Thomas Lloyd, one of the first representatives from Orange county to the general assembly, was foremost among the

Welsh who built homes between Hillsboro and present Chatham county. His grant on Mark creek was entered in 1757.

Quakers constituted a considerable portion of the early population of Orange county. There were 950 white taxables in 1755 but there were only 490 on the militia list, which may be explained by the fact that many Quakers were pacifists. Quakers settled north of Hillsboro but they were most numerous in the Cain creek and the Stinking Quarter creek areas, in present Alamance, Chatham and Randolph counties. Jonathan Lindley of the Cain creek section and William Courtney of Hillsboro were prominent pioneers of the Quaker faith.

From its beginning Orange county was the home of farmers or yeoman. From 1752 to 1800, more than 75 per cent of the property holders owned between 100 and 500 acres of land; approximately 5 per cent held less than 100 acres, and only 5 per cent had 1,000 acres or more. John Morgan returned 9,049 acres in 1781. James Williams owned 16,320 acres in 1785 but only 6,243 acres were in Orange county. According to the United States Census of 1790, only 55 citizens of Orange owned more than 1,000 acres. The three largest landowners in 1800 were William Cain who had 4,417 acres, Richard Bennehan with 4,065 acres, and William Strudwick with 4,000. By the Census of 1860 the landholding ratio was as follows:

Less than 50 acres	45 per cent
50 to 100 acres	32 per cent
100 to 500 acres	21 per cent
1,000 acres or more	about 1 per cent

At no time did slaves constitute more than 31 per cent of the total population of the county. In 1755 only 8 per cent of the families owned slaves and the largest slaveholder, Mark Morgan, had only 6 slaves. By 1780 only 3 per cent of the masters owned 20 or more slaves; 95 per cent owned less than ten. By 1860, 48 per cent of the landowners had slaves, but 21 per cent had only one slave; only 7 per cent had 20 or more. The largest slaveholders by the Census of 1860 were Henry Whitted who had 78 slaves and 9 slave houses, Paul Cameron with 98 slaves and 25 slave houses, and I. N. Patterson with 106 slaves and 20 slave houses.

COUNTY ORGANIZATION

Orange county and the parish of St. Matthew were formed in 1752 from the western portions of Granville, Johnston and Bladen counties. The organization came twenty-three years after the crown purchased the Carolinas from the lords proprietors and two years before the outbreak of the French and Indian War. Phenomenal growth in population between 1740 and 1752, made a new county a necessity. It was organized for convenience of the new inhabitants, to shorten their travel over poor roads, to make it easier for them to get to their county seat. The county lay in Lord Granville's district and was named to honor William III of the House of Orange, who ruled England from 1689 to 1702.

At the time of its organization, Orange was bounded on the north by the colony of Virginia, on the south by Lord Granville's line, 35° 34', and on the east by Granville, Johnston and Bladen counties. After the creation of Rowan in 1753, Orange had a definite western boundary. By act of the general assembly of North Carolina in 1752, the eastern boundary of Orange extended from the Virginia line, near Hico creek,

> to the Bend of Eno river, below the Occanechas, near to the Plantation where John Williams now dwelleth; thence down the South side of Eno River, to Neuse River; thence to the Mouth of Horse Creek; thence a direct line to the Place where Earl Granville's Line crosses Cape Fear River; thence along the said Line, to the Eastern Bounds of Anson County.

There have been many subtractions from Orange county. Originally it included the present counties of Orange, Chatham, Caswell, Person, and Alamance and also portions of Wake, Guilford, Randolph, Rockingham, Durham, and Lee. Segments of Orange, Johnston and Cumberland were united to form Wake county in 1771, for a new county would make it easier for the inhabitants to attend the courts, general musters, and other public meetings. Governor Tryon explained in a letter to the Earl of Hillsborough that Guilford county was formed in 1770 from Orange and Rowan in order to separate the "Insurgents" during the government's trouble with the Regulators. The eastern portion of Rockingham county, which was established in 1785, was originally Orange territory.

Chatham county was carved from southern Orange in 1771, during the Regulator uprising, to encourage its inhabitants in their "public duties," with its northern boundary sixteen miles south of Hillsboro. Randolph, established in 1779, included part of Chatham county which was originally Orange territory. As early as 1770 the inhabitants of northern Orange petitioned the general assembly for a new county because they found attendance at the general musters and courts "very burdensome," but the organization of Caswell was postponed until 1777. The dividing line between Orange and Caswell ran twelve miles north of Hillsboro. Eastern Caswell was organized as Person county in 1792.

For more than a decade there were citizens who tried to form a new county in western Orange. Their proposal was overwhelmingly defeated in a county referendum in 1836. In public meetings, the proponents emphasized the fact that western Orange had industries; whereas eastern Orange was an agricultural area. Political leaders in eastern Orange contended that a large county insured greater justice in the courts since jurors were less likely to know the parties concerned. The *Hillsborough Recorder* of September 6, 1838, insisted that Orange was too large "to be influenced by large and wealthy families, by town influences, corporation influences, or any other influence except the public good." It further argued that the large county would have a low tax rate because it had a large number of taxpayers. After securing the approval of the state legislature and a favorable county referendum, the vote being 1,257 to 1,001, Alamance county was established in 1849. The dividing line between Orange and Alamance ran nine miles west of Hillsboro. On June 4, 1849, the first Court of Pleas and Quarter Sessions of Alamance county convened in Providence meeting house.

One more loss in territory and population came to Orange county. Following the Civil War, Hillsboro landowners gave little encouragement to the tobacco industry which had been started in Hillsboro and Durham. Its monopoly by Durham and the carving of a new county—Durham county—from Orange and Wake in 1881 left Orange economically poor but with a glorious yesterday. This was the result of a favorable vote in a popular referendum in the townships that were to be incorporated into the new county—Durham, Patterson, Lebanon and Mangum. The two townships of Wake county that voted to yield land to Durham sought relief from a heavy county debt.

These many subtractions left Orange a small county, **an area of 398 square miles**. Today Orange is bounded on the north by Caswell and Person, on the south by Chatham, on the west by Alamance, and on the east by Durham.

The Court of Pleas and Quarter Sessions of Orange county held its first session at the home of John Gray near the Eno river, September 9, 1752, with eight Justices of the Peace present. The members of that court voted to build a courthouse on the north side of the Haw river, within two miles of Piney Ford. Marmaduke Kimbrough was awarded the building contract and William Miers and John Sidwell were named as Kimbrough's security. According to the County court minutes, their contract called for a building "thirty two feet long, twenty two feet wide, and eleven feet thick, framed and weather boarded with feather edge plank and shingled Roof." The justices of the county met in December, 1752, on the site that was chosen for the courthouse, but it is improbable that a building was completed there. The organization of Rowan county in 1753 placed Piney Ford only fifteen miles from the western boundary of Orange.

The site of the present town of Hillsboro was chosen as the permanent county seat, where the old Trading Path crossed the Eno river, near the picturesque Occoneechee hills. William Churton in 1754 laid out four hundred acres as a town and commons, on land that had been granted to him that same year. The County court named James Watson, Josiah Dixon and Lawrence Thompson commissioners and trustees for the county seat which was known as Corbin Town, in honor of Francis Corbin, member of the governor's council and the Earl of Granville's land agent. The County court minutes of October, 1754, indicate that John Patterson as town treasurer was instructed to withhold "ten shillings sterling out of each lot to be applied to use of the publick." The General Assembly authorized the building of a courthouse in 1754. Corbin Town was incorporated as Childsburg in 1759, in honor of Dr. Thomas Child (Childs), Attorney-General of North Carolina, 1751-1760, and also the Earl of Granville's land agent. In 1766, the town's name was changed to Hillsborough to honor the Earl of Hillsborough, British Secretary of State for the Colonies. In 1770 it was recognized as a "borough" and thereafter was entitled to a representative in the House of Commons. It was really a pocket borough, created to counteract the influence of the two Regulators, Herman Husband and John Pryor, who had been elected from Orange county to the General Assembly in 1769.

Considerable growth was anticipated for Hillsboro because of its healthful and central location. In a letter to the Earl of Shelburne in 1767, Governor Tryon prophesied that Hillsboro would

> tend much towards the increase of the settlement of that part of the back country, as well as to civilize the inhabitants thereof. Its situation is upon a rich red clay soil ... distant from the Virginia Line twenty five miles. It lies almost centrical to the towns of Halifax and Salisbury being one hundred miles from each and is one hundred and sixty miles N. W. of Newbern and one hundred and ninety nearly north of Wilmington. Tho' there is at present scarce twenty families inhabitants [*sic*] I am of opinion it will be in the course of a few years the most considerable of any inland town in this province.

There have been four courthouses in Hillsboro. The first was ready for use in December, 1756. Prior to that date the County court held its sessions at the home of James Watson. In 1778 the legislature authorized the building of a district courthouse on the site of the first courthouse. Citizens of Orange, Granville, Wake, Chatham and Caswell counties paid taxes "to take care of the building costs." Nathaniel Rochester—who later founded a New York town by that name—and William Courtney announced in the *North Carolina Gazette,* June 26, 1778, that a contract would be let for a brick building; however a frame building may have been erected. After the district courthouse was destroyed by fire either late in 1789 or early 1790, the County court used a room at the home of John Taylor. The building of a third courthouse—second district courthouse—was authorized by the legislature in 1790. That body in 1799 permitted the County court to levy any tax that it deemed necessary for improvements on public buildings, provided the annual rate did not exceed six pence on each poll, two pence on every hundred acres of land, and six pence on every hundred pounds value of town property.

On September 7, 1844, the corner stone was laid for a fourth courthouse, a building which has now been used for more than a century. Members of the County court had talked about a new courthouse for almost twenty years. It was propaganda for the establishment of Alamance county that postponed the new building. Carrying out instructions from the County court, the new courthouse was built near the center of the public square in Hillsboro. Its cost was not to exceed eight thousand dollars, a sum which was to be paid within four years. According to the County Court minutes of February, 1844, the building committee consisted of Harrison Parker, Edwin Holt, Dr. O. F. Long, William Murray, Dr. Michael Holt, Cadwallader Jones, Sr., John M. Kirkland and Dr. James S. Smith. Captain John Berry was the architect and contractor for the brick building. In charge of the ceremony when the corner stone was laid were members of the Eagle Masonic Lodge of Hillsboro and the University Lodge of Chapel Hill. Dr. James S. Smith served as Deputy Grand Master for the occasion. The *Hillsborough Recorder*, September 12, 1844, gave the following report of the ceremonies:

> Under the stone were deposited the different species of the coin of the United States from one dollar to half a dime, a copy of the proceedings of the Grand Lodge, and a copy of the *Hillsborough Recorder*. The stone was firmly cemented; and according to ancient custom, corn, wine and oil were poured on it as symbols, and the ceremonies closed. The brethren of the lodge and the citizens then repaired to the old court house, a few yards distant, to hear the oration. The court house was, for the most part, filled with ladies, while the gentlemen who could not crowd in, occupied seats without the door. From a platform erected in the south door of the court house, the Rev. William M. Green then pronounced his oration . . . .
>
> From the court house, the citizens and masons repaired to the Masonic Hall, where an excellent dinner was served . . . by Richeson Nichols, esq. of which one hundred and thirty persons

partook. The dinner was on the temperance principle, and no excess marred the happiness and enjoyment of the social repast.

This last courthouse is an example of classical architecture with doric columns. Its cost exceeded the builder's contract by two thousand dollars, making its total cost ten thousand dollars. Dennis Heartt, as editor of the *Hillsborough Recorder*, was expressing the pride of the local citizens when he wrote in 1846 that the present courthouse "is not surpassed by any courthouse in the State; and . . . it is perhaps not surpassed in the Union." Editor Heartt was particularly proud that the architect and builder was a native of the county.

Twentieth-century visitors to Hillsboro are told the hour of the day by an eighteenth-century clock which hangs in the cupola of the courthouse. This clock has an interesting history though the identity of its donor is obscure. There are some who believe that it was a gift from George III; while others say that it was given by the Earl of Hillsborough through the influence of Edmund Fanning or Governor Tryon. According to tradition, parts of the clock were thrown in the Eno river in 1781 to prevent a band of Tories from converting them into war material when David Fanning and Colonel Hector McNeill raided Hillsboro. The clock first hung in the steeple of the old Episcopal church and then for many years in the tower of the market-house. When the market-house was torn down about 1826, the clock was stored until the present courthouse was completed. According to items in the *Hillsborough Recorder*, on October 8, 1846, August 13, 1851, and April 10, 1861, Lemuel Lynch was paid $250 to repair the clock in 1846, and later received $25 annually to keep it well regulated.

In a hundred years Orange county had at least five jails. In 1752, Marmaduke Kimbrough was given a contract to build a prison, as well as a courthouse, near Piney Ford. The specifications given in the County court minutes of September, 1752, called for a prison "20 feet Long and 12 feet wide with a partition in the middle to be made of hewed logs eight Inches thick weather boarded with feather Edged plank, with a shingled Roof and floored above and below of hewed Logs." That contract was evidently not carried out. According to the County court minutes,

Alexander Mebane, Josiah Dixon and William Churton laid out the first prison in Hillsboro in 1755. Lot No. 1 in the town was reserved for a market-house, courthouse, prison, pillory and stocks. Joseph Maddock built the first prison and "ground pinned" it in 1757 to make it stronger. That same year the sheriff was instructed to provide stocks, a pillory and a whipping post. By an order from the County court in 1758, the sheriff was to purchase three pairs of bolts and four pairs of hand cuffs.

A second jail was erected either in 1764 or in 1765. Around the jail and stocks John Donrtt built a stockade ten feet high at a cost of twenty-four pounds. Its construction was superintended by Thomas Hart and Francis Nash. After the second jail burned, a district jail was built in Hillsboro in 1771. Another district jail was authorized by the legislature in 1798. Building commissioners were appointed for a new prison in 1836, which was to be forty-five feet long, twenty-four feet wide and two stories high—its cost not to exceed four thousand dollars. John Berry was awarded the contract for the stone building which was completed in 1837. In 1846 John Christmas erected new gallows which were moved in 1850, by order of the court, to "the old place called gallows hill within the Town Commons"— in the western part of Hillsboro.

CHAPTER IV

ORANGE COUNTY AND THE WAR OF THE REGULATION

BY HUGH T. LEFLER

Professor of History, University of North Carolina

The first decade of Orange county's history was relatively peaceful, orderly, and undramatic. People were settling all over the county, clearing the wilderness, developing an extensive though somewhat crude agriculture, and beginning to build up a few household industries. Population increased rapidly. The number of white male taxables rose from 1108 in 1753 to 1595 in 1757 to 2627 in 1761 to 3064 in 1765 and 3870 in 1767. By the latter date, Orange had become the most populous county in the colony, and its rate of population increase during the first two decades surpassed that of any similar period in its whole history.

Within a few years after settlement began, churches were established and there was talk of a "seminary of education." A law of 1755 ordered the laying out of a road "from Orange courthouse to the Cape Fear," but the provisions of this law were not carried out immediately. Meanwhile the Orange farmers were constructing crude roads throughout the county. Some years later, Governor Josiah Martin said that the roads in this area were "the most wretched he had ever seen," and that the region west of Hillsboro was "the most broken difficult and rough country I have ever seen." But there were signs of improvements in economic and social life. Several Scots began to do business in the county in the 1760's and thus "changed the state of things for the better." The Glasgow firm of Buchanan, Hastie and Company operated a store in the county—as well as at many other places in North Carolina—and the Wilmington firm of Hogg and Campbell had business conections in Hillsboro, which was rapidly becoming the political, social, and economic center of the whole back country. In 1764 the county seat contained "only thirty or forty inhabitants," but a few years later it was enjoying "a good share of commerce for an inland town," and was "in a very promising state of improvement."

All of Orange county lay within the Granville district and the quit rents in this district were twice as high as in the southern half of North Carolina, where rents were paid to the royal governor. Granville's agents, notably Francis Corbin and Dr. Thomas Child were accused by Orange farmers of many abuses in granting lands. These men and their subordinates were charged with taking excessive fees; and there can be no doubt of the accuracy of these complaints. No accurate rent or collection records were kept, and sometimes the same tract of land was granted to two or even three different parties and fees were charged for each entry, followed naturally by litigation over the title to the lands thus granted. The hatred of the Orange inhabitants manifested itself in the change in the name of the county seat from Corbinton (Corbin Town) to Childsburg in 1759, and to Hillsborough in 1766. Due to the negligence of the second Earl of Granville, the land office in the district was closed from 1766 to 1773. This fact may explain why the Regulator documents contained few references to the land system.

The peaceful and happy condition of Orange changed rapidly after 1763 and for the next ten years the county was the leader in the East-West sectional controversy which highlighted North Carolina history for the decade preceding the American Revolution. As Hermon (Herman, Harmon) Husband, best known of the Regulator leaders and writers, said in his *Impartial Relation* (published in 1770): "In Orange county the first disturbance is generally ascribed to have arisen, but Granville and Halifax counties were deeply engaged in the same quarrel many years before Orange."

The land problem was a cause of unrest in Orange and the whole back country, but the Regulator documents said little about this grievance of the poeple. There were basic economic, social, and religious differences between Orange and the counties of the East, which promoted sectional rivalry and conflict. Orange was settled largely by Scotch-Irish, Germans, and Welsh; its prevalent religious outlook was non-Anglican—being largely Presbyterian, Baptist, and Quaker; its small farm economy emphasized free labor, although plantation slavery was developing and something of an incipient aristocracy was beginning to emerge.

The major cause of sectional rivalry and conflict was political and centered around the domination of the provincial government by the Eastern planter aristocracy. All other problems—land, religion, trade, and local government—were related to this question and could not be solved until Orange and other western counties had more equitable representation in the legislative, executive, and judicial branches of the government.

In colonial North Carolina, the county was the unit of representation in the legislature and there were more counties in the East than in the rapidly growing back country. Since counties were created by the General Assembly, this situation was likely to continue. As population increased rapidly in the Piedmont, the Eastern dominated legislature created more counties in the West, but it also created additional counties in the East in order to guarantee Eastern dominance. Most of the counties had two representatives in the legislature, but the older counties of Pasquotank, Chowan, Currituck, Perquimans, and Tyrrell had five each—a total of 25 members; while Orange county, which by 1766 had more "white male taxables" than all five of these counties combined, had only two. Even on the basis of total taxables (whites and Negroes) Orange had more than one-half the population of these five counties. This was perhaps the most glaring illustration of inequitable representation in all North Carolina history.

The East likewise had complete control of other branches of the provincial government. From 1765 to 1771—the "Regulator period"—the Governor, the Treasurer, the Speaker of the House, and all the councillors and judges lived there.

But the undemocratic character of local government was the chief cause of complaint of the Orange county farmers and of the Regulators in general. Justices for the county court were appointed by the governor. The sheriff was appointed by the governor from a list of three names sent him by the justices of the peace, who were also appointed by the governor. The register, clerk, and all other civil officials were appointed by the governor and council, as were the militia officers above the rank of colonel.

The only officials chosen by the qualified voters were the two county members in the assembly; not a single local official was chosen by popular vote. The inevitable result of this undemocratic system was centralization of political power and the evolution of what came to be called the "courthouse ring" and the "sheriff and his Bums."

Some of the local officials were natives of the county, but some were "foreigners." As one writer put it: "To it (the county) come the merchant, the lawyer, the tavernkeeper, the artisan, and the court officials, adventurers all in the perennial pursuit of gain." Edmund Fanning, the most hated man in Orange—and perhaps in the whole colony—was a native of New York, a graduate of Yale, and holder of honorary degrees from a number of universities.

Multiple officeholding was one of the obvious and deplorable results of this system and a constant source of irritation to the Orange farmers. This practice was permitted by law, but this did not make the people like it. Fanning, the great friend of governor Tryon, and the recognized leader of the "courthouse ring" in Orange, was lawyer, Assemblyman from Orange county —and then from the borough of Hillsboro—register of deeds, judge of the court, and colonel in the militia. Francis Nash, perhaps considered a native, though he was born in Virginia, was member of the General Assembly, clerk of the court, justice of the peace, member of the county court, and captain of the militia.

In defense of these and other officials, who became the targets of the Regulators, it might be observed that the eighteenth century concept of public office was quite different from what it is now. An office was then considered as a gift of the king—or his agent, the governor—and the property right of the officeholder. Hence one could buy and sell an office, civil or military. Likewise, officials were paid by fees, and not salaries. These fees were fixed by law but most of the people were ignorant of the amounts prescribed and were suspicious that illegal fees were being levied, and illegal "distraints" being made of their property for non-payment of fees and other dues. Sheriffs, "sub-sheriffs" and clerks were accused in affidavit after affidavit of charging higher fees than the law allowed, and there were many charges of illegal "distraints" of property.

County and provincial officers, especially Fanning, were satirized in popular verse, particularly by Rednap Howell, "poet of the Regulation." Perhaps the best known verse from Howell's pen was the one which ran:

> When Fanning first to Orange came
> He looked both pale and wan,
> An old patched coat upon his back,
> An old mare he rode on.
> Both man and mare warn't worth five pounds
> As I've often been told;
> But by his civil robberies
> He's laced his coat with gold.

By 1765 there was general unrest—though no organized movement of protest—in Orange and other western counties. There were charges of corruption, illegal fees, and excessive taxes, and there were occasional protests against these evils of local government.

The passage of the Capital Act by the legislature of 1766 did not help matters any. For many years before the creation of Orange county in 1752 the governors and other colonial leaders had realized the necessity of a "fixed seat of government." The Assembly had been an "itinerant body" meeting at Edenton, New Bern, Wilmington, Bath, or at any place where the governor called it to assemble. The governor lived at one place, the councillors at various places, the treasurer at another. There were not suitable buildings and records were scattered and carried from session to session in a "common cart." Governor Gabriel Johnston in 1747 said "It is impossible to finish any matter as it ought to be while we go on in this itinerant way. We have now tried every Town in the Colony and it is high time to settle somewhere." In 1758, Governor Arthur Dobbs succeeded in getting the legislature to pass a law locating the capital at Tower Hill on the Neuse (near present Kinston), but when the British Privy Council learned that the capital was to be located on lands which belonged to the governor himself, the law was disallowed.

The East was apprehensive that the capital might be located at Hillsboro, which had become something of the capital of the whole back country, and this led representatives from the Albemarle and Pamlico Sound region and the Cape Fear to unite in favor of New Bern. Tryon recommended that town as a "central location" and the Assembly in November, 1766, passed "An Act for erecting a Convenient Building within the town of New Bern for the residence of the Governor." For this purpose, the Assembly appropriated £5,000, a sum increased by an additional £10,000 the next year. Work was begun on the "Governor's Palace" in 1767 and when this beautiful brick and marble structure was completed in 1770, it was considered the finest "government house" in all English America.

The construction of the Palace met with general approval in the East; the Assembly referred to it as "truly elegant and noble," but it met with strong and vehement opposition from Orange and other western counties. Complaints were made of the great distance to New Bern, and its lack of trade connections with the back country. One westerner wrote in 1768: "not one man in twenty of the four most populous counties (Orange, Mecklenburg, Rowan, and Anson) will ever see this famous house when built, as their trade connections do, and ever will more naturally center in South Carolina." A poll tax of eight pence proclamation money was levied by the legislature to pay for the Palace and this action brought forth bitter complaints from Orange county farmers. They considered all poll taxes inequitable, odious, and operating "to the prejudice" of the western counties, which had more white people, but less wealth, than the eastern counties. One farmer declared that "a man that is worth £10,000 pays no more than a poor back settler that has nothing but the labour of his hands to depend upon for his daily support." On August 3, 1768, James Thackston, an Orange county justice of the peace, reported to Tyree Harris "late Sheriff of Orange" that he heard William Butler say "We are determined not to pay the tax for the next three years, for the Edifice or Governor's House. We want no such House, nor will we pay for it." Thackston declared that Ransom Sutherland said that some two hundred Regulators had gathered and had told Harris "that if he should distrain on them for their lives that they would abuse him and kill any Person that should distrain for their levies."

The first organized effort of the back country farmers to redress their grievances had been made by the citizens of Orange county two years before. In August, 1766, a paper, later called "Regulator Advertisement, Number One," was circulated at the meeting of the County court in Hillsboro calling on all North Carolinians to resist local oppression and put an end to the extortion of county officers and asking the people of Orange to elect delegates to "attend a general meeting on the Monday before the next November court at a suitable place where there is no Liquor (at Maddock's Mill if no objection) at which meeting let it be judiciously enquired whether the free men of this County labor under abuses of power or not. . ." Husband said this document was publicly read at court and that Thomas Lloyd, one of the Assemblymen from Orange, "declared his approval of it, and the rest acknowledged it was reasonable."

Meanwhile at a meeting on Deep River, in Husband's home community, Regulator Advertisement, Number Two, was drawn up and William Cox and William Masset were delegated to attend the meeting at Maddock's Mill on October 10, the date having been changed to that time by Lloyd. The county representatives in the legislature, vestrymen, and other officers were requested to give the members of the meeting "what Information and Satisfaction they can." According to Husband's narrative, "about twelve Men met, but none of the officers appeared." Late in the day James Watson, prominent officer, came alone and brought word from Fanning, the Register of Deeds at Hillsboro, that he considered the meeting "as an Insurrection."

The delegates, after hearing Watson's message, and in his presence, drew up another paper, Regulator Advertisement, Number Three, which they read to Watson and which he said was "so just, and reasonable, that no Man could object to it." This document reiterated the need for "a publick and free Conference," and again asked the people to send delegates to a meeting and offered to meet the county officials at any time and place they might select. A copy of this paper was given to Watson and he promised to present transcripts of it to all of the county officials. Fanning, however, as spokesman for the officials, refused to see any justice in the people's complaint and reported at the court in Hillsboro in November, 1766, that he had written to the leaders of the movement "a statement that would silence them."

The people of Orange then appealed to the General Assembly, but this body turned a deaf ear to their appeals and the agitation continued.

The year 1768 was the turning point in the whole controversy and marked the formal organization of the Regulators. Regulator Advertisement, Number Four, drawn up about January of that year, is perhaps the clearest statement of the evils these people proposed to "regulate."

1. That we will pay no Taxes until we are satisfied they are agreeable to Law and Applied to the purposes therein mentioned unless we cannot help and are forced.
2. That we will pay no Officer any more fees than the Law allows unless we are obliged to it and then to shew a dislike to it and bear open testimony against it.
3. That we will attend our Meetings of Conference as often as we conveniently can. . .
4. That we will contribute to Collections for defraying necessary expenses attending the work according to our abilities.
5. That in Cases of differences in Judgment we will submit to the Majority of our Body.

The word Regulator did not appear in this document; it was first used in Advertisement, Number Six, March 22, 1768.

Soon after this a Regulator had his horse, saddle, and bridle "distrained" for non-payment of taxes. On April 8, about seventy Regulators rode to Hillsboro, took the horse away from the officer, and fired "a few guns into the Roof of Colonel Fanning's House, to signify they blamed him for all this abuse." Fanning was indignant and on April 23 wrote Tryon that

> the late orderly and well regulated County of Orange, is now (O my favourite County and people how art thou fallen) the very nest and bosom of rioting and rebellion—The People are now in every part and Corner of the County, meeting, complaining, and confederating by solemn oath and open violence to refuse the payment of Taxes and to prevent the execution of Law, threatening death and destruction to myself and others, requiring settlements of the Public, Parish, and County taxes to be made before

their leaders—Clerks, Sheriffs, Registers, Attorneys and all Officers of every degree and station to be arraigned at the Bar of their Shallow Understanding and to be punished and regulated at their Will, and in a word, for them to become the sovereign arbiters of right and wrong.

He said that he expected "an attack from the whole united force of the regulators or rebels" at which time he intended as "do also the aforementioned Officers" (Colonel Gray, Major Lloyd, Captain Hart, Adjutant Nash, and Captain Thackston) "to *bravely repulse them or nobly die.*"

In Tryon's reply to Fanning, four days later, the governor referred to the *"many deluded* people" in Orange and denounced their leaders as the "invaders of public peace and private happiness." Tryon also issued two proclamations: one to the people and the other to the militia officers of the colony. He ordered the Regulators to disperse to their homes and the militia to be called in Bute, Halifax, Granville, Rowan, Mecklenburg, Cumberland, and Johnston counties, and "that they be held in readiness" to march to the aid of Fanning.

Yet Tryon realized that the Regulators had grounds for complaint against the existing local regime. In 1767, he wrote the Earl of Shelburne that "The Sheriffs have embezzled more than one-half of the public money ordered to be raised and collected by them... in many instances the Sheriffs are insolvent or retreated out of the province." In a message to the legislature, he called attention to the need for further regulation in the control of county officials. And the Assembly agreed that

> The abuses in the Sheriff's office cry aloud for and shall receive the strictest attention and correction, nor shall the embezzlement and irregularities committed by other collectors of the public revenue escape the most exact inquiry.

The legislature passed laws to regulate the fees of inferior court clerks and to correct certain other evils in the administration of local justice. The governor thought that these laws should stop the temptations that led to fraud, embezzlement, and other irregular pactices, and he asked the people to petition the legislature for a "redress of grievances."

But the situation in Orange did not improve. During the

spring and summer of 1768 scores of depositions were made by Orange county farmers against the sheriff, sub-sheriffs, and against Francis Nash "Clark" of the court. John McVey swore that a sub-sheriff had seized "eight large prime deer skins" from him. John McDonald testified that another sub-sheriff did "ketch one of his creatures" for a charge of writ of ejectment. One Regulator said that Sheriff William Nunn and his sub-sheriff "came to my house and broke open the roof of it and took a piece of linen cloth"; another charged the sub-sheriff with seizing "a Gunn valued at thirty two shillings." Several charges were made of "false impressment," of "seizing a mare"; and one Regulator swore that he paid Francis Nash "two pounds, seventeen shillings and four pence for a letter of Administration and got none."

The Regulator leaders took Tryon at his word about a "redress of grievances," and began to prepare a petition to the Governor and the Assembly. At a "general meeting of the regulators" on April 30, they appointed twelve men to meet on May 11 at Thomas Lindley's, where they "hoped some representatives of the county officials would meet them." Due to the arrest of Husband and Butler and the ensuing confusion, this meeting was never held. Meanwhile, Regulator Advertisement, Number Nine, was drawn up and signed by 474 people, 31 of whom wrote their names "in Dutch." This document, addressed "To the Governor and Councill," was the climax of the Regulator's attempts to obtain justice by peaceful means. It declared:

> We the Inhabitants of Orange County pay larger Fees for record-in Deeds than any of the adjacent Counties and many other Fees more than the Law allows by all that We can make out from which a jealosie prevails that we are misused and application has been made to our representatives to satisfy us But we were disregarded in the said application upon which the said discontent growing more and more so as to threaten a disturbance of the public peace, we therefore beg that those matters may be taken under your serious consideration and interpose in our Favour so that we may have a fair hearing in this matter and (be) redressed where we have been wronged.

The Regulators assured Tryon that neither disloyalty nor disaffection was the cause of their troubles, but the corrupt and arbitrary practices of nefarious and designing men who being put into posts of profit and credit among us, use every artifice, every fraud, and where these fail, threats and menaces are not spared to squeeze and extort from the wretched poor.

They rebuked the "heated unruly spirits" who had fired several shots into Fanning's house a short time before.

James Hunter and Rednap Howell carried this petition to Brunswick and presented it to Governor Tryon on June 20. After consulting with his council, the governor replied to the petition, saying that the Regulator grievances did not justify their actions, and ordered them to give up the name of Regulators, cease organized activities, pay their taxes, and not molest officers. As Husband later wrote, Tryon was "inclined to the other side, multiplying all our faults to the highest pitch he was capable of."

Yet Tryon realized that there was justice in the Regulators' demands and he issued a warning to all officers and lawyers against charging excessive fees; he ordered the publication of a list of legal fees; and he directed the attorney-general to prosecute all officers and lawyers charged with extortion. He also promised to go to Hillsboro in person in July, where he hoped to "find everyone at peace."

The governor kept his word and went to Hillsboro—though he did not arrive until August. Meantime Fanning had been indicted for taking excessive fees as Register and his trial had been set for the September session of court. Husband and Butler had been arrested for "inciting the populace to rebellion" and were to be tried at the same court. Two other Regulators, Samuel Devinney and John Phillip Hartzo, were also to be tried for "a riot and rescue" (of a horse). Rumors began to fly that Tryon was raising the militia to suppress the Regulators and that he was calling out the Indians to attack them from the rear. Threats of rescue of the imprisoned Regulators and reports about a general Regulator rising prompted Tryon to call out the militia, and a force of 1,461, largely from Mecklenburg, Orange, Granville, and Rowan counties, marched to Hillsboro for the September session of court. This action only angered the Regulators and increased the debt of the poor colony £4844-19-3.

The Hillsboro Court of September 22-October 1, 1768, was a perfect illustration of the centralization and power of the courthouse ring to which the Regulators had objected. Fanning, the defendant to be tried, and Maurice Moore, the presiding judge, were both colonels in the militia. Six other militia officers were members of the governor's council, and eighteen members of the Assembly were also among the militia officers.

A large number of Regulators were present for the session of court—3,700, according to Husband's account. Husband was tried and acquitted of being a party to the recovery of the horse, which had been "distrained." Butler was fined £50 and sentenced to six months' imprisonment. Devinney and Hartzo were fined £25 and given three months' imprisonment. Governor Tryon, apparently eager to quell the disturbances, released the prisoners and suspended the payment of their fines for three months. There was no serious disorder and the "Battle of Eno" did not materialize. Fanning was convicted of taking a six shilling fee for registering a deed when the legal charge was only two shillings and eight pence. (Tryon said Fanning's action was due to a "misconstruction of the fee bill.") He was fined the nominal sum of "one penny and costs." Though he promptly resigned his office, the Regulators' wrath was not appeased by this obvious miscarriage of justice.

On October 3, Tryon issued a proclamation "out of compassion to the misguided multitude," pardoning all those involved in the "late insurrection" except "James Hunter, Ninion Hamilton, Peter Craven, Isaac Jackson, Harmon Husbands, Matthew Hamilton, William Payne, Ninian Bell Hamilton, Malachi Fyke, William Moffitt, Christopher Nation, Solomon Gross, and John Oneal." On September 9, 1769, Tryon issued a "Proclamation of general pardon extending to Fines and forfeitures to all persons concerned in the late Insurrection."

But the Regulators continued their agitation for reform in local government. Again they decided to carry their case to the legislature, and this time they hoped for better results because, in the 1769 elections, Orange, Granville, Anson, and Halifax counties elected solid Regulator delegations. Husband and John Pryor were elected from Orange, receiving 642 and 455 votes respectively, to 314 for Fanning. Ironically enough, Fanning was chosen to the legislature from Hillsboro, recently created a "borough," through the influence of Governor Tryon.

Meanwhile the Regulator organization was gaining new recruits and spreading into new areas. There were disorders in Rowan and Edgecombe counties, and attacks on the courts in Anson and Johnston. But the most dramatic incidents in 1770 were the "Hillsborough riots" of September 24 and 25. Court convened on the 22nd, but Judge Richard Henderson immediately adjourned it until September 24. The court docket was filled with cases both for and against Regulators, some of whom—according to Henderson—had been coming into town for several days "until the place was filled with a great number of these people called Regulators shouting, halooing and making a considerable tumult in the streets." When court opened, the Regulators marched in and took possession of all the available seats. Then, Jeremiah Fields, acting as the Regulator spokesman for the occasion, informed Judge Henderson that the Regulators had reason to believe that they could not obtain justice in his court, and hence they were determined to obtain justice by their own means. According to Henderson's account, all went well for about half an hour; most of the Regulators withdrew from the courthouse, but within a short time bedlam broke loose. John Williams, local attorney, was beaten as he attempted to enter the building. Fanning was chased, and when he hid behind the judge's bench, he was dragged forth and pummeled through the streets in a vigorous manner. Both Williams and Fanning finally escaped by running into a store. Henderson, fearing for his own safety, left for his home in Granville county, leaving "poor Colonel Fanning and the little Borough in a wretched situation."

The next day, the Regulators took over the deserted court and tried their own cases, with Fields acting as clerk. The Regulator entries made on the court docket were bitter, sarcastic, and vulgar, usually ending with "plaintiff pays cost," but with a little profanity interspersed. The Regulators also took out their vengeance on Fanning by almost wrecking his house, after which they dispersed to their homes.

When the Assembly convened at New Bern on December 5,

1770, panic was running through the province. Tryon hastily summoned his council, which urged him to use military force to quiet the disturbances. In his address to the Assembly, the governor denounced the "seditious mob" at Hillsboro and urged the passage of laws to meet the emergency.

In a state of high tension and reported uprisings, the Assembly, on January 15, 1771, passed The Johnston Riot Act, named for its author, Samuel Johnston, later governor of the state of North Carolina, which provided that prosecutions for riots might be tried in any county, even though the riots did not occur there; outlawed any person resisting or avoiding arrest; and authorized the governor to suppress the Regulators by military force. Professor Bassett, writing about the War of the Regulation, observed that this Assembly, "born as it was in terror, it is not surprising that it should have passed away in blood." (Governor Martin was later notified by the King and Privy council that portions of this law were "irreconcilable with the principles of the constitution, full of danger in its operation, and unfit for any part of the British Empire.")

Husband was expelled from this legislative session on charges of libel and as "not being a credit to the Assembly." But Tryon and the council were afraid to let Husband return to Orange and they jailed him at New Bern on the charge of a libellous attack against Judge Maurice Moore. The Craven county grand jury failed to find a true bill against him and he was released. About this time reports reached the governor that the Regulators were marching on New Bern to rescue Husband and to burn the town.

Regulator reaction to the "Bloody Johnston Act" was swift and defiant. The organization increased in numbers and many strong resolutions were drawn up, such as those in Rowan and Orange, which denounced this "riotous act," and in which the Regulators promised to pay no more taxes, declared Fanning an outlaw to be killed on sight, forbade any sessions of court and threatened to kill all lawyers and judges. The situation seemed to be getting out of hand.

Tryon, who had already been appointed governor of New York, decided to take drastic and dramatic action. He issued orders for a special term of court to be held at Hillsboro in

March, 1771, and, as his council had advised, called out the militia "with all expedition" to protect the court and to suppress the Regulators. 1452 militiamen responded, of whom 1068 were from the East, and the remainder from Orange, Rowan, and a few other western counties. Tryon marched from New Bern to Hillsboro and, on May 16, encamped on Great Alamance creek, a few miles west of Hillsboro, where he was met by a force of about 2000 Regulators. The latter petitioned the governor for an audience, but he refused to communicate with them "as long as they were in arms against the government." He gave them one hour to lay down their arms and disperse. At the end of the hour, he gave the order to fire and after a two-hour battle, the Regulators were defeated and scattered. Tryon's losses were nine killed and sixty-one wounded; the Regulators lost nine killed and an undetermined number wounded. Tryon's terse report about the battle was "a signal and glorious victory was obtained over the obstinate and infatuated rebels."

Twelve Regulators were tried for treason and all were convicted. Six were hanged and the rest pardoned by the governor. Tryon offered clemency to all Regulators who would lay down their arms and submit to authority. Within six weeks 6,409 submitted and later received pardons from the King through Governor Martin.

Husband, Howell, and several other leaders of the Regulation had left North Carolina before the battle of Alamance. Many Regulators, perhaps thousands, moved to the Tennessee country within a short time after their crushing defeat. Morgan Edwards, noted Baptist preacher, traveler, and author, writing in 1772, said that these people "despaired of seeing better times and therefore quitted the province. It is said that 1,500 families have departed since the battle of Alamance and to my knowledge a great many more are only waiting to dispose of their plantations in order to follow them." Tryon and Fanning, the Regulators' arch enemies, had also left North Carolina for good.

There is a vast literature on the War of the Regulation and the Regulators. Scores of poems, songs, articles, pamphlets, and books have either praised or damned these "simple and greatly abused farmers." Many myths have grown up around the movement, its leaders, and the rank and file of Regulators. Some writers, past and present, have described the Regulation as a "great democratic movement." Others have called Alamance "the first battle of the American Revolution." It was not a democratic movement in the modern sense of that term. Its leaders insisted that they were not fighting for a change in the "Form or Mode of Government," but were contending for relief from the malpractices of judges, sheriffs, and "mercenary tricking Attornies, Clarks, and other little Officers," who were usually American-born adventurers of English descent, and "who had sniffed from afar opportunities for wealth and power in a new country." One Regulator writer had referred to the court officals and lawyers as "these cursed hungry Caterpillars, that will eat out the very Bowels of our Commonwealth, if they are not pulled down from their Nests in a very short time."

It is claiming too much to maintain that Alamance was "the first battle of the American Revolution." It was simply the climax of a revolt of the western people against oppressive laws and corrupt local officials. There was not a single British redcoat at Alamance creek in 1771. Nor was North Carolina the only colony where discontented people in the back country organized, agitated and even fought for a redress of their grievances against provincial and local officials. South Carolina, for instance, had a Regulation movement by the same name and at the same time as North Carolina. Its *Plan of Regulation* was adopted in June, 1768, and the organization continued its activities for two years after the North Carolina movement had subsided.

Another myth associated with the Regulation movement is the idea that all, or even most, of the Regulators became Tories in the Revolution, which broke out four years after the battle of Alamance. An examination of the records reveals that of 883 of the known Regulators, 289 were Whigs, 34 Tories, and 560 Revolutionary status unknown.

The Regulation movement in North Carolina collapsed in 1771, but not the cause for which the Regulators had been fighting. Alamance was only a temporary defeat for a revolt against sectional political domination and maladministration in local government. The movement for justice to the back country was interrupted by the American revolution and its aftermath, but the later renewal of the East-West controversy reached its grand climax and victory for the West in the Constitutional Convention of 1835.

Chapter V

ORANGE COUNTY IN THE ERA OF THE AMERICAN REVOLUTION

By Hugh F. Rankin

*John Motley Morehead Scholar
University of North Carolina*

The year 1775 marked the beginning of an era for Orange county and the town of Hillsboro. The widening chasm between Great Britain and her colonies became less of an abstraction and more of a reality. Here, as in the rest of North Carolina and the other colonies, people were beginning to align themselves with others who held similar political beliefs. Those who supported the authority of the King adopted the title "Tory," while others who were in opposition to British measures appropriated the name of "Whig," both appellatives being derived from the political parties in England which followed, basically, the same principles. There was also a third party, the neutrals, who withheld an indication of their allegiance until they were able to determine which faction would be able to muster the greater strength.

The first definite break between the authority of the king and the people of North Carolina occurred far from Orange county—in New Bern, the town then serving as colonial capital. The first step on the road to rebellion had been taken by the North Carolina legislature in December, 1773, when that body had appointed a Committee of Correspondence as a means of maintaining contact with other colonies and coordinating resistance to policies of the English government. This was followed by the meeting of the first Provincial Congress which convened in New Bern August 23, 1774. Thomas Hart represented Orange county, but Hillsboro, although entitled to a seat, sent no delegate. This congress appointed delegates to the first Continental Congress which was to meet in Philadephia. It also made provisions for "a committee of five persons to be chosen for each county." These Committees of Safety were to direct the training of the militia and regulate the activities of both Whigs and Tories in their respective counties.

On April 4, 1775, the regularly scheduled meeting of the legislature was to be held in New Bern. John Harvey, who had been authorized by the first Provincial Congress to call a meeting whenever he should deem necessary, issued a call for the second Provincial Congress, to be held in New Bern on April 3, one day earlier than the legislature. The two bodies held practically joint sessions with the Congress meeting at nine o'clock and the legislature at ten, and with the same officer presiding over both bodies. The Royal Governor, Josiah Martin, failed in his attempts to block the proceedings of the Congress. On April 8, 1775 he dissolved the legislature, the day after it had selected the delegates to the second Continental Congress. In the legislature for this session, Orange county was represented by Ralph McNair and Thomas Hart, while the borough of Hillsboro had sent Thomas Nash. As delegates to the Provincial Congress the county had sent Thomas Burke, John Kinchen and Francis Nash.

In early May, 1775, came the electrifying news of the battles of Lexington and Concord on April 19. Before the end of the month word was received that Governor Martin had abandoned his responsibilities and had fled to a British war ship in the lower Cape Fear river. The flight of the governor, however, did not interrupt local government activities as these functions were performed by the Orange County Committee of Safety. There is little known of the personnel of this body as the records of the Committee have been lost, but it is known that James Hogan was chairman and James Hogg served as secretary.

The political event of the year, insofar as Orange county was concerned, was the meeting of the third Provincial Congress in Hillsboro on August 23, 1775, with 184 delegates in attendance. This assembly opened with the delegates signing an oath professing allegiance to King George III. In three weeks this Congress accomplished much toward establishing a pattern for government. It made provisions for the raising of 10,000 men and for the issuance of £50,000 proclamation money to be used for the subsistence of the troops. In addition, the enlistment of 3,000 Minute Men was urged. A Provincial Council of Safety of thirteen members was established for the regulation of the army and to provide a defense against both the external and internal enemies of the province. In provisions for local government the colony was divided into a number of districts with a Committee of Safety of thirteen members for each district. On Friday, September 8, two days before the Congress was dissolved, William Hooper presented a resolution which declared that the members of the convention were ready to "spend their blood and treasure when constitutionally called upon, in support of the succession of His Majesty, George III, his crown and his dignity . . . ." Although this resolve was unanimously adopted, it is apparent that this was but a formality. Possibly the best gauge to the tempers of these men can be found in a letter which Joseph Hewes wrote some time later in which he said, "Although the storm threatens I feel myself quite composed. I have furnished myself with a good musket and bayonet. When I can no longer be useful in council, I hope I shall be willing to take the field." Among the acknowledged leaders of this Congress were William Johnston, William Hooper, Joseph Hewes, Richard Caswell, Archibald Maclaine, Thomas Jones and Thomas Burke.

The Congress had established the Hillsboro District which was to be composed of Orange, Granville, Chatham and Wake counties. The Committee of Safety for the district included among its members William Taylor, Joseph Taylor and Samuel Smith of Granville county; John Atkinson, John Butler and William Johnston of Orange county; John Hinton, Joel Lane and Michael Rogers of Wake county; Ambrose Ramsey, Mial Scurlock and John Thompson of Chatham; and with John Lark as a member at large. Thomas Person and John Kinchen served on the Provincial Council as representatives of the Hillsboro District.

On September 1, 1775, Francis Nash, a prominent leader of Orange county, was appointed Lieutenant Colonel of the First Regiment of the North Carolina Continental Line which was then being formed in the eastern part of the province by Colonel James Moore. Other military activities in the waning months of 1775 included the formation of three companies of militia for Orange county under the command of James Thackston, who had been appointed Colonel of militia for the Hillsboro District. Other officers of the regiment were Lieutenant Colonel James Hogan, and Majors John Butler, William Moore and Nathaniel Rochester.

The year 1776 had no more than become a reality before the political parties of North Carolina found that they had become military opponents. Reports from the eastern part of the province indicated that the Tories were gathering under the leadership of Donald MacDonald, a British officer who had been commissioned Brigadier-General of Loyalist militia by Governor Martin. All of North Carolina soon presented the picture of marching men. Many militia detachments on their way to the east rendezvoused at Hillsboro. This uprising culminated in the Battle of Moore's Creek on February 27, 1776 and the rout of the Tories. Orange county was represented on both sides of the struggle. On the side of the Tories were Dr. John Pyle, James Hunter, Robinson York and the Reverend George Micklejohn. Michael Holt accepted a commission from Governor Martin and marched for the Tory rendezvous at Cross Creek (present-day Fayetteville), but experienced a change of heart and returned home, accompanied by a number of his men. After his subsequent arrest Holt was allowed to take an oath of allegiance to the cause of the Whigs. This same concession was also later extended to James Hunter. The Whig militia of Orange county were not participants in the actual battle, but they still played an important role in the ultimate victory, as it was the Orange county contingent under James Thackston which occupied Cross Creek and prevented the Tories from using that town as a refuge.

The smashing victory over the Tories lulled the Whigs of Orange county and North Carolina into a false sense of security. In the summer of 1776 General Griffith Rutherford was ordered to march against the Cherokee Indians who at that time were raiding the frontier settlements of North Carolina. For this campaign the militia quota for Orange county was 500 men, but it was soon discovered that so large a number of men could be embodied only with difficulty. When the number was reduced to 300, the quota was met and these recruits participated in the subsequent campaign in which the Indians were subdued. Among the Orange county officers and men who served in this campaign were Major Hugh Tinnin; Captains William Williams, William Murray; Lieutenants Joseph Thompson, Peter O'Neal; Ensigns Edwin Gwin, Elias Powell; Corporals George Holt, John Williams; and Jacob Albright, who went along as drummer.

On April 4, 1776 the Provincial Congress had met in Halifax and Orange county had sent John Kinchen, James Saunders, John Butler, Nathaniel Rochester and Thomas Burke, while William Johnston had represented the town of Hillsboro. This assembly considered the very important question of a permanent constitution. They had, on April 12, instructed the North Carolina delegates to the Continental Congress to vote for independence, a measure which had made the old Committees of Safety obsolete and had created the necessity for a permanent state government. Thomas Burke played a significant part in preparing a "temporary Civil Constitution." During the debates on the nature of the constitution a bitter dispute arose over the questions of the limitation of the suffrage and the method of electing state officials. Tempers flared so high that final action on the constitution was postponed until the next meeting of the Provincial Congress.

During the summer and fall of 1776 there was active campaigning against the conservatives in the Congress, as it was feared they were conspiring to take away the liberties of the people. In the election for the delegate from Hillsboro, William Johnston won by a very narrow margin and his election was protested. Near riots marked the county elections on October 15. At this time Orange county included the territory of present day Orange, Caswell, Alamance, Person and Durham counties. The only polling place was the court house in Hillsboro, and the eligible voters arrived in such droves and so crowded the voting facilities that four times during the day the polls were temporarily closed as a means of restoring order. By sunset only about one-fourth of the voters had been able to cast their ballots. The election of James Saunders, William Moore, John McCabe, John Atkinson and John Paine resulted in the presentation of a petition to the Congress to prevent them from taking their seats. When the fifth and last Provincial Congress convened at Halifax, November 12, 1776, the first report on the petition by the Committee of Privileges and Elections favored the duly elected members, and the recommendation of the Committee was adopted. Thomas Burke, although not a member, attended all the sessions of the Congress, and it was possibly because of his influence that the decision in regard to the Orange county election was rescinded and a new election was ordered. In this special election Thomas Burke, Nathaniel Rochester, Alexander Mebane, John Butler, and John McCabe were elected, taking their seats on December 16, seven days before adjournment, and just in time to participate in the adoption of the Bill of Rights on December 17 and the Constitution itself the following day.

The year 1777 was the first year under the new Constitution for North Carolina. Richard Caswell had been elected as first governor of the state. There was little difficulty experienced in the transition in either the state or local government. Under the new administration the first commissioners for the town of Hillsboro were William Johnston, James Hogg, John Sheels (Shields), William Courtney and James Watson. Local justice returned to the county in May when the county court resumed its sittings in Hillsboro, but there was little activity other than county matters and the probate of deeds, as the legislature had enacted no general court laws. The court officials of the county were Nathaniel Rochester as clerk of the court, Alexander Mebane, Jr., as sheriff, and James Watson as register.

At the meeting of the last Provincial Congress, Thomas Burke had, on December 20, 1776, been elected to represent North Carolina in the Continental Congress along with William Hooper and Joseph Hewes. With the exception of the period from April to August, 1778, he represented the state in the national Congress until April 12, 1781. He was one of the more active members of the body, serving on 108 different committees during his tenure of office, and was a constant protector of the rights of the individual states.

In April, 1777 Orange county lost some of its territory. In that month the General Assembly of the state designated the northwest portion of Orange as a new county and named it Caswell to honor Governor Richard Caswell.

Orange county, primarily an agricultural community, was beginning to take on some of the aspects of industrialization. In April, 1776, the Provincial Congress had designated Ambrose Ramsey of Chatham county (formed from Orange in 1770), Nathaniel Rochester, William Johnston and Thomas Burke as commissioners for the establishment of a gun factory in the Hillsboro District. An allotment of £1,000 was granted for the initiation of this project. This sum of money was inadequate, but the absence of sufficient funds was not the only difficulty that the commissioners experienced. A machine for the boring of gun barrels and skilled operators were both necessary for the chief operation in the manufacture of muskets, and neither could be obtained. Despite this obstacle, the project was inaugurated, and as a temporary expedient, local blacksmiths were at first employed to make different parts for the guns. When a rifle-boring machine was eventually acquired, a shop was erected near a creek on the property of Burke about two miles northeast of Hillsboro.

There had also been a severe paper shortage in the state. With this in mind the General Assembly had offered a bounty for the production of that article. A paper mill was established a mile and a half northeast of Hillsboro with John Holgan (Hogan) as proprietor. Agents were established in several localities throughout the state to collect the necessary rags. An advertisement which appeared in the *North Carolina Gazette* of November 17,1777 stated that "the young Ladies are assured, that by sending to the Paper Mill an old Handkerchief, no longer fit to cover their snowy Breasts, there is a Possibility of its returning to them in the Form of a Billet Deaux from their Lovers. . . ."

In October the war had been brought home to the inhabitants of the county by the reception of the news that Francis Nash, who had been promoted to the rank of brigadier-general, had been killed in the battle of Germantown at the head of his North Carolina troops on October 4. With the death of Nash, Orange county, Hillsboro and the state of North Carolina lost one of their most promising political and military leaders.

In the spring of 1778 the General Assembly met in New Bern

and several acts were passed which directly affected Orange county. One was an act of state-wide scope to secure supplies for North Carolina troops in the field. A quota was established for each county. Orange county's share included 73 hats, 306 yards of linen, 146 yards of wool, 146 pairs of shoes and 146 pairs of stockings. On April 20 the Assembly passed an act authorizing the construction of a new court house in Hillsboro, and Nathaniel Rochester and William Courtney were designated as commissioners to supervise the construction. It was first proposed that the new edifice be constructed of brick, but this was soon discarded in favor of lumber because of the war-time shortages in building materials. The building was constructed near the site of the present day court house and contained only one large room with dimensions of about 40 x 25 feet. This building served as court house for Orange county until late 1789 or 1790 when the structure was destroyed by fire. The need for this building had been justified in March when the Superior court had met in Hillsboro for the first time in five years with Judges Samuel Ashe and James Iredell presiding and with Waightsill Avery prosecuting.

The summer of 1778 was a period of rather severe drought, and the infant industries of the county suffered along with the farmers. The gun factory was forced to cease operations due to the lack of water to turn its wheel. The drought also hampered the activities at the paper mill, but Holgan was allowed an extension of time by the General Assembly in which to start production and obtain the premium which had been offered for paper making.

Although there was a great deal of interest in military matters and recruiting was in "great forwardness," there were domestic disturbances. The religious life of the community was experiencing a period of uncertainty. The Reverend Alexander McMillan had for some time held regular Presbyterian services in the court house in conjunction with the congregations of Little River and New Hope. However, in September, 1778, the pastor was deposed by the Presbytery for drunkenness and other acts of immorality. For a number of years following there were no regular Presbyterian services in Hillsboro, but it is assumed that the communicants visited one of the churches at Eno, New Hope, Little River, or Haw Fields, all of which were located within a radius of fourteen miles.

In August of 1778, the General Assembly met in Hillsboro for a rather short session. In the eleven days that they met the Senate sat in St. Matthew's church, while the House of Commons held its meetings in the court house.

For the town, the county, and the state, the tempo of the war quickened in 1779. Militia units from Orange county served in South Carolina under the command of General John Butler and distinguished themselves under Major-General Benjamin Lincoln when the latter made his attack on the British at Stono Ferry. Hillsboro itself became a depot for the collection and storage of supplies for the army, and the town was soon teeming with activity. The Governor of the state divided his time between the towns of Halifax and Hillsboro. In April, 1780, Abner Nash had assumed the responsibilities of the state, replacing Richard Caswell, who had served three successive terms as governor and was ineligible to succeed himself.

The town of Hillsboro became something of a focal point for the military activities of the state. In late May, 1780, had come the news of the surrender of Charleston, South Carolina by General Lincoln to the British forces under the command of Sir Henry Clinton and Lord Cornwallis. In June, the Baron de Kalb, temporarily serving as commander of the Southern Department, halted in Hillsboro with 2,000 troops which had been marching to the relief of Charleston. The hungry soldiers exhausted all provisions of the vicinity before they resumed their march to the southward.

In July, the new commander of the Southern Department, Horatio Gates, arrived in Hillsboro. He was greeted with a group of ragged and hungry Virginia militia and the remnants of Colonel Buford's command which had fled to this sanctuary after they had been cut to pieces in South Carolina by the British Legion of Banastre Tarleton. For a number of weeks Gates made the town his headquarters, busily collecting available supplies and concentrating troops. The new governor, Abner Nash, aided greatly in the collection of provisions and when an inadequate number of wagons were reported, he made arrangements that the surplus supplies be stockpiled along Gates' proposed route of march. The hungry militia had a tendency to pillage the inhabitants, but their activities were greatly curbed by the efforts of Thomas Burke, who dispatched letters to both Gates and the Continental Congress which declared that the citizenry would defend their property by force of arms if necessary. It was with a sigh of relief that the people watched the army march south towards Salisbury.

In August, disaster struck. Word of General Gates' defeat by Cornwallis at the battle of Camden, South Carolina on August 16 reached the town on August 20. The dispatch rider who brought the information was probably Gates himself, who arrived in Hillsboro long before any of the remaining survivors of the battle. He had covered the approximately 180 miles between Hillsboro and Camden in the near record time of three days and a half, a feat which "does admirable credit to the activity of a man in his time of life. But it is a disgrace to the general and the soldier. . . ." All the preparations and the carefully collected supplies had gone for naught. Governor Nash, then very ill, was too exhausted to aid Gates in the rehabilitation of the army. He had requested the General Assembly to create a Board of War to cooperate with him in the conduct of the war. The Assembly had gone beyond the request and designated greater powers to the Board than had been anticipated by Nash. This action so antagonized the governor that henceforth he cooperated with the board no more than was absolutely necessary. The first members of the original board as appointed by the assembly were Archibald MacLaine, Thomas Polk, John Penn, Oroondates Davis and Alexander Martin, but both Polk and MacLaine refused to serve. The board began to hold formal meetings on September 14, 1780 and assumed the entire responsibility for the military activities of the state. They met in Hillsboro continuously until December 1, 1780, after which they removed to Halifax.

General Gates had designated Hillsboro a rendezvous for his shattered army. The town was soon swarming with soldiery, who boasted confidently that, despite their recent disaster, they were able to whip the British. The army was soon so large that they overflowed into the surrounding countryside. There were frequent clashes between the civilians and the soldiers. The military seemed to have little respect for civil authority and the officers of the army apparently made little effort to acquaint the rank and file with their responsibilities toward the inhabitants. The Board of War authorized the issuance of certificates for the grain taken for the use of the army, but wandering bands of foragers often confiscated or impressed grain from the farmers without resorting to the formality of a certificate. All roads leading into Hillsboro were soon crowded with wagons bringing in supplies for the army. The Board of War designated the court house as a storehouse, but many critical items were still impossible to secure. The church was also ordered to be renovated and used as a hospital.

It was a ragged army that was trying to pull itself together under the command of Gates. The 400 or 500 members of the Maryland line, one of the crack units of the Continental army, were without shoes. The Virginia militia were not only barefooted, but were not suitably clothed and many of their number were without arms and ammunition. Virginia did send some food for her troops, but little clothing and no ammunition. The Board of War collected all available hides and leather, placed the local tannery under state authority and established a shoe factory under the superintendency of John Taylor. Everyone capable of doing leather work was pressed into service. Cobblers were exempted from militia duty. Leather was often secured by barter. Not only was the factory engaged in the manufacture of shoes, but also they repaired all shoes that were in need of that service. Tailors and those women known to be handy with a needle were pressed into service making or repairing uniforms. Letters begging for aid were dispatched to every conceivable source of supplies. A desperate search for salt was initiated. Despite these very efficient operations, the Board of War went beyond the supply problem and made something of a nuisance of themselves. They prepared minute instructions for the military, detailing operations on how to approach the enemy, how to fight and, if necessary, how to retreat. These instructions were possibly an indication that the Board of War had lost confidence in the ability of Gates. To add to the confusion in Hillsboro, Governor John Rutledge of South Carolina, who had fled before the advance of the British, was attempting to run the affairs of his state by remote control from within the protection of Gates' army.

The intelligence that Lord Cornwallis in South Carolina was making preparations for an invasion of North Carolina and Virginia alerted the army. A detachment of the British army under Major James Craig had already captured the port city of Wilmington. To restrict the activities of the Tories in that area, the Hillsboro Brigade of militia was ordered to the eastern part of the state. Other units of Orange county militia were stationed in several areas over the state. With the news of the contemplated British invasion of the state, Governor Nash had hurried to Halifax to rouse the populace in that section. Gates held his army under marching orders after it was discovered that Cornwallis had advanced into the state as far as Charlotte. In the meantime, the Board of War had come to the conclusion that Hillsboro and Orange county were unable to support the army during the approaching winter. They persuaded Gates that an adequate supply of provisions could be found farther south in the vicinity of Salisbury. With the news that Cornwallis had retreated back into South Carolina as a result of the battle of King's Mountain and sickness within his army, Gates marched his force toward Salisbury in late November.

Later that month another general appeared in Hillsboro in search of the army. General Nathanael Greene of Rhode Island had been appointed by General Washington to succeed Gates and had come searching for his command. Finding the army gone, he hurried after them. Both the town and the county settled back to enjoy what they hoped would be a period of relative peace and quiet.

This period was all too short. In late January, 1781 dispatches arrived reporting that Brigadier-General Daniel Morgan had decisively defeated Banastre Tarleton at the battle of the Cowpens on January 17, but had been unable to consolidate his victory and had immediately fled northward. This was followed closely by the news that Greene and the southern army were retreating across North Carolina with Cornwallis and the British army in full pursuit, determined to wipe out the humiliation of Cowpens. As the British had attempted to cross the Catawba, Brigadier-General William Lee Davidson of the North Carolina militia, had attempted to slow the pursuers at Cowan's Ford on the Catawba, and had lost his life in the effort. Part of his little force had been composed of Orange county militia. As a result of this defeat, orders soon arrived to remove the supplies and British prisoners of war confined in Hillsboro out of danger into Virginia. Refugees from the southern part of the state were soon crowding into the county. Greene was reported to be at Guilford Court House, but it was soon learned that he had continued his retreat and had crossed the Dan river into the comparative safety of Virginia. Cornwallis had halted at this barrier and all indications were that his next move would be to Hillsboro.

Unknown to the Whigs, Hillsboro was the foundation stone of the British invasion of North Carolina. Possibly because of the Regulator faction living within the borders of the county, Orange county was considered by the British as being basically loyalist in sentiment. As early as June, 1780, Cornwallis had contacted the known Tories of Orange county, who had responded by dispatching emissaries who reassured him of the fidelity and loyalty of the inhabitants of the county. These representatives had suggested to the British General that he delay his proposed invasion of North Carolina until the crops were harvested. Cornwallis had agreed to this proposal, but had in turn suggested that they prepare secret magazines of supplies and remain quiet until the appearance of the troops of the King.

There was an early spring in 1781, and the fruit trees were beginning to blossom when the British army marched into Hillsboro on February 20. On February 22, Cornwallis raised the Royal Standard and issued a proclamation to the accompaniment of a twenty-one gun salute. This proclamation called for loyal subjects to repair immediately under arms to Hillsboro, bringing with them a ten days supply of provisions. The loyalists were assured of the full cooperation of the British army in "the re-establishment of good order and constitutional government," and Cornwallis declared that he had come to rescue His Majesty's "faithful and loyal subjects from the cruel tyranny under which they have groaned for many years." Ex-Governor Josiah Martin, who had accompanied the red coats, busied himself with the details of re-establishing the authority of the King, but his efforts apparently met with little success.

Despite the claims of the Royalist newspapers of the day that Tories were flocking to the Royal Standard and their proud boast that as many as 700 recruits had joined the British army in one day, there was actually little local strength added to the invading army. Many loyalists had ridden into town to learn the news, inspect the King's troops, and discuss the proclamation, but few expressed a desire to enter the service of George III. Many were bitter toward Britain because little effort had been made to aid them since the beginning of the war and the defeat at Moore's Creek Bridge, and as a result they had suffered much from their neighbors and political rivals. Others expressed the opinion that the British army was spread out too thin over too large an area to afford any degree of security for the supporters of the King. Cornwallis soon discovered that he had relied too heavily on the optimistic reports of the loyalist emissaries in June. He had failed to discount those loyalists who were lost by premature uprisings, or who had become fearful and had journeyed to South Carolina to enjoy the protection of the British army. Many had grown cautious because of the miscarriage of British plans in the past. The activities of local Whigs had broken the spirits of others. The slim response to his proclamation bred disgust in the British general and he later wrote of the North Carolina Tories, "Our experience has shown that their numbers are not so great as has been represented and that their friendship was only passive."

To keep his men busy and out of mischief, as well as to deprive them of the opportunity to plunder the countryside, Cornwallis directed that the streets of Hillsboro near his artillery park be paved. Stones were collected and the intersection of King and Churton streets was paved for 150 yards in all four directions. But it was during their off-duty hours that the soldiers managed to get into trouble. After dark they often left the protection of the picket lines in search of whiskey and rum. These strays were often shot or kidnapped by small groups of Whigs who had concealed themselves around the fringes of the camp. These nuisance raids eventually necessitated the issuance of an order confining the thirsty rank and file within the limits of the encampment area after nightfall.

A critical deficiency in supplies developed. The Tories had not established the magazines as they had pledged. The large number of American troops which had been stationed in the county after the defeat of Gates at Camden had improverished the surrounding area. The only cattle left in the vicinity were the draught oxen owned by the loyalists, who had managed to conceal them from the American foraging parties. These were impressed and slaughtered by the British Commissary department despite the bitter protests of their owners. Foraging detachments were sent out into the county in search of additional beef, but they met with little success. Only the discovery of a quantity of salt beef and a number of hogs allowed the British army to remain as long as it did. The situation became so acute that a number of horses belonging to the army were slaughtered to provide fresh meat.

The North Carolina militia were growing bolder. A group of mounted militia under the command of Captain Joseph Graham attacked the garrison at Hart's mill within a mile and a half of Hillsboro. This detachment had been stationed at the mill for the purpose of grinding meal for the British army and was composed largely of British regulars. Graham and his company boldly attacked the mill, killed and wounded nine of the defenders and escaped with nineteen prisoners.

One of the most violent of the Tories operating in Orange county at this time was the notorious partisan leader, David Fanning. Although he had been born in Johnston county, Fanning had spent much of his early life in Orange county. He was afflicted with a disease then known as "scald head" which made him repugnant to the sight of others. He always wore a cap and was so self-conscious of his affliction that he seldom ate at a table with the family or slept in the house. He had early left his father's home in Johnston county and had come to

Orange where he had been taken in by John O. Deniell. At the outbreak of hostilities he had secured a commission in the loyalist militia. Prior to the arrival of Cornwallis he had, without authority, distributed a circular promising many inducements to those who joined the forces of the King. This circular, along with the proclamation of Cornwallis, had resulted in the embodiment of a large number of Tories in the area between the Deep and Haw rivers under the leadership of Dr. John Pyle. To afford protection and an escort for this group, Cornwallis dispatched Banastre Tarleton and the British Legion to make a junction with them at the plantation of John Butler. The Tories made a picnic of their assembly, strolling around the neighborhood in a group, bidding their friends farewell and drinking numerous toasts to each other and their cause.

Tarleton's departure from Hillsboro had been noted and reported to Lieutenant-Colonel "Light Horse Harry" Lee and Brigadier-General Andrew Pickens whom Greene had ordered back across the Dan to harass the British and report their movements. Pickens and Lee decided to execute a surprise attack on Tarleton. One attempt failed when they charged a reported noonday stop. Their quarry had halted here, but had moved on. They did, however, discover that Tarleton was planning to bivouac that night on the plantation of Colonel William O'Neil.

As they were hastening towards Col. O'Neil's plantation they were suddenly challenged by two of Pyle's men who had mistaken the green uniform of Lee's Legion for the similar dress of Tarleton's British Legion. But Lee and Pickens were after bigger game. They sent a message to Pyle requesting him to station his men on the side of the road and allow their troops to pass, stating as their excuse that their men were tired and wished to reach camp before nightfall. The Tory leader, completely duped by the Americans, obligingly stationed his men alongside the road. Henry Lee, with a flair for military dramatics, carried the deception to its limit by extending his hand to grasp that of Pyle, when the sounds of battle from the rear of the column curbed further histrionics. Prior to this, Lee and Pickens had not time to reveal the deception to all of their subordinates. The militia units at the rear of the column recognized the red strips of cloth in the hats of the men alongside the road as the badge of Toryism and after one of the officers had drawn his sword and struck one of the strangers in the head, rushed to the attack.

The terrified Tories thought that they were the victims of a horrible mistake and filled the air with cries of "You are killing your own men!" "I am a friend to his Majesty!" and "Hurrah for King George!" When they finally did attempt to protect themselves, their hasty shots flew wild and did no damage. Seeing that further resistance was useless, the survivors fled, leaving ninety of their number dead. The loss of the forces of Lee and Pickens was one horse. The two American leaders, now feeling that there was no chance to surprise Tarleton, returned to their camp of the night before.

Tarleton first learned of this "hacking match" when several of the wounded Tories arrived in his camp. Still under the impression that they had been attacked by British troops, these men complained bitterly to the British leader of the cruelty of his dragoons. That night, under the cover of darkness, Tarleton hastily moved his detachment back within the protection of the British lines at Hillsboro.

Hillsboro had now become untenable for the British and Cornwallis was forced to make his preparations for departure before the expiration of the time allowed in his proclamation. The supply situation became so critical that his commissary-general was forced to lead a file of men from house to house requisitioning those provisions which were discovered, regardless of the political affiliations of the owners. The commissary-general made a survey and declared that the town and county were no longer able to support the British army. On February 25, Cornwallis moved his army out of Hillsboro and retired to a new position on Alamance creek between the Deep and Haw rivers. Although this new position was intended as a protection to the Tories of the area, plundering of the inhabitants, especially by the women of the army, became such a problem that frequent reprimands were issued decrying the practice.

Tarleton was detached to observe the movements of Greene's army which had recrossed the Dan. Tarleton camped on the old

Alamance battle ground, and was constantly harassed by small units from the American army which skirmished with his outposts. So nervous did the British cavalry leader become that one night he charged out of his camp and killed several of a group of Tories who were marching to join the British army. On another occasion he attacked another group who were driving cattle to Cornwallis. These two hasty actions succeeded in alienating many of the friends of the King in the county.

As Cornwallis approached the boundaries of the county and moved into Guilford, many of the militia of the county shouldered their muskets and hunting rifles and hurried to join General Greene. There was a sharp skirmish with the British general at Clapp's mill on Big Alamance creek, in which the militiamen from Orange county distinguished themselves. But even before Cornwallis had won his pyrrhic victory over Greene at the battle of Guilford Court House, many of the Tories of Orange county who had enlisted in British service and who were now "convinced of the Folly of their Conduct" were returning to their homes and were petitioning the local government for legal forgiveness.

As the British marched toward Wilmington and the coast, civil affairs occupied the attention of the people. In June the General Assembly met at Wake Court House and on the 25th of that month elected Thomas Burke as Governor of the state. For the first two months of his administration Burke administered the duties of his office from Halifax. He received a report that Tories in the southern part of Orange county were active and were plundering their Whig neighbors. Coupled with this report was the news that David Fanning was once again operating in the county and attacking fortified plantations which he usually subdued and plundered, often executing the defenders. In September Burke returned to Hillsboro to organize an extensive campaign against the Tories. One of his first measures was the embodiment of a combination infantry and cavalry company under the command of a Captain Allen of New Hope. It was hoped that this group would be able to furnish protection for the Whigs in the vicinity of Hillsboro.

General John Butler was in command of a small body of

militia which was located on the south side of Haw river. Burke had been in town only three days when he received intelligence that Fanning was planning to surprise Butler and his men. Fanning was acting in conjunction with the famous Colonel Hector McNeil, and was in command of a group of 500 men. Burke immediately dispatched a messenger to warn Butler and ordered him to move to a position which offered greater security. As Butler initiated a retreat in the direction of Hillsboro he was pursued by Fanning. During the course of the march, Fanning was informed that Burke had returned to Hillsboro and that there was an inadequate guard stationed at that place. The Tory leader immediately set his course for that town. Fanning determined to employ the same tactics which he had used when he had captured Pittsboro on July 18, 1781. The night was dark and cloaked the Tory movements as they approached the town. The morning of Wednesday, September 12, 1781, was one of heavy fog which further obscured the movements of Fanning and his men. The 500 men quietly entered the town from all directions, and by the time the inhabitants were aware of their danger there was no opportunity to present an organized resistance. The majority of the townspeople remained in their homes to defend their families and possessions and the steady fire of the invaders kept them divided. The Tories gradually converged on the eastern part of the town where Burke's home was located. Burke put up a vigorous defence, aided by his aid-de-camp, a Captain Reid, his secretary, John Huske, and an orderly sergeant of the Continental Line. This little group was soon overpowered, but Burke refused to surrender his sword because of the hostile attitude of many of the Tories. Only after the assurance of a British officer accompanying the Tories that no harm would be done him did the Governor give up his weapon. Fanning claimed that, in addition to the Governor and his Council, he had taken over 200 prisoners. The doors of the local jail were forced and about thirty loyalists were released, one of whom was to have been hanged that day. The guards were locked in the jail in the places of their late prisoners. Many of the homes of the town were plundered and tavern doors were forced and the rum stores were brought out. It was 2 p.m. when the

Tory officers finally gained control of their rioting men and marched them out of Hillsboro before the countryside was alarmed.

Alexander Mebane, a colonel in the local militia, rode to warn Butler. Butler immediately marched in an attempt to intercept the Tories and recapture their prisoners. Near Lindley's mill on Cain creek, about eighteen miles from Hillsboro, he placed his force in ambush. Butler posted his men on high ground on the south side of the stream commanding the approach to the ford. The advance guard of the Tories was commanded by Colonel Hector McNeil; their earlier success had made them careless and usual precautions were neglected. At the opening fire of Butler's men, McNeil fell with three musket balls in his body, and his men began a precipitate retreat until they were rallied by Fanning. Fanning, after sending off the prisoners, took one group, crossed upstream from the scene of the action and came in on the rear of Butler's group. The Whigs were thrown into confusion, but soon rallied, and the ensuing engagement developed into a running battle which lasted approximately four hours. At the end of that time, Butler and his militia withdrew, leaving behind twenty-four killed and ninety wounded, ten others having been taken prisoner by the Tories. Fanning had lost twenty-seven killed and sixty of their number were so badly wounded that they were left behind on the field of battle. An additional thirty wounded were able to walk and continued with the main group. Fanning himself was wounded in the left arm and lost so much blood that he was hidden in the woods, with a guard of three men, while the remainder of his group continued on to Wilmington with the prisoners, who were turned over to Major Craig, the British officer in command of that city. Butler, after his retreat from the battlefield, turned and pursued the Tories but he was intercepted by a group of British regulars from Wilmington at Hammond's creek, and after a slight engagement retired to Campbell Town in Cumberland county.

When Burke was captured, Alexander Martin of Guilford county and Speaker of the Senate, became acting Governor of the State. The town of Hillsboro soon recovered from Fanning's raid, and affairs fell into their regular orderly processes. Seven of Fanning's men had been captured, and despite the local feeling, they were held for trial. Court was held when Judge John Williams of Granville county passed through Hillsboro on his way to hold court in Salem. He was accompanied by two young lawyers, Alfred Moore and William R. Davie. Judge Williams was persuaded to hold court, with Moore acting as prosecuting attorney and with Davie as defense attorney. Davie had just secured his license to practice law and this was his first case. His inexperienced pleas were not enough to save his clients who were convicted and sentenced to death. Despite the dire threats of Fanning who threatened retribution "tenfold to one" if his men were harmed, three of the men were hanged on February 1, while Burke later commuted the sentences of the remaining four on the condition that they serve twelve months in the Continental army.

In late January, Burke had returned to Hillsboro and had once again assumed the duties of Governor. After he had been turned over to Major Craig at Wilmington he had been escorted to Charleston, South Carolina, and had been allowed a parole to James Island, outside the city. There were a number of renegade loyalists on the island who had taken a particular dislike to Burke and on one occasion fired into the house where he was staying, killing one of his companions and wounding another. Burke's protest to British authorities went unnoticed. Burke, fearing for his life, escaped from the island and returned to North Carolina. As breaking a parole at the time involved personal honor and integrity, Burke was censured by many of his constituents, although many of the more influential leaders around the state defended his action. Hot charges were levied by both sides, and the matter became a point of controversy between General Greene and the British authorities. Burke, however, busied himself with his duties, found a number of irregularities within the state government and soon began "calling our over-grown fellows in the Public Departments with a very becoming Severity, and is really making some Surprising discoveries."

Before the return of Burke, Acting Governor Martin had issued a proclamation calling upon all Tories to surrender themselves and submit to the laws and the government of the state, and offering amnesty and pardon to all those who should enlist in the Continental army. On February 29, 1782, Fanning made a counter proposition which requested that he and his adherents should be granted a "truce ground" similar to that which had been set aside for the Tories in South Carolina by General Francis Marion. He proposed that this area should extend "from Cumberland twenty miles South and thirty miles East and West, to be free of your light horse, etc." This offer was rejected and then Fanning, as if he were making one last desperate move, redoubled his efforts in depredations against the people of the state. He reported that he had been issued a new commission, which stated that all who refused to join him should be put to death. For a short period he terrorized the Whigs in the Hillsboro District. A number of people were killed by his group and it was reported that the women who fell into his hands were "abused in a barbarous manner." But despite these operations, the career of David Fanning was fast drawing to a close. The General Assembly was supposed to meet in Hillsboro in April. As protection, Governor Burke ordered out the State Legion, with such additional horsemen as could be embodied, to advance against the Tories in the vicinity of Deep river, while General Butler was directed to assemble 200 of the county militia at Hillsboro for the immediate protection of the General Assembly. Despite these precautions, there was an alarm on the night of April 30 (later proved to be false) that Fanning was planning to attack the town. The legislators were roused from their beds and paraded in the streets before it was discovered that the report was false. But Fanning, unknown to the Whigs, had quietly gotten married and had fled to the truce grounds in South Carolina, where he remained until the British evacuated Charleston and in 1784 he went to Nova Scotia where he was to spend the remaining years of his life.

In the April General Assembly Burke was not a candidate for re-election. He at first indicated that he would be, but when he found that the prevailing sentiment was against him, he retired from public office and Alexander Martin was elected to succeed him. Burke began to dissipate rather heavily and brooded over the criticism of his escape from the British and of his public career. In December, 1783 he died at his home in Hillsboro at the age of thirty-six years.

One of the many problems which confronted the April assembly was the disposition of confiscated Tory estates. A number of commissioners were appointed to handle this matter. William Moore was elected Commissioner of Confiscated Estates for the Hillsboro District. One other event of local interest occurred on May 18, the last meeting of the Assembly. Thomas Davis was appointed public printer for the state and directed to establish his press in Hillsboro as soon as possible, and there he was to publish the laws and legislative journal of North Carolina.

Although for all practical purposes the war was over, General Greene was still obliged to maintain an army of observation in South Carolina, and it was necessary that the army be supplied with provisions. Alexander Mebane served as Commissioner of Specific Supplies for Orange county. Hillsboro served as a collecting point, and over 2,000 pounds of salt and fresh meat were collected throughout the county for the use of the army. The local jail also was used to confine a number of British and loyalist prisoners of war during this period, while negotiations were being carried forward for their exchange.

As the county and the state were slowly collecting themselves and the wounds of war were being healed, the General Assembly once more met in Hillsboro on April 19, 1783. St. Matthew's church and the court house were again used as assembly halls for the legislators. Alexander Martin was reelected governor of the state, despite strong opposition by Richard Caswell, who was now again eligible for that office. There were a number of problems which confronted the Assembly. There was the very important consideration of strengthening the union with the other states, and there was a strong movement for the establishment of better educational facilities. A remnant of the Whig-Tory conflict was still evident; the matter of the expulsion of the Tories had to be dealt with. A movement to establish Hillsboro as the permanent seat of the state government was gaining momentum. It was with this in mind that a post route was established between the town and Richmond, Virginia, and there was agitation to move some of the public offices to Hillsboro. But in this matter of location, Hillsboro was vigorously opposed by the towns of New Bern, Tarboro, Smithfield, and Fayetteville.

The people of Orange county were also becoming versed in the democratic processes of government. Objecting to the practices of John Steel, a Justice of the Peace in the Hawfields community, they submitted a memorial to the House of Commons protesting his conduct. The memorial was referred to a committee for study, but before any action was taken, Steel resigned his commission.

There was also evidence that the people of Orange county were beginning to think in terms of national problems. In 1784 there had, throughout the United States, been a strong movement against the Society of the Cincinnati, an organization composed of ex-officers in the Continental army. Although Archibald Lytle, the representative of the town of Hillsboro had been a delegate to the national convention of the society which had met in May, 1784, in Philadelphia, the people of the county still voiced their protest against the organization. In the session of the General Assembly which met in New Bern in November, 1784, the citizens of the county presented a petition asking that members of this "self-erected aristocracy" be prohibited from holding seats in the General Assembly. As a result of the petition, John Butler, representative from Orange county, introduced a bill embodying the mandates of the declaration, although Butler himself was eligible for membership in the society. The introduction of the bill may possibly have been the reason for Butler's subsequent resignation as Brigadier-General of militia for the Hillsboro District. There was no action taken on the bill.

The struggle to establish Hillsboro as the capital of the state carried over from one meeting of the Assembly to the next, despite the opposition of other ambitious communities. In 1785 a bill to this purpose was barely defeated by a vote of 41-37. In the Fayetteville General Assembly of November, 1786, the Treasurer and the Comptroller of the state were directed to move their offices and records to Hillsboro "in order that those offices may be convenient to the greater part of the inhabitants of the State." The Comptroller apparently procrastinated, for a year later the General Assembly issued a similar directive to that officer.

Hillsboro, because of its location, was continuing to play a prominent part in the economy of North Carolina. It was the most convenient place for business men of the eastern and western areas of the state to meet and discuss their affairs. It was probably with this in mind that the General Assembly, on December 3, 1781, passed an act levying a tax on the residents of the Hillsboro District and the town of Hillsboro, the returns to be used in the repair of the court house and stocks, and for the repair of the streets within the town limits.

In 1788 an event of national importance occurred in Hillsboro. This was the convention which met in that place and which had been called to consider the ratification of the Constitution of the United States. Orange county was represented by Alexander Mebane, William Mebane, William McCauley, William Sheppard and Jonathan Lindley, while Absalom Tatom was the delegate from the town of Hillsboro. The majority of the delegates who attended the convention were Anti-Federalists, and were led by Willie Jones of Halifax. This faction controlled the convention, as their majority numbered an even 100, but they did elect a Federalist, Samuel Johnston, as presiding officer of the body. Prominent names among the Anti-Federalists were Timothy Bloodworth, Joseph Caldwell, Judge Samuel Spencer and Major Joseph McDowell. The outstanding leaders of the Federalists were James Iredell, Samuel Johnston, William R. Davie, Richard Dobbs Spaight and Archibald MacLaine. The Anti-Federalists hoped that their opposition to the ratification of the Constitution would give greater weight to the general demand for amendments to that document. Every important phase of the Constitution was discussed and argued, but when ratification was put to a vote it was revealed that there had been no changes in the original sentiments of the delegates—ratification was defeated by a vote of 184-84. The convention then recommended that a Bill of Rights be included in the Constitution and submitted a total of twenty-six amendments for consideration. They also recommended that retaliatory tariffs be instituted against the United States in the event that the Union should levy duties on exports of North Carolina. It was proposed that the General Assembly take action "as speedily as may be" on the tremendous amount of paper currency which had been issued to finance the operations of the state during the war. The last matter taken under consideration by the convention during its eleven day session was of great interest to the people of Orange county. An ordinance was adopted which declared that the convention would not fix a seat of government for the state, but the matter should be left to the discretion of the General Assembly—provided the site would be within ten miles of Isaac Hunter's place in Wake county. This was the general area in which Wake Court House was located, then known locally as Bloomsbury.

In spite of this action by the convention, the struggle to establish the capital in Hillsboro was still carried forward in the General Assembly. At this date there was a definite need for a permanent site. From November, 1787 to November, 1788 the state paid a total of forty pounds for the transportation of the records of the Treasury office from Hillsboro to Tarboro to Hillsboro to Fayetteville. There was also the additional expense of five pounds each for the nine mounted members of the Orange county militia who escorted the treasury funds from Hillsboro to Fayetteville.

By the end of 1788 the citizens of North Carolina were becoming apprehensive over their status as members of an independent state surrounded by members of the federal union. Imports from North Carolina into the United States were charged the same tariffs as those levied on European goods. Alexander Mebane, delegate from Orange county, labored for a new convention when the General Assembly convened at Fayetteville in November, 1788. When the issue was put to a vote, it was decided that a new convention should be held in Fayetteville in November, 1789. Jonathan Lindley and Absalom Tatom of Orange county joined with Mebane in voting for the new convention. The legislature also considered the ordinance of the Hillsboro convention in regard to a permanent state capital.

Orange county delegates conducted an energetic campaign on final action. The matter was deferred until a later meeting.

On November 17, 1789 the second constitutional convention met in Fayetteville. Orange county delegates were James Christmass, Alexander Mebane, Thomas H. Perkins, William F. Strudwick and Joseph Hodge, while Samuel Benton represented the town of Hillsboro. This time the majority was in favor of the Federalists, and when the vote was taken the Constitution of the United States was ratified by North Carolina by a vote of 195-77. Among the Orange county delegation, Christmass and Benton were the only members who cast their votes in the affirmative. After adopting the twelve amendments which had been proposed by the national Congress, the convention adjourned on November 22.

The fight for the location of the capital still flourished. One hundred and nineteen members of the legislature entered a protest against the selection of Isaac Hunter's plantation. Nevertheless, in 1791 the ordinance was carried out and the Assembly appointed a commission of ten members to locate the new capital within ten miles of Hunter's place. On April 4, 1792, the commission purchased 1,000 acres from Colonel Joel Lane of Wake county and laid out a city of 400 acres. The struggle for the location of the capital was terminated. For Hillsboro and Orange county it signified the end of an era.

CHAPTER VI

THE FOUNDING OF THE UNIVERSITY OF NORTH CAROLINA

BY BLACKWELL P. ROBINSON, PH. D.

*Former Holder of the William R. Davie Scholarship
North Carolina Society of the Cincinnati*

The Orange county delegates, Thomas Burke, Nathaniel Rochester, Alexander Mebane, and John Butler, took their seats in the fifth Provincial Congress at Halifax on the eve of a dramatic moment. The following day, December 17, 1776, they had just been joined by their fifth colleague, John McCabe, when the Bill of Rights for the Constitution of the new State of North Carolina was passed. The next day, the Constitution itself was adopted by this constituent body.

The framers of the Constitution, realizing their great responsibility to unborn generations, had seen fit to lay the basis for state patronage and support of education by incorporating into that instrument Section Forty-One. A literal analogue of Section Forty-Five of the recently adopted Pennsylvania Constitution of 1776, it provided "that a School or Schools shall be established by the Legislature for the convenient Instruction of Youth, with such Salaries to the Masters paid by the Public, as may enable them to instruct at low Prices; and all useful Learning shall be duly encouraged and promoted in one or more Universities."

Little did the Orange county delegation realize how profoundly this mandate would affect their county, as well as the state as a whole.

Immediate compliance with this mandate was of course impossible. Even after the surender of Cornwallis and the return of peace, the resources and energies of the state were so nearly exhausted that it was not until 1784 that an abortive attempt was made to implement it.

The cue was given by Governor Alexander Martin in his opening address to the General Assembly October 26, 1784, when he exhorted: "Your schools of learning. . .are great objects of Legislative attention which cannot be too often repeated and held up to your view, that the mists of Ignorance be dissipated and good morals cultivated."

Shortly thereafter, on November 8th, William Sharpe, of Rowan county, presented to the House of Commons the first bill for establishing a state university in North Carolina. Drafted by a Presbyterian divine of Rowan, Samuel Eusebius McCorkle, it was intended to be presented by another Rowanite, Judge Spruce Macay, who, however, was riding the recently created Morgan district, which stretched from Salisbury to what is now Jonesboro, Tennessee. The bill had short shrift in the Assembly. Its defeat may be attributed to the fact that the conscientious author had eschewed, as a source of revenue, such mundane devices as a tax on spiritous liquors, employed by Queen's college in Charlotte and by the New Bern Academy. Instead, he proposed a scheme by which a poll tax was to be levied upon professional men, merchants, county officials, and salaries. Its defeat may also be attributed to the financial stringency and the general confusion of the times, the woeful scarcity of hard money, and the fear on the part of the more radical republicans, who were in the ascendancy, that this proposed University might become a bulwark of aristocratic privilege.

The succeeding years, in which the forces of conservatism were gaining strength, saw a concomitant efflorescence of popular interest in both secondary and higher education. This interest was fanned and inflamed in western North Carolina by such leaders as Joseph Alexander, Thomas Polk, Waightstill Avery, Ephraim Brevard, Alexander Martin, Samuel Eusebius McCorkle, and David Caldwell. The eastern and central portions were represented by such men as Hugh Williamson, a graduate of the College of Philadelphia, student of science and medicine at Edinburgh, London, and Utrecht; William Hooper, a Harvard graduate and founder of Science Hall at Hillsboro in 1785, the two Eton-bred Jones brothers, Willie and Allen, of Halifax and Northampton; and the conservative triumvirate, William

Richardson Davie of Halifax, Alfred Moore of Wilmington, and Samuel Johnston of Edenton.

Contemporary evidence is scant as to the persuasive campaign waged by these men in behalf of securing a charter for the University. At this same time Davie and James Iredell, of Edenton, were using their powerful influence to obtain the ratification of the Federal Constitution, which had been defeated in Hillsboro in July, 1788 by the state rights forces, led by Willie Jones. It is interesting to note that the Constitution was finally ratified by the people in convention at Fayetteville, November 21, 1789. Twenty days later, the General Assembly, composed of a great many of the same men, passed the act to establish the University. William Richardson Davie introduced both measures.

The fight to secure the passage of this latter measure had been a hard one. Greatest credit, according to Archibald De Bow Murphey in an oration delivered in 1827 in the old chapel, now Person Hall, must be given to Davie and Alfred Moore, who had done most to prepare the public mind for the establishment of this University. Davie, a prominent lawyer and orator, who had taken the lofty flowing style of Lord Bolingbroke as his model, and Moore, the Attorney General, who had adopted the plain and precise style of Dean Swift, succeeded in arousing "the ambition of parents and their sons; they excited emulation among ingenuous youth; they depicted in glowing colours the necessity of establishing a public school or university."

Apparently by a preconceived arrangement, the important bill for the establishment of the University was entrusted to Davie. A more natural choice could hardly have been made. He had been instructed in his youth by his Glasgow-bred maternal uncle, for whom he was named, who had been the leading Presbyterian minister of the South Carolina back country. He had been educated at two Presbyterian strongholds, Queen's college and the College of New Jersey, later Princeton. Finally, after marrying Sarah Jones, of Northampton county, he had been under the aegis of her father, General Allen Jones, who, with his brother Willie, had attended Eton and who represented the aristocratic forces of the Roanoke valley. A popular partisan leader during the Revolution, and efficient commissary general of the state, who served under General Nathanael Greene, a conservative statesman, and a framer of the Federal Constitution, Davie possessed the physical and mental attributes to make him a leader.

The Assembly to which Davie presented the University bill was strongly Federalist in complexion, in contrast to the Assembly which had killed the former impracticable and visionary bill. It was therefore with a sanguine confidence that, on November 12, 1789, he introduced a measure so close to his heart. His optimism was reflected four days later in a letter to Iredell: "The University Bill will certainly pass."

In the preamble to the bill, Davie set forth the premise that "in all well regulated governments it is the indispensable duty of every Legislature to consult the happiness of a rising generation, and endeavour to fit them for an honourable discharge of the social duties of life, by paying the strictest attention to their education." It followed that "an University supported by permanent funds and well endowed, would have the most direct tendency" to answer this purpose.

The proposed charter provided for a coöptative board, composed of the most prominent men in the state, who were declared to be a body politic and corporate. These trustees, in order to carry the charter into effect, were to meet at Fayetteville during the session of the next General Assembly. Davie, a practical Scot, realized that the University should be "well endowed" and supported by "permanent funds." Yet he realized, no doubt, that an outright request for money would mean defeat. The bill therefore sought to encourage gifts and subscriptions by a provision to the effect that anyone subscribing, within the next five years, ten pounds, at five equal annual payments, should be entitled to have one student educated at the University free from any expense of tuition. Article X, moreover, provided that "the public hall of the library and four of the colleges shall be called severally by the names of one or another of the six persons who shall within four years contribute the largest sums towards the funds of the University, the highest subscriber or donor having choice in the order of their respective donations."

Contemporary evidence is unfortunately lacking concerning the debates which ensued upon the bill. Fordyce M. Hubbard, Davie's ante-bellum biographer, asserted that they encountered "much resistance," since "men of liberal culture were many indeed, but not common." In fact, a great many of those who were called upon to vote, either directly or indirectly, had "never enjoyed the benefits of learning, and could not easily appreciate them." Many saw the plan as "one step towards a permanent aristocracy," while others objected to the expense. An additional difficulty lay in the fact that the bill "mingled itself. . .with party politics."

Despite these objections, Davie was able, through a combination of tact, logic, satire, and eloquence, to gain its passage through both houses of the Assembly. An act was also passed conferring on the University the proceeds from escheated property.

Seven days after the passage of the University charter, the first meeting of the Board of Trustees was held in Fayetteville. A manuscript volume of "Trustee Minutes" in the Carolina Room of the Library of the University reveals that the Speaker of the Senate, Charles Johnson, of Chowan county, was the chairman of this first meeting. Orange county was represented by Alexander Mebane and James Hogg. Other trustees present were Stephen Cabarrus of Chowan (Speaker of the House), Benjamin Smith of Brunswick, Hugh Williamson of Edenton, Thomas Person of Granville, William Lenoir of Wilkes, Robert Dixon of Duplin, John Hamilton of Rutherford, John Stokes of Surry, William Blount of Tennessee, William Porter of Rutherford, Joseph Dixon of Lincoln, and William R. Davie of Halifax.

It was fitting that Davie, assisted by James Hogg, should have been entrusted at this meeting with the first labor in its founding. They were charged with the responsibility of having "a sufficient number of Copies" printed of the two subscriptions which were to be opened. One was to be conducted in the manner specifically directed by the charter and the other "on the principle of a mere donation."

It was also Davie who announced to the assembled trustees the donation of twenty thousand acres of land by Colonel Benjamin Smith of Brunswick county. This generous grant, representing Colonel Smith's reward for his services in the Revolution, was located in what was to become Obion county, in the extreme northwest part of Tennessee. It might be added, parenthetically, that it was not until twenty-five years later that a sale of these lands was effected, by which the University realized $14,000. Smith Hall, originally the library, later the law school, and today the Playmakers Theater, commemorates the munificence of Colonel Smith.

In the absence of a direct appropriation by the Assembly, the Board of Trustees realized at a later meeting in New Bern, in December, 1791, that a loan from the Assembly would be necessary. Accordingly, they appointed two Superior court judges, John Williams of Granville county and Samuel Ashe of New Brunswick, John Sitgreaves of Craven, later a United States district judge, Richard Dobbs Spaight, governor the following year, and William R. Davie to the all-important committee to prepare an address, soliciting the loan of five thousand pounds.

Davie was chosen to present the appeal to the Assembly. Describing the power of his oratory on that occasion, Archibald De Bow Murphey later wrote:

> I was present in the House of Commons, when Davie addressed that body upon the bill granting a loan of money to the trustees for erecting the buildings of this university; and although more than thirty years have since elapsed, I have the most vivid recollections of the greatness of his manner and the powers of his eloquence upon that occasion. In the House of Commons he had no rival, and upon all great questions which came before that body, his eloquence was irresistible.

Yet the loan was not secured without a hard-fought struggle. Again Davie had to overcome the same prejudices which characterized the opposition to the charter. By a close vote of 57 to 53 in the House of Commons and 28 to 21 in the Senate, the University champions were able to carry the loan.

Two days had not elapsed before the first trouble ensued.

On the last day of the year, 1791, John Leigh, of Edgecombe county, presented a bill to withhold the payment of this sum to the trustees. Ordered to lie on the table until the next Monday, this motion for economic strangulation was rejected January 9, 1792.

No further action was taken towards implementing the progress of the University until the next session of the Board at Hillsboro in August 1792, when twenty-five of forty trustees answered the roll call—a demonstration of their interest in the problem of locating the University. As a solution, Willie Jones offered a motion, which was adopted, that "the board will not determine on any given place; but the ballots shall be taken for a given point, with a latitude of erecting the buildings within fifteen miles of said point." In accordance with this, Davie secured the passage of a motion to the effect that the balloting should take place the next day, "whereupon the following places were nominated, the Seat of Government [just established at Raleigh], Pittsborough in Chatham County, Williams-Borough, Hillsborough, Charlotte, Goshen, Smithfield, and Cipritz Bridge on New Hope."

The following day, August 3, pursuant to this resolution, Cipritz bridge on New Hope creek in Chatham county was chosen as the geographical center, within fifteen miles of which the University was to be located. This bridge, later Prince's bridge. the remains of which are still discernible, was on the old great road from New Bern, by Raleigh, to Pittsboro. This choice represented the desire to place the University as near the center of the state as possible—as was also true of the location of the capital.

The more tedious business of preparing an ordinance fixing the seat of the University was left up to Davie, Willie Jones, and Alfred Moore, who on August 4, submitted their ordinance, which was unanimously passed. Accordingly, one person from each district was to be elected by ballot from the trustees and those so elected were "to view the Country within the limits aforesaid, and determine on the spot or place most proper. . . and to contract with, and purchase from the owner or owners the place they shall so fix or determine on, together with not less than six hundred and forty acres of land thereto adjoining." They were also empowered to purchase "one thousand four hundred acres so conveniently situated in the neighborhood thereof as to answer the purposes of a farm and a sufficient supply of firewood and timber for the University."

Five of the eight commissioners accordingly met in Pittsboro on November 1, 1792, prepared to visit all places deemed eligible. "An excellent committee," according to Dr. Kemp P. Battle, the University's historian, it was composed of Frederick Hargett of Jones, Alexander Mebane of Orange, James Hogg of Cumberland, William H. Hill of New Hanover, David Stone of Bertie, and Willie Jones of Halifax.

These commissioners viewed several places within the fifteen mile radius of Cipritz bridge, and received several offers of donations if the University were fixed at those sites—several places near Pittsboro, the confluence of the Haw and Deep rivers, Tignal Jones' place, and Nathaniel Jones' place (the latter being at the cross-roads in Wake county). On the 5th of November they "proceeded to view New Hope Chapel Hill, in Orange County." Here, due to the exertions of James Hogg, they received offers of donations of land amounting to 1,390 acres, on and adjoining Chapel Hill, and subscriptions for donations in money amounting to £798 or thereabouts—all conditioned upon the seating of the University there.

These donors, according to Dr. Battle, were of "plain, honest, unambitious stock," who were "possibly more moved to their generosity by the hope of increasing the value of the broad acres retained by them than by love of letters and far-seeing patriotism." Despite their motivation, the largest of these donors deserve mention. Leading the list was Christopher Barbee, who donated 221 acres of his large holdings. Familiarly known as "Old Kit," he lived three miles east of the village on an eminence called "The Mountain." The next two largest donors were Colonel John Hogan and Edmund Jones, who gave 200 acres each. Colonel Hogan, a Revolutionary officer, lived in Randolph county, while Edmund Jones settled for a short while on a farm near Chapel Hill, but soon moved over into Chatham county. His son, Atlas Jones, was a University alumnus, tutor, and trustee. The McCauley brothers, Matthew and William, gave 150 and 100 acres respectively. Immigrants from the north of Ireland, Matthew established a large holding on Morgan's creek, where he had a mill and a blacksmith shop, while William lived a few miles west of Chapel Hill in the district called the "Great Meadows." The former served as a lieutenant in the Revolution, while the latter represented the county in the House of Commons during most of the war, in the Senate from 1784 to 1788, and in the Hillsboro Convention of 1788 which refused to ratify the Federal Constitution.

Hardy and Mark Morgan, also brothers, donated 125 acres and 107 acres respectively, and were among the older inhabitants of this section. Mark lived three miles southeast of the village on land, bought from Earl Granville, which extended up to the summit of Chapel Hill. His brother's land lay along Bowlin's creek, east of the village.

Another deciding factor in the selection of Chapel Hill was the fact that the great roads or highways from Petersburg to Pittsboro and the country beyond, and from New Bern towards Greensboro and Salisbury crossed at this point. It might be added that at the northeast corner of the crossing there was a chapel of the Church of England, hence the name "New Hope Chapel Hill or the Hill of New Hope Chapel."

While these purely mercenary considerations had great weight with the selecting fathers, another factor surely had its effect—the idealness and enchantment of the "Hill" itself. Davie, in a graphic description, written the following September, in announcing the sale of lots, seems to have felt this charm:

> The seat of the University is on the summit of a very high ridge—there is a gentle declivity of three hundred yards to the village; which is situated on a handsome plain, considerably lower than the site of the public buildings, but so greatly elevated above the neigbouring country, as to furnish an extensive and beautiful landscape, composed of the heights in the vicinity of Eno, Little and Flat Rivers.
>
> The ridge appears to commence about half a mile directly east of the buildings, where it arises abruptly several hundred feet: the peak is called Point-Prospect; the flat country spreads off below like the ocean, giving an immense hemisphere, in which the eye seems to be lost in the extent of space.

There is nothing more remarkable in this extraordinary place, than the abundance of springs of purest and finest water; which burst from the side of the ridge, and which have been the subject of admiration both to hunters and travellers ever since the discovery and settlement of that part of the country—several of the lots on the north side of the town have the advantage of including a spring.

The University is situated about 25 miles from the city of Raleigh, and 12 from the town of Hillsborough; and is said to be the best direction for the road—the great road from Chatham, and the country in the neighbourhood of that county, to Petersburg, passes at present directly through this place, being the nearest and best direction.

This town being the only seat of learning immediately under the patronage of the public, possessing the advantages of a central situation, on some of the most public roads in the state, in a plentiful country, and excelled by few places in the world either for beauty of situation or salubrity of air, promises with all moral certainty, to be a place of growing and permanent importance.

There is an apocryphal story to the effect that it was Davie who led this group of trustees in their quest for a suitable location for the University. The legend conjured up a hot summer day on which these men relaxed in a cool, grassy spot beneath a giant poplar. Having regaled themselves with mint juleps, or other intoxicating beverages, and gorged themselves with a picnic lunch, they were easily persuaded by Davie to settle on this spot as the object of their search. To commemorate this story, Mrs. Cornelia Phillips Spencer supposedly gave it the name, the "Davie Poplar."

As a result of the recommendations of this committee, the trustees on December 5, 1792 ordained that "the said Newhope Chapell Hill" was to be the seat of the University. On the same day they appointed commissioners "to erect the buildings of the University and lay off a Town adjacent thereto." These commissioners, Davie, Alfred Moore, Frederick Hargett, Thomas Blount, Alexander Mebane, John Williams, and John Haywood, were charged with the responsibility of laying off "in the most pleasant and commodious part of the Tract. . .a proper quantity of Land to erect the buildings of the said University upon. . . and to lay off and survey adjacent thereto a town containing twenty four lots of two acres each and six lots of four acres each," which were to be sold at public vendue on twelve months' credit. They were also empowered "to cause to be built. . .a House or Houses sufficient if practicable from the sum appropriated for that purpose to accomodate fifty students."

Meanwhile, the champions of the University had turned their attention to the laborious and seemingly thankless job of gaining subscriptions for the University. Early in January, 1793, Davie and Willie Jones issued a joint appeal in the [Halifax] *North Carolina Journal,* in which they "flattered" themselves "that the Gentlemen of Halifax county, will not, on this occasion, so interesting to the rising generation, suffer any county in the state to exceed it in making efforts to promote an institution of such vast and general utility." They held up the example of Orange county which had already subscribed "near *one thousand pounds* towards the endowment of this important institution."

By July these two political antagonists, Davie and Jones, were able to report that Orange county had contributed nine hundred and nine pounds and four shillings, while Halifax contributed eight hundred and four pounds. Moreover, a grand total of $6,723.00 had been subscribed in amounts running from five dollars to two hundred. Three contributors subscribed the latter figure—Alfred Moore of Brunswick and two men from Orange county, William Cain and Walter Alves. Alves, who was the son of James Hogg and who had changed his name at his father's request, had added his donation to a legacy willed by his father-in-law. Among the $100 subscribers were Jesse Neville of Orange, Willie Jones, William R. Davie, and Governor Richard Dobbs Spaight.

In April, 1793 the building commissioners met in Hillsboro where they "contracted with Mr. George Daniel of the County of Orange for the making and delivering three hundred and fifty thousand Bricks at the rate of forty shillings per thousand." In July they contracted with an "undertaker," James Patterson of Chatham county, to "undertake" the construction of "a house of ninty six feet seven inches long and forty feet one Inch and a half wide" for two thousand five hundred pounds. This represents the beginning of Old East Building—the first building to be erected on the campus of any state university in the United States.

By July 22, 1793, Commissioners Davie, Moore, Mebane and Thomas Blount were able to announce that the lots laid off would be sold on the premises on Saturday, the 12th of October and that "considerable time will be allowed for payment, the purchasers giving bond with approved security." On August 10 they met again and "proceeded to lay off . . . a proper quantity of Ground to erect the buildings on; the particular sites of which were fixed and accurately marked off, together with the necessary quantity of Land for offices, Avenues, and ornamental grounds." They were pleased to report, moreover, that "much might justly be said of the beauty and natural advantages of the grounds laid off for the public buildings and for the Village."

Still zealous for the weal of the University, Davie assured the public on September 25, that "the cornerstone of the building of the University, undertaken by Mr. Patterson, will be laid on the 12th of October next; when the Commissioners and a number of gentlemen will attend to assist at the ceremony." Announcing again the sale of the lots on the same day, he described the town as consisting "of one principal street, laid off in lots of two acres each, parallel with the north front of the buildings" and that there were also "six lots of four acres each, located on the most elegant situations contiguous to the University."

At long last the auspicious day—October the twelfth—arrived. The only extant contemporary account of the proceedings, appearing first in the *North Carolina Journal,* was presumably written by Davie:

> On the 12th inst. the Commissioners appointed by the Board of Trustees of the University of this State, met at Chappel-Hill [*sic*] for the purpose of laying the corner-stone of the present building, and disposing of the lots in the village. A large number of the brethren of the Masonic order from Hillsborough, Chatham, Granville and Warren, attended to assist at the ceremony of placing the corner-stone; and the procession for this purpose moved from Mr. Patterson's at 12 O'clock, in the following order: the Masonic Brethren in their usual order of procession, the Commissioners, the Trustees not Commissioners, the Hon. Judge Macay

and other public officers, then followed the gentlemen of the vicinity. On approaching the south end of the building, the Masons opened to the right and left, and the Commissioners, etc., passed through and took their place. The Masonic procession then moved on round the foundation of the building, and halted with their usual ceremonies opposite to the southeast corner, where WILLIAM RICHARDSON DAVIE, Grand Master of the fraternity, etc., in this state, assisted by two Masters of lodges and four other officers, laid the corner-stone enclosing a plate to commemorate the transaction.

The Rev. Dr. McCorkle then addressed the Trustees and spectators in an excellent discourse suited to the occasion. . . .

This discourse was followed by a short but animated prayer, closed with the united AMEN of an immense concourse of people.

The Commissioners then proceeded to sell the lots in the village, and we have the pleasure to assure the public, that although there were but twenty-nine lots, they sold for upwards of one thousand five hundred pounds, which shews the high idea the public entertain of this agreeable and healthful situation.

This was indeed a prosaic account of a proceeding so important in the annals of the history of North Carolina. Surely a more glowing picture of this day could have been painted. Anyone who has known Chapel Hill in the fall could well imagine the beauties of the natural setting, which formed a fitting background for the procession of earnest men who marched with stately tread along the narrow road. At the head of this procession was the commanding, almost marmoreal, figure of Davie, resplendent in his Grand Master's regalia. One can imagine his mixed emotions at this point—honest and deserved pride in the success of his achievements thus far so nobly advanced, weighed against deep humility in the face of the herculean task yet ahead.

Next to Davie was his great rival, Alfred Moore, described by Murphey as "a small man, neat in his dress, and graceful in his manners."

Next might be seen William H. Hill, a descendant of Governor John Yeamans, an able lawyer of Wilmington, and later state senator and member of Congress.

Conspicuous in the group also was John Haywood—for forty years Treasurer of the State (1787 to 1827). Described by Battle as "the most popular man in North Carolina" for many years renowned for his hospitality, kindness, and charity dispensed from his Raleigh seat, he served the University faithfully and well for almost thirty years.

By his side was General Alexander Mebane. Of Scotch-Irish descent, he had been a member of the constitutional convention at Halifax, 1776, an able officer in the Revolution, a member of the state legislature and was to be elected to Congress the following year.

Next might be seen Judge John Williams, founder of Williamsborough, in Granville county, judge of the first court under the Constitution of 1776, and a member of the Confederation Congress.

Thomas Blount and Frederick Hargett completed the list of the commissioners. The former, a member of the state legislature from Edgecombe, was soon to enter Congress. The latter, a senator from Jones county, was described by Dr. Battle as "plain, solid, but eminently trustworthy."

Next in the procession came the other trustees, not commissioners, followed by the State officers, not trustees (among whom was Spruce Macay), officers of the county and gentlemen of the vicinity. Truly this was an imposing array of North Carolina's great.

Dr. McCorkle's address was one worthy of the occasion. Following the philosophical creed of Beccaria and Jeremy Bentham, he laid down the proposition that "Happiness is the center to which all the duties of man and people tend" and "To diffuse the greatest possible degree of happiness in a given territory is the aim of good government and religion." This happiness of a nation, he reasoned, "depends on national wealth and national glory;" they in turn depend on "liberty and good laws," which in like manner call for "general knowledge in the people and extensive knowledge in the ministers of the state, and these in turn demand public places of education."

Prophetic and optimistic was his peroration:

> The seat of the University was next sought for, and the public eye selected Chapel Hill—a lovely situation in the centre of the State, at a convenient distance from the capital, in a healthy and fertile neighborhood. May this hill be for religion as the ancient hill of Zion; and for literature and the muses, may it sur-

pass the ancient Parnassus! We this day enjoy the pleasure of seeing the cornerstone of the University, its material and the architect for the building, and we hope ere long to see its stately walls and spire ascending to their Summit. Ere long we hope to see it adorned with an elegant village, accommodated with all the necessaries and conveniences of civilized society.

After the "short but animated prayer," the sale of lots ensued. Undoubtedly the impassioned plea of McCorkle had its effect upon the auction. Later, in a report to the Board of Trustees, it was announced that all the lots were sold with the exception of one which was held in reserve for the president's house. The commissioners observed "with pleasure" that "although many were present from different parts of the State at the laying of the corner stone and sale of the lots as aforesaid, all appeared satisfyed and content, and they are willing to believe, that the amount of sales furnishes a pleasing and undeniable proof of the high estimation in which this healthful spot is held."

Two years later, despite vicissitudes and reverses in construction and staffing, the University of North Carolina opened its doors on January 15, 1795, with the Presbyterian minister, Dr. David Ker, as the "presiding" and only professor and with no student body. It would not be until February 12th of that year that Hinton James, the first student, walked in from Wilmington to claim the distinction of being the first student to enter the first state-supported university in the nation to open its doors.

CHAPTER VII

ORANGE COUNTY POLITICS, 1789 - 1860

ELMER L. PURYEAR

*Research Assistant, Institute For Research in Social Science
University of North Carolina*

In 1789 the boundaries of Orange county included present day Alamance, Orange, and nearly all of Durham. The people were mostly small farmers, strong believers in local control, and somewhat suspicious of a strong central government. When the question of ratification of the new Federal Constitution came before the people, it was only natural that they would be opposed. At the Convention of 1788 the delegates from Orange, as well as the delegate from the borough of Hillsboro, voted in opposition to the new Constitution, and it should be noted that Hillsboro was the only borough in the state to be Anti-Federalist. By the time of the second convention, which met at Fayetteville, sentiment in the state had become more favorable to the Constitution. The delegates from Orange, however, were still opposed to the document by a ratio of four to one.

With the organization of the federal government, Orange county in the matter of national politics cast its lot with the opposition party of Thomas Jefferson. In 1793 Alexander Mebane, a resident of Orange who had voted against the Constitution in the Fayetteville convention, was elected to Congress. He has been described as belonging to the agricultural interest and being a representative of agrarian democracy not remarkable for his ability. Absalom Tatom (Tatum) from Hillsboro, an Anti-Federalist, was the next congressman from Orange. Beginning in 1796 Richard Stanford, not a native of Orange, represented the Hillsboro district in Congress for about twenty years. Stanford was a Jeffersonian Republican even before Republicanism became fashionable, but by 1806 he had broken with Jefferson and joined the faction of the party known as Quids and was therefore acceptable to the Federalists in that year's election. Duncan Cameron of Hillsboro, one of the leading Federalists in the state, was his opponent in 1808, but Stanford was elected by a huge majority. Due to the fact that Stanford opposed the War of 1812, Republicans of undeviating faith were bitter in their complaints against him. In the Congressional election of 1813 James Mebane, an ardent Republican of Hillsboro, gave Stanford a vigorous but unsuccessful battle. In the next election Stanford, by now branded a full blooded Federalist, was opposed by Roger Tillman, a Democratic Republican, who missed election by 103 votes. Dr. James S. Smith, a native son of Orange and a Democrat, was elected to represent the Hillsboro district in the fifteenth and sixteenth Congresses (March 4, 1817-March 3, 1821). Smith, who was never very popular politically and sometimes referred to by Willie P. Mangum as the "Puffin doctor," was defeated by a Democrat from Caswell county, Romulus M. Saunders, who served only one term. Saunders was succeeded by Willie P. Mangum who entered politics as a Democrat but soon became a Whig.

In state politics, 1789-1824, Orange was represented in the state legislature by many outstanding men, some of whom were Federalists, others Democratic Republicans, and some apparently without definite party affiliation. In the Senate her representatives included such men as William Cain; William F. Strudwick; David Ray, who served for six terms; William Shepperd; Archibald D. Murphey, who served in seven successive sessions from 1812 to 1818; Duncan Cameron, the Federalist leader; and Michael Holt. In the House of Commons the borough of Hillsboro and the county of Orange were served by such prominent men as: Absalom Tatum, Thomas Ruffin, James S. Smith, Thomas Clancy, John Scott, Alexander Mebane, William Nash, William F. Strudwick, James Mebane, John Thompson, Michael Holt, Duncan Cameron, John Craig, Frederick Nash, and Willie P. Mangum. Four of these representatives were chosen speakers of the House of Commons. They were Frederick Nash, 1814; John Craig, 1815; Thomas Ruffin, 1816; and James Mebane, 1821-1822.

Between 1824 and 1836 the colorful personality of Andrew Jackson tended to dominate the national scene, and in many cases a candidate ran as a Jackson man or as an anti-Jackson man. The presidential election of 1824 showed the Democratic leanings of the people of Orange. In spite of the fact that Congressman Willie P. Mangum was committed to the Crawford ticket the vote stood at 591 for Crawford and 638 for Jackson. In the election of 1828 Mangum was the Jackson elector and James S. Smith was the Adams elector, but again the county cast its vote for Jackson 1036 to 440. In 1832 the county was overwhelming for Jackson giving him a vote of 759 to only 170 for Clay. Between 1832 and 1836 many of the leading men of the county broke with the Jackson party and in that year the vote for Van Buren, the Democratic candidate, was 1103, and Hugh L. White, the Whig candidate, polled 905 votes.

In the congressional elections of the period 1824-1836, as in local elections, there were no clear party lines. In 1825 Orange gave Willie P. Mangum 1553 votes to only 716 for Josiah Crudup, and in 1827 Archibald D. Murphey secured a huge majority over Daniel A. Barringer of Wake, who nevertheless was the successful candidate. Barringer defeated John Craig in 1829, but Craig had a good majority in Orange. The election of 1833 brought John G. A. Williamson into the fray against Barringer and Barringer again won even though Williamson received 1518 votes in Orange to only 908 for his opponent. Dr. William Montgomery, a tried and true Jackson Democrat, defeated Barringer in 1835 and received from his own county 1501 votes to 900 for Barringer.

In the field of state politics from 1824 to 1836 Orange was represented in the state Senate by Dr. William Montgomery for ten of the twelve years. James Mebane and Joseph Allison each served one term. Prominent members of the House of Commons were John Boon, John Stockard, William McCauley, James Mebane, Priestley Mangum, Joseph Allison, John Scott, Frederick Nash, Thomas J. Faddis, William Phillips, Hugh Waddell, and William A. Graham.

There were two questions on the state level that vitally concerned Orange in this period. One was state aid for internal improvements. Orange county being located above the fall line felt a great need for roads and river improvement in order to get her goods to market. Dennis Heartt, editor of the *Hillsborough Recorder*, constantly ran editorials favoring state aid and copied widely from other papers which urged such aid. In 1829 a mass meeting of the people of Orange county was held at which James Webb was chosen chairman and Dennis Heartt secretary. An address to the people of Orange County advocating internal improvements was adopted and five hundred copies were printed for distribution within the county. Practically every candidate for any office from sheriff to congressman felt the pressure of public opinion and went on record as approving state aid for the construction of roads and the improvement of navigation. Many of the citizens of Orange invested money in companies which undertook to accomplish such improvements and quite a few were brought to dire financial straits because of the failure of various projects.

The second issue was that of a convention to amend the state constitution so as to give the western counties a fairer share of representation in the state legislature. Agitation for such a convention began as early as 1820 and continued until a convention was called. When a measure was passed by the legislature allowing the people to vote for or against a convention, the *Hillsborough Recorder* urged the people of Orange to vote in full strength for the convention. The plea did not go unheeded. Orange voted 1648 for a convention and 111 against a convention while Hillsboro, which stood to lose its borough representation, voted 228 for and 23 against a convention. There was no shortage of candidates to represent Orange in the convention. At various meetings throughout the county the following men were nominated. Thomas Ruffin, who was then Chief Justice of the North Carolina Supreme Court, Frederick Nash, James S. Smith, James Mebane, William Montgomery, Herbert Sims, Michael Holt, Cadwallader Jones, Joseph Allison, and Alexander Albright. From this list the voters selected two doctors: William Montgomery and James S. Smith. These two men ably represented Orange and both voted with the majority to end borough representation which meant that Hillsboro lost its member of the House of Commons.

From 1836 to the Civil War Orange county was a hotbed of politics and all elections followed strict party lines. The split among the Jacksonians led to a great deal of bitterness. Many of the leaders in Orange such as Willie P. Mangum left the party of Jackson and became Whig leaders.

In every presidential election after 1836 and before the Civil War a majority of votes in Orange was cast for the Whig candidate. The majority was usually small, averaging around two hundred votes. While voting the Whig ticket in the Presidential campaign, the people still voted, perhaps due to his personal popularity, for a Democratic congressman, Dr. William Montgomery, as long as he sought office. Beginning in 1841, when Orange cast its majority vote for James S. Smith, until 1855 the county voted for a Whig congressman each election, except in 1845 when the expansionist fever was rampant. In 1855 the vote favored the Know Nothing candidate, and as the Civil War approached and the Whig party disintegrated, the county in 1857 and 1859 voted for the Democratic nominees. It is apparent that in national politics Orange was essentially Whig in the period; and it is also worthy of note that two of her sons, both Whigs, Willie P. Mangum and William A. Graham represented the state in the United States Senate. Orange, in fact, reached its political summit in 1840 when she had both of the United States Senators, the Representative from the district, and the Chief Justice of the North Carolina Supreme Court, and the Speaker of the House of Commons.

In regard to local and state politics the Whigs and Democrats were nearly equal in strength with perhaps a slight edge going to the Whigs. In the gubernatorial races the Whig candidates secured a majority in each election from 1836 to 1846. In 1844 and 1846 Orange was jubilant when one of its citizens, William A. Graham, was the successful candidate. From 1848 through 1852, when David S. Reid from nearby Rockingham county was the Democratic candidate, Orange gave him a majority. Dennis Heartt stated that his majority was won because of his advocacy of free suffrage which was popular with the people of interior North Carolina. In 1854 Orange was back in the Whig column, but in 1856 the Democratic candidate edged the Know Nothing John A. Gilmer by a slight majority even though Hillsboro had elected a Nativist slate in the municipal elections of 1855. In the last two elections preceding the Civil War the county again cast a Whig vote.

In the matter of state senators Orange seemed to have a slight preference for Whigs. Between 1836 and 1846 Hugh Waddell represented her in the Senate three sessions and was Whig Speaker of the Senate in the session of 1836 and 1837. Other Whig senators were Willie P. Mangum, William A. Graham and Josiah Turner Jr., who also ran as a Know Nothing. The Democratic senators included Joseph Allison, John Berry and Paul C. Cameron. Altogether the Whigs won seven senatorial elections and the Democrats six.

In the House of Commons from 1838 to 1861 the Democrats of Orange had a slight edge. They won a majority of the representatives in six elections; the Whigs won five, and in one election each party elected two members. During this period the Democrats had 21 terms of office to nineteen for the Whigs. The Whigs were strongest in the decade of the forties and the Democrats in the fifties. Leaders of the Democratic ticket included John Stockard, Benjamin Trollinger, Cadwallader Jones Jr., Julius S. Bracken, Sidney Smith, Patterson McDade, Daniel A. Montgomery, Bartlett Durham, George Patterson, John Lyon, and Pride Jones. The Whig candidates included Willie P. Mangum, William A. Graham, Speaker of the House of Commons for two sessions, Nathan J. King, James Graham, Michael Holt, Henry K. Nash, Giles Mebane, John B. Leathers, Loftin K. Pratt, Chesley Faucett, Josiah Turner, Samuel F. Phillips, and Hugh Guthrie.

No political history of Orange county would be complete without a discussion of her sons who became state and national leaders. A roll call of such leaders must include the names of Archibald D. Murphey, James S. Smith, William Montgomery, Frederick Nash, Thomas Ruffin, Willie P. Mangum, and William A. Graham.

Archibald D. Murphey was important to the state, not for the offices held, but for his visionary projects to improve social and economic conditions in North Carolina. Born in Caswell county, Murphey attended David Caldwell's "Log College" and graduated from the University of North Carolina in 1799. After teaching two years at the University he was admitted to the bar and began practice at Hillsboro. Murphey soon won distinction as an equity pleader and from 1818 to 1820 was a Superior court judge. Many young men who were later to become famous studied law with this eminent lawyer. They included Thomas Ruffin, Bartlett Yancey, Governors John M. Morehead and Jonathan Worth, James T. Morehead, John A. Gilmer, William J. Bingham, Judge Henry Y. Webb of Alabama, and Charles Pendleton Gordon of Georgia. It was not in the field of law, however, that Murphey was chiefly interested. From 1812 to 1818 he was a member of the state Senate from Orange and during this period he became the leader for many public causes. Believing that the backwardness of North Carolina was due to its lack of adequate transportation facilities and a public school system, he worked untiringly for both. He advocated a comprehensive system of internal improvements with aid from the state for dredging rivers, constructing canals, building turnpikes, and draining swamp lands. In 1817 he wrote a *Report on Education . . .to the General Assembly of North Carolina* which was the first definite plan of public education submitted in North Carolina, and proposed a school system with primary schools and academies and more support for the University. Murphey was also interested in revision of the state constitution, humanizing criminal law, and abolishment of imprisonment for debt. After he retired from the legislature, Murphey began to collect materials for the writing of a history of North Carolina but death intervened in 1832 with only the introductory chapter completed. Archibald D. Murphey was a visionary and idealist too far advanced for the period in which he lived and he died with his ambitions unrealized and his efforts unappreciated.

Two of Orange's doctor-politicians had strangely parallel careers. Dr. James S. Smith and Dr. William Montgomery were both practicing physicians and seekers of public office. Smith was perhaps the better doctor and Montgomery the better politician. James S. Smith was born near Hillsboro in 1790 and obtained his degree from Jefferson Medical college. At an early age he entered politics and represented his district in Congress 1817-1821. When he was defeated for Congress in 1821, he entered the campaign for a seat in the House of Commons and was elected representative from the borough of Hillsboro. Smith was frequently a candidate for various offices but was not again elected until 1835 when he was a delegate to the Constitutional Convention. In the Convention he was one of the leaders of the fight to end borough representation and had considerable influence since he had been a borough representative. Smith began politics as a Democrat but ended as a Whig running in 1841 for Congress against Romulus M. Saunders.

Dr. Montgomery was an extremely successful politician. He represented Orange in the state Senate for ten sessions between 1824 and 1835, winning every election except one when he was defeated by James Mebane. Starting in politics as a Democrat he remained a Democrat all his life. Running for Congress in 1835 as a strong supporter of Jackson he was elected and served three successive terms. When he was a candidate for a delegate to the state Constitutional Convention of 1835, he polled approximately twice as many votes as his nearest rival who was Dr. Smith. The people of Orange may not have called upon him to heal their bodies, but they consistently year after year gave him a huge vote for whatever office he sought.

North Carolina has produced many outstanding jurists, and two of the most able, Frederick Nash and Thomas Ruffin, were residents of Orange. Nash was not a native son but during most of his public life he was a resident of Hillsboro. Graduating at the College of New Jersey in 1799 and then studying law in the office of Edward Harris, his public career began in 1804 when he was elected to the House of Commons from New Bern. Moving to Hillsboro in 1807 he began an extensive law practice and a career of public service in his new home. He represented Orange county and Hillsboro in the House of Commons for six terms and in 1814 was elected Speaker. During his legislative career he sponsored legislation to prohibit dueling and to provide a state penitentiary. Frederick Nash's chief distinction came, not as a legislator, but as a jurist. He had a notable career as a superior court judge from 1818 to 1826 and again from 1836 to 1844. Upon the death of William Gaston in 1844 Nash was appointed to the Supreme Court of the state and after eight years was selected by his associates as Chief Justice. On the bench, though not as powerful in logic as Ruffin, his opinions were characterized by clearness of legal conception, terseness of style, and cogency of reasoning.

Like Nash, Thomas Ruffin was not a native, and like Nash he was educated at the College of New Jersey, graduating in 1805. Moving to Hillsboro in 1807 he began the study of law under Archibald D. Murphey. After being admitted to the bar he represented Hillsboro in the House of Commons in 1813, 1815, and 1816 serving as Speaker the last year. At the end of his legislative career he was appointed a superior court judge but resigned after two years in order to augment his income. He returned to the bench in 1825, and in 1828 he again resigned, but this time to head the state bank which was having financial difficulties. With the bank in sound shape Ruffin was elected as associate justice of the Supreme Court in 1829 and Chief Justice in 1833, in which position he served until 1852 when he retired to his farm. He was called from retirement in 1858 to again become Chief Justice, but he served for only one year. Ruffin, during his tenure on the court, became known as an authority on constitutional law, being ranked with John Marshall and Lemuel Shaw. He was a busy judge, writing over fourteen hundred opinions covering every topic of criminal and civil law. These opinions are remarkable for broad viewpoint, full discussion, sound reason, strong and simple language, and their lack of citation of authority. Justice Ruffin, relying heavily upon logic, was no great respecter of precedent if it stood in the way of justice. As an executive officer of the court he greatly increased its efficiency and improved its procedure.

Probably the two most widely known political figures in the political history of Orange county were Willie P. Mangum and William A. Graham. Both attended the University of North Carolina, both were lawyers, both were United States Senators, and both stood high in the councils of the Whig party.

After graduation from the University in 1815 Mangum began the study of law under Duncan Cameron and received his license in 1817. He had scarcely started his practice when he entered politics. In 1818 and 1819 he was a member of the House of Commons where he actively supported the cause of education and constitutional reform which was very popular in the western region of the state. At the end of the session of 1819 Mangum was elected a superior court judge, but after two years resigned because of the "intense labor, great responsibility" and financial difficulties. In 1823 he began a service of two terms in the federal House of Representatives but resigned in 1826. He was soon appointed judge but failed to secure the confirmation of the legislature. Mangum served as a Jackson elector in 1828 and on a wave of popularity was again elected a judge only to once again resign after a year of service.

In 1830 Mangum was a candidate for the United States Senate and was duly elected by the legislature. Except for a brief period in the late thirties he remained in the Senate until 1853, and it was in this body that he made his great reputation. At the time he entered the Senate he was a Jacksonian Democrat, a champion of state rights, and a foe of the protective tariff and the Bank of the United States. Changing his political position rapidly the senator voted to recharter the bank, and while being opposed to nullification, voted against the Force Bill. He broke with Jackson over the removal of deposits from the bank, voting for the resolution of censure. Denying the right of instruction, he refused to vote to expunge the censure resolution when instructed to do so by the North Carolina legislature, but when the people elected a Democratic legislature he resigned. In the presidential election of 1836 South Carolina cast its electoral vote for him. Mangum remained in private life until 1840 when he served in the state senate and the same year he was again elected to the United States Senate where he remained until 1853. After his break with Jackson Mangum was closely identified with the Whig party, being one of the chief Whig leaders in the state. He was offered the vice-presidential nomination in 1840 but refused and then became active in the Whig quarrel with Tyler, finally offering the resolution reading him out of the party. Mangum served as president *pro tempore* of the senate from May 31, 1842 to May 4, 1845. On the floor of the senate he seldom spoke, but he was noted for his astute political leadership, his personal charm, and his power as a campaign speaker.

William A. Graham, after his graduation from the University in 1824, studied law under Chief Justice Thomas Ruffin and within a few years was a leader of the bar. His political career began in 1833 when he became the borough representative of Hillsboro in the House of Commons. Graham served continuously as a member of that body until 1840 and twice was honored with the speakership. During his legislative career he worked persistently for internal improvements and public education. In 1840 he was elected to the United States Senate, but he retired to private life when the Democrats controlled the General Assembly of 1842-43. He was again called upon to hold public office when in 1843 he was unanimously chosen by the Whigs as their candidate for governor. Graham served for two terms as governor (1845-1849) demonstrating superior ability as an administrator.

In the summer of 1849 he was offered his choice of missions to Spain or Russia, but he refused both and instead was tendered the post of Secretary of the Navy by President Fillmore. While he was Secretary of the Navy, (1850-1853), his department undertook four measures of great importance: the reorganization of the coast survey, reorganization of the personnel of the Navy, the Perry expedition to Japan, and the exploration of the Amazon. By 1852 William A. Graham had become so important to the Whig party that he was nominated for vice-president to run on the ticket with General Winfield Scott. The Whig party was doomed to defeat, but Graham's service to his native state was not at an end. As the Civil War approached Graham was a leader of the moderates, condemning secession and acting to preserve the Union, but once war came he devoted himself to the cause of the South and served in the Confederate Congress.

There are many other men who were prominent in the affairs of state and political history of Orange county, but space forbids more than mention of their names. Such men as John Umstead, Councillor of State from 1807-1820; Duncan Cameron, judge, member of both houses of the legislature, and president of the state bank; and James Mebane, member of the General Assembly at various times from 1798 to 1828 and Speaker of Commons, are but a few of these.

In conclusion Orange county contributed richly to the political life of the state and nation between 1789 and 1860, and in the field of politics was perhaps the outstanding county of the whole state. What other county can claim five Councillors of State, five Speakers of the House of Commons, seven Judges of Superior Court and two Supreme Court Chief Justices? In addition a Speaker of the Senate and a governor of the state were residents of Orange. The county sent six representatives to Congress and gave the county two Senators, a vice-presidential candidate and a Secretary of the Navy. Truly in the field of politics Orange was second to none.

Chapter VIII

SLAVERY IN ORANGE COUNTY

By Fletcher M. Green

Kenan Professor of History, University of North Carolina

The institution of slavery had been firmly established in North Carolina long before Orange county was created in 1752. The first Negro slaves were brought into the colony by Virginians who settled along the shores of the Albemarle Sound in the 1650's. As new settlers came they brought slaves with them, purchased some from their neighbors after their arrival, or imported them from Virginia or New England. As planting developed the demand for slaves increased; some planters considered it a "hopeless task" to "settle a new plantation without negroes."

The Lords Proprietors recognized the importance of slave labor in settling the colony and offered, in the Concessions of 1665, to give a master fifty acres of land for each slave, fourteen years of age or above, imported into North Carolina. This practice was continued throughout the proprietary period, and partially accounts for the growth of slavery. The institution grew more rapidly in the tobacco planting area than in the subsistence farming region. Orange, a small farmer county, had a slave population of only fifty Negro polls when first organized. Thirty-five of the Negroes were men and fifteen were women. In 1755 only about eight per cent of the whites of Orange county owned any slaves; Mark Morgan with six slaves was the largest slaveholder at that time. By 1780, however, some three per cent of Orange slaveholders owned more than twenty slaves each. The slave population grew more rapidly during the early years than did the white, and in 1765 the population was 3,324 whites and 649 Negro slaves. The first federal census of 1790 gave Orange 10,055 whites, 2,060 Negro slaves, and 101 "other free persons," presumably free Negroes. Orange had a larger slave population than any other Piedmont county. Fourteen white citizens owned ten or more slaves in 1790. Four of them lived in Hillsboro, the others in the country round about. William Hooper with twenty-two was the largest slaveholder in Hillsboro, and Richard Bennehan, a planter of St. Mary's district, with twenty-four was the largest slaveholder in the county. Others who owned ten or more were George Allen, John Taylor, Matthew McCauley, John Hogan, and Thomas H. Perkins with ten each; Walter Alves with eleven; William Sheppard and William O'Neal with twelve each; Hardy Morgan with thirteen; William Cain with fourteen; Alexander Mebane with sixteen; and an unnamed person with twenty slaves.

The slave population of Orange county continued to increase more rapidly than the white during the nineteenth century. The figures for 1800 were white 12,222 and slave 3,327; for 1810, white 15,102 and slave 4,701; for 1820, white 16,777 and slave 6,153; for 1830, white 15,918 and slave 7,339; for 1840, white 16,772 and slave 6,954; for 1850, white 11,330 and slave 5,244; and for 1860, white 11,311 and slave 5,108. It is to be noted that both white and slave population declined during the latter decades, but the slave decline was less drastic and came later than the white. Some of the slave decline resulted from migration of slaveholders to other parts of North Carolina or to other states; to the loss of territory cut off to form new counties; to sale of slaves to non-residents of the county; or to the manumission of slaves. Some few slaves also bought their freedom. The free Negro population of Orange increased from 101 in 1790 to 631 in 1840, declined to 481 in 1850, and increased to 528 in 1860.

The slave population of the county was highest in 1830, but at that time it amounted to a little less than thirty-one per cent of the total population. Slave ownership was widely dispersed throughout the county. In 1860 forty-eight per cent of all land owners were slaveholders, but twenty-one per cent of the owners possessed only one slave, and only seven per cent possessed twenty or more. In 1860 the three largest slaveholders were I. N. Patterson with 106, Paul Cameron with 98, and Henry Whitted with 78. Cameron was reputed to have owned a total of 1,900 slaves in the 1850's, but all except the 98 were on absentee owned plantations. It is interesting to note that whites, free

The Courthouse in Hillsboro erected in 1844 by Captain John Berry.

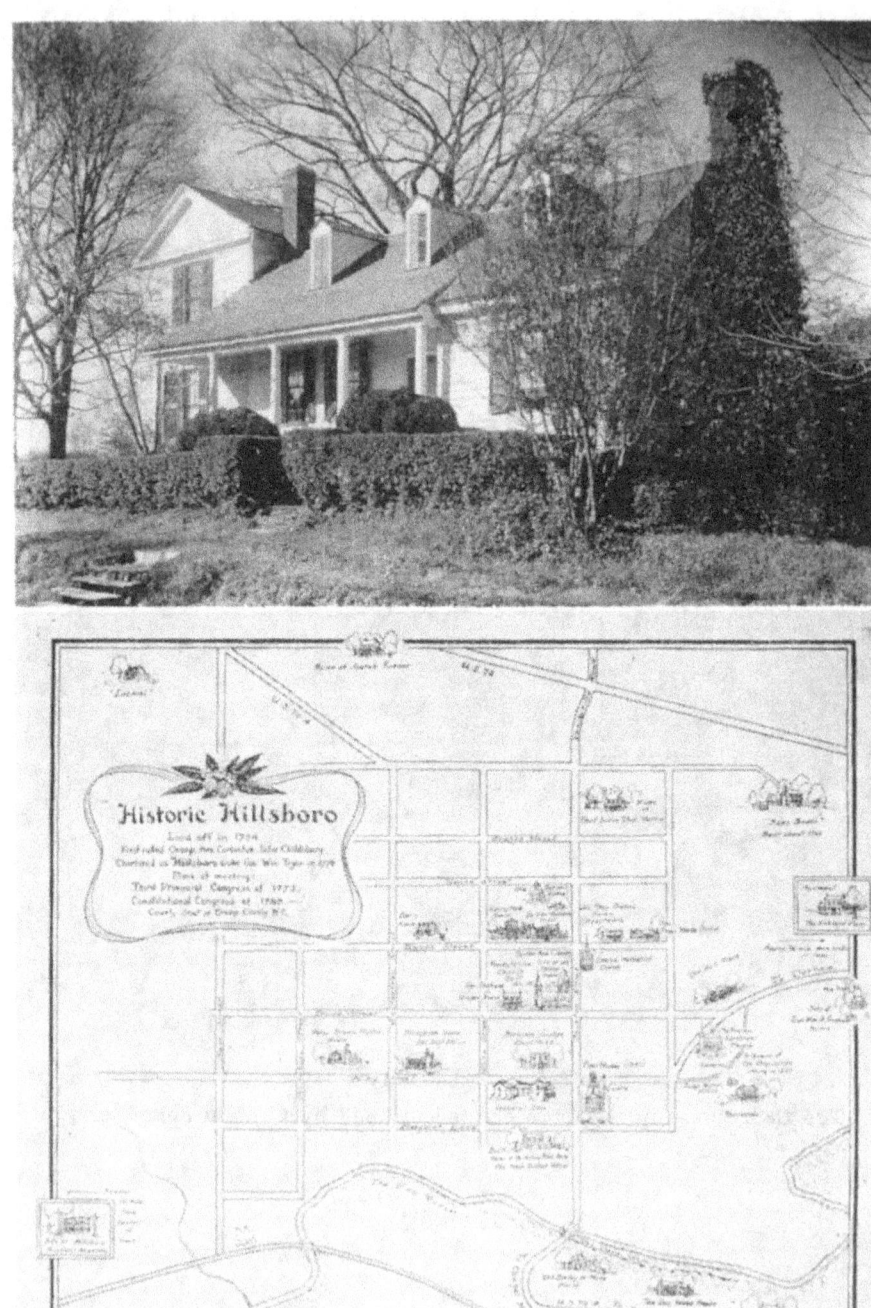

Top: Thomas Burke and Dennis Heartt home in Hillsboro. Bottom: Map of Historic Hillsboro, drawn by Lucia Porcher Johnson.

Top: NASH-HOOPER-GRAHAM HOUSE: Built by General Francis Nash as his home in 1772; the home of William Hooper from 1782 to 1789; the home of William A. Graham during the 1860s; now the home of Mr. and Mrs. H. H. Brown. Bottom: MOOREFIELDS: Built by Alfred Moore of Wilmington as his summer home in 1785; Alfred Moore was appointed by President John Adams to the United States Supreme Court in 1800 to succeed Mr. Justice Iredell. Moorefields is the birthplace of Senator Thomas Hart Benton and of Mrs. Henry Clay; it is now the home of Edward T. Draper-Savage.

Top: Colonial Inn, Hillsboro, erected in the 1780s. Bottom: Chandelier in Lodge Room of Eagle Lodge No. 19 Hillsboro, formerly in Occoneechee home of Julian S. Carr.

Top: Old Scott home in Hillsboro about 1896. Bottom: Miss Sarah J. Kollock's School in Hillsboro about 1897.

Top: University Inn, U.N.C. about 1898, site of Graham Memorial Building. Middle: Old Central Hotel, U.N.C., about 1898, site of Battle, Vance and Pettigrew Dormitories. Bottom: University of North Carolina about 1907.

Top: Old Memorial Hall, U.N.C., erected about 1889, demolished in 1929.
Bottom: Recent aerial view of Chapel Hill.

Top: Old Burwell School, Hillsboro. Bottom: Nash-Kollock School, Hillsboro, from pen sketch by Hope S. Chamberlain.

Top: Smith's Bar in Hillsboro about 1896. Middle: Hayes Drug Store in Hillsboro about 1896. Bottom: Churton Street, Hillsboro, about 1914, showing old town pump.

Top: The Bennett Place where General Joseph E. Johnston surrendered to General William T. Sherman on April 26, 1865. Bottom: The Dickson Place near Hillsboro, before remodeling by Mrs. Mary R. Few, Johnston's Headquarters.

Top: Burnside in Hillsboro, built by Paul C. Cameron. Office of Justice Thomas Ruffin. Regulators were hanged nearby, now the property of Rebecca Wall. Bottom: Sessions House, Hillsboro.

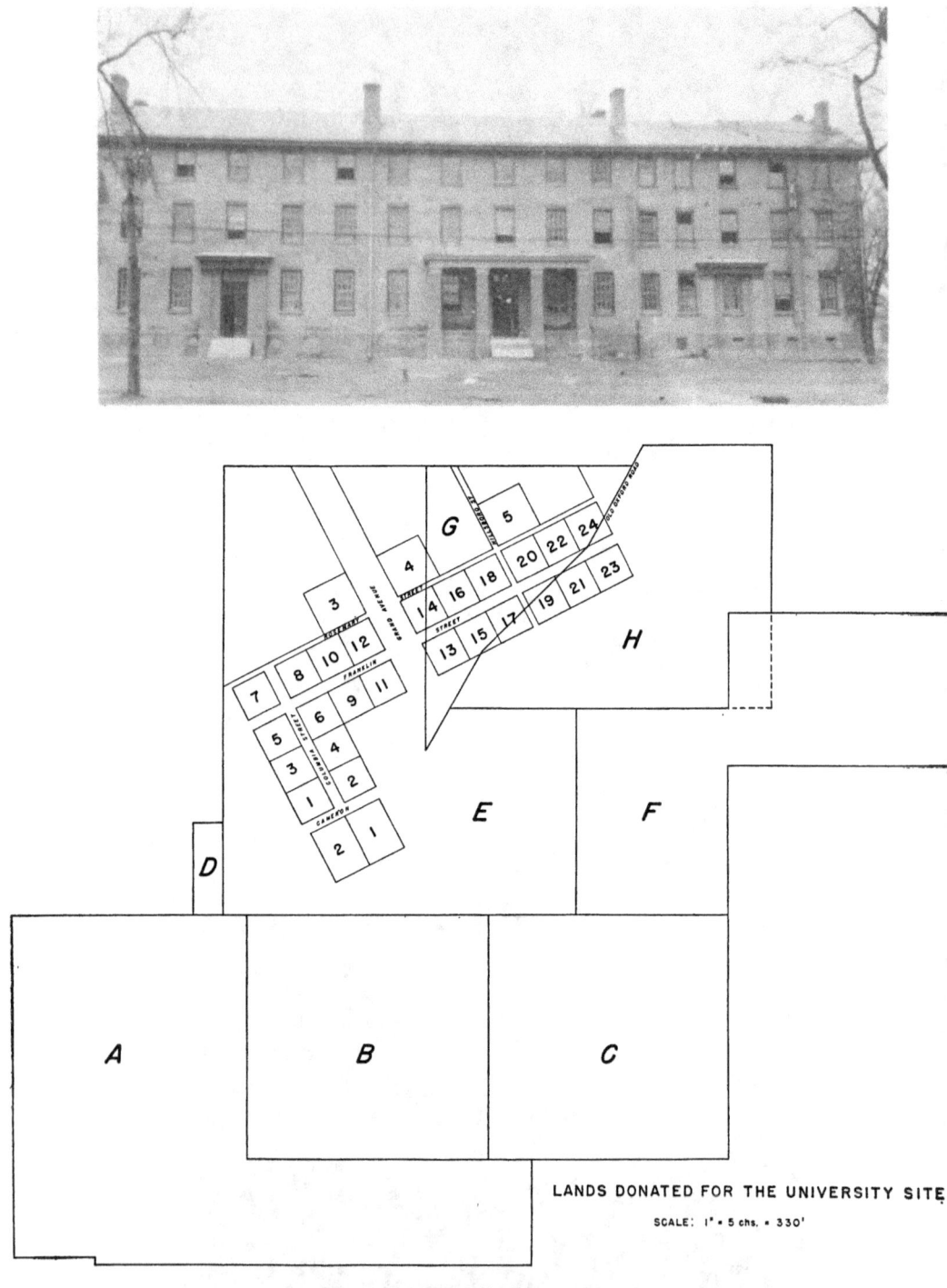

Top: Old East Building, U.N.C.
Bottom: A, donated by Edmond Jones, 200 acres; B, donated by John and Solomon Morg 107 acres; C, donated by John Daniel, 107 acres; D, donated by James Craig, 5 acres; E, nated by Christopher Barbee, 221 acres; F, donated by Hardy Morgan, 125 acres; G, p chased by Benjamin Yeargin, 50 acres; and H, donated by Hardy Morgan, 80 acres.

THIS INDENTURE made the nineteenth Day of October One Thousand Seven Hundred and Ninety Nine BETWEEN the following Commissioners, to wit, Alfred Moore, John Hayward, William Richardson Davie, John Haywood, Richard Stone, of the one Part, and Christopher Barbee, of the other Part, WITNESSETH, That the said Alfred Moore, John Haywood, William Richardson Davie, and Alexander Matson Commissioners as aforesaid by Virtue of the Powers and Authority to them given by an Ordinance of the Board of Trustees of the University of North-Carolina, made on the eighth Day of Decem. N. One Thousand seven Hundred and Ninety-one, entitled, "An Ordinance for appointing "Commissioners to erect the Buildings of the University, and by-laws (very near thereto), and for the Confirmation of One hundred and fourteen pounds ten shillings Currency of North-Carolina, to them paid by the said Chris. Bett. Barbee HAVE granted, bargained and sold, aliened, enfeoffed, released and confirmed, and by these Presents DO grant, bargain and sell, alien, enfeoff, release and confirm unto the said Christopher Barbee one Lot of Ground in the Town adjacent to the Buildings of the University in Orange County, which Lot doth contain two acres and fifty feet, and numbered two (2) in the Plan of the said Town: And all Woods, Trees, Waters and Appurtenances to the said Lot of Ground belonging. TO HAVE AND TO HOLD the said Lot, together with the Appurtenances, to the said Christopher Barbee his Heirs and Assigns forever. And the said Alfred Moore, John Haywood, William Richardson Davie, and Alexander Matson, for and on Behalf of the Trustees of the University of North-Carolina DO covenant and agree to and with the said Chris. topH. Barbee and his Heirs, that the Trustees of the University of North-Carolina, shall warrant and defend the said Lot of Ground granted to the said Christopher Barbee his Heirs and Assigns to whom so ever the lawful Claims of all Persons forever. IN WITNESS WHEREOF, the said Alfred Moore, John Haywood, William Richardson Davie and Alexander Matson have hereto set their Hands and Seals the Day and Year first above written.

Signed, Sealed and Delivered
in the Presence of

M Slate
Jno: H. Clark
James Patton

A. Moore (Seal)
J. Haywood (Seal)
W. R. Davie (Seal)
Alex Martin (Seal)

Deed from first Trustees of U.N.C. to Christopher Barbee for Carolina Inn lot.

Top: Sans Souci, built about 1760 by William Cain, now the property and home of S. T. Latta, Jr. Middle: Ayrmont, erected by William Kirkland. Bottom: Confederate Memorial Library, Hillsboro.

Top: Franklin Street in Chapel Hill, October 12, 1925.
Bottom: Franklin Street, Chapel Hill, about 1914.

Top: Main Street, Carrboro, about 1920. Middle: The first garage in Orange County about 1913, Strowd's Garage in Chapel Hill. Bottom: "Strowdmobile" built by Bruce Strowd when he was 16 years old. Diagram made by the late William Meade Prince from description by Bruce Strowd.

Negroes, and slaves were almost equally divided between the two sexes. For instance in 1820 the male slaves numbered 3,057 and the females 3,096. In 1860 there were 2,529 male and 2,579 female slaves. The total value of slaves was approximately two thirds the total value of the land of the county in 1815. The slaves were valued at $1,216,347 and the land at $1,917,993.

Most slaveholders owned a small number of slaves, hence the relationship between master and slave was very close. The master knew his slaves by name, took a personal interest in them individually, and looked upon them almost as members of his family. Many masters in fact spoke of their slaves as their "black family." Thomas Ruffin described the personal relationship between master and slave as follows:

> Often born on the same plantation, and bred together, they have a perfect knowledge of each other, and a mutual attachment. Protection and provision are the offices of the master, and in return the slave yields obedience and fidelity of service; so that they seldom part but from necessity. The comfort, cheerfulness and happiness of the slave should be, and generally is, the study of the master.

Most slaves, even on the larger plantations, were housed in log or frame houses designed for small families. I. N. Patterson had twenty houses for his one hundred and six slaves, and Paul Cameron had twenty-five houses for his ninety-eight slaves. The masters were generally interested in happy marriages for their slaves and took pains to arrange satisfactory marriages between their own slaves, or with slaves of their neighbors. For instance Jeremiah Holt of Alamance county wrote Thomas Ruffin of Hillsboro as follows: "I am informed by my Boy Thomas that he wants your Negro girl Emily for a wife if it is agreeable with you and wants a recommendation. I can say that Thomas is a boy of good character sober and honest as far a I no [sic] of and is permitted to pass and repass to your house and home."

Some Orange county planters made provision by will for mulatto slaves, probably their illegitimate offspring. One bequeathed such a slave $500, and another, Jehu Whitted, gave instructions that his mulatto slave Fanny "be put to school for the Term of Six months and the expenses thereof be defrayed by my executors." Other planters took care of free Negro relatives of their slaves. One kindly master advertised in the Hillsboro *Recorder* for Patty, a free Negro woman, sixty years of age, homeless, insane, and in feeble health. She had been living with her slave relatives on a farm owned by the subscriber for several years, but had strayed away. "Diligent search," said the planter, had "been made for her, but without effect . . . .Any information concerning her will be thankfully received, and any person who will bring her home will be paid for his trouble."

Household servants were plentiful in Hillsboro and Chapel Hill. Some of them were interesting characters. Davidge, popularly called "Dr. November," was the carriage driver for Dr. Joseph Caldwell of Chapel Hill for many years. He boasted that he had blacked boots for senators, made beds for governors, and even waited on President James K. Polk. Dave Barham, janitor for Dr. Elisha Mitchell, declared that his master had never spoken a harsh word to him. Many family servants in Chapel Hill took pride in their position and looked upon themselves as the aristocracy of Orange county slaves.

The most distinguished Orange county slave was George Moses Horton. He had learned to read from a spelling book, hymnal, and the Bible while working on his master's farm in Chatham county. He hired his time from his master and went to Chapel Hill where he served as a janitor for the University of North Carolina. At Chapel Hill he read books supplied by President Caldwell, picked up a wide store of information from his associations with faculty and students, and learned to write good idiomatic English from James K. Polk, Professor Manuel Fetter, and Caroline Lee Hentz, the authoress. He wrote poetry and love letters for the college students for which he charged twenty-five cents, fifty cents "when an extra amount of warmth and passion [was] demanded." His love letters were eloquent and often, it was said, "not only touched but captured the fair hearts for which they pleaded." He published several compositions in the Raleigh *Register*. One of his pieces was "The Pleasures of College Life." Horton also wrote for Horace Greeley's New York *Tribune*. Joseph Gales of Raleigh published Horton's *The Hope of Liberty* in 1829. It was expected that the volume of verse would bring Horton money with which to purchase his freedom. A second edition was published in Philadelphia in 1837, and a third in Boston in 1838. Dennis Heartt of Hillsboro published a volume of Horton's *Miscellaneous Poems* in 1845.

Another Chapel Hill slave who attained some recognition was Sam Morphis, a hack driver and a waiter at the University of North Carolina. Sam, a mulatto, belonged to James Newlin of Alamance county. He hired himself and "earned a fair livelihood." His major weakness was an inclination to alcoholic drink, but he was popular with faculty, students, and townspeople; and he endeared himself to the students when he saved the life of a Virginia student. A petition, signed by President David L. Swain, 43 townspeople, and 309 students, asked the legislature to emancipate Morphis. The legislature denied the petition, but "the small college town accepted once again the popular slave who enjoyed virtual freedom." Sam married Judge William H. Battle's slave girl and spoke of himself as Battle's son-in-law.

The great majority of slaves, however, lived on the farms and plantations and worked as field hands. They had few diversions to lighten the monotony of their existence. Many of them were often mistreated by their masters. The slave code gave the master almost complete control over the slave; the master might whip the slave at will, and if the slave resisted the master might kill with impunity; the master might work the slave from dawn to dusk, and might regulate his every action. In return the master was required to feed, clothe, provide housing, and safeguard the slave's health. If the slave committed a crime he was tried, not in the regular courts but before a special court of two justices and four freeholders. Should a Negro give false testimony he was to have one ear nailed to the pillory for one hour and then cut off, then the performance was repeated for the other ear. Finally the slave was given thirty-nine lashes on the bare back. For rape of a white woman the slave was punished for the first offense by castration, for the second offense the penalty was death. The code forbade the slave to bear arms, or to be taught to read and write. Fortunately the harsh penalities were often ignored, and in time some of them were abolished.

The state law authorized the county courts to establish rules and regulations for county patrols. The Orange county court required the patrol to visit each slaveholding farm and plantation at least twice each month. The patrol was to search for arms and stolen goods, to enforce the curfew, to prevent free Negroes from entertaining slaves in their homes at night, or on Sunday, without the written permission of the owner. If a slave was found to sell any goods without his owner's permission the patrol was to punish with thirty lashes on the bare back. No slave was permitted to possess firearms. The patroller was to confiscate all guns and swords for his own use and to punish the offender with twenty lashes. No slave was to visit the slave quarters of another plantation for dancing without written permission of both his owner and the owner of the slave quarters. Punishment of the slave for violation of this regulation was twenty lashes. At the end of each year the county court appointed a committee "to adjudge the services of the patrollers in said county for the last year." Those who performed patrol service, and expected pay for same, were required to submit proof of such service.

Hillsboro had a special town patrol. The magistrate of police required the captain of patrol to summon all members of his company to patrol the town for one week, "at least three times in said week, in the night time, and three hours in each night, after nine o'clock; and you are to apprehend . . . all such white persons, free negroes, mulattoes and slaves as shall be found acting contrary to the ordinances of said town, and bring them before me to be dealt with according to the ordinances established by the commissioners of said town." Country slaves were forbidden to spend the night in town except with written permission to visit their family, or on Sunday to attend church services. The curfew hour was nine o'clock. The penalty for violation of either ordinance was fifteen lashes.

Despite the severity of the penalties Orange county slaves committed many infractions of plantation rules, city ordinances, county patrol, and state laws. The 1828 session of the Superior

Court found Jim, slave of Willie P. Mangum, guilty of manslaughter in killing a slave belonging to Francis Epperson. He was sentenced to receive thirty-nine lashes on the bare back. The same court sentenced Sherod, slave of Ezekiel Brewer, to fifteen lashes for larceny; and Harry, slave of Samuel Kilpatrick, was given the death sentence for burglary. Kilpatrick appealed and Harry was granted a new trial. James Bass and Jesse Heathcock, both free mulattoes, were found guilty of larceny and sentenced to thirty-nine lashes, imprisonment for three months, a second thirty-nine lashes, and then required to pay court costs and upkeep while in jail. Beth Crabtree, a white girl who lived on the Hillsboro common, and Harry Wall, a Negro slave, were jailed in 1821 to await trial for murder of Beth's illegitimate child begotten by Wall; and an unnamed Negro slave was committed to the Hillsboro jail for rape on a white woman of Chatham county.

Whites also disobeyed the law which forbade trading with slaves. In 1822, John Faddis published the following notice in the Hillsboro *Recorder*: "I hereby warn all persons not to trade with any of my negroes, particularly Jim, Joe, Alfred and Peter, in any way whatever, unless it be by permission from me in writing. Some persons, unknown to me, have been in the habit, for some time past, of letting my negroes have spirituous liquors, and thereby have rendered them useless to me in a considerable degree; I am determined hence forward to enforce the law to the utmost extent against all persons who may trade with them, in however slight a degree."

Financial difficulties and the death of slaveholders often led to the sale of Negro slaves in Orange county. Most owners who advertised slaves for sale because of debt preferred to sell their slaves in family groups and to people in the vicinity. Thomas Clancy's advertisement of November 18, 1829, is typical of many such notices. It reads as follows: "I wish to sell my negro woman Lucy and her five children, four of whom are boys, the eldest about thirteen years of age. I would prefer selling them together and to some person in Hillsboro or vicinity. They are well known as a family of first rate negroes, and I should not sell them were it not for the want of money." William Hooper advertised nine Negroes, the property of the late Mrs. James Craig, as a family that "is well disposed and accustomed to the usual varieties of business." He, too, desired to sell them as a unit. On the other hand William M. Adams offered to sell his family of six, either singly or together.

Most advertisements of slaves for sale spoke of them as "likely negroes." Other slaves were described as skilled artisans, including blacksmiths, carpenters, masons, and wagon makers; some were "well trained house servants," "excellent cooks," a "good ironer and washer," and "waggoners." One pathetic advertisement offered "For sale Ben, 60 years old, grey and very black, has one hat and two suits. $2." Most public sales were of only a few slaves, ofttimes a single one. Occasionally the number exceeded ten. William Spanhour and Thomas Ruffin each offered for sale sixteen slaves belonging to a single client. Archibald D. Murphey offered the unprecedented number of forty slaves for sale in 1821.

Some would-be purchasers made known their wants through the columns of the Hillsboro *Recorder*. For instance William Holt "Wanted to buy a negro woman servant raised and well acquainted with house business, cooking, washing, etc., and also who can weave." For such a well trained servant he was willing "to pay a liberal price." One master, residing in York District, South Carolina, purchased Fred at a public sale in Hillsboro. A year later he offered Fred for sale in Hillsboro because the slave wished "to return as his wife and children reside there." Occasionally a commercial slave trader visited Hillsboro. In 1835 George Lewis did so, and advertised that he would "pay cash for 100 young Negroes."

There was much hiring of slaves in Orange county. Agents often advertised skilled artisans, including blacksmiths and carpenters, as well as field hands and house servants for hire. James Webb, James Mebane, and Thomas Ruffin were agents who offered to hire slaves of deceased clients by the year. Their hire was by private or individual transaction, and they made every effort to find employment that would be satisfactory to the slaves. Some groups of slaves were advertised for hire year after year, thus indicating that the groups were hired as a whole and not individually. Occasionally Negro slaves were offered at the Hillsboro Market House for public hire to the highest bidder. The hire for an able-bodied worker during the 1850's ran from $95 per year for a field hand to as much as $250 for a skilled laborer.

Orange county Negroes, unhappy in chattel slavery, often resorted to hiding out and running away to escape bondage. Judging by the advertisements for runaways in the Hillsboro *Recorder*, most runaways were men in the prime of life, from twenty to fifty years of age. Many of them were described as well dressed; several carried extra new clothes; some had money, one $50 in cash; and others possessed horses, probably stolen from their masters. Some were mulattoes, and were able to pass as free. Some few had traveled to Maryland, Virginia, and South Carolina. Many runaways were recent purchases, and were suspected of trying to return to their old homes. Most hideaways were thought to be lurking in the vicinity of their wives and children. James, a runaway, "who for the last four years attended Chapel Hill in the capacity of college servant," was "well dressed, and has considerable quantity of clothing . . . and a sorrel horse." He was thought to be making his way to Richmond or Norfolk "for associating himself with the Colonization Society."

The rewards offered for runaways ranged from $5 to $50. Most of them were either $10 or $25. In the case of Nan, about fifty-five years old with one bad eye, the reward was only one cent. One master offered only $20 for the return of Priscilla, a girl eighteen or nineteen years old, "very black and stout," but $50 for the return of a stray mare nine years old.

During the 1820's and 1830's the manumission and colonization movements were strong in Orange county. The editor of the Hillsboro *Recorder* noted in 1821 the "deteriorating effects of slavery" on the well being of the state, and declared that "the existence of this class of people [slaves] among us is a misfortune of great magnitude." He thought, however, to free them and leave them in the state would increase the evil. He did not think it wise to throw upon the public "a mass of improvident and helpless individuals, unfitted by their habits and their want of education to provide for themselves." He recommended that the free Negroes be transported to Africa at public expense, and suggested that the legislature take action. And Judge William Gaston, in a commencement address at the University of North Carolina in 1832, predicted the overthrow of slavery. His audience applauded his oratory but turned away from his abolitionist views. As early as 1819, the Reverend William Meade reported a flourshing auxiliary Colonization Society in Chapel Hill, and Duncan Cameron, a leading citizen of Orange county, was elected president of the States Colonization Society in 1834. Numerous individuals, various Presbyterian and Episcopal churches, and at least one textile factory contributed to the support of the Society between 1819 and 1856. Among the individual contributors were the Reverend James Caldwell, William Hooper, Dr. S. D. Scofield, and Professor Solomon Pool. Among the largest contributions was $240 by John Kelly, and $1,000, by an unnamed person to go toward the payment of transportation costs of free Negroes to Liberia. One Orange county lady, the owner of the wife and several children of a free man of color, offered her slaves their freedom provided they would go to Liberia. In 1825 the former slaves of David Patterson of Orange county sailed for Liberia under the auspices of the Colonization Society. In 1858, however, the General Assembly passed "A Bill for the Relief of Emily Hooper. That Emily Hooper a negro, and citizen of Liberia, be and is hereby permitted, voluntarily, to return into a state of slavery, as the slave of her former owner, Miss Sally Mallet of Chapel Hill."

The Colonization Society bore little fruit, but the Manumission Society was strong and effective in Orange county. It found much support among the Friends. Meeting at Trotter's creek in 1825, a branch society adopted "An Address to Our Fellow Citizen" in which it expressed "unshaken confidence in the goodness of the cause," and called upon all citizens "to unite in a common exertion for the removal of one of the principal grievances of our land." The Address admitted that manumission would bring added hardships, including "hard work and drudgery" for women and girls, but predicted that it would bring infinite good. Among its benefits would be better educational facilities, which should be opened to Negroes as well as whites so that they might have a chance for cultural and moral improvement. An educated Negro citizen, said the Address, would lessen the fear of free Negroes and bring greater prosperity to all the people. The Address closed with an invitation to the people to unite with the Society in the promotion of its "object, to the end that slavery may be done away by the voluntary consent of the people, and not by the hand of avenging justice."

This humanitarian spirit led a goodly number of citizens to manumit their slaves, and some slaves were able to buy their freedom. The number of free Negroes increased from 108 in 1800 to a maximum of 631 in 1840. Because of the rise of radical abolition and the fear of slave insurrections sentiment began to turn against free Negroes and the number in Orange county decreased to 487 in 1850. The county nevertheless had more free Negroes than any other Piedmont county in the state. Free Negroes of Orange were generally of the lower economic class, although only two were inmates of the county poor farm in 1860. A goodly number of free Negroes were property owners and a few owned slaves. In 1860 David Moore, a free Negro barber of Chapel Hill, owned property valued at $4,400. Six free Negroes of the county owned real estate and twenty-three owned personal property. Three owned and operated farms. The twenty-nine free Negro property owners were possessed of a total of $16,175. In 1830 Fred Hartgrove, a free Negro owned three slaves and Lucy Peters owned one. No free Negroes owned slaves in 1860. By far the larger part of free Negroes were mulattoes. In 1860 their number was 361 out of a total of 528.

Business relations between whites and free Negroes were generally good. Sam Morphis who bought his freedom and David Moore, the barber, were both held in high esteem by the Chapel Hillians. But there was little social relations between the two groups. One white farmer, being destitute of land of his own, rented a farm from a free Negro. Later, in 1832, he sued for divorce on the ground that his wife had fallen in love with his Negro landlord.

The coming of the Civil War led to much unrest among the

slaves, and when abolition came in 1865 the Negroes began to wander away from their old homes and to seek new opportunities away from the scenes of their slave existence. The former slaves were a source of worry to many whites. For instance, Mrs. Cornelia Phillips Spencer reported that the Phillips Negroes were "inclined to do as little as possible," but that they looked to Phillips for their upkeep. Phillips reserved one of the small buildings for the old Negroes when he rented the place to others. Uncle Ben and Aunt Dilsey who had been trusted family servants since 1826 remained faithful to their master, and refused to leave his service. The end of the institution of slavery, however, left many problems of race relations for future settlement.

CHAPTER IX

CIVIL WAR AND RECONSTRUCTION IN ORANGE COUNTY

By J. G. de R. Hamilton

Kenan Professor of History and Director of the Southern Historical Collection, Emeritus, University of North Carolina

During the anxious period preceding secession, Orange county was, on the whole, Unionist in sentiment. In the state elections of 1860, John Pool, the Constitutional Union candidate for governor, carried the county by a majority of 129. Josiah Turner Jr. was elected to the state Senate, and Hugh B. Guthrie and W. N. Patterson were elected to the House of Commons. In the national election John Bell carried the county by 169. Few people were declared secessionists, but with the election of Lincoln, secession sentiment began to make itself manifest.

In the legislature the members from Orange voted against the submission to the people of the call of a convention, and when the election was held upon the question, it resulted in a vote of 1436 against the call to 458 for it. At the same time William A. Graham and John Berry were elected delegates over Henry K. Nash and Pride Jones by overwhelming majorities. There was general recognition of the accuracy of Josiah Turner's statement, contained in a letter to the people of Orange, that the issues in the election were Union or Disunion, and clearly the county was not ready for secession.

But then came the fall of Fort Sumter and Lincoln's call for troops, and even as staunch a Unionist as William A. Graham yielded. The legislature met and called a convention, and in the resulting election of delegates, Graham and Berry defeated Paul C. Cameron and Nash by substantial majorities. Upon the meeting of the convention Graham was defeated for president by Weldon N. Edwards of Warren county by a vote of 65 to 47. Graham and Berry both voted for the ordinance introduced by George E. Badger, which ignored the issue of the right of secession by a declaration of independence from the United

States, and after the defeat of this, both voted for and signed the Craige ordinance of secession.

Graham played a large part in the deliberations of the convention. His speech opposing a proposed test oath secured the defeat of the proposal. Opposing such extreme measures, he was entirely loyal to the confederate cause, and the people of the county, as always, trusted him implicitly and relied upon his leadership.

In the politics of the war period, Orange county pursued an undeviating course. In 1862 a strong movement developed in the state for the election of Graham as governor, but he quickly declined the consideration of his name. The county gave Zebulon B. Vance a majority of 748 over William Johnston for that office, Graham was elected to the state Senate without any organized opposition, and Berry and William N. Patterson were elected to the lower house. Early in the session Graham was elected to the Confederate Senate, for the term beginning in May, 1864, but retained his seat in the state Senate until December, 1863. Berry was elected to succeed him, his place in the lower house being taken by James S. Leathers.

When George Davis, whom Graham was to replace in the Confederate Senate, resigned to become attorney-general, Governor Vance offered the place to Graham, who declined it. He took his seat at the opening of the second Confederate Congress.

In 1864, the county, unaffected by the peace movement, fostered so vigorously by William W. Holden, himself a native of Orange, gave Vance a majority of 885 over Holden, and elected Berry to the state Senate and Samuel F. Phillips, outwardly conforming, but at heart a peace man, and Patterson to the House of Commons. Josiah Turner was elected to the Confederate Congress as an anti-administration candidate.

In the Confederate Senate Graham took an important place. His efforts there, aided somewhat by Turner's resolutions in the lower house, were largely responsible for the Hampton Roads conference. He ably opposed the suspension of the writ of habeas corpus, and defended the state against the campaign of slander against it.

The lines drawn during the War were maintained during reconstruction in Orange. In 1865 it would have elected Graham to the so-called Johnson convention of 1865-66, but his pardon was held up after being signed through the influence of Provisional Governor Holden, and he therefore wthdrew from candidacy, and Berry and Phillips were elected. In the resulting election of 1865 the county gave Jonathan Worth a majority of 724 over Holden, and Graham was elected to the state Senate, and Phillips and Colonel Robert F. Webb to the Commons. Because of the lack of a pardon Graham did not present his credentials, but he was almost immediately elected to the United States Senate, and at once resigned from the legislature, where he was at once replaced by Berry. With the others elected to Congress Graham was denied his seat. His pardon was not delivered until 1867.

The county voted 816 to 37 for Worth over Alfred Dockery in 1866, and elected Berry state Senator and W. W. Guess and S. D. Umstead to the Commons. In the meantime in 1865 the county voted 169 to 73 for the amendment abolishing slavery, and 170 to 55 for the amendment repudiating secession. In 1866 it voted 494 to 392 against ratification of the proposed constitution submitted to the people that year.

No sooner had the news of President Lincoln's call for troops reached Orange county than military preparations and organization were begun. The Orange Light Infantry, commanded by Richard J. Ashe became Company D of the Bethel Regiment, the Flat River Guards, under Captain Robert F. Webb, and later under Captain William K. Parrish, became Company B of the Sixth Regiment, and the Orange Grays, commanded successively by William G. Freeland, W. G. Guess, and H. B. Lowrie, became Company C of the same regiment. Company D of the First Regiment, commanded first by Edward M. Scott and later by J. W. Williamson, was an Orange company, as was Company G of the Eleventh, commanded by James A. Jennings, and later by John F. Freeland. The Orange Cavalry, commanded successively by Josiah Turner, Jr., William A. Graham, Jr., and John P. Lockhart, was Company K of the Nineteenth Regiment. The Orange Guards, commanded successively by Pride Jones,

Joseph C. Webb, Stephen Dickson, and James A. Graham, was Company A of the Twenty-seventh Regiment. The Orange Light Artillery, commanded by William Cameron, and later by Henry Dickson, was Company E of the Fifth Battalion. Company G of the Twenty-eighth Regiment, commanded successively by William J. Martin, George B. Johnson, E. Graham Morrow, and George McCauley, was an Orange company, as were Company E of the Thirty-first Reigment, commanded by Jesse Miller, and later, Julius F. Allison. Company F of the Thirty-third Regiment (partly composed of men from Hyde County), commanded by Thomas W. Mayhew and James A. Allston, both of Hyde; Company G of the Forty-fourth Regiment, commanded by Robert Bingham; and Company D of the Fifty-sixth Regiment commanded first by John W. Graham, and then by Robert D. Graham.

In addition there were men from Orange in the Second, Third, Fourth, Seventh, Eighth, Tenth, Twelfth, Thirteenth, Fifteenth, Sixteenth, Eighteenth, Twenty-third, Twenty-fourth, Twenty-sixth, Thirty-fifth, Thirty-seventh, Forty-third, Forty-fifth, Forty-sixth, Forty-seven, Forty-eighth, Fiftieth, Fifty-first, Fifty-second, Fifty-fourth, Fifty-fifth, Fifty-seventh, Sixty-third Regiments, and the First, Seventh, and Eighth Battalions.

I have identified in Moore's Roster 1260 men from Orange, but it is practically certain that in the numerous companies where the counties of origin are not listed that a considerable number of men came from Orange. It is also well known that others were to be found in the troops from other states. Of those listed 249 were killed or died in service and 139 were wounded, but both numbers represent fewer than the actual losses.

Of field officers Orange furnished to the army one brigadier-general: William W. Kirkland; three colonels: Charles C. Tew, William J. Martin, and William L. Saunders; three lieutenant-colonels: Robert F. Webb, Joseph C. Webb, and Joseph H. Saunders; and three majors: D. H. Hamilton, John W. Graham, and William A. Graham, Jr.

Many of the soldiers were men of small means, and there was early recognition of the necessity of making provision for their families, and also of furnishing the soldiers with clothing.

In May, 1861, the county court made an appropriation of $50,000 for soldiers' families. This fund lasted until late in the war. Tremendous and valuable service was rendered the cause by Ladies Aid Societies. Soon after secession two were established, one in Hillsboro and one in Chapel Hill. Later others were organized. They continued their work until the end of the war. Through their efforts a vast amount of material aid was rendered to the soldiers in camp, in the hospitals, and in the field, and to those in need at home. They met trains with food and drink for soldiers, sick and well. The doors of homes were opened to the sick and wounded, and many a private home became, to all intents and purposes, a private military hospital. The women made bandages, socks, shirts, suits, caps, and gloves, collected food, money, and materials, and nursed the sick, in the meantime undergoing themselves much of privation and hardship. Mrs. Cornelia Phillips Spencer thus described this work:

> Few were the hearts in any part of the land that did not thrill at the thought that those who were fighting for us were in want of food. From the humble cabin on the hillside where the old brown spinning-wheel and the rude loom were the only breastworks against starvation, up through all grades of life, there were none who did not feel a deep and tender, almost heart-breaking solicitude for our noble soldiers. For them the last barrel of flour was divided, the last luxury in homes that had once abounded, was cheerfully surrendered. Every available resource was taxed, every expedient of domestic economy was put in practice. . . . . I speak now of central North Carolina, where many families of the highest respectability and refinement lived for months on cornbread, sorghum, and peas; where meat was seldom on the table, tea and coffee never; where dried apples and peaches were a luxury; where children went barefoot through the winter, and ladies made their own shoes, and wove their own homespuns; where the carpets were cut up into blankets, and window-curtains and sheets were torn up for hospital uses; where soldiers' socks were knit day and night, while for home service clothes were twice turned and patches were patched again; and all this continually, and with an energy and a cheerfulness that may well be called heroic.

Life, however, of course went on as it does when people become accustomed to war. With almost every house one of mourning, gloom hung over the county as indeed it did over all the South. Yet young people danced and were gay, there was marriage and giving in marriage, and birth in the midst of wounds, disease, and death.

Peace, or rather cessation of war, finally came to a well-nigh exhausted people, the end coming within the county itself where at the Bennett house (now in Durham County) General Johnston surrendered to General Sherman. The soldiers came home, most of them on foot, and slowly the people began to adjust themselves to new conditions. There were many problems. Slavery was gone, and the whole labor system had to be reconstructed. The Negroes were unsettled, many of them roaming about, and living on the land. The state government was destroyed and replaced by military rule, as always ignorant and inept. Rumors of every sort concerning the future abounded, and added to the confusion. And on almost every one was pressing the necessity of acquiring daily bread.

Slowly things settled down. The Negroes were placed under the direction of agents of the Freedmen's Bureau, which was manned by soldiers, nearly all of whom were unfitted by lack of experience and knowledge, by character, and by temper of mind, for a tremendous and nearly impossible task. Most of them began at once to do everything possible to alienate the Negroes from not only their former owners but also from the white people generally. No effort was spared to demonstrate the authority of the agents. The venerable former Chief Justice Ruffin, once more a resident of Orange, was compelled, for some time, to report daily at the office that he had behaved himself since his last visit. Practically every question between a white and a Negro was decided in favor of the latter, regardless of the facts of the case. And the agents busied themselves organizing the Negroes into the Union League.

The President set in motion the restoration of civil government by appointing William W. Holden, the editor of the Raleigh *Standard*, provisional governor. He appointed state and local provisional officers, called a convention, which met in 1865 and again in 1866, and restored the regular government of the state. But Congress refused to recognize the states as restored, and finally passed the succession of so-called reconstruction acts by which military rule was restored, a convention was called, elected by a limited electorate which included the Negroes, and excluded most of the experienced men in the state. The convention included in its membership a number of persons newly arrived in the state, most of them of evil character, soon to be known as carpet-baggers, and a larger group of Negroes, many of them completely illiterate and unfit for any office. A new constitution was adopted in 1868 and submitted to the same limited electorate, varying greatly from the former, and in many ways unsuited to the needs of the state.

Orange voted by a majority of 550 against the call of a convention, and elected Dr. Edwin M. Holt and John W. Graham, both Conservatives, as delegates. It voted 1863 to 1324 against ratification of the resulting constitution, and cast 1834 votes for Thomas S. Ashe for governor against 1310 for W. W. Holden. In the legislative election Turner was chosen Senator, but was excluded because his disabilities under the 14th Amendment had not been removed. John W. Graham, whose ability had been manifested in the convention, was elected in his stead. John J. Allison and Thomas M. Argo, both conservatives, were elected to the lower house, now the House of Representatives. Allison resigned in 1870, and was succeeded by Frederick N. Strudwick.

Allusion has been made to the Union League. Because of its activity in Orange county, it requires some description. It was founded in the North in 1862 with a view to organizing and strengthening loyal sentiment, and spread quite widely. It came south with the Union armies, and from time to time new members were admitted from Union men in the state, and a few Negroes were also admitted. No attempt to extend it widely was made until 1866 when it became evident that Congress would control reconstruction in the interest of the Republican party, and that Negro suffrage was inevitable. By that time, while progress had been made by the carpet-baggers in the alienation of the freedmen from the native whites, it was apparent that further steps must be taken in order to control them, to bind them to the interest of the ambitious Northerners by something which would appeal to their pride and their emotions, and would at the same time organize them. The Union League, because of the effect of its ritual upon the ignorant and emotional Negroes, and through the discipline of its organization furnished an ideal instrument to the end desired. Introduced by carpet-baggers, it was for the entire period of its existence in the state controlled by them, chiefly for their own aggrandizement.

During the latter part of 1866 and the early days of 1867, a campaign of extension was carried on, and by August, practically every Negro who would vote at the election was a member. Some few declined to join, preferring to be guided by natives in their entrance into political life. This species of ingratitude, not to say treason—for so it was regarded by the carpet-baggers— was seen to be a grave menace to the political solidarity of the race, and the colored members were not only encouraged but ordered to deal with the dissenters in such a way as to convince them of the wisdom of submitting to northern guidance, and to acceptance of a policy to hostility to native whites. So effective was the treatment that few Negroes dared to remain out of accord with the majority of their color. Those who did were subjected to every type of violence and intimidation. An Orange example of this can be seen in a notice posted on the door of a Conservative Negro in Hillsboro.

Notice for Thomas Green

> A d - n Consurvitive . . . . , we understand you were out with Consurvitive lys, but d - n your time if you don't look out you will catch h -l shure. We herd you come very near catching it in Sharlot and if you don't mind you will catch it in Hills Boro shure enough and that Right. If you d - n Consurvitive friends can protect you, you had better stick near to them in that hour for great will be your Desterny. This is the last of our example. The next time will tell you your will on good behavior.
> Postscript. You mind me of the Sun of Esaw and who sold his birth Right for one morsel of meat and so now you have sold your wife and children and yourself for a drink of Liquers and have come to be a Consurvitive boot licker.
> Thom. I would not give a d—n for your Back in a few days; you Consurvitive . . ."

The man looked simply to a complete and unyielding organization which would force the Negroes to register, arouse them to a high pitch of enthusiasm for the Republican party, and a corresponding degree of hostility against the Conservatives, and for that matter, in many cases, against all white natives, lead them to the polls in an unbroken phalanx which would secure Republican supremacy in the state, and, in the process, put into positions of honor, trust, and profit—with due emphasis upon the last—the would-be statesmen who had dominated the organization from the beginning.

In the process the organization lost its character, and became the symbol of most that was evil in the period. Through violent and incendiary speeches by the leaders, calculated and intended to arouse the Negro Conservatives at whatever cost, the meetings tended to be incitements to crime, the Negroes regarding the gospel of "Kill and burn," so constantly preached, as a command with authority behind it.

Albion W. Tourgée, who organized the League in Guilford, Alamance, and Orange, was the first state president. He was succeeded by William W. Holden, who retired when elected governor in 1868. He was succeeded by Milton S. Littlefield, but the Negroes continued to regard Holden as the head as long as the League lasted, and the Raleigh *Standard* as his mouthpiece. All the violent threats contained in that paper were regarded as authoritative utterances.

Public parades, frequently under arms, were frequent, and violence increased. It became almost impossible to arrest a member, and difficult to hold him. Even when convicted, a pardon was almost certain.

The most common of the graver outrages committed was barn-burning, and there was a mass of evidence to prove that in many instances it had been decided upon at a meeting of the League, and in many more by members following its teachings.

Orange was among the counties which suffered most from League activities, and there were many scattered cases during 1868 and 1869. Organized and directed violence tended powerfully to increase individual violence, and this must also be charged to the League's account.

Throughout its existence life and property increasingly lost security in Orange as well as in a large portion of the state, and it was only to be expected that counter-organization followed, equally beyond the law, but intended to preserve public order. A retaliation so violent, and a retribution so swift came, that in a very short time after the appearance of the Ku Klux the activities of the League became decidedly less, and they vanished altogether by the end of 1870.

The most startling happenings in Orange county during the period of reconstruction grew out of the existence there of three secret organizations, the Constitutional Union Guards, the White Brotherhood. and the Invisible Empire, all of them operating under the general title of the Ku Klux Klan, although that, properly speaking, belonged only to the Invisible Empire.

The first of these organizations to appear in North Carolina was the White Brotherhood, which came late in 1867 or early in 1868. It spread widely, and at last, to all intents and purposes, became in fact but not in name, a part of the Invisible Empire. Its origin is unknown, but it had no vital connection with the original Tennessee Invisible Empire, but was probably an imitation of it. Its purpose was at first purely the protection of the homes and families of its members and of all Confederate soldiers, and its entrance upon an aggressive campaign was a departure from its original intent, so grave in its nature that the Hillsboro camp was at once disbanded because the large majority of its members were opposed to the active agressions of some of its members, who acted without authority of the camp. Later that element continued to operate without warrant, enlisting new members without unanimous consent. The activities of these, along with similar elements of the other organizations, brought the whole movement into deserved disrepute. The Orange county chief of the White Brotherhood was Colonel Joseph C. Webb, succeeded by Frederick N. Strudwick.

The Constitutional Union Guard was organized in the North in 1868 with a political purpose. Its object was to secure the presidential election of the Democratic candidates, Seymour and Blair. Organized into "Klans," it existed, side by side, or blended with other orders until the movement had spent its force. Nothing is known of its leaders, either in the county or state.

The Invisible Empire was the original of the Ku Klux orders, having been founded in Pulaski, Tennessee, in 1865. In its origin it had only a social purpose, but its possibilities as an agency for suppression of crime and violence by the Negroes were soon recognized, and it spread with inconceivable rapidity. General Nathan Bedford Forrest became its Grand Wizard and did much to direct its activities and to spread its organization and membership. It was first brought to the state by one of his emissaries, who visited many counties and began the work of organization by initiating some chosen person in each. The date of this visit is unknown, but it was in 1867, or early in 1868.

The constitution and ritual of the Invisible Empire were the most elaborate of those of any of the orders, and apparently were the only ones ever printed. At the head was the Grand Wizard, each state had a Grand Dragon, any district that might be set up, a Grand Titan, and every county, a Grand Giant, who in North Carolina was usually called a Grand Mogul, and each "deer," or local organization, a Grand Cylops. Numerous subordinate officers were supposed to be associated with these. The provisions for effective organization were never carried out, because, from its very nature, its officers could not control the activities of the members.

Whatever may have been the intent of its founders, its ritual shows that it could not be other than political in character. As a preparation for taking the oath, the novice had to deny that he had ever been a member of the Radical Republican party, the Loyal, or Union League, and the Grand Army of the Republic, and that he had fought against the South. He had to affirm his opposition to the organizations mentioned, to Negro equality, social and political, and declare his belief in constitutional liberty, a free white government, and the inalienable right of self-preservation of the people against the exercise of arbitrary power.

At the head of the Invisible Empire in the state was Colonel William L. Saunders of Chapel Hill, who, although he directed it, and through it, to an extent, the other two orders, for the membership was often, and the leaders nearly always, identical, never took the oath of membership and hence was, strictly speaking, not a member. There are few more convincing tributes of confidence than this and well did he deserve it. Summoned in

1871 to appear before the joint committee on "affairs in the insurrectionary state," he, in spite of threats of punishment, declined to answer fifty-three questions relating in any way to the Ku Klux, quietly defying the committee to punish him for contempt.

The full extent of the organizations will never be known, and probably no one ever knew it. Forty thousand members was a usual estimate of the membership for the state, and Orange was said to have eighteen hundred. The latter figure was undoubtedly an exaggeration though the county was probably better organized than any other. But certainly no such numbers were active in either state or county. It was essentially a movement of the Piedmont region. The only counties with Negro majorities in which the Ku Klux appeared were Caswell, Lenoir, Jones, Franklin, and Wayne, and only in Caswell were they active. Orange and its daughter Alamance were centers of the movement, which Daniel R. Goodloe described as "hereditary anarchy, dating back to the Regulation."

Of violence on the part of the Ku Klux there was considerable, for severe punishment was inflicted upon evil-doers. Five persons were put to death in 1869, none for any political reason. Late in July three barns were burned in the same locality, and at the same time. The owner of one of them, with complete ruin staring him in the face, committed suicide the next day. A few nights later two Negroes, accused of another barn-burning, were taken out of jail. One was released, but the other was shot and died of his wounds. Suspicion fell upon Dan and Jeff Morrow, as the barn burners, and they were hanged on a tree by a public road in the southern part of the county, and left with the inscription "All barn burners and women insulters, we Ku Klux hang by the neck until they are dead, dead, dead. K. K. K." Later in the year, Wright Woods, who had threatened rape, was found hanged with a paper on his foot, upon which was written, "If the law will not protect virtue, the rope will." Later still Cyrus Guy was hanged for the same offence.

The discipline of the movement was good at first. Nearly all the manifestations of its power were carefully planned, executed with silence and dispatch, and not mentioned by the members.

As a result, a large part of the population had lifted from it a burden of terror. Crime of all sorts grew rapidly less, and so by illegal methods the observance of law was maintained. But as the organizations became more political in character, the membership increased, and, the mass of members realizing their power, discipline relaxed until there was none. The Ku Klux continued to be a terror to evil-doers, but it was also a terrible menace to the personal quiet of its active political opponents. The orders were officially disbanded, but they were beyond the control of leaders, and the best element having withdrawn, the name of Ku Klux by 1870 had come to be associated with much of unjustifiable violence, of injustice, and of wrong. It became the cloak for private vengeance of those who were unworthy, and in many instances of those who had never been connected with it.

The acts of the Klan in Orange at first excited more attention in the state than those of any other county, and Governor Holden decided to send troops to Hillsboro, but changed his mind after receiving good advice from there. On November 3, the *Standard,* declaring that it was speaking for the Governor, threatened a proclamation that the county was in a state of insurrection. A week later it closed an editorial on the subject with the following sentence: "They will be dealt with as traitors by both the state and general government, even if there has to be a gibbet for every tree in the forests of Orange." Finally the governor issued a proclamation, warning the people of Orange and of three other counties that if the disorders did not cease he would proclaim them in insurrection, and exert the whole power of the state to enforce the law.

Public sentiment in the county was divided. With the mass of the white population, grateful for protection, the Ku Klux were popular, but many were opposed seeing the dangers inherent in the movement. William A. Graham, Thomas Ruffin, John W. Norwood, George Laws, James Webb, Henry K. Nash, Henry N. Brown, Octavius Hooker, and others condemned the movement, and most of them joined on March 5, 1870 in a recommendation to Governor Holden that Pride Jones be given a captain's commission to attempt to suppress it. The governor at once sent the commission, and night riding quickly ceased. After four weeks he resigned, his work having been completed.

When in 1870, in an attempt to carry the election by force, Governor Holden raised an illegal military force, declared Alamance and Caswell in a state of insurrection, and declined to obey the writ of habeas corpus, issued for a large number of persons illegally arrested, the only person arrested in Orange was Josiah Turner, who was seized at his home and confined in jail in Yanceyville. All were finally released by Judge Brooks of the Federal district court.

In the election of 1870 John W. Graham was elected to the state Senate, and Strudwick and Matthew Atwater to the lower house. Samuel F. Phillips, who accepted the Republican nomination for attorney general, was defeated. Strudwick offered the resolution impeaching the governor, William A. Graham headed the counsel for the board of managers, planning a large part in the conduct of the trial, and John W. Graham offered the judgment of the Senate, sitting as a court of impeachment, removing Holden from office and declaring him incapable of again holding office.

In politics the county remained staunchly Democratic throughout the period. It cast 1945 votes for Augustus S. Merrimon in 1872 to 1321 for Tod R. Caldwell, and 2410 for Vance to 1675 for Thomas Settle in 1876.

In legislative elections John W. Norwood was elected Senator in 1876, and Pride Jones and Jones Watson Representatives. In 1874 Calvin E. Parish was chosen Senator and Joseph W. Latta and Matthew Atwater Representatives. In 1876 John W. Graham was elected Senator over Josiah Turner who ran as a Republican endorsed candidate. John K. Hughes and Parish were elected Representatives.

In national elections the county was also Democratic, voting, in 1868, 1907 to 1453 for Seymour over Grant; in 1872, 1483 to 1265 for Greeley over Grant; and in 1876, 2428 to 1668 for Tilden over Hayes.

For the convention of 1875 William A. Graham defeated Washington Duke 1908 to 1528, and Josiah Turner defeated John T. Hogan 1777 to 1518. Graham died before the convention met, and in a special election William N. Patterson defeated Duke 2000 to 1297. The amendments submitted by the convention were adopted 2,335 to 1,691.

The two outstanding figures in the county during the reconstruction period were William A. Graham and Josiah Turner. Graham, long a trusted leader, retained this place in the Conservative party and held it until his death. His speech before the Conservative convention in 1868 settled the policy of the party with respect to Radical reconstruction, and his advice was sought and heeded on every public question. He would, undoubtedly, have been elected to the United States Senate except for the fact that he still labored under the disabilities imposed by the Fourteenth Amendment.

Josiah Turner's editorial policy with the *Sentinel* made that newspaper the outstanding organ of the Conservative party, and through it he played a large part in the overthrow of the Republican state administraton whch was entirely under the control of the Radical carpet-bagger and scalawag elements. He was a man of positive genius for warfare, sparing not and caring little where he struck. His ingenuity seemed little short of diabolical to his opponents. Quick-witted, ingenious in putting opponents on the defensive and keeping them there, at the same time ignoring counter-attacks, gifted with a keen sense of humor, he saw the ridiculous side of everything, and employed it as a means to an end, realizing that in politics a dangerous enemy is often rendered harmless by laughter and ridicule. No man was so bitterly hated by the spoilsmen, or so intensely feared. Cunning as a serpent, writing with a pen that seemed dipped in gall, he relentlessly pursued what now became the chief aim of his existence, the overthrow of the Republican party in the state. No man was ever better adapted to such work, for his genius was destructive always, and he naturally belonged to the opposition. He was the inspiration of the Conservative party in its deepest gloom, and to him, more than to any other one man, belongs the credit for the speedy overthrow of the carpet-bag rule in the state.

Orange county, thanks to the fact that the carpet-baggers and scalawags never obtained a foothold there, had an economical government throughout the reconstruction period and remained without debt. Times were hard but adjustment to new conditions came, and the people, with the redemption of the state completed in 1876, faced the future with hope.

The following figures from the census returns of 1860 and 1870 are of interest. It should be remembered that values listed in 1870 are in greenbacks which were still a highly inflated currency.

	Population	
	1860	1870
Total	16,947	17,507
White	11,311	11,087
Free Negro	528	6,420
Slave	5,108	
	Property	
	$7,336,296	$2,040,903
	Land	
Improved	101,354 acres	73,745 acres
Unimproved	246,040 acres	174,156 acres
Value Implements & Machinery	$129,292	$71,707
Value Farms	$2,141,690	$977,308
	Stock	
Horses	3,199	2,006
Mules	552	662
Milk Cows	4,081	3,216
Oxen	375	294
Other Cattle	5,622	3,110
Sheep	11,314	7,171
Hogs	27,444	14,618
Value	$513,353	$287,631
	Crops	
Wheat, bu.	157,794	29,023
Corn, bu.	400,242	193,161
Oats, bu.	81,825	92,061
Tobacco, lbs.	1,159,764	530,442
Cotton, bales	848	383

Crops

	1860	1870
Potatoes, bu.	12,754	18,157
S. Potatoes, bu.	46,716	18,559
Peas and Beans, bu.	8,506	1,949
Butter, lbs.	105,884	179,995
Hay, tons	1,390	1,337
Flax	4,584	
Honey, lbs.	16,924	10,083
Wax, lbs.	2,165	760
Wool, lbs.	15,004	11,106

Manufacturing

	1860	1870
No. Establishments	61	92
Capital	$185,943	$201,857
Cost of raw material	$241,770	$276,385
Value of Products	$336,846	$420,970
Cost of Labor	$ 36,324	$ 31,120
Laborers, Male	181	277
Laborers, Female	35	39

Churches

	Organizations	Sitting	Organizations	Sitting
Methodists	10	2700	30	3400
Baptists	8	2140	9	3300
Presbyterian	7	2198	8	1900
Episcopal	2	650	2	900
Christian			1	250
Value of Property		$27,100		$38,150

CHAPTER X

PERIODICALS AND EDITORS IN ORANGE COUNTY

By Phillips Russell

Professor of Journalism, University of North Carolina

Journalism in Orange county may be said to have begun with the establishment of a paper mill near Hillsboro in 1777, which mill seems to have been short-lived; but the first regularly established newspaper in the county was apparently the *North Carolina Gazette* of Hillsboro, which first appeared in 1785, the same year in which died James Davis, North Carolna's first printer and publisher. Not much is known about this paper. The only surviving copy with an imprint is dated February 16, 1786, "printed by Robert Ferguson for Thomas Davis."

The father and dean of Orange county journalism was Dennis Heartt, founder of and for nearly fifty years editor of the *Hillsborough Recorder*, which was as well edited a newspaper as North Carolina ever had.

Heartt was a Whig, a Unionist, and a sane and tolerant eighteenth century gentleman, writing with something of the literary flavor of Joseph Addison and Richard Steele and the clarity and humor of Benjamin Franklin. It is doubtful if he ever enjoyed a circulation above 1,000, yet he had a great following of respectful readers and what he said carried weight throughout the state.

Like so many devoted North Carolinians of the period, Heartt came not from the land below the Potomac but from New England. He was born at New Bedford, Connecticut, November 6, 1783, the son of an English sea captain. Little is known about his early life, and for the information used here we are drawing mostly upon the sketch prepared by W. K. Boyd in 1898 and printed in the *Papers of the Trinity College Historical Society*, Series II. Heartt learned the printing craft from Read and Morse, New Haven printers, and in 1802 moved to Philadelphia where American journalism, encouraged by the Federalists on the one hand and the Jefferson party on the other, was gathering strength. He married Elizabeth Shinn of Springfield, New Jersey, and in 1810 began publishing the *Philadelphia Repertory*, a literary periodical.

Such things had small chance of success along the sparsely settled Atlantic seaboard, and in 1820, probably having learned that in Orange county, North Carolina, was a center of enlightenment, he moved to Hillsboro and on February 20 of that year issued the first copy of the *Recorder*. The town then had a population of only 805, but it still remembered it had once served as the colonial capital. It possessed schools, lawyers, and learned men. Belonging to the bar were such figures as Thomas Ruffin, Duncan Cameron, and William Norwood, and judges like George E. Badger, Archibald D. Murphey, Willie P. Mangum, and Francis Nash still lived there.

Heartt engraved the heading of his paper, illustrated its columns with lead cuts, made his own composition sticks out of Orange county walnut, and often took a hand with the cumbrous old press, which had to be inked with buckskin bags.

The files in the University of North Carolina Library are incomplete, but we have spent enjoyable hours poring over the early numbers beginning with March 20, 1820. The old *Recorder* was a weekly of four pages, five columns, $3 a year. The letterpress was clear and distinct, the quality of the paper high. The advertisements—fourteen lines three times for $1—reveal the community's business and social life. William Kirkland ran a dry goods "cash store," and James Andrews was a tailor and ladies' dressmaker who boasted "the art of cutting to fit the human shape." William Hannah proclaimed that "whereas it was my unfortunate lot to be married to a Mrs. Nancy Dunnegan," she had left his bed and board and he would not be responsible for her debts. A. Mason advertised the Eagle Hotel at Mason Hall; David Price, coppersmith, offered "stills and materials," and the Hillsborough Academy, J. Witherspoon, principal, announced its resumption of session in July.

There is a legend that one of the *Recorders's* classified advertisements offered five cents reward for an apprentice boy in "blue home-made coat, tow trowsers, and a wool hat." This boy is said to have been William W. Holden, an Orange county lad who apprenticed himself to Heartt at an early age and learned the printing trade under him, then moved to Raleigh where he later became the Federal governor of North Carolina at the end of the Civil War and subsequently was impeached, convicted, and removed from office. Holden is said to have replied to this advertisement by slipping into the shop and altering the type of a certain issue so as to offer the editor and plant for sale for fifty cents.

The editorial contents of the *Recorder* were well chosen and dignified. A note to correspondents appearing in the issue of June 28, 1820, said:

> Pieces calculated to improve the moral or political condition of society, either by addressing the reasonable faculties or the fine feelings of our nature, or by the sometimes more potent means of ridicule in indicating the foibles and follies so frequently exhibited, we shall be thankful to receive. . .though an editor cannot at all times conduct himself so correctly as to give universal satisfaction, yet if he pursue an even course, unbiased by prejudice and unawed by fear, he will obtain the approbation of a liberal and free people.

No one could ever accuse the *Recorder* under Heartt of addressing aught but the reasonable faculties. Heartt drew his news for page one largely from the *National Intelligencer* of Washington, the Philadelphia *Gazette,* and the New York *Commercial Advertiser.* He gave considerable space to extracts from current debates in Congress, especially those relating to efforts to curb slavery.

It was on the last or fourth page that Heartt indulged his literary tastes and filled its columns with lively sketches, essays, comments, and anecodotes. For example, there is an account clipped from the Norfolk *Herald* of a pettish young lady who was heard one Sabbath morning to exclaim: "I'd rather go to H—than go to church without having my hair done to please me," whereupon she fell dead; plainly a judgment and warning from Heaven. And this is a sketch of a stroll on Broadway, New York, towards Central Park:

> Lots of dandies, their fine large bushy hair gracefully hanging beneath their hat, and their thin and pale faces peeping out of their tangled tresses, half buried and concealed; their enormous

chains and seals, mincing steps, and neatly padded coats, black ribbons and eye glasses, ogling the whole world, and eyeing the milliners and confectioners, with their fine, drawling, silver-toned salutations. . . .The ladies with black and velvet caps, gold bands and tassels, and splendid merino dresses and shawls, looked beautiful and extravagant.

By 1828 the *Recorder* had so prospered as to be able to afford enlargement and improvement. In 1839 it proclaimed its support of "the Union, The Constitution, and the Laws, the Guardians of our Liberty." In 1844 it announced its support of Henry Clay, a bank of the United States, and a sound national currency. In 1848 it supported the Whig ticket of Zachary Taylor and Millard Fillmore. As the war clouds approached, the *Recorder* engaged in occasional controversies with the North Carolina *Democrat*, a secession paper briefly published at Hillsboro.

All through the Civil War Heartt kept the *Recorder* going, but in 1867 hard times compelled him to cut down its size. However, he announced, "We shall pursue the same lights hereafter that have guided us hitherto."

In 1869 Heartt sold the *Recorder* to C. N. B. Evans, a former journeyman printer of his who had set up the Milton, North Carolina, *Chronicle*. He then retired from active journalism. W. W. Holden later wrote of him, "He was the best man in all respects whom I have ever known."

It should be mentioned that the *Recorder* shop occasionally issued pamphlets as well as news sheets. Among those that have survived are "Letters on Popular Education Addressed to the People of North Carolina," 1832, and "The Discipline of Friends" (for the use of Quakers), and "A Solemn Address to Youth, with Serious Reflections and Remarks," both issued in 1823.

Following the end of the Civil War, Orange county, like the rest of North Carolina, was too impoverished and dispirited to support any marked cultural life, but in 1878 the *Orange County Observer* appeared at Hillsboro with Joseph A. Harris as editor and proprietor. It lived to about 1917.

The county's only woman editor was Mrs. Cornelia Phillips Spencer, who for some months in 1879 edited the *Chapel Hill Weekly Ledger*. She had as her assistants two University students, R. P. Pell, who subsequently became president of Converse College, Spartanburg, South Carolina, and Francis D. Winston, who became a superior court judge and lived for years at Windsor, North Carolina, as not the least interesting member of the intellectual Winston family. Mrs. Spencer, although otherwise successful as an author, seemed not to enjoy editing a small town paper and she soon yielded her place to Charles B. Aycock, later governor of the state and a leader in its educational revival.

Chapel Hill as a town seemed not able to support a strong paper until a native son, Louis Graves, returned to it after several active years as a journalist in New York. In 1923 he established the *Chapel Hill Weekly*, which soon acquired a loyal following as having a unique and highly individual flavor and which has grown stronger with the years.

On the paper's seventeenth birthday Graves, after chronicling the event, added that he was "very tired of it," an outburst that startled the nation, for the statement was copied all over the land and freely commented on. However, the tired editor did not, as was feared, give up the paper or his much-read column, "Chaff."

Graves's older brother, Ralph, was also a journalist, serving as city editor and Sunday editor of the *New York Times* at a time when it was beginning to be one of the world's foremost newspapers.

Another long-lived paper published in the county was the *Chapel Hill News*, established in 1894 by W. B. Thompson, who published it until 1944 when he sold it to J. Roy Parker. Its name was changed to the *News of Orange county* and it was in 1948 sold to E. J. Hamlin. Mr. Thompson was also editor for seven years of the Hillsboro News. He died in 1946.

Over the years there have been frequent attempts to establish literary periodicals in Orange county, but not all of them have been successful, due to scanty financial support. One of the first was the *Harbinger*, published by Isaac C. Partridge in 1833. Its aim was to give space to the sciences as well as the arts and it relied chiefly on the contributions of two University professors, Dr. Elisha Mitchell, and Dr. William Hooper. It failed to live long. Three years later the *Columbian Repository* was born, with

Hugh McQueen as editor, but no copies exist and it seems not to have survived beyond one issue.

The University at Chapel Hill has of course been the source of many periodicals, including the student newspaper, the *Tar Heel,* established in 1894, and its non-fraternity rival, the *White and Blue,* which was short-lived. But the campus editors and writers gave the state one of its proudest possessions in the form of the *University Magazine,* which was established in 1844 and except for one brief period was published continuously for 104 years before an ill-informed student body gave it up. It was one of the oldest and best edited college magazines in the nation, had many notable names among its contributors, and for a long time was the state's sole cultural periodical. Particularly noteworthy were its historical and biographical studies, which are now much sought by researchers. Its traditions have been in some measure preserved and carried on by the *Carolina Quarterly.*

CHAPTER XI

EDUCATION IN ORANGE COUNTY

BY EDGAR W. KNIGHT

Kenan Professor of Education, University of North Carolina

Before North Carolina established its first public school system in 1839, educational facilities in Orange county were provided as elsewhere in the state chiefly by means of the apprenticeship system, local "old-field" or neighborhood schools, Sunday schools, private academies, and perhaps also for some children of the well-to-do by the tutorial system, although little is known about this practice in Orange.

The apprenticeship practices were attempts to provide some educational training for poor and dependent children, under arrangements inherited from England and developed into a form of compulsory education for such children in all the American colonies. These arrangements seemed to have been in operation in those parts of North Carolina which were earliest settled, before legislation on the subject was enacted by the colony. Records of the latter part of the seventeenth century show that orphans or poor children were then being bound out or apprenticed by the precinct courts, although legislation in the colony was not enacted on the subject until later. In 1715 a colonial law was enacted which gave the precinct courts sole authority to bind out and apprentice dependent children to responsible masters or mistresses until they became of age, the girls at eighteen and the boys at twenty-one.

In 1762 legislation noted the experience of the courts in each county in the matter of apprenticing dependent children, and transferred to the grand jury of each county authority which formerly belonged to the church wardens of each parish. Legislative revisions were gradually made but the principal features of the law of 1762 remained in force until far into the nineteenth century. A legislative act of 1889, which continued until the public welfare system was established in the 1920's, required the master of an apprentice to provide:

"Diet, clothes lodging and accommodations fit and necessary; that the apprentice be taught to read and write and the rules of arithmetic to the double rule of three; six dollars in cash, a new suit of clothes and a new Bible at the end of the apprenticeship and such other education as may be agreed upon and inserted in the indenture by the clerk."

The full extent of the apprenticeship practices in Orange county may never be fully known. But those students, teachers, or other citizens of the county who are interested in the subject will find material on it in the records of the Clerk of the Court in Hillsboro or in the Department of Archives and History in Raleigh in which many of the old county records have been collected.

So-called "old field" schools in Orange were local neighborhood or community schools which many children seemed to have attended before interest was developed in education provided by taxation. Such schools were set up voluntarily at convenient points in the neighborhoods as private cooperative activities. An "old field" school might be conducted at the residence of the teacher, but most frequently it was found in some neglected or abandoned old field, from which it got its name. The salary of the teacher was paid by the parents who sent their children to him, each parent paying according to the number of children he sent. In the "old-field" school generally only the rudiments were taught - reading, writing, arithmetic - but occasionally more "advanced" subjects seemed to have been taught. Most of the teachers in these schools were men, and many of them were clergymen, or "lay readers" in the church, who tried by teaching to supplement their earnings. Now and then no doubt an "old-field" school was locally known as "academy."

The Secular Sunday school. The secular Sunday school also furnished some means of education, especially for poor and underprivileged children, in the days before the idea of schools by public taxation became popular. The beginnings of such educational work were generally made by voluntary effort. Such schools were numerous in North Carolina and seemed to have been very widely used in Orange County.

In 1825 the Orange County Sunday School Union made a

memorial to the General Assembly of the State to get aid for twenty-two schools which were being conducted under the direction of that organization. According to this petition, from 800 to 1,000 children were being instructed in these schools on Sunday, many of whom, "the children of the poor, who would otherwise have been brought up in utter ignorance and vice, have been taught to read and trained to habits of moral reflection and conduct." The House rejected the petition, which asked for twenty-five cents annually for each "Sunday school learner" under the care of the petitioning organization. The petition, which was presented to the House of Commons by John Scott, of Hillsboro, was signed by J. Webb, president; William Kirkland, first vice president; William Norwood, second vice president; John Kirkland, treasurer; J. W. Norwood, recording secretary; J. Witherspoon, corresponding secretary; and Dennis Heartt, William Huntington, J. G. Bacon, Elam Alexander, William Bingham, managers; and twenty-eight other citizens of the county, testifying to the wide interest in the work of the organization. Two years later a bill was introduced in the General Assembly, and passed by the Senate on first reading, to appropriate twenty-five cents for each poor child or indigent person who was being instructed in Sunday schools "in the art of reading and writing" but the bill failed to pass.

Academies and boarding schools - Academies and boarding schools were very numerous in Orange in the nineteenth century. It appeared that at least twenty-one were established there by 1832. Apparently the oldest of these schools in the county was the "Hillsborough Academy," which as early as 1801 carried an advertisement in *The Raleigh Register* signed by the following trustees: Walter Alves, William Kirkland, William Whitted, William Cain and Duncan Cameron. It was open to "youth of both sexes," and was under the direction of Reverend Andrew Flinn, who had "a proper assistant," and was prepared to teach Latin, Greek, English, reading, writing, arithmetic, geography, bookkeeping, "and the plainer branches of mathematics." Tuition was $16.00 a year for the advanced subjects and $12.00 for the elementary subjects. Board could be had in private families "on very reasonable terms." The "healthiness" of the location, "plentifulness of provisions," the abilities of the teacher, and the "cheapness of board" recommended the school.

Early in 1803 the trustees announced that "George Johnson, A. M., lately of Edinburgh," would be principal, but he seemed not to have kept his contract, and later Thomas Baron, who held the master's degree from Harvard, was announced as principal. In 1804 Richard Henderson, a former professor in the University of North Carolina, was announced as head of the academy. In 1812 the name of Reverend William Bingham appeared as principal, with Elizabeth Russell, who was in charge of the "female department," offering elementary subjects and needlework, painting and drawing. A Mr. Graham and a Miss Farly were in charge in 1815, and three years later J. Witherspoon was principal, and announced a list of rules to govern the conduct of the students. John Rogers was in charge of the school from 1822 until 1826, when W. J. Bingham took over and continued its direction for several years. This school acquired a high reputation, enlarged its curriculum, and prepared young men for the University of North Carolina.

This academy paid close attention to discipline, as the following rules, which appeared in *The Raleigh Register* for December 11, 1818, indicated:

> Each scholar must be present at morning and evening worship, at the opening and closing of the exercise of the day.
> No profane, abusive, or indecent language shall be permitted among the pupils but each conduct himself with propriety and decorum on all occasions.
> The use of ardent spirits is strictly forbidden, unless as a medicine, and the severest discipline will be used when such cases occur.
> No scholar shall be permitted to lounge about any store or tavern, or the public streets, nor play therein.
> Every student is required to pay strict regard to the Lord's Day, attending regularly public worship, refraining from ordinary studies and every kind of amusement, as riding, walking, visiting, and the like."

The most eminent of the academies in Orange County was the Bingham School, founded by Reverend William Bingham, who had been graduated by the University of Glasgow in 1778, and who began his work as teacher in Wilmington apparently in the early 1790's. He moved to Pittsboro and on June 10, 1800, *The Raleigh Register* contained an advertisement of the "Pittsborough Academy," which was in charge of Bingham. Later, he moved to Hillsboro, where he continued a school, which was later moved to Mt. Repose, about five miles from Mebane, then back to Hillsboro and then to Oaks, apparently about 1814, then to "Mebaneville" in 1863, and about 1891 to Asheville where it continued under the name of Bingham School for several years. The founder of the famous school was succeeded in its management by his son, William J. Bingham, who was graduated from the University of North Carolina in 1825; and his sons, William and Robert, also graduates of the University of North Carolina, joined with their father in the operation of the school.

An early catalogue of the school at Mebane said that Bingham School was "situated in a quiet, moral, and very healthy country neighborhood in Orange County, three-fourths of a mile from Mebaneville Depot, on the North Carolina Railroad. It was incorporated by Act of Assembly, and the officers are commissioned by the State." While at Oaks and also at Mebane, the Bingham School was attended by young men from several states. The Binghams were effective teachers and William Bingham, grandson of the founder, was widely known as the author of Latin and English texts.

Dr. Kemp P. Battle, in his *History of the University of North Carolina*, wrote of Bingham as "that progenitor of a line of able and cultured teachers and founder of a school eminent for nearly a century for its widespread and multiform usefulness,. . ."

In *The Raleigh Register* for August 10, 1839, appeared an article, signed "Atticus," which highly praised the work of the "able and indefatigable principal, Mr. Bingham," whose reputation rested upon the proficiency and success of his pupils. The article also said that the trustees had issued a small pamphlet containing an outline of Mr. Bingham's methods of teaching and managing the school. "Atticus" thought well of Bingham's plan of studies and in his article in the Raleigh paper criticized the educational "short cuts" which apparently, in his opinion at least, were already threatening "sound education." In this criticism, which has a modern ring, he wrote:

"It is common to hear American scholarship depreciated, and perhaps when contrasted with European, it may not be without truth, but there is abundant reason to account for it." Thorough elementary instruction and the time devoted to classical studies, he said, accounted for the superiority of European education. He said experience showed that sound learning in advanced studies could not be attained except by "a perfect mastery of the primary studies. More good minds have been wrecked, by attempting a *northwest passage* to learning than ever failed to arrive at it by the old route. The impatience of this age, and particularly of this country, have [*sic*] become proverbial, and in nothing is this more seen than in the discoveries of short systems of education; a species of quackery, which panders to the public appetite." It will be noted that this was written in 1839, nearly eighty years before the advocates of soft and easy going educational methods organized themselves into the Progressive Education Association.

Other academies in Orange County in the early part of the nineteenth century included Mrs. Gregory's Boarding School for young ladies, which offered them instruction in such "arts and sciences" as reading, writing, arithmetic, grammar, geography, plain sewing and sampler, embroidery, lace-work, fine needlework, filigree, artificial and scrap work, wax-work, drawing and painting, and music, with "board, washing, and tuition of every description, music excepted, $100." The fees were to be paid quarterly in advance.

Hawfield Academy, about ten miles west of Hillsboro, was in charge of Reverend William Paisley, and offered a curriclum somewhat similar to that given in the Hillsborough Academy. From 1812 to 1814 its principal was John H. Pickard.

In 1818, Union School, "about one mile south of Woody's Ferry on Haw River, Orange County," was in charge of Mary Mendenhall. Six miles northwest of Hillsboro, at Long Meadows, Mrs. Graves' Female School was announced by Rev. Elijah Graves in 1819, and in 1829 he announced "A Female School" under his direction at Walnut Grove, "twelve miles from Hillsborough, near the road leading from that place to Pittsborough, where every necessary and useful branch of literature, and some of the ornamental," would be taught. In 1820 James A. Craig, of Chapel Hill, announced in the press the opening of Chapel Hill Academy, with a course of studies so arranged "as to render it in every respect preparatory to the University."

Hillsborough Female Seminary was under the direction and inspection of Reverend William M. Green and Lavinia Brainerd in 1825, and offered, in addition to the usual academic subjects, "ancient, modern and sacred Geography," Euclid, astronomy, natural philosophy, moral philosophy, evidences of Christianity, botany, chemistry, mineralogy, logic and United States history. In 1826 Mr. Green said in his announcement of the school that "everything taught shall be taught thoroughly and with a view to practical life. And although the lighter gratifications of female education, usually called 'accomplishments,' shall be attended to in their proper place and measure, yet the chief aim of the instructors shall be to fit their pupils for usefulness, by inculcating, both by precept and example, moderation, forbearance, good temper, self-control, and the morality of the Gospel." Green continued to announce the work of this school until 1838. The following year the trustees (James S. Smith, William Cain, Cadwallader Jones, Sr., P. H. Mangum, Hugh Waddell, Nathan Hooker, Stephen Moore) announced that Maria L. Spear was the principal. The course of study contained many subjects.

Reverend John Witherspoon's Private Boarding School was announced in *The Raleigh Register* for opening in 1826, and two years later it was announced in the same paper that "The Reverend John Witherspoon of Hillsboro, has been unanimously elected to the Pastoral Office, by the Presbyterian Church in the vicinity of Hampden Sydney College," Virginia, but the school seemed to have continued until 1830 or later.

Other academies and private schools were conducted in Orange County before the establishment of the public system under legislation of 1839. Bethelehem School, "on Cain Creek, twelve miles from Hillsborough," under the direction of George W. Morrow, in 1829 offered studies preparatory to college. The following year W. Anderson announced Anderson's Female

Boarding School "within one mile of Hillsboro," and this school seemed to have continued at least through 1836. It was described as a family institution, in which the pupils met, "in every respect, with the same treatment to which they have been accustomed at home, so far as consistent with a strict though mild discipline." The number of pupils was limited.

In 1836 James Phillips of Chapel Hill announced Phillips' Female School there, with Mrs. Phillips and "a lady from Mrs. Willard's Seminary at Troy" (New York) doing most of the teaching. James Phillips was Professor of Mathematics and Natural Philosophy in the University. This school continued for several years. It recommended itself because of its location in Chapel Hill and opportunities "for mental improvement" which the libraries and public lectures of the University offered.

Daniel W. Kerr in 1837 announced Mount Pleasant Academy "twelve miles northwest of Hillsborough, six miles north of Mason Hall, and six miles west of Prospect Hill in Caswell County." This school, which continued for several years later changed its name to Junto Academy. Burwell's Female School in Hillsboro in the late 1830's was highly recommended by citizens of that community and Virginia. Among those endorsing the school were Judge Nash, Dr. James Webb, William Cain, Sr., J. W. Norwood, Judge Mangum, Rev. D. Lacy, of Raleigh; Rev. F. Nash, of Lincoln; Rev. William S. Plumer, of Richmond, and Rev. W. M. Atkinson, of Petersburg, Virginia. Thomas W. Holden announced Holden's English School at his residence in Orange County in 1838, and James P. Clark announced Fairfield School, six miles northwest of Hillsboro, in that year. John R. Holt announced Union Academy in the western part of Orange County in 1839. From 1858 to 1892 the daughters and niece of Judge Francis Nash conducted a school for young ladies, known as the "Select Boarding School of Misses Nash and Kollock."

Public school system established—As already noted, the academies and private schools provided most of the educational facilities for Orange County children whose parents were able to pay for the privileges. This continued to be the practice until the public school system was established by an act of the Legislature in 1839 when elections to ascertain the voice of the people on the subject were held. Most of the counties approved the plan and the principle of supporting schools by a combination of local taxation and the income from the Literary Fund which had been established in 1825. Only seven counties failed to ratify the plan. Orange was among those that approved it. The counties which voted for schools were required to levy a tax amounting to $20 for each school district which was to be supplemented by twice that amount from the proceeds of the Literary Fund.

Weaknesses of the new state system—The chief weakness of the system thus established was the lack of any central supervision. This defect was removed in part by an act of the legislature in 1852 which provided for a state superintendent of common schools, and in January of the following year Calvin H. Wiley became the first executive head of the public schools of North Carolina. Improvements were made from time to time in the educational legislation of the State, which applied to Orange County along with the other counties, and by the outbreak of the Civil War North Carolina was reported to have had the best state school system in the South and one of the best in the entire country.

But many difficult problems faced this new state system. The academies and the "old field" schools, which were numerous in the middle of the nineteenth century, were somewhat jealous of the public school system. Also, public education was not highly favored by certain classes of people. Schoolhouses were primitive, the teachers did not have excellent preparation, the methods of teaching were poor, and textbooks and other materials of instruction were inadequate. Nevertheless, there was an educational revival in the State toward the end of the antebellum period, in large measure promoted and strengthened by the leadership of Calvin Wiley, who visited every county, organized the teachers of the State, began the publication of an educational journal, and made use of other means of improving educational conditions. Orange county shared along with the other counties of the State in this educational advance.

Then came war and the tragic period of Congressional Reconstruction which followed, and public education in North

Carolina was seriously retarded. It was not until around 1900 that the public schools of Orange county and the state as a whole reached again the level which they had attained by 1861.

The school system as Wiley found it—The first written record of the operation of the public schools in Orange was for 1853, the year that Calvin H. Wiley took office as the first state superintendent of the public school system of North Carolina. There were at that time fifty-one districts in the county and schools were taught in all except one. The number of children in the districts was 4,447, of whom 2,507 attended school. Thirty male teachers and one female teacher were that year licensed to teach. In 1860 fifty-seven district schools were taught in the county, thirty-eight male and seven female teachers were licensed, state school funds received by the county amounted to $7,410.89 and about $1,800 came from county taxes. The sum of $5,300 was expended for the schools whose annual term was about four months.

The state system during Reconstruction—As already noted, the effects of the war and Congressional Reconstruction were ruinous to schools in the South. North Carolina suffered along with the other states in this region and Orange along with the other counties in the State. The funds available for schools in the county in 1884 were considerably less than these had been in 1860. There were thirty-three white and thirty-one Negro schools, in which there were 1,369 white and 1,134 Negro children; the school term was less than ten weeks. Most of the schoolbuildings were log structures, and the total value of all the public-school property of the county was $3,500 (white) and $2,500 (Negro). In 1900 the white children enrolled were 1,516 with an average daily attendance of 918; Negro children enrolled were 667, with an average daily attendance of 404.

As early as 1895 there had been 1,678 white children enrolled in the schools, but enrollment in the Negro schools had considerably decreased. So also had the school term (for both races). This was ten weeks as compared with twelve weeks in 1890. It appeared also that the average salary was lower than it had been in 1890. The school funds were apportioned on a per capita basis, the sum of $3,930 for the whites and $2,087 for the Negroes.

Beginning of improvements—Some improvement in education in Orange county began to appear after 1900, under the influence of the "Aycock Revival." In the early years of this century there were thirty-eight white schools and ten Negro schools giving work through the seven elementary grades. Apparently the only public high school work provided in Orange at that time was given at Chapel Hill and Hillsboro. The salaries of the teachers and their educational preparation were very modest. President Francis P. Venable of the University of North Carolina suggested to the County Board of Education that the white teachers of the county would profit by attending the Summer Session of the University and he proposed to admit them at a cost of $75 per person, and the Board accepted the proposal. It also voted to pay a salary of $35 a month to those teachers who made a grade of 95 on the examination at the end of the Summer Session and $40 a month to those who made a grade of 98 on such examination. In 1904 there were fourteen white teachers and twelve Negro teachers in the county with some normal or professional training. Twenty-five white and fifteen Negro teachers had had four years' teaching experience, and six white and two Negro teachers held collegiate diplomas.

In 1905 the school fund of the county amounted to a little less than $15,000. The salary of the county superintendent was $750 a year in 1908. In his report for 1910 Superintendent T. Wingate Andrews showed a school fund of about $20,000. There were forty-two children in the high school grades in Chapel Hill and nineteen in Hillsboro. Rural schoolhouses for the white children numbered forty-two and those for the Negro children twenty-five. There were forty-eight one-room schools in the county, twenty-four white and twenty-four Negro, and the average annual school term was eighty-six days. At that time there were thirty-nine white and one Negro school libraries reported in the county, with about 3,000 volumes. There were six special local tax districts in the county, and the sum of about $500 came from such sources.

Orange County's superintendents—In 1885 Orange County provided for its first Board of Education after the Civil War. Under legislation of that year the Board was to be elected by the justices of the peace and the county commissioners in joint session. Since that time the county has had a Board of Education continuously, except for the period from 1895 to 1897 when the schools of the county were in charge of the county commissioners. Also, except for that two-year period, the county has had a superintendent of schools. This office has been held since 1885 by the following men: Reverend J. L. Currie from June 1885 to June 1889; B. C. Patton from June 1889 to June 1890; John W. Thompson from June 1890 to June 1895; John W. Thompson from June 1897 to July 1901; Reverend Charles E. Maddry from July 1901 to September 1904; Reverend J. C. Hocutt from September 1904 to October 1908; T. Wingate Andrews from October 1908 to August 1911; S. P. Lockhart from August 1911 to September 1917; R. H. Claytor from September 1917 to July 1947; G. T. Proffit from July 1947 to July 1951; and G. P. Carr since July 1951.

Before World War I Orange had many one-teacher schools, but after that time consolidation was so effectively made that in 1952-53 the county school system contained only eight white and three Negro schools (outside of the administrative unit of Chapel Hill), none of them one-teacher schools. There were then two white and one Negro high schools. The schools, with the number of teachers in each, were:

White	Elementary	High School
Hillsboro H. S.	23	11
West Hillsboro	7	
Murphey	3	
Efland	9	
Aycock	6	4
Carrboro	11	
White Cross	4	
Caldwell	3	
Negro		
Central H.S.	16	9
Efland	5	
Cedar Grove	14	

It was under the administration of Superintendent Claytor

that effective consolidation was developed. This was one of the first tasks that he set out to do. A survey of the county was made by the County Board of Education and Superintendent Claytor and by 1930 most of the small white schools of the county were consolidated, with adequate means of transportation. But progress was slow, for as late as 1925 the county had twenty-one one-teacher white schools in which 30 per cent of the rural children of the county were enrolled, and several one-teacher Negro schools. The average daily attendance (based on enrollment) in the one-teacher schools was only about 67 per cent. At that time Orange ranked sixty-second among the one hundred counties of the State in the number of its children in one-teacher schools.

In order to bring about further improvements in education, a county-wide committee was formed in October of 1948 to make a study and report of conditions in the county. A part of that report was published in February, 1949, and may be found in *The News of Orange County,* of February 10 and in subsequent issues of that paper, as well as in the Durham Morning Herald papers of March 6 and November 20, 1949. This careful and comprehensive report disclosed many important facts about the administrative organization of public education, taxation for schools, school population, attendance, and other conditions. A result of this study was a call by the county commissioners for a special election to authorize bonds not to exceed $1,250,000. This was approved by the voters November 22, 1949, for improvements and enlargements of old and the erection of new school buildings, and for a new courthouse building. At an election in 1947 the voters had defeated similar proposals, but by approval in 1949 several school buildings were nearing completion by 1952 and others were being projected, and work on the new courthouse and offices was going forward.

In 1952-1953 the county was using fifty-six buses, thirty-four for the transportation of white children and twenty-two for Negro children. These transported 1759 white children and traveled 1280 miles a day, and 1102 Negro children and traveled 940 miles a day.

Improvement in the quality of certificates held by the school personnel has been gradually made. In 1952-53 the superintendent, the supervisor, three principals and four teachers in the white schools held graduate certificates; two principals held principal's certificates; sixty-seven teachers held A certificates, five B certificates, and only two teachers held C certificates. In the Negro schools the supervisor, two principals, and one teacher held graduate certificates, one principal held the principal's certificate, and forty teachers held A certificates.

Chapel Hill a separate unit—Chapel Hill is the only separate educational administrative unit in Orange County. The schools in that community were organized many years ago under a special charter from the Legislature under which it has operated continuously. Prior to the establishment of a public school in Chapel Hill, there were several teachers in the village who helped prepare boys and girls for college. One of the most important educational agencies in town was the "Canada School," organized by John W. Canada, soon after his graduation from the University in 1896. Canada, assisted by his brother, Charles S. Canada, Mrs. Sallie Wilson, and a Miss Hendon, operated the "Canada School" until John W. Canada moved to Texas soon after 1900. Among the students at the "Canada School" were Charles E. Maddry, Eben Alexander, Louis Graves, Foy Roberson, Louise Manning Venable, John Manning Venable, Birdie Pritchard, Nellie Roberson, Junius Thomas Harris, Isaac Foust Harris, and Bunn Hearn. In the Chapel Hill school district were a high school building and an elementary school building for the white children and the Orange County Training School, both elementary and high school, housed in one building for the Negroes. The high school building for white children was destroyed by fire August 8, 1942. All of the high school library books and the laboratories for home economics and science were destroyed. It was impossible promptly to replace the building and the high school pupils were housed in the Baptist Church, the basement of the elementary building, the Cone House and a small residence used for home economics. This makeshift arrangement continued until the classroom wing of the present high school and a new shop were occupied during the spring of 1947. The classroom wing had thirteen rooms including five basement rooms which were intended to be a cafeteria. This space enabled the high school to move out of the basement of the elementary building and thereby release some very much needed room for the elementary children, but the high school continued to use the Cone House and the small residence, which in 1952-53 was still being used for Home Economics and was very over-crowded. This condition continued until portions of the new high school were occupied in the fall of 1951.

The white schools in 1952-53 had an elementary building approximately thirty-five years old, yet in good condition, and a modern high school building complete except for the gymnasium. These properties had a value of $734,500 for insurance purposes.

The needs of the Negro children had not been neglected during this period of improving school facilities. Two new rooms were added to Northside (formerly known as Orange County Training School), a new cafeteria was built, and a new high school (without the auditorium-gymnasium) was completed and occupied in September, 1951. The properties occupied by the Negro children had an insurance value of $365,100.

The plans for expansion of the schools in Chapel Hill contemplate the completing of the two high schools and the construction of additional elementary buildings in other sections of the community such as the one under construction in the fall of 1952 in the Glen Lennox area. When these plans have materialized it is contemplated that the present elementary building will be converted into a junior high school and then it will not be necessary for the small children to come into the congested town traffic.

The enrollment in the white schools in 1952-53 was 1096 and in the Negro schools 738, with thirty-nine teachers employed in the former and thirty-two in the latter. The white elementary school library contained approximately 4321 volumes, the white high school library approximately 6220, and the Negro school library approximately 3400 volumes. Seven buses operated to the white schools and five to the Negro schools. The white schools provided the School of Education of the University of North Carolina with facilities for supervision and practice teaching.

Superintendents of the Chapel Hill Schools have been E. M. Highsmith, 1908-1910; W. H. Rhodes, 1910-1912; H. B. Marrow, 1912-1914; Fred W. Morrison, 1914-1924; Lettie Glass, Acting Superintendent in Mr. Morrison's absence and again in 1923-1924; L. R. Sides, 1924-1926; E. R. Moser, 1926-1927; H. F. Munch, 1927-1928; B. A. Stevens, 1928-1929; C. A. Hoyle, 1929-1932; J. Minor Gwynn, 1932-1933; H. F. Munch, 1933-1934; George Howard 1934-1935; J. Minor Gwynn, 1935-1937; A. W. Honeycutt, 1937-1945; C. W. Davis, 1945 to the present.

Sources of revenue and expenditures for the schools in Chapel Hill 1945-1947 were as follows:

	Actual	Budget
Sources of Revenue	1945-1946	1946-1947
State	$70,459.15	$82,500.00
Federal and State for Vocational Education	4,374.73	5,942.00
County taxes	5,946.98	6,364.00
County fines	7,572.00	8,243.00
District taxes	15,689.90	12,555.00
Share of tax on intangibles	682.21	660.75
Miscellaneous	46.31	40.00
Total	$104,771.28	$116,304.75
Expenditures		
Current Expenses	$90,246.47	$107,704.24
Capital Outlay	2,581.90	6,600.00
Debt Service	4,415.90	4,282.50
Total	$97,244.27	$118,586.74

In 1952-53 the expenditure figures were as follows:

Current expenses:
State	$213,241.37
County and local	81,659.65
Total	$294,901.02

Capital outlay: $34,395.82. There were no expenditures for debt service.

Indebtedness to Murphey — Orange County and the entire State owe a deep debt to Archibald D. Murphey, who is known as "The Father of the Public Schools of North Carolina." Although he was born in Caswell County, Murphey spent most of his adult life in Orange. The son of a Revolutionary officer, he was born a few miles from Milton in 1777, attended the famous academy of Dr. David Caldwell, known as "Log College", near Greensboro, where he was prepared for the University at Chapel Hill from which he was graduated with high honors in 1799. Murphey taught in the University for two years and then began the practice of law in Hillsboro, soon rising to a position of leadership in his community and State. In 1812 he entered the State Senate as a representative of Orange and remained in that body until 1818, when he became a judge of the Superior Court of the State. While in the Legislature he advocated many measures for the advancement of the material, educational, and moral resources of the State, including internal improvements, constitutional reform, and a state public school system, and was the author of the well known legislative report in 1817 which proposed a state-wide public educational plan. This report led to the creation of the Literary Fund in 1825 and to the passage of the law of 1839 on which the State's ante-bellum public school system was established. For Murphey, who died and was buried in Hillsboro in 1832, Murphey Hall at the University of North Carolina is named, and so also is Murphey School which is located a few miles east of Hillsboro on the old Durham-Hillsboro road. For his work and his general interest in the State, Orange County and North Carolina should keep fresh the memory of the name of this distinguished citizen.

Chapter XII

THE UNIVERSITY OF NORTH CAROLINA IN CHAPEL HILL

By Robert Burton House

Chancellor of the University of North Carolina at Chapel Hill

[Adapted from Kemp Plummer Battle, *History of the University of North Carolina*, 2 vols., Raleigh, 1907-1912, and from Archibald Henderson, *The Campus of the First State University*, Chapel Hill, 1949.]

A previous chapter has told of the founding of the University of North Carolina. It is important to emphasize here that the University opened its doors to students in 1795. It thereby became the first State University in the United States to admit students and to send them out into the nation bearing a State University diploma. Without any pretense at originality of research or expression, this chapter endeavors to outline the evolution of the most significant institution in Orange County and in the State of North Carolina and to mark its rise as one of the distinguished Universities in the world of learning.

"The University of North Carolina," said Edward Anderson Alderman, "was chartered by the legislative action of a pioneer people in a primitive wilderness to furnish impulse and light to an agricultural community of English people." Dr. Alderman was right except in the phrase "English people." North Carolina was a pioneer community of English, Scotch and German people, along with a few surviving Indians and a large contingent of Negroes.

In colonial days, a chapel of the church of England stood on top of a wooded hill in Southern Orange county where the road from Petersburg to the south crossed the road from New Bern to the west. The name of this sanctuary was New Hope Chapel. About the middle of the eighteenth century, James Hogg, a Scotch merchant of Fayetteville, kinsman of the Scotch poet of the same name, was influential in bringing to this section of Orange county a number of families from Scotland and neighboring sections of England. Among these families were the Hogans, the Yeargans, the McCauleys, the Pipers, the Craigs, the Barbees, the Jones, the Morgans, and the Daniels. There were others, but these families are mentioned particularly because they gave land and money and labor in building the new University. They also were prominent in building the village of Chapel Hill. Their descendants have remained in the community, showing a canny conservatism in holding, selling and developing their lands and practical statesmanship in building the village of Chapel Hill and in serving the University and the State. They brought with them from their native highlands a love of nature and a desire to preserve its beauty. This impulse has found beautiful fruition in the hills of the region around Chapel Hill itself. These early settlers called the hill of the Chapel, New Hope Chapel Hill. Later they shortened the term to Chapel Hill.

It was a beautiful spot. A granite promontory jutted out from the north and west three hundred feet above the valley to the east and south. Two bold creeks at the foot of the hill, Bolin's on the north, Morgan's on the south, were ready to turn the gristmills and sawmills of farmers and lumbermen. A profusion of springs and brooks gushed from the hillside and had carved the terrain into bends, glens and meadows. All of this was covered with a mountain growth of oak, hickory, ash, laurel and rhododendron. Chapel Hill was already a beautiful place. It would have become an important town in southern Orange even if there had been no University. Chapel Hill became the site of the University of North Carolina because of its beauty and the healthfulness of its location, since it was already qualified as being easily enough within range of the geographical center of the State as provided by the Trustees' regulation. Furthermore, the citizens of the community, under the stimulus of James Hogg, had made the greatest donations of money and lands and had demonstrated the most practicable skill in making the brick and in doing the carpentry to get the building of the University and the village under way.

The University, the village of Chapel Hill, and Orange county all grew up together. James Hogg moved his family into the county, many other settlers came as the University increased economic opportunities in the region and, of course, hundreds of professors and staff members of the University came in the course of the years. All of these also became ardent lovers and citizens of Chapel Hill and of Orange county. While this story concerns itself primarily with the evolution of the University itself, it is important to note that the village of Chapel Hill grew as the University grew and demanded housing and business services. Chapel Hill has never depended upon any business other than this service to the University, although the neighboring industrial community of Carrboro demonstrated also the economic importance of the location. Chapel Hill residents furnished boarding houses, stores, clothing shops and other businesses such as a University community would need. Most of the buildings served their purposes, disappeared in the course of the years, and have been replaced by others, but East Franklin Street, for several blocks from the President's house toward Durham, still preserves in the Chancellor's house on the north side of the street and in the Kay Kyser home on the south side of the street, two surviving original houses of the period. The first permanent brick structure in the village still stands. It is the Kluttz Building in the center of the town. The old freestone walls bounding the campus on the north and east and bounding the yards of the old houses on East Franklin Street were laid during the administration of President David L. Swain. The great professor, Elisha Mitchell, laid them out and did a great deal of the work with his own hands. Franklin Street, named for Benjamin Franklin, has always been the main street of the village. Cameron Avenue, running through the campus and called after the Orange county family of that name, was the original southern boundary of village and campus. Columbia Street, named for the spirit of the Republic, was the western boundary, and Hillsboro Street was the eastern boundary as well as the main artery of business and commerce connecting Chapel Hill with the county seat at Hillsboro. Rosemary Street, named because Lady Rose lived at one end and Lady Mary lived at the other, marked the most outlying district of the infant village. Although Chapel Hill has grown tremendously, the terrain has remained practically unchanged. The coming of the automobile and the cutting of new highways have done more to change the surface appearance of Chapel Hill of the last ten years than in all the years preceding. The ancient springs and brooks have been piped underground. The campus was almost original forest until after the Civil War. It has been gradually graded to something approaching a level appearance. Trees have been thinned and replanted, but the original Davie Poplar and many of the original oaks are still standing.

The following "Historical Sketch of the University of North Carolina" is from the *University Catalogue* for 1952-1953:

The University began its career with a gift of land warrants for 20,000 acres, cash amounting to $2,706.41, and a loan of $10,000 (afterward converted into a gift) made by the legislature in 1791 as a result of the interest and leadership of Davie as a member of the House. By constant struggle and periodic appeals for private benefactions, the institution grew despite general poverty, opposition to taxation, denominational hostility, and sectional controversies between eastern and western North Carolina. The General Assembly made no specific appropriations for its maintenance until 1881, but through the act passed in 1789 it exempted the University from taxation and made it the beneficiary of escheats and arrearages due the state; and in 1867 it appropriated $7,000 to pay to officers' indebtedness incurred during and immediately after the Civil War.

Before 1804, the University was under a succession of "presiding professors." This was not a satisfactory system, and in 1804, Joseph Caldwell was elected the first president. Under Caldwell (1804-1812, 1817-1835), the University grew from a small classical school into a creditable liberal arts college. After 1815, natural sciences were placed on terms of equality with the humanities.

When Caldwell was succeeded by David L. Swain in 1835, the University was widely known as a center of sound scholarship and teaching. During his long tenure (1835-1868), Swain devoted his administration to a program of drawing the institution and the state close together. More emphasis was placed on subjects designed to prepare men for public service—history, law, rhetoric, and public speaking. The ideal of public service overshadowed general culture prior to 1860. During these years, the enrollment of the University reached a peak of 456 (1858), and its alumni included one president of the United States, one vice-president, seven cabinet officials, ten United States senators, forty-one representatives in Congress, fifteen state governors, and many state judges and legislators. From 1814, when a University alumnus first became governor, until the present time, twenty-six of the forty-six governors of North Carolina have studied at Chapel Hill.

The University remained open during the Civil War, although most of its faculty and students joined the Confederate armies. Reconstruction, however, closed its doors for nearly five years (1871-1875). Through the efforts of the alumni and Mrs. Cornelia Phillips Spencer, a Chapel Hill resident, the University was reopened in 1875.

By the constitution adopted in 1868 the General Assembly has "power to provide for the election of Trustees of the University of North Carolina, in whom, when chosen, shall be vested all the privileges, rights, franchises and endowments thereof in anywise granted to or conferred upon the trustees of said University; and the General Assembly may make such provisions, laws and regulations, from time to time, as may be necessary and expedient for the maintenance and management of said University." The governor of the state is, ex officio, president of the Board of Trustees.

The same constitution, in connection with "Benefits of the University" further states: "The General Assembly shall provide that the benefits of the University, as far as practicable, be extended to the youth of the State free of expense for tuition; also, that all the property which has heretofore accrued to the State, or shall hereafter accrue, from escheats, unclaimed dividends, or distributive shares of the estates of deceased persons, shall be appropriated to the use of the University."

In 1875 the University was reopened with the Reverend Dr. Charles Phillips as Chairman of the Faculty (1875-76). From

1876 to 1949 the University had seven presidents, each of whom made a distinct contribution to its expansion and progress. Dr. Kemp Plummer Battle (president 1876-1891) reorganized the University in 1876, established the first summer normal session in the South (1877), secured the first regular appropriation for maintenance (1881), and wrote a two-volume history of the University. George Tayloe Winston (1891-1896) "made its campus the dwelling place of dynamic democracy and a citadel against the forces of intolerance and bigotry." Edwin Anderson Alderman (1896-1900) opened its doors to women. During the administration of Francis Preston Venable (1900-1914), the University's financial condition improved, the physical plant was considerably expanded, athletics were encouraged, and creative scholarship was required of the faculty. The brief administration of Edward Kidder Graham (1914-1918) was notable for the enlargement of the University's service to the state at large, increased resources for administrative and building purposes, and a strengthening of student morale and honor standards. President Harry Woodburn Chase (1919-1930) guided the University through a period of rapid physical expansion, and during this time the University achieved an international reputation for high standards of scholarship and freedom in research and teaching. Student enrollment increased rapidly, and maintenance appropriations reached $894,379 in 1928-1929, the high point up until that time. Increasing emphasis was shown in the social sciences and graduate work. The Graduate School was reorganized in 1920. The Institute of Government was founded in the 1920's. The University of North Carolina Press was incorporated in 1922, and the Institute for Research in Social Science was organized in 1924. Professional schools of law, medicine, pharmacy, engineering, education, and commerce attained a standing which gave the University its widening reputation.

Under President Frank Porter Graham (1930-1949) the University continued to make progress. The administrative consolidation of the University, the North Carolina College for Women at Greensboro, and the North Carolina State College of Agriculture and Engineering at Raleigh into the University of

North Carolina was effected in 1932. New schools and divisions were added at Chapel Hill—Library Science in 1931, the General College in 1935, and Public Health in 1936. The Institute of Government became a part of the University in 1942, the Communication Center was established in 1945, and the School of Education, discontinued in 1933, was re-instituted in 1948. New departments were added—City and Regional Planning in 1946, Radio in 1947, Religion in 1947, and Astronomy in 1950 in connection with the $3,000,000 Morehead Building and Planetarium which was completed in 1949.

The Division of Health Affairs was organized in 1949 and includes the schools of Medicine, Public Health, and Pharmacy; the new schools of Nursing and Dentistry; and the University Hospital. It was established for the purpose of integrating the work of all of the health professional schools and the hospital in their teaching and research programs within the University.

In 1950, by action of the Board of Trustees, a School of Social Work and a School of Journalism were established, and the School of Commerce became the School of Business Administration.

In the development of the consolidation process, Robert Burton House was selected by President Graham and duly confirmed by the Trustees in 1934 to serve as Dean of Administration of the University at Chapel Hill. In 1945, Dean House's title was changed by the Trustees to Chancellor of the University at Chapel Hill.

In World War II the service of the University and its alumni was particularly noteworthy. More than 10,000 students and alumni, not including Navy and Army personnel sent to Chapel Hill for training, entered the armed forces. More than 300 lost their lives in service. Some 20,000 officers and cadets in naval aviation were trained in the United States Navy Pre-Flight School, established in 1942. A naval ROTC unit, which was established in 1940 and still continues, was the core of the Navy's V-12 program at the University. Army and Army Air Corps groups were trained on the campus. An Air R. O. T. C. was installed in 1947. Many members of the faculty were given leaves of absence for war service, and a number of University departments were engaged in research programs for the armed forces, for government, and for industry. Throughout the war period the University maintained also its normal curriculum offerings.

On March 22, 1949, Governor W. Kerr Scott appointed President Graham to the Senate of the United States. Pending the election of a new president, Controller W. D. Carmichael, Jr., was designated Acting President. By the unanimous vote of the entire membership of the Board of Trustees, Gordon Gray was elected President of the University on February 6, 1950. He assumed full responsibility for the office on September 23, 1950, and was officially inaugurated as president on October 10, 1950.

On May 22, 1951, upon the recommendation of President Gray, two new positions were created in the general administration of the University. Under the by-laws passed at that time by the Board of Trustees, the Controller was made Controller and Vice-President and an additional vice-presidency was created. The chancellors and vice-presidents of the several branches of the University became chancellors of those branches. Dr. Logan Wilson was chosen as the new vice-president and assumed his duties in the fall of 1951. He resigned to become President of the University of Texas in 1952.

With the growth of the University has come a need for the redefining of the relation of the faculty to the University. On November 6, 1942, the General Faculty authorized the appointment of a committee, under the the chairmanship of the late Professor John M. Booker, to study faculty government and prepare a report embodying a uniform set of principles defining the powers, duties, and status of the various divisions which constitute the University. The committee, known as the Committee on University Government, submitted its report in sections during the next eight years. On May 10, 1950, the General Faculty adopted, in its entirety, the new instrument known as "Faculty Legislation on University Government," with the provision that it go into effect in January, 1951.

The chief departure from previous legislative practice in University government made by the new legislation is in its establishment of a Faculty Council as the governing body. The Council, elected for three-year staggered terms from all the divisions of the University and embracing all ranks of professorship on a proportional basis, has assumed all the legislative functions of the General Faculty except the power to amend the "General Faculty Legislation." Consisting of ex-officio and elected members, the Council meets on the first Friday of each month during the academic year for the transaction of University business.

Growth of the University at Chapel Hill is depicted in enrollment figures. In the fall of 1920 students in residence numbered some 1,300; in 1930, 2,700; and in the fall of 1941 enrollment reached 4,108—up to then an all-time high. Because of the G. I. Bill and the general pressure for university and college education at the conclusion of the war, enrollment at Chapel Hill increased rapidly and in 1948-1949 reached 7,603, the highest figure to date.

In the past thirty years there have been three notable periods of expansion in the physical plant of the University. The first occurred in the 1920's, the second in the late 1930's and the early 1940's, and the third during World War II, when the University expanded its facilities to accommodate Navy and Army training programs on the campus. The 1947 and 1949 legislatures projected a fourth period of building activity when they made appropriations totaling $20,028,800 for permanent improvements. These improvement include the expansion of the two-year School of Medicine at Chapel Hill to a four-year school with a teaching hospital; four new dormitories for men; a great increase in the capacity of the library; expansion of the University's utilities and service plants; buildings for the schools of Nursing and Dentistry; living quarters for nurses, internes, and residents; a Public Health research laboratory building; additions to the Law and Chemistry buildings; and new quarters for the School of Business Administration. The total value of the physical plant when these facilities are completed and in use is estimated at approximately $42,000,000.

The University of North Carolina in Chapel Hill opened in 1795 with one building, one professor and one student. In 1953 that one student is represented by 5,218 students in residence and many thousands of students in some form of extension education. That one professor is represented by 800 members of the faculty with the rank of instructor or higher, that one building is represented today by 77 permanent buildings on a campus of 150 acres in a total property of 1,200 acres. Some 2,400 people are on the total staff of the University and the annual overall budget is $12,000,000.00. The village of Chapel Hill has expanded far beyond its corporate limits and is a community of some 18,000 citizens. The University has already embarked upon a new era of service to the State with a bright past and opportunities for an even more brilliant future. The University of North Carolina looks ahead with confidence and challenge.

CHAPTER XIII

ORANGE COUNTY'S CONTRIBUTIONS TO MEDICAL PROGRESS

BY C. SYLVESTER GREEN

Executive Vice-President, The Medical Foundation of North Carolina

When Orange county was established two hundred years ago there was not a single School of Medicine in the United States. The few physicians who practiced medicine in the county had either been trained abroad, as were most of the physicians of the Albemarle section of the state, or had learned medicine by attaching themselves to other reputable practicing physicians.

There were no state organizations of medical men when Orange county was established. The first State Medical Society of record was in 1766 in New Jersey. The medical profession was scarcely recognized and yet the men who lived and worked in Orange county left reputations as scholars and artisans of high skill, far superior to the rumored evidences of quackery and witchcraft prevalent in so many parts of the nation. These early doctors in Orange county were in the main educated men, cultured and refined by any standard, and upright citizens in their communities.

In its two hundredth year, Orange county is the site of a four-year School of Medicine - a school that has offered two years of medicine since 1879. In addition, the county boasts through the expanding Division of Health Affairs of the University of North Carolina at Chapel Hill, a School of Pharmacy (1887), a School of Public Health (1937), a School of Dentistry (1950), a School of Nursing (1951), and their teaching adjunct, the North Carolina Memorial Hospital (1952).

During all of these years, Orange county has enjoyed a better average in the number of physicians and the availability of medical care than has been true in many other counties in the State.

Two contributions must be credited to Orange county in the

general field of medicine. The county's early physicians, and mainly those of 155 years ago, provided the leadership out of which came the organization of the State Medical Society, the eighth such organization in the nation. Then, through the University of North Carolina, both at the undergraduate and graduate level, even before the actual beginnings of medical instruction, there has been an intelligent emphasis on medical training. This latter has seen new and vastly extended emphasis in the progress of the past ten years.

In the early years physicians were professional "jacks-of-all-trades" - and were good at most of them in the light of the then knowledge of drugs, operative procedures and therapies. They substituted for their uncertainty about certain illnesses, an intelligent inquisitiveness that gained for them leadership in the profession, and brought recognition to many of them personally.

The name of Dr. James Webb appears early in the records of medicine in the state. He was the leading physician in Orange county in the closing years of the eighteenth century, and was one of the principal figures in the establishment of the State Medical Society. He was in that small group that attended the organizing session in Raleigh, December 17, 1799.

A charter of incorporation was dated December 23 of the same year. Designed to encourage a spirit of inquiry, the physicians also sought a chance to set up certain standards that would outlaw "ignorant pretenders" and give the true physician a sure recognition in every community. This effort was their reply to "the fatal and criminal practice of quacks and empyrics," who still held forth in some sections of the state.

That this Society, after five years, ceased to exist is no discredit to the men of that period. They found transportation next to impossible. They were discouraged by the heavy demands of their own practice, and some professional complacency that disturbed Dr. Webb and others like him. The 1804 meeting was the last one held until 45 years later.

Dr. Webb himself was one of the "censors" appointed by the early Society to examine men who wanted to practice medicine, and to approve them, upon acceptable examination. This approval quickly became recognized and appreciated. It was obviously the forerunner of the present system of medical examiners, and it is reported that North Carolina was the first state in the union to make any attempt to regulate the practice of medicine in this fashion.

It was Dr. Edmund Strudwick, also of Hillsboro, who was responsible in a large measure for the revival of the State Medical Society. He advanced the idea and was active in the call for the meeting in 1849. Dr. Strudwick had studied under Dr. Webb, and the affection of the younger man for the preceptor is a touching story.

Dr. Webb was born in 1774 and died in 1855. After graduation at the University of North Carolina, he had gone to the University of Pennsylvania for his medical training. When the new Society was organized he was made an honorary Charter Member and was paid high tribute and recognition by Dr. Strudwick and others.

Orange county has provided continuous leadership for the State Medical Society. Many of its presidents have been graduates of the University of North Carolina, and a large number of them studied medicine at Chapel Hill. Orange county physicians have held positions of trust in every capacity in which the Society has operated, and members of the faculty of the University have consistently found places of recognition and service on its annual programs.

Dr. Strudwick was the first president of the revised Society. Dr. Hubert A. Royster wrote of him in a paper presented to the Society many years later that he was "a man of great courage and energy morally, mentally, and physically." He also spoke of his unfailing charity as exemplified by service to the indigent, as well as his skill and daring as a surgeon.

In his service to his profession, Dr. Strudwick advocated prolonged pre-collegiate study under a preceptor, something comparable to the first and second years in the colleges of the present. He would also have restricted medical schools "to those fully equipped," - the advocacy of which was surprising in a day when a will to be a doctor was about the principal requirement for entering the profession. It was this urging on Dr. Strudwick's part that brought about the first Board of Medical

Examiners set up by law in 1859. The Board of Censors of 1799 had been a substantial predecessor, although the earlier board lacked the authority of the State. Dr. Strudwick and his associates also stressed the importance of internship and postgraduate study and recommended that as many of the men as possible go abroad for study and training.

Of added significance was Dr. Strudwick's advocacy of autopsies by which he believed even then that much added medical knowledge could be gained. He wanted laboratories set up at as many places as possible. He advocated museums of multiple scientific phases. He urged frequent meetings of physicians throughout the state, and insisted that knowledge should be preserved through publications as fully and adequately presented as possible. These techniques of professional advancement are all taken for granted today. They have become the pattern of professional growth. It is revealing that more than a hundred years ago Dr. Strudwick should have advocated so wisely and insistently.

Dr. Strudwick was born at Long Meadow, five miles north of Hillsboro, March 25, 1802; studied early at Bingham School and later took his medical degree from the University of Pennsylvania. He did a two-year residency at the Philadelphia Alms House and Charity Hospital, and returned to Hillsboro in 1826. Soon a recognized surgeon, his fame spread around the state. Various newspaper accounts from many sections relate how he traveled to widely scattered areas for special practice. In addition, it is reported that hundreds came from other sections of the state to Hillsboro to consult him and be treated by him. There is no record of a hospital there. His home was his office. No doubt, it was also the place where he treated and cared for many who came to him for his professional services.

An often quoted paragraph from his presidential address in 1850 is of interest as an indication of his capacity of thinking and expression. "Neither the apathy of friends, the cold neglect and deep injustice of legislation nor pampered quackery and empiricism can stay its onward course. True medical science will like the majestic oak stand the shock and storm of every opposition. It has been beautifully compared to a star whose light though now and then obscured by a passing cloud will shine forever and ever in the firmament of heaven."

There is no record of anything Dr. Strudwick ever wrote, not even a case history. In his work as a country practitioner he was apothecary, physician, obstetrician, and surgeon. His fame as a physician and surgeon would be of comparable command even in this advanced day.

In early records of the State Medical Society there are mentioned other doctors from Hillsboro (then spelled Hillsborough), including Walter A. Norwood, Thomas H. Turner, William Webb, J. E. Williamson, H. O. W. Hooker, and from Chapel Hill, Johnston B. Jones and L. D. Schoolfield. Dr. Jones was also prominent in the work of the Society, serving as officer several times, and as stated orator, and delegate to the national medical meetings. The name of Dr. William H. Moore also appears in the early records. He was a physician in Chapel Hill, too.

Dr. Williamson was president of the Society in 1852 and 1853. He was born in Caswell county in 1799 and died in 1867. He was a colleague of Dr. Strudwick and was called an extremist for cleanliness and fresh air.

Unfortunately, the records are unusually scarce on these men and their activities. Had it not been for their activity incident to the State Medical Society the names of both Dr. Webb and Dr. Strudwick would never have been as well known as they are, and the knowledge of them is all to limited. Surely there ought to be some energetic soul who would find it most interesting to do some research in the annals of the State for more adequate information about the great medical men of a hundred years ago.

In the minutes of the Society for 1858 are listed the schools at which North Carolina doctors were trained. The list includes Pennsylvania, Charleston, Jefferson, New York, Harvard, Yale, Columbia, Medical College of Virginia, Rutgers, Hampden-Sydney, Maryland, Virginia, College of Physicians and Surgeons. Predominantly the men went either to the University of Pennsylvania or to Jefferson.

> Dr. John Wesley Long wrote in 1917: "In reviewing the work and men of the early periods of our medical history, there are

many things worthy of consideration. In the first place, it is to be noticed that the vision of those early fathers was quite as clear and farsighted as our own. If we have gone further in scientific development, it is simply because we have stood upon the shoulders of the dead past and profited by the wisdom and experience of progenitors. Practically everything that we stand for today was inaugurated and practiced by them.

They not only stood for all that was good, but they set their faces like a stone wall against all that was evil; against quacks and empiricisms; against secret remedies, and the giving of certificates; against patentees; against advertising and against contract practice.

To say of these pioneers that many of their theories and practices have been proved to be erroneous is only to anticipate what posterity shall say of us. They lived up to the best lights, the most advanced science of their day. If we are in any sense better than our fathers were, it is only because "a live dog is better than a dead lion."

Orange county was just twenty-eight years old when the first medical school was established in America: the school at the University of Pennsylvania. Between the years 1789 and 1800 five or six medical schools had been established in the United States, and as many State Societies. Of the latter the first one was in 1766 in New Jersey. North Carolina's Society in 1799, is regarded as the eighth such in the country. And that record stands, if one wishes to blink at its dormant 45 years until its reorganization in 1849.

But it was not until 1879 that a School of Medicine was established at the University of North Carolina. From that date the University offered the first two years of medicine, and only in 1952 expanded its two-year school to a fully recognized four-year School of Medicine. Since 1879, of the doctors who have practiced in North Carolina, many of them have had both their undergraduate work and two years of medicine at Chapel Hill. Only during the eight years - 1902-1910 - did the University attempt to offer the two clinical years and confer a medical degree. And those courses were taught in Raleigh, and not at Chapel Hill. So the class that will graduate as Doctors of Medicine in 1954 will be first such to receive their degrees from Chapel Hill.

The alumni of the School of Medicine have been especially loyal, and have supported various programs of service for the enhancement of the School. Many of them are directly responsible for the expansion of the School from a two-year unit to a four-year School. They created public sentiment that made the expansion possible. They have cooperated with their interest and their incomes to advance its work.

The picture in Chapel Hill today is a brilliant one, born of years of travail and consecration. Several of the former deans, dreamed, talked, and even drew plans for the expanding School of Medicine, but it remained for Dean Berryhill to spend much time during the past thirteen years focusing his attention and energies on this possibility, now a reality. Much of the credit for the advance belongs to his leadership.

The pioneer in medical education at Chapel Hill was Dr. T. W. Harris, who came from Chatham County in 1878 to open a private School of Medicine in the University town. Within a year, the administration and trustees of the University of North Carolina had asked Dr. Harris to join the faculty and associate the School of Medicine with the University"s curriculum and operation.

Dr. Harris thereby became the first Dean of the School of Medicine in 1879, and continued in this capacity until 1886. The School was closed for three years because of financial difficulties, but was reopened in 1890, under the deanship of Dr. Richard H. Whitehead, and called "the Medical Department" of the University. Other deans in succession have been Dr. Isaac H. Manning, 1905-1933; Dr. Charles S. Mangum, 1933-1937; Dr. W. deB. MacNider, 1937-1940; and Dr. W. Reece Berryhill, since 1940.

But uncounted others had a part in this progress. From the private conversations as to medical needs in the State came the Medical Care Study Commission, the subsequent Good Health Association composed of private individuals working tirelessly to educate the people of the State on these needs. The appropriation by the General Assembly of North Carolina of millions of dollars for the building of the vast medical center at Chapel Hill is the end result of all of this energetic and intelligent program to inform the people.

More than 2000 students have already had part of their medical training at Chapel Hill. In excess of 1500 of them are still in practice.

The School of Medicine at Chapel Hill is a worthy tribute to the leaders who thought wisely and planned nobly in those long years ago. They loved the University, and they often dreamed of the day when the State-owned institution would fill its place in the complete education for their profession.

Now, surely, they would be pleased. At Chapel Hill is a great health center, a center of medical education, medical research, and medical services that is imbued with a ready willingness to fulfill the mandate of the people of the State to serve the health of all of the people of the State.

The Division of Health Affairs at Chapel Hill is headed by Dr. Henry Toole Clark, Jr. Under his direction are six facets of medical education and services: the School of Medicine, headed by Dean Berryhill; the School of Pharmacy, Dean E. A. Brecht; the School of Public Health, Dean E. G. McGavran; the School of Dentistry, Dean John C. Brauer; the School of Nursing, Dean Elizabeth L. Kemble; the North Carolina Memorial Hospital, Dr. Robert R. Cadmus, director. The schools of Dentistry and Nursing, and the hospital are brand new. The first class in Dentistry will graduate in 1954. The first class in Nursing will graduate in 1955. The hospital opened in September, 1952. The dedication of the Hospital, and exercises in recognition of the Schools of Medicine, Dentistry, and Nursing were at Chapel Hill, April 23-24, 1953. The General Assemblies of 1945, 1947, 1949, and 1951 made possible the development of this center. The people of North Carolina are watching its development with interest and appreciation.

During the depression years of 1933 and 1934 a group of outstanding North Carolinians, representing the medicial profession, the hospitals, and the progressive-minded lay public, made a study of the need for an organization which would provide hospital service to people of small means. Dr. I. H. Manning of Chapel Hill, a former president of the State Medical

Society and for more than a quarter of a century dean of the medical school of the University of North Carolina, was the leading spirit in this movement which resulted in the establishment in 1935 of the Hospital Saving Association of North Carolina, better known as the Chapel Hill Blue Cross plan. Dr. Manning was the first president of this association, which by May 1, 1953, had an enrollment of over 450,000 Blue Cross members and over 420,000 Blue Shield members in more than 5,700 employee groups scattered through virtually every community in North Carolina. As of this same date, over $34,000,000 had been paid to the hospitals and surgeons of the state by the association.

The lengthened shadows of men make institutions. The pervading influence of men like Webb, and Strudwick, and their worthy successors lives on in the progress of the profession they loved and lived.

CHAPTER XIV

HISTORY OF THE COUNTY GOVERNMENT

BY PAUL W. WAGER

Professor of Political Science and Research Professor Institute for Research in Social Science, University of North Carolina

The Colonial Period

On April 9, 1752 an act was passed by the North Carolina House of Commons which provided for the formation from Granville, Johnston and Bladen counties of a new county to be named Orange for Prince William of Orange who later became King William III of England. It was a very large county embracing an area ten times that to which it was eventually to be reduced.

At that time, administrative as well as judicial power at the county level was vested in the county court made up of the justices of the peace. The court met quarterly. Its judicial power extended to criminal cases below the grade of felonies and to civil actions involving not more than twenty pounds. Its non-judicial powers included the assessment and levying of taxes; the establishment and care of roads, bridges, ferries; the licensing of taverns and fixing the prices of foods and drinks served; and control of the erection of public mills.

The justices of the peace were appointed by the Governor with the approbation of the Council. This method was only nominal, however, for appointments were usually made on the recommendation of members of the Assembly, members of the council, or by members of the county court itself. Whatever the source of the recommendation, it amounted to the same thing, for the county court was made up exclusively of prominent merchants, planters, and slave-holders, and the justices in turn dominated the Assembly.

The first court held in the county was in September, 1752, and it met at the home of John Gray on the Eno River. The justices present were Lawrence Bankston, Andrew Mitchell,

James Dickey, Mark Morgan, John Patterson, John Pittman, Marmaduke Kimbrough, and Joseph Tate. The sheriff was Alexander Mebane and the clerk was Richard Caswell, both probably serving under temporary appointments.

At the first meeting of the court fifteen men, including six of the justices, were named commissioners of the roads, each to supervise the roads in a designated portion of the county, presumably in the area in which he resided. Several others were named constables, each with a given jurisdiction, that of John Williams, for example, being "from the trading path down the Eno River to New Hope." Two other interesting items of business are recorded. A tax of one shilling proclamation money was to be collected by the sheriff on each and every tithable inhabitant of the county. And it was decided that the courthouse, prison and stocks be located near the Piney Ford on the North side of Haw River.

At the December court seven justices were present when it convened and four at the time of adjournment, two of the number—James Allison and Thomas Lovelatty—not having been present in September. William Churton presented a commission from the governor appointing him public register. He had served as Lord Granville's surveyor and within a short time was to employ his talents to lay out the new county seat. Several persons appeared and requested that they be allowed to keep an ordinary (tavern). Several others had their marks and brands recorded. William Martin came into court and "acknowledged himself indebted with our loving Lord the King 20 pounds proclamation money." Mark Morgan and Timothy Sorrel went on his bond.

Six justices were present at the March, 1753 term, the only new name being that of James Watson. At the June term fifteen justices qualified by taking the oath, but only six remained to hold court. Richard Caswell presented his commission from the Secretary of the Province appointing him clerk of the county court and clerk of the peace. During most of the colonial period each county court seems to have had two clerks—a clerk of the court for civil cases and for the general business of the court and a clerk of the peace (or clerk of the Crown) for criminal cases. Both were appointed by the Secretary of the Province until 1761, when a provincial officer known as Clerk of the Pleas was given the power to appoint the clerks for civil matters. Often the same person held both clerkships and this seems to have been the case in Orange County. It is believed that the clerk of the court acquired the second position for a financial consideration.

The method by which the clerk of court secured his office, and particularly the practice of "farming out" the office of clerk of the crown invited abuses. Since compensation was by fees the clerks were under the temptation to charge what the traffic would bear and apparently they did.

At the December, 1753 term the names of John Gray, Lawrence Thompson and James Dickey were submitted to the Governor as a panel from which to appoint a sheriff for a term of two years, Alexander Mebane's term being about to expire. The entry reads, "Ordered that John Gray, Lawrence Thompson, and James Dickey be recommended to the Hon. Mathew Rowan, Esquire, President's Commander in Chief, for the next two years." The record shows 10 votes for Gray, who was appointed, eight for Thompson, and 6 for Dickey. It is not clear how there came to be 24 votes, for it seems unlikely that there were that many justices in the county; but it is significant that Gray, who was the most favored by the justices, got the appointment. Two years later, in 1755, the nominations of John Patterson, Lawrence Thompson, and Alexander Mebane were submitted and Thompson was appointed.

The early court records reveal a constant succession of constables. Either the office was unpleasant and unrewarding or it was difficult to get dependable officers. An entry in March 1753 reads, "Ordered the sheriff to summon John Williams, John McGee, and John West, constables, to attend the next court." Possibly persons whom they had arrested were to be tried.

Evidence of the court's administrative work is found in an entry of January, 1754. It reads, "Ordered that county made beer be sold at 4 pence per quart in the ordinaries of this county till further notice."

For the first two years after the formation of the county, causes beyond the jurisdiction of the county court had to be tried in the Provincial, or General Court, at New Bern. But in 1754 this court was replaced by Supreme Courts which sat in five different places. After 1760 these courts were known as Superior Courts, and in 1768 Hillsboro became the seat of one of these higher courts. There was thus a need for a resident clerk of this higher court, the first clerk of the superior court in Orange County being Francis Nash. The Superior Court might also have its clerk of the crown, but, as in the case of the county court, the office seems to have been delegated or sold to the clerk of the court. At any rate, there is no record of its being held by a separate person in Orange County. It should be explained that the Superior Court at this time was both a trial court and an appellate court.

At their first meeting the justices had voted to locate the courthouse on the north bank of the Haw River at Piney Ford, within 15 miles of the west boundary of the county. However, the Assembly, in 1754, took the position that the courthouse had been located too far to the west and directed that it, with prison and stocks should be located on, or near where the Western path crosses the Eno River on a piece of land on which James Watson then lived. This was just east of the present courthouse and the selection of this site represented the beginning of Hillsboro. That same year a town was laid out by William Churton, and, like the country, was first called Orange. It was named Hillsborough in 1766. The first courthouse, a frame structure, was built in 1755, sessions of the court being held in private homes until that time.*

When sitting as a county court the justices not only exercised judicial functions, but performed the services now performed by the board of county commissioners, and, in addition, certain duties which grew out of the conditions of the time. The court was authorized to levy and assess annually such tax on the taxable persons of the county as should be sufficient to defray the

---

* A second courthouse, built of brick in 1782, was destroyed by fire seven years later. In 1790 a third courthouse was built, it, like the first one, being of wood. It was replaced by the present courthouse in 1846.

"contingent charges" of the county. It is to be noted that the tax was assessed on polls and not on property. Other administrative functions included the laying out and construction of roads and bridges, and the operation and control of ferries; the construction of public buildings, mainly jails and courthouses; the licensing of ordinaries (eating houses) and fixing the rates on the foods and beverages to be served; determining the location of mills; the regulation of weights and measures; the protection of slaves and indentured servants; granting letters of administration; the oversight of orphans and orphans' estates; proving headrights; granting marriage licenses; establishing and marking the boundaries of land ownerships; recording deeds and mortgages; and approving and recording cattle marks or brands. The only important public function not directly under the county court was the care of the poor. In 1764 the colonial assembly authorized the vestry of each parish to lay a tax on the taxable persons in their parish, not exceeding ten shillings on each poll, for parish purposes including support of the poor. The oversight of poor relief was in the hands of the wardens of the poor chosen by popular vote in the parishes. Since St. Matthew's Parish and Orange County were coterminous, their selection was by the county electorate. Incidentally, they were the only popularly elected officials other than the representatives to the General Assembly.

Most of the county officials were appointed by the county court. This body appointed the constables, overseers of the roads, searchers, patrolmen, inspectors, and sometimes town commissioners. As explained earlier, the court virtually appointed the sheriff. In fact, it appointed all the important local officers except the clerk of court and public register.

Since the county court was the main organ of county administration during the colonial period, the most important officials of the county were the court officials, especially the sheriff and the clerk.

The sheriff, or his deputy, was required to execute all writs directed to him by the county court and return them within the prescribed time. He was required to be in constant attendance at the county court when it was in session, and to attend, in turn with other sheriffs, the sessions of the general court. It was his duty to arrest any person who was a disturber of the peace or suspected of treason. He had custody of the county jail, imprisoned criminals, inflicted corporal punishment, and attended executions. He held the elections for burgesses and summoned juries for the inferior and general courts. He was also the collector of public duties (taxes) both for the county and the parish, a service for which he was allowed a commission at one time of 8 per cent.

No other single officer exercised such plenary powers as the sheriff, nor did any other officer enjoy such handsome fees. Hence, his office became the prize bit of patronage at the disposal of the county court. His political influence was so great and his control over the conduct of elections so complete, that he was frequently able to return to the Assembly the person of his choice rather than that of the electorate. He was also very lax in the collection of taxes, irregular in his settlements with the treasurer, and sometimes guilty of embezzlement. That the fiscal powers of the sheriff were very much abused is evidenced by the numerous acts passed by the Assembly to curb these excesses, Orange being among the counties from which complaints had come.

Whether true or not, many Orange County citizens felt that they were the victims of extortion by both the sheriff and the clerk. But the chief object of their dislike and distrust was Edmund Fanning, the public register from 1763 to 1768.

In 1765 citizens of the neighboring county of Granville issued a formal complaint setting forth their grievances against the officials of that county. The next year similar complaints were made in Orange County. Protests were sent to the General Assembly, but this body offered no redress. The colonial legislature was itself composed largely of the same "clique", a handful of men from each county who alternately occupied a county office and a seat in the legislature. Angered and exasperated, the colonists were in a mood for resistance by force, and in 1766 the so-called War of Regulation began. This struggle is described fully elsewhere in this volume.

As a result of the revolt attorney's fees were more carefully regulated, sheriffs were restricted in the manner of collecting taxes; inferior courts were authorized to establish tobacco warehouses wherever needed; county officers of importance were placed under heavier bond; and provision was made for a quicker and cheaper method of collecting small debts. These improvements came during the last years of colonial government.

During the colonial period the poll tax was generally the only means of raising funds for local government. The tax was imposed on all tithable persons, which included all free males 16 years of age and over and all slaves, both male and female, twelve years old or above. Ordinarily the heaviest poll tax was that levied by the parishes for the support of the established church and to care for the poor. Funds for other public undertakings, such as building courthouses, jails, roads, bridges and public gates and meeting the other costs of town and county government were derived from poll taxes. The amounts varied widely. A poll tax of one shilling annually for two or three years for some one or more of the above-mentioned purposes was frequently authorized by the legislature.

The colony itself also relied mainly on the poll tax, the rate in 1752 and for several years thereafter being one shilling per poll. For the year 1754 Richard Caswell, the clerk of the county court, reported 950 white polls, 35 black males, and 15 black females. Thus the county contribution to the support of the provincial government did not exceed 50 pounds. Yet these taxes were bitterly resented by the colonists and of course were one of the main causes of the Revolution.

The Period from 1776 to 1868

Independence from England after 1776 had little effect on the conduct of local government. The Court of Pleas and Quarter Sessions remained the dominant institution in the county. All went on as before except that the sheriff opened court in the name of the State instead of in the name of the King, and criminal cases were docketed "The State vs. John Doe" instead of "The King vs. John Doe."

The Halifax constitution of 1776 did not provide for any particular form of county government, with the result that the existing form was continued. The county court retained its control over the administration of the affairs of the county. The court was composed of all the justices of the county, but any three justices could hold court. A common practice was for a majority of the justices to meet at the beginning of the year, appoint a chairman, and designate five of their number to hold the court for the year. As before, the justices were commissioned by the governor on the recommendation of the General Assembly to hold office during good behavior. They might be removed by the General Assembly for misbehavior, absence, or inability.

At the court held in May, 1777 the names of 22 persons who had been commissioned justices of the peace by Governor Richard Caswell are recorded. They were John Butler, Nathaniel Rochester, Thomas Taylor, Eli McDaniel, William McCauley, John Hawkins, Hugh Twining, William Courtney, John Steel, William Cain, Charles Abercrombie, Thomas Hart, Alexander Mebane, Sr., Alexander Mebane Jr., James Freeland, John Hogan, Robert Abercrombie Sr., Richard Bennehan, Richard Holleman, William Rainey, John Ray, and John Nichols. Of these, the first eleven listed, appeared, took the state oath and also the oath of a justice of the peace, 'subscribed the test', and took their seats. The others qualified later.

Alexander Mebane Jr., a son of the county's first sheriff, was commissioned as the first sheriff under statehood. His bondsmen, for 1,000 pounds, were John Butler, James Mebane and Nathaniel Rochester. He was also named treasurer, James Freeland and Eli McDaniel going on his bond for 2,000 pounds.

The court then proceeded to the choice of a clerk, Nathaniel Rochester being unanimously elected. He 'qualified agreeable to Law, and subscribed the test.' It then named no less than 33 persons, none being justices of the peace, as overseers of the roads, indicating the road for which each man was responsible. Other entries of that court include the following:

> Charles Richardson being called upon by the court as a suspicious person, and refusing to take the oath of allegiance to this State agreeable to the directions of an act of General Assembly. Ordered that he be committed to the common gaol there to remain until he takes the said oath, and pays the lawful fees thereupon, and that the gaoler receive him accordingly.

Ordered that the gaoler of Hillsborough District so receive into the public gaol all soldiers belonging to the Continental Army who may be apprehended and sent to him as deserters, by any Justice of the Peace in Hillsborough District.

Ordered that John W   be appointed overseer to clear out the road intended to be cleared as per former order of court, from Richard Bennehan's to New Hope Chappel, the said road being only cleared as far as John Patterson's.

Before adjournment the court also probated several deeds, received an inventory of an estate exhibited by the executor, and appointed several constables.

At the next term of court, in August, 1777, there appear these entries, which reflect the issues and conditions of those uncertain days.

In pursuance of an act of the General Assembly directing the Justices of the respective counties to issue citations to all merchants who have traded to Great Britain, Ireland or the British West Indies and their factors, agents and storekeepers to appear at this court and take the oath prescribed by law or otherwise be dealt with as the law directs, the following persons have been cited, viz: James Hogg, David Robinson, Nathaniel Rochester, Peter Smith, James Monro, John Mounair, Henry Maxwell, John Hogan, James Reed, George Mack, Gilbert Eccles, Henry Cooper, William Ross and John McClellan of which Nathaniel Rochester and John Hogan appeared and took the oath of allegiance.

Ordered that Thomas Rice have leave to keep a tavern at the place where he now lives, he giving John Hincher security in the sum of fifty pounds, and that a license issue accordingly.

Ordered that James Empey find security for his good behavior in future, that he shall not evade the Act of Assembly of this State by endeavoring to recruit any man within this state for any other state. Robert Baker and William Armstrong, his sureties, is bound each in fifty pounds.

Ordered that the sheriff safely convey William Grimes for horse stealing, and Williarm Rains for robbery, to Salisbury gaol immediately in order that they may be tried for the said offenses at the next court of oyer and terminer to be held at Salisbury on the 2nd day of next month, and that the gaoler of the said gaol receive them into his gaol and safely keep until discharged by due course of law, and that the sheriff summons sufficient guard for that purpose.

Ordered that all persons who have been cited to appear at this court pursuant to an act of the Assembly of this State passed at Newbern in April last, and having failed to appear agreeable to such citation (Quakers excepted) or having appeared and failed to take the oath prescribed by such act, depart this State to Europe or the West Indies within sixty days from this present term, and that the clerk furnish the sheriff of the county with a copy hereof, together with the names of such persons, and that the sheriff when so furnished make known this order to them, and make a return thereof to the next court.

At this same term of court, the several assessors within the county exhibited an account of their assessments in the several districts, to wit:

The district of Hillsborough	£313	
The district of St. Thomas	80	
The district of Tryon	101	16s
The district of Orange	117	
The district of Chatham	68	
The district of St. Mary's	216	
The district of St. Mark's	94	13s
The district of St. Alophs	87	12s
	£1078	1s

The following justices were appointed to take the lists of property for the next year's taxes.

William Courtney Esq.	Hillsborough
William Rainey Esq.	Chatham
Thomas Taylor Esq.	Orange
Charles Abercrombie Esq.	St. Mark's and St. Mary's
John Hawkins Esq.	St. Alophs
John Butler Esq.	Tryon
William McCauley	St. Thomas

The constitution provided that there should be in each county a sheriff, one or more coroners, and constables, but it did not specify how they should be chosen. For some time all continued to be appointed by the county court. The court also appointed a clerk, a register, a county attorney, a standard-keeper, an entry-taker and surveyor, rangers for estrays, and overseers of the roads. In 1777, the office of clerk of the Crown was abolished, and thereafter each Court of Pleas and Quarter Sessions had only one clerk and, as just indicated, he was appointed by the local court. The first clerk of court in Orange County to be appointed by the local magistrates was Nathaniel Rochester.

The office of county trustee (treasurer) was in existence in Orange county almost from the beginning, for in August, 1778 there is this entry in the minutes of the county court:

> Ordered that John Hogan, Esquire, be appointed Trustee for this County, and that he enter into bond with William McCauley and William Cain securities in the sum of one thousand five hundred pounds, for the faithful discharge of the trust reposed in him.

There seemed to have been a general expectation that freedom from England would mean freedom from taxes. For this reason the state had to rely heavily on borrowing during the Revolution and for several years thereafter. Nevertheless the General Assembly of 1777, laid the foundations of a tax system whose most significant feature was an ad valorem tax on most types of property. The first state tax levy, in 1777, was at the rate of a half-penny on each pound valuation, or the equivalent of 21 cents on $100 valuation. The rate increased steadily during the war years until it reached the staggering height of $20.00 per $100 valuation in 1781 for all taxables except money, on which the rate was $1.67. Of course many could not pay their taxes, and those who could pay paid partly in continental currency which was rapidly depreciating in value. A shift to specie payment in 1782 was accompanied by a sharp reduction in rates, and in 1784 the ad valorem principle was abandoned and a land tax at a uniform rate per acre and a poll tax substituted.

The legislature which met in 1777 delegated to the counties the right to levy an annual tax to raise funds for paying the contingent expenses of the county government. The maximum rate was one shilling on the 100 pounds valuation of property, and all freemen who did not possess taxable property paid a poll tax of one shilling. Two years later the maximum rate on property was raised to five shillings per 100 pounds and unmarried men without property were required to pay a poll tax equivalent to the levy on 400 pounds valuation of taxable property. In addition to the taxes for contingencies there was a levy in each county to care for the poor. The maximum fixed for this levy in 1777 was 6 pence on the 100 pounds valuation and 6 pence on polls without property. To keep pace with inflation the rates rose sharply during the War years but with a return to specie payment in 1782 the maximum for this purpose was placed at 1 shilling for each 100 pounds valuation and a like amount on those who were subject only to a poll tax.

In 1784 the principle of ad valorem taxation was abandoned for both state and county purposes except in respect to town lots and improvements. Thenceforth all rural land was taxed according to the number of acres without regard to value. All personal property was exempt from taxation except slaves which were taxable as polls. The tax rate on 100 acres of land was equal to one-third of the rate levied on each poll or one third of the rate levied on a town property with a valuation of 100 pounds. Stated differently, three hundred acres of land, a slave, a white poll, or a town lot which with improvements was worth 100 pounds were taxed the same amount. This means, in effect, that for tax purposes a slave was given a value of 100 pounds ($250) and land a value of 6 shillings and 8 pence (83 cents) an acre.

After 1784 the tax on polls was not limited to those who did not pay a minimum tax on other property. It was levied on all free men and servants above 21 years of age and on all slaves, both male and female, between 12 and 60 years of age. The result was that the poll tax produced far more revenue than the land tax.

After 1796 the legislature allowed the counties more discretion in fixing the local tax rates. Beginning with that year the county courts were authorized "to lay and collect taxes from year to year as long as may be necessary, for the purpose of building, repairing, and furnishing the several courthouses and gaols in such manner as they shall think proper."

The taxes collected to care for the poor were not a part of the regular county tax levied by the county court but were determined by the wardens within the limits set by the legislature. This maximum was fixed at 4 pence on the poll and 1 shilling on each 100 acres of land in 1793. Sometimes this general levy might be supplemented by special taxes at a much higher rate for short periods to pay for the erection of buildings to house the poor and the insane.

Some idea of the kind of matters which came before the county court in the post-Revolutionary period may be obtained by examining the minutes of the August term in 1786. The court which lasted nearly a week, was held by three justices—John Butler, William McCauley and William Ansley. A summary of the actions recorded follows:

The sheriff returned a venire for that term of court; a grand jury of fifteen was impaneled; trial juries were impaneled for several criminal cases as well as several civil cases; half a dozen persons were exempted from the poll tax; two children were bound to masters to serve until their maturity; more than twenty deeds were acknowledged and ordered to be registered; two or three administrators were appointed to settle estates; a jury was summoned to divide and lay off an estate; three persons were granted licenses to keep taverns; a jury was named to mark and lay off a new road (it to be the best and most direct from William McCauley's mill to Hillsborough); a tax collector for the District of St. Mark's was allowed insolvents for eleven polls and 433 acres of land; tax collectors were appointed for each of the seven taxing districts; several road overseers were appointed; and jurors were ordered summoned for the next term of court.

Throughout the whole period from the Revolution until the Civil War the county tax structure was closely geared to the state structure. Both relied heavily on the land tax and the poll tax assessed and collected by the same officials. The list-takers, assessors and collectors were all named by and responsible to the county court though the sheriff, as collector, also had a responsibility to the state treasurer with whom he settled for the state taxes. While at first both levels of government taxed the same objects, the state in time levied a variety of occupational or privilege taxes in addition to the taxes on property and polls.

For the purpose of listing and assessing property the county was subdivided into convenient districts, or according to the law of 1784 into captain's districts and towns. The first act regulating the listing of property authorized the county courts to divide the county into districts and appoint a justice for each district to secure a "just and true" list of all taxable property, on oath, as of April 1 of each year. The taxpayers were warned in advance by the constables to meet the justice at a specified time and place within the district to make returns of their property. The time of listing was modified from time to time and in 1801 was designated as the last twenty working days in July.

The justice for each district was required to post a notice at three different places in the district, ten days beforehand, giving the time and place at which he would appear to receive the tax lists. Five days after the end of the listing period, the justice gave the constable of the district a list of the persons who had given in their property and a warrant directing him to search out and summons every person who had failed to make a return to appear before the list-taker and do so within ten days. The returns of the list-taker were made to the county court, and the clerk of the court calculated the taxes and then turned the tax lists over to the sheriff for collection. The clerk also submitted certified copies of the lists of state taxes to the state comptroller who used them as charges against the sheriff.

From 1784 to 1815 there was really little assessing to be done for only town lots were taxed according to value; the tax on rural land was determined entirely by the acreage. Indeed, the task of list taking was simple, for taxes had been removed from all forms of property except real estate and slaves. The duties of the list-takers were to locate and determine the approximate size of each tract of land, to locate the town lots, to list the free and black polls, and to give the names of individuals liable for certain license taxes. The county court was authorized to pay the list-takers and assessors "a reasonable allowance" for their services out of the county tax levied for contingencies.

In 1815 the system of taxing land by the acre regardless of value was abandoned and there was a return to the ad valorem basis. The change represented a victory for the small farmers over the plantation owners, who usually had the richest lands. It was only a partial victory, however, for slaves were treated as polls and were not subject to the property tax. The poll tax applied to all freemen from 21 years of age upward and all slaves from 12 to 50 years of age. The rate of the poll for tax state purposes was fixed at 20 cents in 1817 and so remained until 1854.

Despite this relatively low rate, it produced more revenue than the land tax, in fact, over a third of the state's revenue.

The clerk of court was required to file with the State Comptroller an abstract of the objects subject to a state tax by September 1. The objects and the rate on each established in 1817 were as follows:

Rural land per $100 valuation	6 cents
Town lots per $100 valuation	6 cents
White polls (males 21 to 45)	20 cents
Black polls (both sexes, 12 to 50)	20 cents
Wholesale stores	$16
Retail stores	$ 6
Stud horses and jacks	one service fee
Public gates	$ 5
Pedlars	$ 9 per cart
Itinerant players	$20
Slave traders	$ 5 per slave

From 1815 to 1835 the state was in a continuous state of depression and no doubt Orange County was as badly off as any part of the state. Not until the nineteenth century was nearly half spent was there a real stirring and a general air of prosperity evident. The people of the county certainly did not contribute very heavily to the support of the state government.

In 1826, Thomas D. Watts, sheriff, was charged by the state treasurer with the following taxes to be collected in Orange County:

land tax	$ 999.31
tax on town property	71.95
polls	958.24
other taxes	474.23
Total	$2,503.73

That little money was spent for public purposes in Orange county in these lean years is indicated by the modesty of the tax levies. In March, 1822 is this entry in the court minutes:

> Ordered that a tax of twenty-five cents on each poll and 10 cents on each $100 value of land and town property within this county be levied and collected for the payment of county contingencies for the present year.

Seven years later the rates had increased some on both land and polls and they are broken down by purposes. The minutes of the August, 1829 term include this item:

> Ordered that a tax of twelve cents on each $100 value of land and town property, and thirty-five cents on each white and black poll be levied and collected for the payment of county contingencies.
>
> Ordered that a tax of six cents on each white and black poll and three cents on each $100 value of land and town property be levied and collected for a poor tax.
>
> Ordered that a tax of ten cents on each black poll be levied and collected for the payment of a patroll.

The constitution of 1835 was silent on the subject of taxation except to require that the capitation tax be equal throughout the state, upon all individuals subject to it. Since slaves were subject to the poll tax a constitutional barrier prohibited any ad valorem tax from applying to property in slaves. This constitutional barrier was not removed until 1861.

The creation of Alamance county in 1849 reduced Orange to about half its former size and three-fifths its former wealth. This is shown by comparing the state taxes paid by the two counties in 1950.

	Orange	Alamance
Land tax	$ 628.86	$ 532.28
Town property	88.12	88.12
Polls	664.20	475.46
Other	1,339.02	857.94
Total due by sheriff	$2,720.20	$1,953.80

The Centennial Year

The February term of court in 1852 was held by the following justices: John W. Carr, John U. Kirkland, Harrison Parker, William Nelson, and John J. Freeland, Esquires. Two items of business are of interest.

> The following persons were elected to compose the Board of Superintendents of Common Schools: Messrs. Thomas D. Oldham, Harris Wilkerson, Thomas Lynch, Samuel W. Hughes, William H. Brown, Nelson P. Hall, Stephen Moore, and William J. Hogan.
>
> The court levied the following tax for county purposes:

	Poll	Land
County contingencies	52¾ cents	17¾ cents
Common schools	12 ,,	7½ ,,
Support of poor	10 ,,	7 ,,
	74¾	32¼
To which add		
Former state tax	20 ,,	6 ,,
Tax for lunatic asylum	5¼ ,,	1 cent
	$1.00	40 cents

One hundred years ago there was no such thing as a county budget but an idea of the size of the county's operations may be gained from the record of the settlement with the treasurer, Thomas Faucett. Between the February term of court in 1852 and the February term a year later the treasurer received $3,115.21 and paid out $4,043.25. He retained $178.96 as his commission, 2½ per cent on both receipts and expenditures. The following year, for some reason, the financial operations were considerably greater, the receipts being $7,061.52 and the disbursements, exclusive of the treasurer's commission, $6,146.39. An itemization of the receipts follows:

1851 taxes	$2,177.61
1852 taxes	3,415.64
Forfeitures from clerk and master	1,029.96
Fines	254.22
Tax fees on suits	157.09
Unallocated	27.00

These figures do not include receipts and disbursements for poor relief, for the wardens had their own treasurer.

ROADS

An act of 1784 directed the county courts to appoint overseers of the roads each year. Each overseer was responsible for a particular road or district and he was required to summon all taxable men from the age of 16 to 50 years to appear with tools at a specified place in the district to repair existing roads, open new roads, and clear the river channels for travel. Any person liable for work who did not appear was required to send three slaves or three other workers to take his place, or forfeit 5 shillings (approximately 60 cents) a day.

The county courts were given the power to build public roads and bridges wherever they were necessary. If the cost of building and maintaining bridges was too burdensome contracts might be given for toll bridges. The tolls were fixed by the county court and paid to the builders for a designated number of years. The actual construction of roads and bridges made little progress, however.

An entry of February 27, 1788 reads,

> James Carrington and John Carrington who were appointed to lett and superintend the building of a bridge over flatt river at the Island Ford on the land of John Carrington returns that the said bridge is completed according to contract and exhibits their ―――――――― to the amount of three hundred and seventy pounds which is allowed by the court. Ordered that the county treasurer pay the same.

Another entry of November 24, 1789 reads:

> Agreeable to an order of the County Court and petition of Theophilus Thompson to turn the road round a Hill on the Road leading from Town to Gen'l Persons, the following jury being summoned to wit: John Estis, William Whitehead, John Whitehead, Joseph Moore, Thomas Watts, Joseph Stubbins, Andrew Burke, Henry Thompson, Robert Ferguson, George Clancey, William Newman, Sterling Harris—say on their return they have layed off and mark the said road agreeable to said order. Ordered that Theophilus Thompson open the same and that Richard Williams and the hands under him keep it in repair.

For the first hundred years of the county's history, the public roads were very primitive—indeed almost impassable in wet weather. Such little maintenance as they received was that given them by the district overseers with the help of three days of labor annually from each freeholder. As late as 1848 the governor in his message to the legislature stated that "our method of maintaining the public highways has made no advance beyond that existing in England in the time of Philip and Mary." But about 1850 there was a wave of interest in plank roads and a number were built by private concerns, sometimes with some slight public assistance.

In 1852 the legislature granted a charter to the Chapel Hill and Raleigh Plank Road Company, with an authorized capitalization of $40,000. Among the incorporators were W. J. Hogan and Edward Mallett of Chapel Hill.

An editorial in the *Hillsborough Recorder* of January 19, 1853 bemoans the fact that an application was not made at the recent session of the legislature for a charter for a local corporation to build a plank road from "this place to Milton via Roxborough or Yanceyville or perhaps in both directions." It expresses the hope that a stock company may be organized under the General Act of 1850-51, under which the work can proceed until a charter is secured.

Apparently no companies were organized under the "general act" but in 1855 no less than four were given charters by the legislature to build plank roads which would traverse portions of Orange county. Their titles suggest the terminals of the roads. One was the Chapel Hill and Morrisville Plankroad, Tramroad and Turnpike Company with an authorized capitalization of $150,000, to be subscribed by Edward Mallett, John W. Cain, Isaac Hudson and others. The second was the Chapel Hill and Durhamsville Plankroad Company, with an authorized capitalization of $20,000, to be subscribed by Charles Marcom, Charles Phillips, and others. The third was the Hillsboro and Chapel Hill Plankroad Company, with an authorized capitalization of $25,000. Among the incorporators were Edmund Strudwick, Thomas Howerton and Edwin A. Heartt of Hillsboro, and Andrew Mickle, Patterson H. McDade and Thomas Hogan of Chapel Hill. The most ambitious project was that of the Hillsboro and Milton Plankroad Company, its incorporators being authorized to subscribe $100,000.

It is not known which, if any, of these roads were built. It is known that few of the toll roads were a financial success, though those that were built served the purpose of opening up roads for trade and many of them later became public roads.

Schools

Orange County had no school officials until 1841. In fact, North Carolina's first public school law was not passed until 1839. It called for elections to be held in each county of that year to ascertain the wishes of the people in respect to the establishment and support of public schools. If the vote was favorable the county was to levy a tax amounting to $20 for each school district, which was to be supplemented by twice that amount from the earnings of the State Literary Fund. All but seven counties voted in favor of public schools so supported, Orange being among those voting favorably. The act provided that in those counties which voted for schools the county court should elect from five to ten persons to constitute a county board of superintendents. This board was to divide the county into school districts approximately six miles square. For each district the board was to name a committee of local citizens to assist the county board in erecting a schoolhouse and in establishing a school.

The earliest record of a payment to Orange County from the Literary Fund was in September 1841, when an allotment of $670.14 was made. Twelve years later, in 1853, the allotment to Orange County was $2543, indicating that public school expenditures in a community of 11,800 people (exclusive of slaves) aggregated $3,800.

The county board of superintendents elected their own chairman, who had certain administrative and financial responsibilities. To him the county allotments from the Literary Fund were transmitted. Among the men to hold this position were Stephen Moore, William H. Brown, and O. Hooker.

The public schools of the county were apparently open throughout the war years, for on April 20, 1863 school committeemen for each of the 53 districts were named by the County Board of Superintendents.

Moreover, in the *Hillsboro Recorder* of April 22, 1863 there appears this notice:

> The Examining Committee will meet at the Court House on the first Saturday of May. All who desire to obtain certificates to teach must attend on that day, as there will be no private examinations.
>
> W. H. BROWN, C. B. C.

Poor Relief

It has been explained earlier that the care of the poor was

never directly under the county court, but in the hands of a board of wardens chosen in the parishes. In 1783 an act was passed by the legislature which recognized the ineffectiveness of the colonial system and required that a tax be levied in each county for the support of the poor. The rate of the tax was to be decided by the overseers, though it had to be within the limits set by the legislature. The maximum set by the 1783 act was one shilling specie on each 100 pounds valuation of taxable property. In 1793 the limit was fixed at 4 pence on the poll and one shilling on each 100 acres of land. This general levy for outdoor relief might be supplemented by a much higher levy to be imposed for a limited period for the purpose of erecting buildings to house the poor and the insane.

In December, 1789 a bill was passed by the State Legislature empowering the wardens of the poor in Orange, Franklin and Surry counties to build a house or houses for the reception of the poor. It is not known whether the wardens of Orange County built a poorhouse soon thereafter or whether there was an interval of thirty years before one was built. But on October 18, 1823 a deed was made from Enoch Thompson to the Wardens of the Poor of Orange County, conveying 470 acres, more or less, at a price of $800 "for the purpose of building a poor house thereon and for supporting and maintaining thereon such paupers as said Wardens and their successors from time to time in their discretion take charge of. The poor house built at this location remained in use until 1941. The original poor house may have been a single structure, for in the 1850's there is a reference to "repairing of the west wing" but in the last decades of its existence the poor house was a series of log cabins which it was generally assumed were original buildings.

The Court of Wardens was a body of seven appointed by the justices for three year terms and largely from among their own membership. Complete records of this body are extant for the period 1857 to 1868, from which it is possible to get a good idea of the administration of poor relief in the middle of the nineteenth century. A few scattered minutes follow:

> April 5, 1857:- Ordered that the treasurer pay to the superintendent the balance of the taxes for the year 1856 and that the superintendent pay upon the oldest orders.

Dr. Benjamin F. Mebane was elected physician for the Poor Home.

May 11, 1857:- The Court of wardens held a called meeting this day at the Court House in Hillsborough to take into consideration the condition of the Poor House Building. Members present: John U. Kirkland, James C. Turrentine, Nathaniel Bain, William I. Hogan, D. C. Parrish, R. B. Ruffin, Dr. Pride Jones.

May 25, 1857:- Ordered that application be made to the County Court now in session that an order issue to the magistrates of the county to appear at the Court House on Friday next to take into consideration the condition of the poor in Orange County.

Ordered that the superintendent pay to F. Y. Blalock two dollars for making a coffin for Mrs. Sutton.

Ordered that the superintendent pay to Alex Dickson ten dollars for the benefit of Polly Blackwood for six months from the first Monday of April last.

Susan Clemmons has been ordered to be received at the Poor House and the former order of ten dollars rescinded.

Ordered that the account for burial clothes for Minerva Chamblee of two dollars be allowed.

Ordered that Messrs. Ruffin, Turrentine and Bain be appointed a committee for the repairs of the West building of the Poor House.

Resolved that the superintendent be authorized to borrow the sum of one thousand dollars for Poor House purposes.

September 7, 1857:-Samuel P. Moore was duly elected superintendent for the ensuing year.

February 22, 1858:- Ordered that we recommend to the Court of Pleas and Quarter Sessions to lay a tax for the expenses of the Poor House for the ensuing year of ten cents upon the $100 value of land and 20 cents upon the poll.

April 5, 1858:- The Court of Wardens through their committee-Dr. P. Jones and P. B. Ruffin-proceeded to examine the accounts and vouchers of the superintendent. They find that he has received the sum of $2,886.16 and that he has expended the sum of $2,202.84.

Ordered that hereafter all accounts contracted by the superintendent for the Poor House shall be presented for liquidation to the Court of Wardens at their semi-annual meetings.

April 6, 1862:-Ordered that the treasurer collect from the sheriff all the money due from the first of this month without fail and pay towards our debts except as much as the superintendent is obliged to have for immediate use.

Dr. Pride Jones was elected treasurer of this court for three years. John U. Kirkland was elected chairman.

September 10, 1866:- Ordered that the chairman be authorized to appoint an agent to go to Mrs. Mark Tate's in the County of Wake with proper vouchers to borrow the sum of two thousand dollars according to the order of the County Court at August term.

April 1, 1867:- Ordered that the chairman appoint a committee consisting of James P. Clark and N. P. Hall to give notice to the Sheriff of Orange County that if he fails to pay over to the treasurer of the Court of Wardens the balance of the taxes due the Court of Wardens on or before the 15th of May next that suit will be instituted against him on his official bond.

October 1, 1867:- James M. Bain was re-elected superintendent for the ensuing year at a salary of $150 per annum and $25 for his wife.

Once a year the Court of Wardens made an inventory of property at the Poor House and an enumeration of the inmates. On September 1, 1867 there were 21 inmates. There were three adult males, one of whom was deformed, 13 adult females, and five colored children, three of whom had white mothers.

The last meeting of the Court of Wardens before its work was taken over by the newly established Board of County Commissioners was held June 27, 1868. The members present were James C. Turrentine, Lemuel Lynch, S. M. Wilkinson, Nelson P. Hall, T. D. Oldham, and James P. Clark. One member, John Carr, was absent. It will be noted later that when the Board of Commissioners met at the Poor House three months later Lemuel Lynch was a member of that body, in fact the chairman.

Land Valuations and Taxes

Land was assessed only four times between 1835 and the Civil War—in 1837, 1847, 1855 and 1859. The process of valuing land according to its cash value was carried out in each tax listing or captain's district by a district board of valuation composed of two respectable freeholders associated with one justice of the peace. This board was appointed by the county court and given power to call witnessess and to examine them under oath. In the years between regular assessments the listtakers received a copy of the last assessment list from the clerk of court and used it to arrive at real estate values. The valuation for these years could not be less than that fixed by the previous board of valuation. Until 1858 any person who considered his land assessed too high could present his case to the county court which had the right to reduce the assessment upon satisfactory proof. After 1858 the justices who served on the district boards of valuation were constituted a county board of valuation with power to review the returns of the district boards and to change any or all of the valuations. It also served as a board of appeals. Thus there came into being a body which has been perpetuated as the county board of equalization and review.

County taxes were not reported to the state until 1856. In that year Orange county taxes, all on property and polls, amounted to $9,432.53. The distribution by objects was as follows.

County contingencies	$6,153.98
County poor	1,583.92
Common schools	1,694.63

State taxes collected in the county in 1856 were $8,029.24, but in 1861 they were $14,108.21, and in 1864 the state levy was $40,091.34. County taxes in 1864, still practically all on property and polls, amounted to $35,106.63.

At the February term of the county court in 1865 a resolution was adopted which provided that the same tax be levied on land and polls as levied by the state. Of the proceeds, $15,000 should be used for poor relief, $10,000 for county purposes, and the remainder applied to the relief of soldiers' families.

Several notices which appeared in the Hillsboro *Recorder* in the war years reflect conditions in those dark days.

CONFEDERATE TAX

We will attend at the following times and places, for the purpose of taking a list and assessing the taxes under the Confederate Tax Act passed the 24th of April, 1863. . . . (fourteen places listed, the dates August 18 to September 4)

The following are some of the articles and other matters subject to be listed, viz: naval stores, salt, wines and spirituous liquors, tobacco, cotton, wool, flour, sugar, molasses, syrup, rice and other agricultural products held or owned on the first day

of July, 1863; all moneys, bank notes, or other currency. . . . .etc.
August 5, 1863

H. M. STROUD }
A. M. ANGIER } *Assessors*

NOTICE

To the Justices of Orange County:

It is earnestly requested that all the Justices of Orange County shall meet on Tuesday of August Court to take measures for the support of soldiers' families. The subject requires immediate attention.

August 10, 1864

JAMES C. TURRENTINE, *Presiding Justice*

TAX IN KIND

The subscriber is ready at all times to receive lists of corn, fodder, Irish potatoes, molassess, cotton, peas, beans, and ground peas.

December 21, 1864

J.A.TURRENTINE, *Assessor*

A notice issued to the taxpayers by the sheriff in June, 1866 sheds light on the political practices of the time as well as reveals the desperate condition of the county treasury. It is reproduced below:

NOTICE

To the Taxpayers of Orange County

I shall attend at the following times and places to collect the taxes for the year 1866. . . .(fifteen places designated, each on a day in July.)

It is earnestly requested and expected for all to come up and pay their taxes promptly, for the money is needed, not only for the State but the county, for there is not a dollar in the county treasury, no tax having been levied and collected for the year 1865, and the wardens of the poor are very much in debt and have no money; therefore it is expected of all to be punctual in attending to this matter and not one will, under the circumstances, excuse themselves.

The persons who have been making whiskey, who have already permitted two quarts to pass without paying, will take notice that it will be well for them to come up prepared to pay their tax and save costs as well as trouble.

It is expected to have the candidates, and some fun.

June 25, 1866

H. B. GUTHRIE, *Sheriff*

The End of an Era

Throughout the ante-bellum period the county exercised all the powers of local government except in Hillsboro, chartered in 1770, and in Chapel Hill, chartered in 1851. Even in these two villages governmental functions were very limited. It is true that there were voting districts, tax collecting districts, military districts, and, after 1839, school districts, but none of these had much governmental significance. Civil authority was centered in the county court composed of the justices of the peace. Their office was one of influence and esteem and often attracted the ablest men in the county. Thus, when Justice Willie P. Mangum retired from the Superior Court bench in 1855 and returned to Orange County to live he was appointed a justice of the peace so that he might give the county the advantage of his knowledge and experience. The same was true of Chief Justice Ruffin, when he retired from the Supreme court though his appointment was to the Alamance court since his home was in the area severed from Orange in 1849.

While the county court no doubt consisted generally of able men who were interested in public affairs, the records indicate that only a minority were active. At a given time there might be fifteen or twenty magistrates but only five or six present at a term of court. Indeed at one time three was considered a quorum for the transaction of business. Since appointments to the court were made primarily on the nomination of those who were already members, county government was in the hands of a self-perpetuating oligarchy. Throughout most of the period the number of justices was not large, perhaps indicating a high property and ability test, but strangely the number mounted sharply in the War years. In 1864 Orange County had 62 justices of the peace.

Except for minor changes from time to time the same system of county government had prevailed in North Carolina from the formation of the colony, and it had been transplanted from England. Not until 1868, or during the carpet-bag regime, was this long-established system overturned and a new and more democratic scheme of local government established. Of course, the new system went into effect in Orange as in other counties of the state.

The Reconstruction Period, 1868-1878

The Constitution of 1868, drafted by a convention dominated by Northerners and their sympathizers, provided for a new plan of local government which was borrowed largely from Pennsylvania. It is usually referred to as the Township and County Commissioner Plan. It provided for a board of five county commissioners to be elected at large by the voters of the county. To this body was delegated all the administrative powers and duties which had hitherto belonged to the county court. That is, the commissioners were given control over the public buildings, schools, roads, bridges, taxes and finances of the county. The voters of the county were also to elect the following officers: treasurer, surveyor, register of deeds, clerk of superior court, sheriff, and coroner. All the county officials except the clerk of superior court were to be elected for a term of two years; the clerk's term was made four years. The register of deeds was to be ex officio clerk to the board of commissioners.

The entire court system was radically changed. The Court of Pleas and Quarter Sessions was abolished and its functions distributed among the Superior Court, the clerk of the Superior Court, and the new board of county commissioners. Most civil and criminal cases which had formerly been tried in the county court were henceforth to be tried in the Superior Court. Extensive changes were made in civil procedure, which tended to increase the authority of the clerk. He became, and has continued to be, the chief ministerial officer of the Superior Court, with extensive powers to act for the court between terms. Moreover, he is an independent judge of "special proceedings" not involving a regular suit and of probate matters. In this latter capacity, he appoints administrators, executors, collectors, receivers and commissioners, and audits their accounts and settlements; receives the probate or acknowledgement of deeds, mortgages and wills; and issues all necessary orders and decrees in connection with the administration of estates. He also appoints guardians, binds apprentices, and hears petitions for partition and dower.

William A. Graham, Governor, Secretary of Navy and U. S. and Confederate Senator.

Willie P. Mangum, United States Senator.

William Hooper, signer of Declaration of Independence.

Archibald D. Murphey, Founder of Public School System.

Thomas Hart Benton, born in Efland, United States Senator from Missouri.

Thomas Ruffin, Chief Justice North Carolina Supreme Court.

A. W. Kenion, former Clerk of Superior Court.

S. M. Andrews, former Sheriff and Register of Deeds.

Cicero H. Jones, former Register of Deeds.

Samuel M. Gattis, Sr., Solicitor.

John Laws, for about 63 years Register of Deeds.

Robert H. Claytor, Superintendent of Schools.

Isaac R. Strayhorn, Solicitor.

Josiah Turner, Jr., Editor, *Raleigh Sentinel*.

W. S. Roberson, long Mayor of Chapel Hill.

Richard M. Jones, former Sheriff.

Charles Strayhorn, former Clerk of Superior Court.

Harriet M. Berry, "The Mother of North Carolina Good Roads."

Dr. J. S. Spurgeon, for 63 years a dentist in Hillsboro.

Reverend L. H. Hackney, for nearly 60 years Pastor Rock Hill Baptist Church of Chapel Hill.

John U. Kirkland, former Clerk Court of Pleas and Quarter Sessions.

Thomas F. Lloyd, builder of cotton mills.

Venable (Carrboro) School in 1912; J. F. McDuffie, Principal.

A group of U.N.C. professors in May 1934: Noble, Woollen, Mangum, Graham, Bernard, Wilson and Beard.

Top: Dr. H. H. Bradshaw and others at a Sunday School picnic.
Middle: Hillsboro Post Office group about 1906: Davies, Walker, Haley, J. S. Rosemond, C. G. Rosemond, Postmaster, and Durham.
Bottom: Eno Cotton Mill Baseball Team about 1904. Standing: Roberson, Barton, Stutts, Graham, Dixon, Hunter, Mallett and Boone. Seated: Hughes and Davis.

Top: Chapel Hill Baseball Team about 1905.
Strowd   Temple   Lloyd   Raney
Hearn   Mincey
Harris   Pickard   Lloyd
Bottom: Carrboro Baseball Team about 1913: Brockwell, Pearson, Ray, Crabtree, Andrews, Thrift, Bowden, Ray, J. Gilmore and G. Gilmore.

Top: John W. Canada School in Chapel Hill about 1898.
Middle: White Cross School about 1906.
Bottom: University School about 1916.

Top: Dr. Brack Lloyd and Joe Sparrow at Pace's Mill about 1923.
Bottom: Confederate Veterans at reunion about 1903. Front row: Blackwood, Clemmons, Harward, Davis, Pendergraft, Whitaker and Brockwell. Back row: Smith, Nunn, Sparrow, Fowler, Benton, Garrett, Hunter and Lloyd.

Top: "Prof." Thomas Dunston and his horse "Nellie Bly."
Middle: William Faucett who drove a hack for about 40 years in Hillsboro.
Bottom: Franklin Street, Chapel Hill: J. M. Whitaker, Chief of Police, Robert A. Eubanks, Sr., later Postmaster of Chapel Hill.

Top: Mr. and Mrs. S. J. Brockwell, owners of first movie theatre in the county, and friends in an early Cadillac.
Bottom: Locomotive and crew on yard in Carrboro about 1905, Capt. Smith, Engineer Nesbitt and "Neighbor" Sparrow.

Top: Mars Hill School about 1900, Mrs. Agnes Forrest Bivins, Teacher.
Bottom: Carrboro Baptist Sunday School about 1917.

Top: A bus of the Chapel Hill & Durham Line (C. S. Pendergraft) about 1918.
Bottom: Ed Rosemond's Drug Store in Hillsboro about 1911.

Top: University Athletic Store, Chapel Hill, about 1912; J. M. Neville and J. C. Webb.
Bottom: Carrboro about 1913 when it was one of the largest hardwood cross-tie markets of the world.

Top: Pendergraft's Store, Chapel Hill, about 1918.
Bottom: Storm Damage, Franklin and Columbia Streets, Chapel Hill, January 26, 1906.

Top: Presbyterian Cemetery in Hillsboro, burial place of William Hooper, William A. Graham, James Hogg, Archibald D. Murphey, Sarah J. Kollock, and many other prominent persons.
Bottom: Hillsboro Military Academy.

The duties of the other officers remained unchanged. Although the new constitution did not require it, the sheriff continued to be collector of taxes.

The new constitution also provided for the creation of townships, which were made bodies corporate for purposes of local government. They were to be administered by a board of trustees composed of a town clerk and two justices of the peace, elected every two years by popular vote in the township. These trustees were given control of the roads and bridges of the township and they were also to assess the taxable property of the township and report the same to the county commissioners for revision. The clerk of the board of trustees was made treasurer of the township. Other township officials included a school committee of three and a constable. Townships containing cities or towns might elect more than two justices. All the terms were two years.

The significant changes wrought by the new constitution may be summarized as follows: (1) The administration of county affairs was taken from the justices of the peace and placed in the hands of a board of commissioners: (2) Townships were created as separate units of government; (3) All county and township officers were made elective by popular vote: (4) The justices of the peace were reduced to the position of petty magistrates, with a few administrative duties in connection with the townships; (5) The judicial power of the old county court was distributed among the justices of the peace acting singly, the superior court, and the clerk of the superior court.

The first county election under the new regime was held August 4, 1868 and the next day the first board of commissioners assembled at the courthouse, qualified before the clerk of the court, and organized for the transaction of county business. The body consisted of Lemuel Lynch, who was elected chairman, John U. Kirkland, Jones Watson, Robert F. Morris, and William N. Patterson. At subsequent meetings within the next few days the other officers-elect appeared before the commissioners, produced their certificates of election from General Canby and entered into their respective bonds—John Turner, sheriff; David C. Parks, treasurer; John Laws, register of deeds; and George Laws, clerk of superior court.

The minutes for the meeting held October 19, 1868 contain this entry:

> It is ordered by the board that Silas M. Link be employed to readjust the school districts of the County of Orange and lay the same off into townships and that he be allowed the sum of seventy-five dollars for his services, the work to be completed by November 15, 1868.

The county was divided by Mr. Link into eight townships, and his proposal received the approval of the commissioners. The townships were: Hillsboro, Little River, Mangum, Durham, Patterson, Chapel Hill, Bingham, and Cedar Grove. Some years later (in 1877) the board, acting on a petition, divided Mangum Township at Little River, designating the new township Lebanon.

In his report Mr. Link had specified the school districts by number which were included in each township. There were 53 districts, and at a meeting on November 11, 1868 the board appointed three school committeemen for each of the 53 districts. Presumably they were to serve until township elections could be held.

In a December meeting of this same year reference is made to a report of A. Hooker, late chairman of the board of common schools, giving some facts about the number of school children resident in each district and the condition of the schoolhouses. According to the report, there were 3,667 white children to be accommodated, and 2,235 colored children. There were only 43 schoolhouses, mostly in a dilapidated condition, to serve both races. It was estimated that it would cost an average of $50 each to repair these buildings, and $100 each to build the 63 new buildings required. To accommodate 30 children, it was felt that a structure should be about 18 by 20 feet.

The new constitution provided that the General Assembly, in its first session, should "provide by taxation or otherwise for a general and uniform system of public schools, wherein tuition shall be free of charge to all the children of the state between the ages of six and twenty-one years." In April, 1869, the legislature passed the required legislation. The law provided that the net annual income of the public school fund (the remainder of the anti-bellum school fund) be distributed among the counties of the state in proportion to their scholastic population, and that the county commissioners levy a tax for building or renting schoolhouses. Local township committees were to "establish and maintain, for at least four months in every year, a sufficient number of schools at convenient localities" to accommodate the demand. A county examiner was to be appointed by the county commissioners to examine teachers, issue certificates, and assist in enforcing the prescribed course of study and the rules and regulations governing the schools. In case any township failed to provide for schools to be taught at least four months, the county commissioners were required to levy on the township a tax sufficient for the purpose. However, in 1870 the Supreme Court ruled that the support of schools was not a necessary expense, so no local school tax could be imposed without the consent of the people of the district. Indeed the poverty of the people was so great in the Reconstruction Period that no serious effort was made to maintain public schools except in the cities and towns, and particularly those aided by the Peabody Fund.

Although the oversight of the poor farm after 1868 was under the county board rather than a board of wardens the records reveal no significant changes in management nor in the character of the poor house as an institution. Though the reports invariably stated that the rooms were in good condition and the patients well cared for, an occasionally entry raises some doubt as to this. Note this resolution of the board adopted on March 10, 1870:

> It is resolved by the Board of Commissioners of the County of Orange that a reward of $200 be offered for the apprehension and conviction of those persons who in disguise visited the poor house of Orange County on the night of Tuesday the 8th of March instant and perpetrated outrages upon several of the paupers— men and women—by whipping. It is not to be tolerated and all good citizens are requested to aid the officers of the county in apprehending and bringing to trial said offenders.
>
> The undersigned, one of the commissioners, solemnly enters his protest against the adoption of the above resolution— believing that the parties who visited the Poor House had none other than the public good in view and that other means than

those contemplated by the resolution would better serve the purpose of preventing a recurrence of such unlawful visits to the Poor House.

W. N. PATTERSON

The statistics also throw some light on the kind of "home" it must have been. The enumeration for September 5, 1876 lists six white males, eight white females, four colored males, and six colored females. The ages are not given but it is stated that during the preceding year ten persons had died and there had been two births, also that 12 persons had been received and four had left. The capacity of the institution at this time is not known, but an inventory of the furnishings a few years earlier had mentioned 21 bedsteads and 21 feather beds.

The first election for township officers occured August 5, 1869. In Chapel Hill township, to cite one example, 565 voters registered and 540 votes were cast. The following officers were elected: magistrates—Jones Watson, John W. Carr, Neverson P. Cates, Charles W. Johnson; clerk—Andrew Mickle; constable—Merritt Cheek; school committeemen—John R. Hutchins, Abel Maddry, William S. Kirkland.

The minutes of the board of commissioners for these years record an endless repetition of certain types of transactions—persons relieved of the poll tax because of disability or because of being overage; persons who failed to list their taxables allowed to do so without penalty; somebody admitted to the poorhouse; somebody awarded a small sum, rarely more than two or three dollars a month, for support; a license granted for twelve months to retail spirituous liquors; occasionally a license revoked; delegations heard petitioning for the opening of a new road or the repairing of a bridge; commissions named to inspect a bridge and contract for its repair; juries named to lay out a road; permission granted for the erection of a public gate; juries summoned for the Superior Court; bills against the county audited and ordered paid by the treasurer; and periodically new officers being bonded, fiscal officers making settlement, and list-takers appointed.

Occasionally an item of an exceptional nature appears. A few may be of interest:

March 10, 1870:- It is ordered that the sheriff receive 50 cents per day for feeding prisoners instead of 65 cents as heretofore.

January 5, 1875:- The Board proceeded to consider the propriety of purchasing a new bell for the use of the Court House. And on motion it is ordered that David C. Parks be authorized to contract for the purchase of a bell and to have it put up in a suitable manner for use—also to dispose of the old bell on the best terms he can.

February 1, 1875:- The case of Calvin Clark and others against William Hawkins, overseer, and others concerning that section of Road No. 16 - appeal from the trustees of Cedar Grove Township to County Commissioners - came up for a hearing this day. After hearing the evidence in the case, the Board decided in favor of the Trustees that said William Hawkins is the lawful overseer and that he alone has jurisdiction in the matter in controversy.

The minutes for the meeting of the Board held April 5, 1875 contain this item:

It is ordered that the clerk of the board notify the trustees of the different townships to take the tax list for the year 1875, and also to notify one from each board to meet the commissioners on Thursday, the 15th of April, to agree upon a uniform scale of valuations in the county as required by law.

At the meeting held ten days later the following scale of values for personal property was adopted:

1st class horses and mules	$100
2nd ,, ,, ,, ,,	60
3rd ,, ,, ,, ,,	25
Jacks and jennets according to value	
Sheep and goats	1 per head
1st class catlle	20
2nd ,, ,,	12
3rd ,, ,,	8
Oxen at the discretion of the board of assessors	
Hogs at the discretion of the board of assessors	

In May and early June the board of commissioners, sitting as a board of equalization and review, met for sixteen days "to revise the tax list."

The Justices Share Power with the Commissioners, 1878-1895

In 1875 the state government passed again into the hands of the conservatives, and the Reconstruction era was over. Immediately a constitutional convention was called to undo the work of the previous convention. Regardless of its merits, the scheme of government set up in 1868 was repugnant to the citizenship of the state, or at least to the ruling elements. The dual form of township and county government was something to which the people were not accustomed, and moreover there was apprehension that popular election of all the officials might result in control of the local government by the recently enfranchised Negroes. On the other hand, the more democratic system had gained many supporters, especially among the common people, and there was no certainty that a majority of the electorate would vote for a return to the old order. Therefore the convention decided against drafting and submitting a new constitution. Instead it left the article dealing with county and township government unchanged except for the addition of a significant amendment. This gave the General Assembly "full power by statute to modify, change, or abrogate" any or all of the provisions of the article except those limiting the taxing and debt-making powers of municipal corporations. In effect, it delegated to the legislature authority to modify as it saw fit most of the features of the prevailing system of local government. The only important officers beyond its reach were the clerk of superior court, the sheriff, and the coroner.

On the basis of this constitutional authority, the General Assembly of 1876-77 provided for a new plan of county government. It did not provide for a return in all respects to the prewar pattern. It retained some of the features introduced in 1868, but it restored the powers of decision in all important matters to a small hand-picked group of men.

The board of county commissioners was retained but instead of being elected by popular vote three to five persons were to be selected by the justices of the peace from within or without their own membership to serve as county commissioners. They were to have general oversight of the administration of county affairs, but when fiscal matters of any importance were being considered decision was to be made in a joint meeting with the justices of the peace. Thus, the commissioners could not levy taxes, purchase real estate, remove public buildings, construct or repair bridges costing more than $500, borrow money, or change township boundaries without the concurrence of a majority of the justices. Moreover, the justices were given full control over the election machinery of the county, the establishment of voting precincts, and the appointment of registrars and judges.

The justices of each county were required by the act to assemble and elect a board of commissioners on the first Monday in August, 1878, and every two years thereafter, and this is the way in which county commissioners were chosen in Orange County until 1896, when they again became popularly elected.

The reorganization act of 1877 continued the offices of treasurer, surveyor, and register of deeds, each to be filled by popular election for a term of two years.

The act provided for the retention of townships as magisterial districts, but instead of the justices of the peace in each township being popularly elected for two year terms, as before, they were to be appointed by the legislature for six year terms. Three were to be appointed for each township, with one additional justice for each 1,000 population of the cities and towns.

In addition to the voice which they were to have in county affairs the justices of each township constituted a township board of supervisors. In this capacity they had supervision and control of the public roads and bridges established in the township. They were authorized to divide the township roads into sections, appoint overseers for each section, and allot the hands subject to road duty. They were also given the power to lay out and discontinue cartways, as distinguished from public roads. The county board had this responsibility when the latter were involved.

In February, 1881, the Legislature authorized the formation of a new county from parts of Orange and Wake counties, subject to a favorable vote of the people in the areas effected. The election was held April 14, 1881 and the vote was in favor of the partition. Therefore the new County of Durham was organized May 2, 1881, the magistrates of the county naming five county commissioners, a sheriff, a coroner, six constables, and six tax assessors.

A few entries from the minutes of the board of commissioners, either when meeting alone or jointly with the magistrates, follow:

August 2, 1880:- A majority of the justices of Orange County met with the Board of Commissioners this day for the purpose of laying the county tax for the year 1880. After discussing the matter fully, it was ordered that a tax of 25 cents on the $100 of real and personal property be levied for county purposes.

March 7, 1881:- It is ordered that a gate be erected across the public road leading from Orange Factory to the Durham and Roxboro Road near the old Douglas Place. Also one gate across the public road on the opposite side of the river from Orange Factory on the premises of S. W. Holman.

November 7, 1881:- Ordered that John K. Hughes, sheriff, be allowed thirty-five cents per day for feeding prisoners to take effect as of September 1, 1881.

May 11, 1882:- A petition was presented to the Board asking them to order an election at the various precincts in Hillsboro Township for and against the fence law in said township. The petition was granted and persons were named to hold the election June 10.

June 3, 1889:-The Board held a joint meeting with the justices of the county. John Thompson, W. V. Andrews, and D. S. Parker were elected a board of education. Rev. J. L. Currie tendered his resignation as superintendent of public instruction for Orange County, and B. C. Patent was elected as examiner and superintendent.

An act of 1885 made it unlawful for cattle to run at large in Cedar Grove, Little River, Hillsboro, and Bingham townships, and it was made the duty of the commissioners to erect "a good and lawful fence" around the townships in which such stock law prevails, and to defray the expense of the same from a special tax laid on the property of these townships.

Another act of the same year provided that whenever three-fourths of the freeholders of Chapel Hill township petitioned for a stock law, the commissioners might declare the general stock law in effect without any further election and without any tax to build fences.

An item in the minutes of the board of commissioners for February 6, 1893 reads: "W. A. Maddry was instructed to examine the stock fence between Orange and Chatham counties."

In 1889 the Legislature passed an act (chap. 361) which provided for an alternate method of constructing and repairing the public roads. The act authorized the board of commissioners and the justices of the peace of the county, in joint session, by a majority vote, to adopt the alternative method. This was to levy a county-wide ad valorem tax, not exceeding 15 cents on the hundred dollars valuation, and a poll tax not exceeding 45 cents, the proceeds of which were to be kept separate from other funds and expended only for the construction and repair of the public roads. The adoption of the plan did not relieve able-bodied males from the customary four days of labor on the roads each year but permitted a person, at the discretion of the commissioners, to work out also his road tax at such price per day as the commissioners might prescribe.

The act also made persons confined in the county jail or sentenced to the state prison available for road work at the discretion of the commissioners.

The commissioners of any county were permitted to adopt any system for maintaining the roads of that county not inconsistent with the provisions of this act.

In 1891 Orange county adopted some of the features of the act, most important of which was the imposition of a county-wide tax of 7 cents on the hundred dollars valuation for road purposes. The proceeds were turned over to the township supervisors. A statement of the taxes collected from the road tax in each of the five townships in the two year period during which it was in force, 1891 and 1892, together with the amounts which had been expended when it was terminated follows:

	Received	Expended
Hillsboro	$1105.52	$1014.49
Little River	462.75	388.96
Cedar Grove	496.38	324.89
Chapel Hill	935.43	285.73
Bingham	439.95	187.18

The property-owning class, as represented by the justices of the peace, were opposed to the tax and forced its repeal after two years. The reluctance of the commissioners to yield to the magistrates is reflected in the minutes of the two bodies meeting in joint session.

> June 5, 1893:- The question as to the repeal of the alternative system of working the roads of Orange County, after considerable discussion, was put to the vote and declared repealed, a majority of all the Justices of the Peace in the County voting for its repeal and the entire Board of Commissioners voting against the repeal.
>
> July 3, 1893: - In obedience to the call of the commissioners, on the first Monday in July the Commissioners and Justices of the Peace met again in joint session. As it had been declared that the alternative system of road working had not been repealed as the Commissioners had not concurred. Again (after being) warmly discussed, it was decided by a vote of the Justices of the Peace that they would not reconsider the question as they regarded the system as repealed. .
>
> August 8, 1893:- By a unanimous vote the board of commissioners concur with the Board of Magistrates in the repeal of the alternative system of road working in Orange County.

The last joint meeting of the board of commissioners with the justices occurred June 4, 1894. Three items of business are recorded:

> John Thompson was elected County Superintendent of Common Schools.
>
> The following persons were elected by the Justices of the Peace to serve as commissioners for two years from December 1, 1894:-D. H. Hamilton, W. A. Maddry, M. W. Moore.
>
> The following tax was levied for the year 1894:-county tax, 20 cents on the hundred dollars valuation; school, county and pension, $2.00 on the poll.

Thereafter the justices had no part in the management of county affairs; except for one brief interval they had been the dominant figures for 142 years.

The Period Since 1895

For a few years after the justices were finally ejected from the governing body of the county the commissioners had no competitors; there were no other county boards. Neither did they have to share their powers with others, with a single exception. To constitute a board of equalization they were joined by one trustee from each of the townships. Thus on July 1, 1895 we find the three county commissioners and one assessor (trustee) from each township sitting as a board of equalization and, after comparing relative standards used, raising all assessments in Little River township by one-third. There was no longer a separate board of wardens or a separate school board, and not yet was there a separate board of elections or a separate board of welfare. Thus in the minutes of the commissioners for the early years of this final period we find them naming judges and registrars, a power formerly reserved to the justices. We also find them naming the school superintendent, formerly named in a joint meeting with the justices.

Though the commissioners had the field to themselves county business was pretty humdrum. The monthly meetings of the board were largely taken up with the same petty matters that had been coming before the county governing body for a century—exempting a man from the poll tax or road duty because of disability or being overage, remitting part of a property tax because of an erroneous assesment, committing someone to the poorhouse or granting a dollar or two a month in outdoor relief, granting a license to retail spirituous liquors, ordering the repair of a bridge, auditing and authorizing payment on bills presented for miscellaneous supplies, or granting a petition for a new road. Increasingly frequent were such entries as the following:

> September 2, 1895:- Ordered that the supervisors of Little River Township open the following road, to wit: Commencing at James Roberts at the forks of the Milton Jamison Road running east to the Durham County line, about three-fourths of a mile long.

Indeed, by the turn of the century the work of the commissioners had ceased to be humdrum. The people had become road conscious and for the next thirty years the problem of road construction and improvement was to be a dominant and absorbing one.

Roads

After the magistrates succeeded in securing the repeal of the road tax, the county went back to the old system. Moreover, the township continued as the unit of road administration and the justices of the peace constituted the board of road supervisors. Their road duties were not heavy. The law provided that they should meet at least twice a year (on the first Saturday of February and of August) "for the purpose of consulting on the subject of the condition of the roads in their township." Once in each year, during the week of the August meeting, they were required to go over and examine personally all the roads in the township. At their meeting in August the board of supervisors divided the roads of the township into sections and appointed an overseer for each section. They allotted a certain number of hands to each overseer and designated the section boundaries. Each overseer was required to make a report at each meeting of the board of supervisors, giving the present condition of his road, the number of days worked, the number of hands who attended and worked each day, the number and names of those who failed to attend, whether or not they were legally summoned, and whether or not they had paid the dollar as provided. He was required to make a report of all money collected and how expended.

This system was not unlike that which was in use a hundred years earlier and produced no better roads.

Nevertheless, there continued to be agitation for change. More and more people recognized that good roads could not be built without heavy equipment, and it would require a tax levy to raise the necessary money. The legislature had authorized elections on the question of a road tax to be held in individual townships if a sufficient number of taxpayer so petitioned.

On October 1, 1900 a petition with the required number of signers was presented to the board asking for an election in Hillsboro Township on the question of a special road tax. The petition was granted, the election held and carried, and a tax of 10 cents on the $100 and 30 cents on the poll was levied by the commissioners. A similar petition with a similar outcome was presented from Bingham Township. Other townships followed and by 1903 road taxes were being levied and collected in all seven townships. The levy in Hillsboro township was 25 cents on the $100 valuation; the Chapel Hill levy was 20; and the rate in the other five townships was 10 cents. The poll tax in each case was equivalent to the tax on $300 of property.

The Legislature of 1903 had authorized the county board to create two new townships—Cheeks from the western part of Hillsboro Township, and Eno River Township from Hillsboro and Little River townships. Acting on this authority the board established the two new townships.

A state-wide act of 1901 had authorized any township, upon petition of one-fourth of the qualified voters, to hold an election, and, if the election carried, to issue bonds for road improvement. If bonds were issued the county board was required to levy a special tax on the property and polls of the township to service them. Hillsboro was the only township which took advantage of this privilege, bonds to the extent of $40,000 being floated in 1909-1910 to build a limited mileage of macadam roads.

By this time there were several automobiles in the county and it was becoming apparent that the townships were not suitable units to finance automobile roads. There was increasing demand for county support, and in 1911 the county secured passage in the legislature of a local act authorizing issuance by the county of as much as $250,000 in bonds for road improvement, together with authority to levy a special road tax of 25 to 35 cents on the $100 to service the bonds.

On the first day of January, 1912 the board of county commissioners ordered a county election for March 19th to determine whether bonds to the extent of $250,000 should be issued by the county and the proceeds used "in repairing and grading and improving or macadamizing the public roads of the county." The election carried by a narrow margin, 919 to 831. About a year later the bonds were sold. They were 40 year term bonds bearing 5 per cent interest. Thus a county which was out of debt in 1911, two years later had embarked on an ambitious road building campaign which it was ill-equipped to undertake and had encumbered itself with a staggering debt which was not lifted until 1953.

The same act which authorized the bond issue provided for the election by the board of commissioners of a "good roads commission" of nine members—two from Chapel Hill Township, two from Hillsboro Township, and one from each of the other five townships. This commission was to designate the roads to be improved, taking into consideration the needs of the entire county. It was also empowered to employ an expert engineer.

Since Hillsboro Township had already issued bonds to the extent of $40,000 to build macadam roads in that township, it was reimbursed half of this sum from the county bond issue.

Though the bond issue was to finance the improvement of the major roads by the county, it was soon apparent that the township system of maintenance was too antiquated for an automobile age. In 1915 the legislature passed an act abolishing the township system in Orange County and making the county the unit of administration. The board was authorized to elect some competent man as county superintendent of roads and place him in charge, under the direction of the board, of all the roads in the county.

At a meeting of the board of commissioners held March 2, 1915, A. W. Clarke, the newly elected road supervisor, came before the board and accepted the proposition made him of $65 a month for nine months from March to November and $3.00 per day for every day worked during the months of December, January, and February of each year. It was ordered that the superintendent of roads keep an accurate account of all work done in the townships then having a balance to their credit and that the work done in these townships be charged to the usual township funds until those funds were exhausted.

A few months later the road superintendent was authorized to appoint men in different sections of the county to work both the sand-clay and the unimproved roads, the method of having the work done being left to his discretion. In 1916 he was authorized to purchase the necessary equipment to enable him to work convicts. This same year some of the recently improved roads were placed in the Federal-State system. Note the record:

> April 17, 1916:-Ordered that the road from Chapel Hill to Durham be turned over to the U. S. Government engineer the same as the central highway by Hillsboro, and that $40 per mile per year be appropriated for maintenance.
>
> May 1, 1916:- Ordered that $40 per mile per annum be ap-

propriated for maintaining road from Carrboro to Alamance line via White Cross, work to be done under supervision of engineer furnished by Dr. Pratt of the State Highway Commission.

In 1917 the board appointed a road inspector in each township who was to make a reconnaisance of the roads of his township, suggest their subdivision into sections, and recommend suitable persons to be considered by the board as "contractors" for such sections. On March 6, 1917 the inspectors submitted the following classification of the roads by townships:

Township	Central Highways miles	Class A miles	Class B miles
Bingham	10.0		62.2
Cedar Grove		11.8	72.2
Chapel Hill	10.0	5.0	84.0
Cheeks	8.0	4.5	40.5
Eno	5.0	13.3	27.8
Hillsboro	4.0	18.5	12.5
Little River		9.0	43.0
Total	37.0	62.1	365.2

Although there was now a county-wide road levy, road bills were recorded and paid by townships until 1920 or later. In May, 1920 township road inspectors were still being paid. The county road funds were apparently being allocated among the townships according to some formula, perhaps in proportion to taxes paid. However, as early as 1917 the board provided that all bridges, trunks and pipes, and all tools for use on the roads be paid for out of general county funds.

All through the 1920's road building and road improvement eclipsed all other activities of the county government. The board was besieged with requests for new or better roads. Often requests were granted on condition that the beneficiaries make some contribution in cash or labor. Despite the fact that the county had a road superintendent there might be a dozen projects under way simultaneously under the immediate oversight of local amateur foremen. Each submitted payrolls with little supporting evidence. Prisoners were used on some of the projects, and a frequent item among the bills presented for payment was one entitled "boarding prisoners." The road superintendent, and several held the position while it lasted, was usually neither an engineer nor an administrator. While there may have been no major scandals, there was petty graft, confusion, and waste.

Either projects cost more than anticipated or more were undertaken because of the pressure than the tax revenues would support. As a result, the board was constantly under the necessity of borrowing from the banks. Unable or unwilling to tax high enough to meet current demands and pay off the bank loans, the debts were funded. The first example of this was on August 6, 1923 when a resolution was passed to issue bonds in the amount of $65,000 to liquidate existing indebtedness.

The pressure for roads was terrific and what Orange County was doing was duplicated all over the state. The counties were failing to get their money's worth either in road construction or maintenance, and they were getting heavier and heavier in debt. In fact, the burden was too great to be borne by the counties, whose main reliance was the property tax. Since 1921 the state had maintained the primary roads and gradually it added to the mileage so designated, but the vast proportion of the roads were not in that category. The counties must either get a share of the proceeds from the gasoline and motor vehicle taxes or be relieved of the secondary roads. As the result of the findings of a survey ordered by Governor Gardner, the legislature of 1931 passed an act transferring all the public roads, except city streets, to the state for maintenance. At the same time the State assumed responsibility for the custody and care of all prisoners sentenced for 60 (later 30) days or more, thus largely emptying the county jails. Thus a major function of local government from the beginning of the county and one which for two decades had been increasingly burdensome and vexatious was suddenly lifted from the shoulders of the board.

The Gardner report stated that the previous year (1929) Orange County had spent $48,076 on roads. It had built 12 miles of new roads and rebuilt 26 miles of sand-clay roads. It credited the county with 412.1 miles of roads—of which 107.9 were unimproved, 237.3 miles were improved to the extent of being graded and drained, and 66.9 miles had a sand-clay surface. Obviously all roads which had been hard-surfaced had been added to the primary system.

Schools

With the beginning of the new century there was a revival of interest in education. This found expression in the appearance before the county board of neighborhood delegations requesting authorization to hold district elections on the question of a special tax for an extended school term. The first district to hold an election and vote a tax on itself was the Mebane School District, and on April 4, 1904 the board ordered that "a tax list for Mebane School District be placed in the hands of the sheriff for the collection of a tax of 30 cents on $100 value of real and personal property and 90 cents on polls.

In the next few years there was a steady procession of requests for special elections, often followed by reports of such elections, and by 1910 special school taxes were being levied and collected in six districts. The districts and property tax rates, the poll tax always being equal to the tax on $300 of property, were as follows: Mebane, 30 cents; Fairfield, 30 cents; Efland, 20 cents; Hillsboro, 20 cents; Efland, 20 cents; West Chapel Hill, 15 cents; University, 20 cents. The subsequent development of the public schools of the county is fully treated in another chapter.

Public Welfare

In 1917 North Carolina took a big step forward in meeting the problem of dependency. As a result of the efforts of a few public-spirited and broad-visioned citizens, the legislature of that year was induced to pass a state-wide public welfare act. The North Carolina Board of Public Charities, which had existed since 1868, was replaced by a State Board of Charities and Public Welfare with greatly expanded powers and duties. Moreover, in order to extend the new type of relief work to the counties, the county commissioners were given power to create county boards of public welfare and to elect a county superintendent of public welfare. The law as it related to counties was optional, and only two counties had perfected organizations when the next legislature met. The 1919 legislature amended the act, making it mandatory for every county to create a county board of public welfare. In the more populous counties a superintendent of public welfare was required. In counties which did not choose a superintendent of public welfare, the superintendent of schools was required to perform the duties of the office. A full-time superintendent was not required in Orange County, and on July 7, 1919 the board of commissioners meeting in joint session with the county board of education elected R. H. Claytor, county superintendent of schools, to the position. He was voted an additional salary of $600—one-half to be paid from general county funds and one-half from school funds. This arrangement continued until July 5, 1920, when Wiley B. Sanders became superintendent on a part-time basis. He served only six months, and for the next several years the duties of the position were alternately performed by Mr. Claytor and a temporary and part-time welfare officer. This unsatisfactory arrangement continued until September 3, 1928 when the two boards, in joint session, elected George H. Lawrence as full-time superintendent of public welfare.

The 1919 act gave the superintendent an imposing array of powers and duties. These included the care and supervision of the poor, under the control of the county commissioners; the oversight of dependent and delinquent children; the oversight of prisoners in the county on probation or parole; the enforcement of the child labor law including the issuance of work certificates to minors; finding employment for the unemployed; the enforcement of the laws regulating commercial amusements; and enforcement of the compulsory school attendance law. In the performance of all these duties, the superintendent was expected to investigate into the cause of distress or delinquency in order to effect rehabilitation. Yet for several years Mr. Lawrence had no case workers, only a part-time clerk. His office was in Chapel Hill in an old house owned by the University.

In the early days of welfare work, the superintendent had to go before the commissioners and solicit an appropriation every time he felt that some family should be granted five or ten dollars in relief. But as the depression deepened and the appeals for aid increased the board relaxed its control and allowed him more discretion. Thus a minute of January 7, 1935 reads:

> Ordered that the sum of $150 per month for January and February be paid to George H. Lawrence, welfare officer, to be turned into the ERA fund for expenses of the totally disabled on the list.

And another of two months later:

> The Board arranged with George H. Lawrence to handle all relief help for the month of March and April as was arranged for January and February.

During the depression years the welfare superintendent was actively involved in the several federal relief and recovery programs - certifying persons for the Civilian Conservation Corps, the Civil Works Administration, and the Works Progress Administration. He was also largely instrumental in getting certain WPA projects approved, including the Confederate Memorial Library and the Agricultural Building in Hillsboro and the Negro Center in Chapel Hill.

With the inauguration of the Social Security program in 1937, the county departments of public welfare were reorganized to take care of the vastly expanded work and to meet the more rigid professional requirements of the federal and state laws. The county agency was given responsibility for the administration of old age assistance, aid to dependent children, and certain child welfare services. All were supported jointly by federal, state and county funds, hence the requirement that all workers in the welfare department come under the jurisdiction of the State Merit Council. That is, all personnel must pass a qualifying examination and all case workers must have had professional training in social work.

The reorganization abolished the former advisory board and created a new County Board of Public Welfare consisting of three members—one appointed by the county board of commissioners, one by the State Board of Public Welfare, and one by the other two members. This board was given power to appoint the superintendent, supervise the work of the department, and adopt overall policy. The original membership of the reconstituted board consisted of O. L. Crabtree, Bruce Strowd, and Charlie McDade (colored). Appointments are for three years and no one may serve more than two consecutive terms.

The first superintendent to be appointed after the reorganization was W. T. Mattox. He assumed the duties in July, 1937, and served until his death in May, 1947. He was succeeded by Mrs. Jean Heer and she, on April 1, 1951, by Miss Annie Strowd, the present incumbent.

The staff in 1937 consisted of the superintendent, three case workers, one of whom was a specialist in child welfare work, and two clerical workers. At present the department has, in addition to the superintendent, two child welfare workers, two case assistants, and three clerical workers.

In the fiscal year, 1927-1928, the first year that the county operated under a budget, the expenditures for what would now be called public welfare were as follows:

County home and farm	$ 3,363.21
Outside poor relief	730.50
County aid	962.54
Public welfare	27.50

For the year which ended June 30, 1952, expenditures for welfare purposes, including the cost of administration, aggregated $190,973.26. Of this, $145,679.75 came from State and Federal funds, $41,628.75 from county funds, and $3,764.76 from an unexpended balance of the previous year.

A breakdown of the expenditures will suggest the scope and character of the department's current activities:

General relief	$ 2,039.23
Hospitalization	8,088.06
Pauper burials	150.00
Boarding homes	4,997.18
Aid to the Blind	1,199.51
Aid to Dependent Children	60,543.00
Old Age Assistance	81,078.00
Aid to Permanently and Totally Disabled	8,974.00
Administration	
Salaries	19,559.19
Travel	1,660.18
Other	2,688.91
Total	$190,973.26

It will be noted that the two major items are old age assistance and aid to dependent children. In 1952 the number receiving old age assistance averaged about 290. The number of families without a breadwinner benefiting from Aid to Dependent Children grants was approximately 125. There were 35 persons receiving aid because of being permanently and totally disabled and 25 because of blindness. An increasingly costly item is that of providing hospitalization to the indigent, one of the functions of the department being to certify persons eligible to the benefits of the medical care program. The county home was discontinued in 1941 because most of the inmates were eligible for old age assistance and, with this assistance, could get care in boarding homes. There are no boarding homes for adults in the county, but there are three for children as well as one foster home for children being considered for adoption. Since the welfare office was moved to Hillsboro in 1937 a branch office has always been maintained in Chapel Hill, and the superintendent spends two days a week there. The office is in the building occupied by the School of Social Work and there has always been close and mutually profitable collaboration.

Agricultural Extension Work

Agricultural extension work in the county goes back to September, 1912 when the board of commissioners appropriated $300 to supplement a like amount appropriated by the state. This modest support was discontinued in December, 1915. However, the work was revived after the outbreak of the war and on March 4, 1918 this entry appears in the minutes of the board:

> Ordered that County Agent Chance be authorized to purchase a carload of pigs, weight from 35 to 80 pounds, the same to be sold to citizens of the county at cost for cash, the county advancing the money for the purchase of the same by Mr. Chance.

This first agent was succeeded by E. S. Vanatta who came into the county in 1918 to make the Soil Survey and remained as county agent until February, 1921. The work was supported intermittently for the next few years, but in 1928 Don S. Matheson was employed on a full-time basis and began the splendid work which now after a quarter of a century is bearing such abundant fruit. It took infinite patience but gradually the farmers of the county abandoned antiquated and wasteful practices and turned to scientific methods. Through the years Mr. Matheson has emphasized a shift from soil depleting row crops, except for tobacco where suitable, to grasses and livestock with the gratifying results everywhere apparent.

In addition to being teacher and demonstrator, the county agent has served as the liaison between the U. S. Department of Agriculture and the county in executing the federal crop control and conservation programs and as representative of the Manpower Commission in World War II.

Since 1935, except for a period of 18 months, Edwin P. Barnes has been assistant county agent, devoting much of his time to 4 H Club work. Also since 1935 a Negro agent, M. C. Burt, has worked among the Negro farmers of the county. For a period the Negro agent was shared with Chatham county.

Home Demonstration Work

Extension work among farm women began in Orange County as a part of the Food Will Win the War campaign during World War I. At least we find these early entries in the minutes of the county commissioners:

> July 5, 1915:-The board endorsed the election of Miss Mary Owen Graham of Charlotte as supervisor of the canning clubs of Orange County.
>
> June 5, 1916:- Ordered that the appropriation of $250 a year for tomato club work be continued for another year.
>
> May 7, 1917:- Ordered that remainder of $100 appropriation for Home Demonstration Work be spent for the purchase of a demonstration canner and to pay traveling expenses of those members of the Home Demonstration Clubs volunteering their services in cooking and canning in the community.
>
> April 1, 1918:- Ordered that the board pay two-thirds of the salary of $800 a year of Home Demonstration Agent to be employed by the county, the balance of one-third to be paid by the Board of Education.

After the war ended the work was discontinued and was not resumed until September, 1935, when Miss Grace E. Holcombe was employed jointly by Orange and Chatham counties. Within a year she had organized four home demonstration clubs and nine 4 H clubs in Orange county. Prior to that time all 4 H club work had been done by the county agent. So eager were the farm women of the county for the full services of a home demonstration agent that their request was not long denied and by 1941 there were 17 home demonstration clubs and ten 4 H clubs providing outlets for her instruction. Miss Holcombe had been succeeded by Miss Woodward Byars in August, 1939, who stayed until 1945 carrying on and expanding the work so ably started.

In 1941 an assistant agent of the Negro race was added to the staff to work exclusively among the Negro women, Ruby Crews, who later became Mrs. Ruby Carraway, being the first agent. This work is now firmly established and highly regarded.

Library Service

Since 1942 Orange county has been in a tri-county library district consisting of Caswell, Person and Orange, which with the help of state funds, provides district-wide library service through the facilities of a bookmobile. For a few years prior to that it was in a district embracing Chatham rather than Caswell, the service being supported in considerable measure from WPA funds. The Orange county branch office of the tri-county library district is in the Hillsboro Confederate Memorial Library, which is housed in a handsome stone building erected as a WPA project and dedicated in 1934. The county made small annual appropriations to this library even before state grants were available, at least as early as 1938.

Public Health

Although the legislature made provision for county boards of health as early as 1879, there is no record that Orange County organized such a board until ten years later. The Biennial Report of the State Board of Health for 1889-90 lists for the first time a part-time Superintendent of Health, Doctor D. C. Parris, of Hillsboro. He was succeeded in 1898 by Doctor C. D. Jones, who continued to serve until the organization of a full-time health department in 1935. The activities during these years consisted largely of quarantine of contagious diseases, vaccination against typhoid fever and smallpox, and promotion of sanitation.

Full-time health service was inaugurated in July, 1935,

when the county appropriated $2,500 to the budget of a bi-county district department with Person County. Doctor G. H. Sumner, now Randolph County Health officer, was the first health officer, serving temporarily for about two months. He was followed by Doctor M. H. Rourk who served until Feburary, 1936, and was succeeded by W. P. Richardson. The present health officer, Doctor O. D. Garvin, followed Doctor Richardson in 1944.

The department began in a modest way. Orange County shared the health officer and a sanitarian with Person county and had a local staff of one nurse and a clerk. The original district has grown with the addition in 1937 of Chatham County, and in 1946 of Lee.

Both the budget and staff of the Orange County unit of the district have shown consistent growth. For the fiscal year 1952-53, the county appropriated $14,000, or approximately 48 cents per capita. With the considerably greater amount available from other sources—town and university appropriations, state and federal allotments, and foundation grants—this appropriation provides for the county a staff of ten public health nurses, two sanitarians, three clerks, and the county's proportionate part of the services of three medical officers, a supervising nurse, and a health educator who serve the entire district.

The county has one of the better public health programs in the country. Services provided include communicable disease control, tuberculosis case finding and supervision, venereal disease control, maternal and child health supervision, an active school health program, an organized health education program, sanitary supervision of public food handling establishments, meat markets, dairies and the like, as well as promotion of general environmental sanitation. The newest service is a limited bedside nursing program in the southern half of the county, provided in conjunction with the University Hospital and Out Patient Department.

Because the health department provides important services in public health field training for the State Board of Health and the Schools of Public Health, Medicine, and Nursing of the University, it receives a considerable amount of special financial support.

The county has thus benefited greatly from its strategic location, and has acquired a department and program much more adequate than would be expected in view of its wealth and population.

Register of Deeds

This history would not be complete were not some mention made of the office of register of deeds. The first public register, as the office was then called, was William Churton, Lord Granville's surveyor, who laid out Hillsboro and remained as its most distinguished citizen. His successor, Edmund Fanning, was also a man of great talents but, if the Regulators are to be believed, fattened his purse by charging extortionate fees. At any rate, he was the chief object of their wrath and lost his job and his home as a result of their vengeance. In two centuries the office has been held by a succession of respected, if not eminent, men, one of whom deserves special mention. This is John Laws who was register and clerk of the board for more than sixty years. His service began not later than October, 1849, and except for a two year interval, 1853 to 1855, continued until his death on November 23, 1913 at the age of 92.

The vaults of the register of deeds contain a mine of historical information. The record of deeds is complete from the formation of the county. Until 1930 they were copied in longhand; some are in beautiful script, others are scarcely legible. Since January 1, 1930 deeds and other recorded documents have been typed, and since October, 1951 they have been photostated and microfilmed. That is, when a deed or deed of trust is brought in to be recorded, it is photographed or photostated and the negative sent to Hall and McChesney, Syracuse, New York. This company retains a picture of the instrument on microfilm but returns a positive print of the exact size to fit the binders which Orange county has used from the beginning. Not only does this system insure against error in transcription but leaves a duplicate copy on microfilm in storage at Syracuse in case of loss by fire or any other cause. Moreover, to enjoy the same protection in the case of the deeds recorded prior to 1951, they too have been microfilmed - a total of 136 volumes of deeds and 30 volumes of deeds of trust. Currently the chattel mortgages are being microfilmed, with a miniature print returned to the county; it can be read with the aid of a projector which has been provided. The vaults of the register of deeds also contain the minutes of the board of commissioners since this body was established in 1868, and incomplete records of the early treasurers and wardens of the poor.

The register of deeds is custodian of vital statistics. These are complete since registrations began in October, 1913. The district health officer is the official registrar for the county, and he sends one copy of each birth certificate and each death certificate to the register of deeds of the county and one to the Bureau of Vital Statistics in Raleigh. Many persons born outside the state or born prior to 1913 have established the date of their birth by other documents and had it recorded. The register of deeds issues marriage licenses and keeps a record thereof; in his vaults are records of the marriage bonds of former days.

The register of deeds was clerk to the board of commissioners from 1868 until this duty was assigned to the county accountant in 1928.

Inferior Courts

The abolition of the Court of Pleas and Quarter Sessions in 1868 left the county with a very simple court structure. The superior court became the court of general jurisdiction, trying all cases, both civil and criminal, except the most petty ones, which might be tried by a single justice of the peace. The latter's jurisdiction in criminal cases extends to misdemeanors committed in the county where the punishment prescribed by law does not exceed a fine of fifty dollars or imprisonment for thirty days. He has jurisdiction in civil actions founded on contracts when the sum demanded does not exceed $200 and when the title to real estate is not in controversy, and in cases not founded on contracts involving no more than $50. For the first few years, the magistrates were all elected by popular vote in the several townships, but after 1877 they might also be elected by the legislature, and a bit later the constitution was construed to permit their appointment by the governor. The number that might be chosen by these three methods is very large, but actually the number seeking the post has steadily declined. A few years ago there were only two in the county, but at this writing there are four, all appointees of the governor.

The limited jurisdiction of the justice of the peace and the infrequent terms of the superior court, usually only two criminal and two civil terms a year, led in time to a demand for an intermediate court meeting frequently. Thus, in 1929, the Chapel Hill recorder's court was established with a territorial jurisdiction extending over Chapel Hill township and a subject matter jurisdiction extending to all misdemeanors. The judge (recorder) is elected by the voters of the Chapel Hill municipality for a two year term; the clerk and the prosecutor are appointed by the Chapel Hill board of aldermen. The court meets every Tuesday.

With the growth of population there later arose a demand for a similar court serving the rest of the county. Consequently, the legislature of 1949 authorized an Orange County Recorder's Court, and in May of that year one was established by action of the county commissioners. It is similar to the one in Chapel Hill except that its jurisdiction covers six townships. The county board appoints the recorder, the prosecutor, and the clerk - the last-mentioned office being held presently by the clerk of superior court. This court meets every Monday. Neither court uses a jury except in rare instances.

Sheriff and Jail

The ancient office of sheriff has unquestionably lost prestige in two centuries, though it has probably gained in public confidence. It was once considered the highest office in the county and, being the most lucrative, was passed around among the squirearchy. While, no doubt, the office commanded respect, this was not always true of the incumbent, and many of the early sheriffs were suspected of illicit gains. This was more easily accomplished because they were paid by fees and commissions, their commissions as tax collector appearing most generous by today's standards.

The Orange county sheriff served as tax collector until 1936, though he ceased to be paid by commissions somewhat earlier. Except that he is no longer tax collector the sheriff's duties are not greatly different from those of his predecessors, at least when serving as a court officer. As a police officer, he of course has vastly improved facilities to aid him, such as two-way radio patrol cars and the services and laboratories of the State Bureau of Investigation.

In 1926 the county built a commodious new jail, its earlier one being dilapidated and inadequate. At that time the convicts were being used for road work but of course the jail served as an assembly point as well as a place for confinement in the winter months. Had the county board known that in five years the county jails would be largely stripped of prisoners serving sentence, most certainly it would not have made this $65,000 investment. Except for the last few weeks before a term of criminal court, when there may be several persons in jail awaiting trial, the number of inmates is normally no more than two or three, and not infrequently the jail is completely empty for several weeks at a time. Including the jailor, the sheriff has four full-time deputies, while the services and salary of a fifth one are divided between the county and the cotton mill operators in West Hillsboro.

Clerk of Court

Through the years the office of the clerk of Superior Court has remained an important one. To the many duties placed here in 1868 others have been added. In 1919 a law was passed requiring a juvenile court in each county; in most counties, including Orange, the clerk of the Superior court was made its judge. In Orange, as stated above, he has been made clerk of the county recorder's court. He is judge of probate and judge of special proceedings. He keeps a great variety of records in addition to those pertaining to the several courts, such as election returns, lists of notaries public, surety companies, architects, and many others. Of great historical value are the wills and final settlements of executors, administrators, and guardians filed here since the beginning of the county.

Fiscal Control

A basic principle of good administration is unity in fiscal control, yet this principle has been generally violated in county government. For the first 175 years of its history Orange County had no budget, no central accounting, no fiscal control. It had a treasurer, first called trustee, from 1778 until the office was abolished in 1948 but he was merely the custodian of public funds; he received what was turned over to him and paid out on orders drawn against him. There was usually an annual audit to detect any embezzlement, but often the absence of supporting documents made the audit meaningless. Nor was the treasurer the custodian of all the funds; at times the wardens of the poor and the school board had their own treasurers, and individual officers like the clerk of court retained custody of their own receipts.

Until modern times the only sort of fiscal control which existed was the examination of bills by the board of commissioners, or their counterpart, before an order was drawn on the treasurer. This preaudit, which was necessarily quite perfunctory, acquainted the commissioners with what was being spent but was in no sense a control device. It occurred after the transaction had been completed. In brief, counties in North Carolina operated without a financial plan, and without a fiscal control officer; it is not surprising that the funding of deficits was occurring with increasing frequency. Finally the State found it necessary to do something about it.

In 1927 the legislature enacted the County Fiscal Control Act (chap. 146), one of the most far-reaching acts in the interest of sound financial practice in county government that has been enacted in any state. Its purpose, in brief, was to place a competent accountant in every courthouse, to develop a degree of uniformity in county accounting, and to guarantee a balanced budget in every county every year. The fiscal year was to run from July 1 to June 30; the budget was to be adopted by the fourth Monday in July; and the necessary tax levy was to be made not later than Wednesday after the third Monday in August. The budget officer, called county accountant, had to be "some person of honesty and ability, who is experienced in modern methods of accounting." To prevent deficits no contract or agreement requiring the payment of money, or requisition of supplies or materials, was valid unless endorsed by the county accountant as follows: "Provision for the payment of the moneys to fall under this agreement has been made by appropriation duly made or by bonds or notes duly authorized, as required by the 'County Fiscal Control Act'."

The Orange County commissioners fell in line with the spirit of the act and began searching for an accountant fully capable of meeting its requirements. In the meantime, J. L. Lockhart, deputy clerk of court, filled in on a part-time basis. On September 3, 1928 Gilbert W. Ray was employed as county accountant and purchasing agent and he held the post until August 31, 1947. He immediately installed a system of bookkeeping which was intelligible as well as effective as an instrument of control. He saved the county money through centralized purchasing. In due course he became tax supervisor and for a time tax collector. Even after Carl C. Davis succeeded him as tax collector in 1938, they worked as a team, sharing their clerical assistants. For the first time any information sought about taxes, finances, or county business generally could be obtained in one place. Mr. Ray was succeeded by Ira A. Ward, the present encumbent, who has demonstrated the same high quality of performance in this key position.

After a proper accounting system was installed, a post audit became a much simpler operation and audits have been made regularly since 1927, if not annually at least periodically. They cover all departments of the county government including the schools. Most of these audits, covering a quarter of a century, have been made by Kennon W. Parham of Raleigh. They provide a consolidated and abbreviated fiscal record of county operations which is invaluable.

County Indebtedness

Orange County has been in debt on several occasions in its long history but its early loans were always for short terms. The first three courthouses appear to have been financed by special tax levies, each continuing for only three or four years. The present courthouse, built in 1844, cost about $10,000 but it too was financed through bank loans.

Not until the modern road building era began did the county issue bonds. Although Hillsboro Township had issued some earlier, 1908-1910, the county's first bond issue was in 1913 when it sold $244,000 of highway improvement bonds to undertake a county-wide road improvement program. By 1927 there had been six bond issues aggregating $688,000, all without a vote of the people only by a resolution of the board. This had been quite legitimate because all had met the constitutional test of being for "necessary purposes." Although the constitution was not amended so as to normally require a vote of the people if substantial sums were involved until 1936, the legislature of 1927 enacted a County Finance Act which placed some wholesome restrictions on the flotation of bonds. Among other things, it prohibited the further issuance of term, or sinking fund, bonds; it required all future issues to be serials, some of the principal maturing each year. Orange County had not offended seriously in this particular; except for the $244,000 issue in 1913 its outstanding bonds were all serials which were steadily being reduced.

The first audit made after the employment of a county accountant reveals the indebtedness of the county as of December 3, 1928.

Orange County Debt, December 3, 1928

Character of Obligation	Date of Issue	Amt. of Issue	Outstanding
Highway Improvement Bonds	1913	$244,000	$244,000
Road and Bridge Funding Bonds	1921	99,000	31,000
Jail Bonds	1925	65,000	59,000
Road and Bridge Bonds	1927	166,000	166,000
Funding Bonds	1927	49,000	49,000
School Funding Bonds	1923	65,000	40,000
State Special Building Fund Loan			110,850
State Literary Fund Loan			19,825
Notes payable			77,455
Gross debt			797,130
Less amount in sinking fund			51,635
Net debt			$ 745,495

For the next several years the county's financial position steadily improved; the current debt was paid off and the funded debt payments regularly met. In spite of a school bond issue of $165,000 in 1935 to supplement funds made available by the Public Works Administration of the Federal Government, the county's net debt on June 30, 1940 stood at $401,823 or less than it will ever be again in the foreseeable future. As of December 31, 1952, after the new courthouse bonds had been sold, the net bonded debt of the county was $1,378,000. It is detailed below.

Bonded Debt, December 31, 1952

Purpose	Date of Issue	Amount Issued	Amount Outstanding
Road Improvement	1913	$ 244,000	$ 244,000
Jail	1925	65,000	9,000
Roads and Funding	1927	215,000	66,000
School	1935	190,000	36,000
School	1941	20,000	2,000
School	1950	1,000,000	1,000,000
School	1950	15,000	15,000
Courthouse	1952	250,000	250,000
Total		$1,999,000	1,622,000
Less amount in sinking fund			244,000
Net bonded debt			$1,378,000

Conclusion

The historian of the future may be grateful if this sketch is concluded with a statement of the county's revenues and expenditures in 1951-52, the last year of the second century of the county's history. This will indicate the volume and sweep of its functions in the middle of the twentieth century.

A consolidated revenue and expenditure statement for the year which ended June 30, 1952 follows:

Revenues

Other than for schools
1951 property taxes	$142,828.20
Back taxes	2,640.35
Tax penalities and costs	2,291.53
Tax on intangibles	8,299.48
Poll tax	1,500.00
Beer tax	19,195.65

ORANGE COUNTY—1752-1952

Beer and wine licenses	2,025.00	
Schedule B taxes	1,301.25	
Recorder's court	13,768.77	
Register of Deeds' fees	8,998.35	
Sheriff's fees	3,666.66	
Clerk of court's fees	3,357.69	
Sale of land	1,500.00	
Other local revenues	595.60	$211,968.53
Grants-in-aid		
Old age assistance	71,474.74	
Aid to dependent children	53,219.24	
Aid to disabled	7,505.50	
Boarding Home	2,068.14	
Welfare administration	11,412.13	
Veterans' Service	2,778.03	148,457.78
For Schools		
1951 property taxes	177,926.87	
Poll taxes	5,287.50	
Back taxes	2,532.95	
Tax penalties and costs	246.15	
Tax on intangibles	8,403.05	
Dog tax	2,386.30	
Fines and forfeitures	34,582.73	
Interest	1,446.70	
Sale of land	5,182.25	
Other local revenues	560.30	238,554.80
Grants-in-aid		
Vocational agriculture	8,544.00	
Home economics	8,279.33	
Jeannes Fund	100.00	16,923.33
Total		$ 615,904.44

Expenditures

Other than for schools		
General fund		
Superior Court	$ 4,799.97	
County jail	3,431.87	
Clerk of Superior Court's office	10,974.19	
Sheriff's office	22,828.80	
Register of Deeds' office	11,370.02	
County accountant and tax col.	17,089.23	
Extension Service	10,827.34	
Veterans' Service	2,778.03	
District library	1,700.00	
Other	17,280.28	103,079.73

Courthouse and jail improvements	6,588.62	
Public health	13,107.53	
Public welfare	190,973.26	
Recorder's court	5,073.84	
Debt service	32,866.34	248,609.59
Schools		
Current expense	102,485.24	
Capital outlays	131,258.33	
Debt service	31,213.44	264,957.01
Total		$616,646.33

Orange County remained a poor county until recent times. The creation of Alamance County in 1849 took from Orange the industry on its western edge, and the creation of Durham in 1881 snatched from her the budding industries on its eastern border. Except for the presence of the University, and it was a small institution until after World War I, any increase in wealth had to come mainly from agriculture, and it did not increase very fast. While assessed valuation for tax purposes is not a true measure of wealth, the slow increase in assessed valuation is nevertheless a significant barometer. The valuation for selected years follows:

1902	$ 2,355,792
1909	3,750,123
1913	4,280,276
1918	7,973,283
1920	6,994,966
1930	13,241,854
1940	16,551,426
1952	36,050,070

In 1952 the assessed value of Orange county's taxable property was $36,050,70. This includes only real estate and tangible personal property. Intangibles are taxed separately by the state at a lower rate than tangible property, with 80 per cent of the proceeds returned to the local units. The county tax rate in 1952 was $1.00 on a hundred dollars valuation. The assessed value may have averaged approximately 50 per cent of true value but, with prices rising steadily over a period of several years and with only a hasty reassessment in 1947, the board recognized that valuations probably varied quite widely from a norm. To correct inequalities and get all properties evaluated in accordance with scientific principles, expert appraisers have been employed to make the 1953 assessment.

The 1952 tax levy delivered to the tax collector in October, 1952 for collection in the ensuing eight months aggregated $402,956.30, and consisted of the following elements:

County property tax levy	$360,500.70
Chapel Hill special school district levy	28,594.60
Poll tax	9,184.00
Dog tax	3,946.00
Penalty for late listing	731.00

Orange County enters the third century of its history with a full coverage of public services, a moderate tax rate, only a modest debt, and a steadily growing tax base. Its activities are carried on by competent, devoted, and professionally-minded personnel. A new courthouse is rising to house with comfort and dignity the expanding agencies of a new era.

The new courthouse will neither supplant nor overshadow the present classic structure. It is designed to complement and, in a way, accent the restful lines and quiet beauty of that century old building. Built on the same axis, with a common courtyard, the two units symbolize the continuity of history. Just as the old courthouse reaches back to the middle of the nineteenth century, so the new one picks up in the middle of the twentieth and leads on into the future.

CHAPTER XV

AGRICULTURE AND RURAL LIFE

BY PAUL W. WAGER

With the Assistance of Don S. Matheson, County Agent

Although agriculture plays a less dominant role in the economy of the county than formerly, a third of the people live on farms and 20 per cent of the workers derive their livelihood directly from agriculture. Many others are dependent on agriculture to a greater or less degree.

Quality of Land

The county's natural endowments for agriculture are not particularly favorable. It has relatively little high quality soil. There are scattered spots of good soil, but most of its crop land will hardly rate higher than fair. At least it would have to be so characterized for general purposes. It is true that there is quite an extensive acreage of sandy land that is well adapted to tobacco, which of course is no mean asset. And it is also true that there are limited areas of excellent clay loam soils. But the dominant soils are silt loams which normally cannot be rated higher than fair to good. Some are definitely poor.

The Soil Conservation Service has made land use plans for about 1500 farms of the county based on the potentialities, or use capabilities, of the land. Six "use capability" classes of land are recognized. These are:

Class I. Very good land that can be cultivated safely with ordinary methods of good farming.
Class 2. Good land that can be cultivated safely with moderate conservation treatments.
Class 3. Moderately good land that can be cultivated safely with intensive conservation treatments.
Class 4. Fairly good land that can be cultivated occasionally if handled with great care but is better suited generally to pasture or hay.
Class 6. Land with hazards or limitations not too great generally for close growing forage.
Class 7. Hazards or limitations are so severe that this land is best suited generally for forestry.

The farms for which plans have been made embrace about 142,000 acres, whereas the total acreage in farms is 179,073. Assuming that the land class distribution in the farms which have been examined is representative of all of them, the use capability classifacation of all land in farms can be determined. It is given below, with the acreage in cultivation also shown.

	Total acreage	Acreage in cultivation
Class 1.	1,410	325
Class 2.	48,901	20,447
Class 3.	59,248	20,858
Class 4.	38,602	6,026
Class 6.	13,062	518
Class 7.	17,850	784
Total	179,073	48,958

In addition to inherent limitations, the soil resources of the county were for a long time being steadily depleted by erosion and faulty methods of cultivation. This deterioration began early and was accelerated by the poverty of the War and Reconstruction periods.

In 1869 J. W. Norwood of Hillsboro, in addressing the farmers of the county on agriculture, painted a dismal picture of conditions then existing. In describing the general practices in the county, he said:

> "All three of our great natural laws of agriculture have been disregarded and violated.
> 1. No remains of vegetable matter have by it been supplied as food to the growing crops.
> 2. No rotation of crops has been practiced—or nothing which deserves the name. But a ceaseless succession of corn and small grain without change, and without rest.
> 3. No precaution has been used to prevent the soil from being carried away by every washing rain.
> And behold the melancholy consequence of such a system of cultivation in the exhausted and worn out condition of our lands, as at this moment they lie spread out before us to our view. . .
> My friends, . . .a better system must be adopted, or the coming ruin now hastening with constantly increasing speed will soon be here."

This general impoverishment of the soil continued despite

the demonstrations in sound land use made by a few men like Norwood. If Orange suffered less than some other Piedmont counties, it was partly because, being hillier, less of the land was cleared. Again, Orange County may have fared less badly than some others, for the very mediocrity of its soil operated to check cash crop farming and tenancy and tended to preserve more livestock on the farms. Even so, agriculture continued to decline and the majority of the farms continued to deteriorate until comparatively recent years. Only within the last 20 years has there been notable progress.

The present progress can be attributed in large part to the educational and demonstration work done for the past 25 years by the Agricultural Extension Service. Through the years the County Agent has been observing and experimenting and, on the land of cooperating farmers, demonstrating sound farm practices. While the formula has differed in different parts of the county, it has generally involved more livestock, better breeds of livestock, improved pastures, more legumes and cover crops, less cotton, and in the tobacco areas no exclusive dependence on that crop. In more recent years his efforts have been supplemented by the Federal conservation program and the demonstration work of the Soil Conservation Service. The financial inducement offered for adopting soil-conserving practices plus the increased farm income resulting from crop control has enabled farmers to stop mining their land and begin the process of restoration. But the federal stimuli and the improved financial situation would not have produced such gratifying results had it not been for the foundations laid by the Extension Service.

In succeeding paragraphs a brief picture will be presented of present day agriculture in Orange County, together with some of the evidences of progress.

Land in Farms

Orange County has a land area of 254,729 acres. Of this total, 179,073 acres, or 70.3 per cent, are in farms. Although more than one-third of the land in farms is cropland, much of it is not being cultivated. In 1949 more than 8,000 acres were being used as pasture and over 16,000 acres were neither harvested or pastured. The increasing attention to livestock explains and warrants the use of considerable cropland for pasture. The large acreage which is yielding neither crops nor pasture is not so easy to justify. While no doubt some of it was fallow or being improved by conservation practices, much of it was probably idle. Permanent open pastures accounted for 8,500 acres, woodland pastures for about 14,000 acres, and non-pastured woodlands for 83,000 acres. More than half of the land in farms is therefore in woodland. This suggests the importance of the woodland in the economy of the average farm. Properly managed it can be a stabilizing element in the farm enterprise and an anchor of strength in time of adversity.

Land use on the farms of the county in 1949 is indicated below.

Land in Farms (2038 farms)	179,073 acres
Cropland harvested (1816 farms)	39,741 acres
Cropland pastured (781 farms)	8,624 acres
Cropland not harvested or pastured (1160 farms)	16,357 acres
Open pasture (694 farms)	8,519 acres
Woodland pastured (883 farms)	13,892 acres
Woodland not pastured (1480 farms)	83,204 acres
Other land (1816 farms)	8,736 acres

Size of Farms

In 1950, according to the United States Census, there were 2,038 farms in the County. Their average size was 87.9 acres, though this figure in itself is not very meaningful. The Census Bureau counts as a farm any tract of three acres or more if the value of farm products, exclusive of garden vegetables, raised on it exceeds $150. Even smaller tracts are counted if sales of farm produce exceed $150. Thus, there are in the county 180 farms under 10 acres in size. A classfication of the farms by size follows:

Size Class	Number	Total acreage
Under 10 acres	180	996
10 - 49 acres	667	16,738
50 - 99 acres	557	39,744
100 - 179 acres	405	52,946

180 - 259 acres	132	27,825
260 - 499 acres	79	27,039
Over 500 acres	18	13,785

The farms of the county have tended to become smaller through the years as a result of subdivision. Now, for the first time, at least since slavery days, consolidation of farms has begun to take place. While the trend is not yet pronounced, the awakened interest in livestock has been accompanied by the emergence of several big farms. The 1950 Census disclosed 18 farms of over 500 acres. These 18 farms embraced 13,785 acres, which means they averaged 766 acres. These, it should be noted, are operating units; there are more than 18 ownerships in excess of 500 acres. The dominant type of farm in the county is nevertheless a small one, the median farm being about 63 acres.

Most of the farmers in Orange County are small operators. Sixty per cent of the 1816 farms which reported harvested crops in 1949 harvested less than 20 acres, and less than 8 per cent of them as much as 50 acres. A distribution of the farms by harvested acres follows:

Cropland harvested per farm	No. of farms
Under 10 acres	567
10 - 19 acres	526
20 - 29 acres	307
30 - 49 acres	275
50 - 99 acres	107
100 - 199 acres	27
Over 200 acres	7

The fact that about one-half of the farms raise tobacco, which requires much hand labor, helps explain the small acreages cultivated on so many farms. The 141 farms which cultivate 50 acres or more do, of course, reflect the mechanization which is taking place in the production of most crops.

Land Tenure

About one-fourth of the farmers of the county own none of the land which they cultivate. Nevertheless the tenancy ratio has been declining in recent years. In 1920 there were 765 farm tenants in the county and in 1950 only 528. The change which took place between 1940 and 1950 is indicated by comparing the tenure figures for these two years.

	1940	1950
Full owners	1,211	1,260
Part owners	142	246
Managers	3	4
Tenants	687	528
Total	2,043	2,038

The amount of land held in 1950 under each form of tenure is shown separately below for white and Negro farmers:

White	Farms	Total	Average Acreage per farm
Full owners	1049	104,981	100.1
Part owners	180	28,399	157.2
Managers	3	1,503	501.0
Tenants	236	14,374	60.9
Negro			
Full owners	211	12,368	58.6
Part owners	66	4,338	65.7
Managers	1	170	170.0
Tenants	292	13,040	44.7
Total	2,038	179,073	

The full owners occupy farms which average 93.1 acres whereas those occupied by tenants average only 51.9 acres. The small size of the farms cultivated by tenants is due to the fact that a large proportion of them are tobacco farms. When the farms are classified by race of operator, it will be noted that those occupied by white operators average larger in all tenure categories than those occupied by Negroes.

Value of Farm Products

In 1949 the products sold from Orange County farms brought the growers $3,591,887. Of this sum $3,390,543 went to the operators of 1179 commercial farms and $201,344 to the operators of 611 other farms. Thus the commercial farms had an average cash income of $2,875. When added to shelter, fuel, and a considerable portion of the family food supply, this income, though by no means a net cash income, can support a comfortable standard of living.

The 1949 income is nearly 20 per cent greater than in 1944 when war-time prices prevailed, and therefore reflects mainly increased volume rather than higher prices. The comparative figures for the two years are given below by type of product.

	1944	1949
Field crops	$1,939,720	$2,083,660
Vegetables and fruits	45,425	14,566
Dairy products	404,995	599,431
Poultry and poultry products	367,312	493,036
Other livestock and livestock products	183,495	232,077
Forest products	43,566	169,117
Total	$2,894,513	$3,591,887

It will be noted that there was a more pronounced increase in livestock and livestock products than in crops. Except for a modest but steady expansion in tobacco production, there has been no increase in the production of crops for sale. More hay and grain is fed to livestock, which is a desirable trend.

The 1949 crop production both consumed and sold, as reported by the Census, is detailed below:

Crop	Farms	Acres	Value of Crop
Tobacco	938	4,088	$1,869,830
Corn for grain	1551	12,299	542,205
Cotton	81	220	27,318
Lespedza and red clover seed	111	946	20,846
Corn for silage	59	587	
Wheat	494	4,224	115,914
Oats threshed	337	2,892	76,191
Barley threshed	74	488	12,128
Soybeans ''	44	355	13,726
Cowpeas ''	9	26	404
Alfalfa hay	123	605	55,085
Clover	146	999	35,680
Lespedeza hay	1089	9,693	310,806
Oats cut green	287	1,166	39,061
Other small grains cut green	124	663	18,425

Soybean hay	234	1,107	43,650
Cowpeas cut for hay	27	66	1,937
Other hay	168	881	21,547
All other crops			87,434
			$3,292,187

Crops

Tobacco—Tobacco is Orange county's largest money crop, and for the past ten years its growth has been exceedingly profitable. In 1952 the tobacco growers of the county planted 4,795 acres, from which they harvested approximately 5,175,000 pounds. It brought an average of 50 cents a pound or a total of $2,637,250. Even larger sums were derived from the crop the two previous years. Comparative figures for several recent years are given below:

Year	Acreage	Average Yield	Average Price	Gross Sales
1939	5350	855 lbs.	15.2	$ 693,000
1942	3653	746 lbs.	40.0	1,090,055
1945	4775	1,132 lbs.	45.0	2,148,000
1948	4160	1,192 lbs.	50.8	2,518,330
1949	4088	1,010 lbs.	46.6	1,920,850
1950	4380	1,264 lbs.	55.0	3,044,976
1951	4791	1,284 lbs.	54.0	3,321,887
1952	4795	1,100 lbs.	50.0	2,637,250

Since 1940 tobacco acreage has been allotted to individual growers with compliance enforced as a result of a referendum on compulsory control supported by over 90 per cent of the growers. The control of tobacco acreage has had beneficial effects other than its effect on price. It has improved the quality and yield of the crop. Fifteen years ago most of the crop grown in the county was harvested by cutting, and the average yield was a little over 500 pounds per acre. Now practically all the crop is primed, and in normal years the yield is 1200 pounds or more per acre. Farmers have almost universally improved their fertilization and cultural methods. The use of extra potash is becoming commonplace. Nevertheless, the profitableness of growing tobacco fluctuates widely from year to year, depending on price, weather, and disease. Blue Mold and Granville wilt have been the two most dreaded enemies of the crop, the latter having made its first appearance in 1939. However, new wilt resistant varieties have proven 90 per cent resistant. Good results are also being obtained with a new Blue Mold control spray.

However, a new disease appeared first in 1943 which rivals wilt in its destructiveness. This is the so-called black shank disease which has spread rapidly over the tobacco belt. Already a seed resistant to it has been developed, but experience indicates that plants are not wholly immune to the disease. Its attack appears to be less damaging, however, if tobacco is not planted on land which was in tobacco the year before. With good tobacco land as scarce as it is, growers are naturally reluctant to take this precaution.

The county is fortunate in that so many of its farms contain land suitable to the growth of tobacco, for tobacco constitutes an excellent source of cash income. There is always the danger, however, that the lure of cash will cause concentration on tobacco to the exclusion of food and feed crops, a practice which has often proved to be destructive to the land and disastrous to the people who cultivate it. The enforced curtailment of tobacco production has caused many farmers to expand their feed and livestock operations with the discovery that the more balanced practice yields a more certain income and probably on the average no less total income. It also improves the land, raises the general standard of living, and makes for a more stable community. If crop controls were removed, however, it is not improbable that some of these farmers would be enticed again to stake everything on tobacco.

Cotton—Twenty years ago cotton was a major crop in the county, the Census reporting 3,206 acres grown in 1929 but yielding only 1349 bales. Since then the crop has been steadily displaced by tobacco, livestock and poultry. By 1940 only 179 acres were planted although the acreage allotment under the AAA was 1,893 acres. In 1949 only 220 acres were raised despite the relatively high price. This trend is to be desired, for cotton growing in Orange County is conducive to erosion and soil depletion.

Corn—Corn is the county's most widely planted crop, about 15,000 acres being planted each year. The yields have been low.

From 1910 to 1930 they averaged about 15 bushels per acre, and from 1930 to 1945 only about 20 bushels. Not until the introduction of hybrid corn and new methods of fertilization did there begin to be substantially higher yields.

In 1945, four corn demonstrations were conducted along lines recommended by the North Carolina Experiment Station. The demonstrators were John H. Brown of Rougemont, W. C. Cole of Chapel Hill, Walter Reitzel of Efland, and R. M. Anderson of Cedar Grove. The results of the demonstrations indicated that the yield of corn could be more than doubled by the use of hybrid corn, flat shallow cultivation, thick spacing and plenty of nitrogen.

Then for several successive years a corn growing contest was sponsored by the Bank of Chapel Hill in which at least 50 growers competed each year. In 1947 the winner, Clyde Roberts, made 93.3 bushels of N. C. Hybrid 26 on one acre, while the average yield of all contestants was 61.9 bushels. In 1948 eleven competitors made more than 100 bushels per acre and the winner, J. L. Phelps, of the sandy tobacco section of the county, made 136.4 bushels. The average yield was 86.9 bushels.

While these high yields are still the exception, the county average has been brought up to 30 bushels, and Orange county farmers now produce 100,000 more bushels of corn than they did ten years ago on 2,000 fewer acres.

In addition to there being more corn grown for grain, there has been a pronounced increase in the acreage cut green for silage. There are now at least 85 silos on Orange county farms.

Small Grain—For a long time the county witnessed a progressive decline in the acreage devoted to small grain. The acreage in wheat is still decreasing though the yield per acre is improving. The growing of oats had almost reached the vanishing point when about 1930 the tide turned, and there has been a sharp upswing in both acreage and yield since. The decennial census figures are revealing.

	Wheat		Oats	
	Acreage	Yield per A	Acreage	Yield per A
1889	15,538	7.1 bu.	9736	8.0 bu.

1899	13,052	5.0 bu.	6066	7.4 bu.
1909	10,234	7.8 bu.	3057	9.2 bu.
1919	13,464	6.6 bu.	493	10.0 bu.
1929	7,750	9.0 bu.	210	16.7 bu.
1939	5,831	10.0 bu.	1217	22.8 bu.
1949	4,224	14.1 bu.	2892	32.1 bu.

The old practice was to follow corn with small grain, but the yields were so pitifully small that it is not surprising that less and less was sown. With better seed, better land use practices, and low cost fertilizer, there have been better yields and, as a result, a new interest in small grain. The shift from cotton production to live stock and dairying has, of course, increased the demand for feed.

Small grain, either wheat or oats, with lespedeza, is now a part of the rotation on almost every farm. The yields from improved varities of oats have been particularly impressive. On 30 demonstrations in 1951 growing the New Arlington variety, the average yield was 68 bushels per acre. To stimulate the use of superior varieties of seed, the Chapel Hill Rotary Club each year offers $50 in prizes for the best yields on fields on which experiment station recommendations are followed.

The growing of barley is also on the increase and several new varieties offer great possibilities. The renewed interest in small grain is encouraging, for in addition to providing feed for livestock it means a cover crop on more land during the winter months.

Hay—One of the most encouraging developments in Orange county agriculture has been the steady improvement in the quality of the hay crops and pastures without which there could not have been the expansion which has taken place in dairying and live stock. The decennial census figures are illuminating. Listed below are the types and acreages of hay reported cut in 1909, 1929 and 1949.

1909		1929		1949	
Type	Acres	Type	Acres	Type	Acres
Tame hay	1185	Alfalfa	68	Alfalfa	605
Grain cut green	198	Clovers	870	Clover	
Coarse forage	105	Lespedeza	2135	and timothy	999

Wild hay	1423	Grain cut green	130	Lespedeza	9693
		Other tame grasses	684	Grain cut green	663
		Wild grass	525	Other hay	825
	2911		4412		12785

Forty years ago some clover was grown, alone or in mixture, but sixty per cent of the limited amount of hay cut consisted of the wild native grasses. By 1919 Korean lespedeza had been introduced and numerous farmers had been induced to try it. Nearly a thousand acres were grown in the county that year. This valuable legume was soon in wide use as a winter cover crop and soil builder as well as the chief source of hay. It is probably fair to state that the renaissance of agriculture in Orange county, as in the South generally, began with the widespread use of this plant. It has been called the poor man's alfalfa. It is still the most important hay crop.

There has nevertheless been a steady expansion in the growth of alfalfa, the choicest of all hays. In 1919 only 32 acres are reported, and ten years later only 68 acres. However, by 1949 it was being grown on 123 farms, a total of 605 acres. It is not grown more extensively partly because of the expense involved in getting it started and partly because farmers have had the impression that their soil was not adapted to it. The latter is not usually the case, for it has been demonstrated that alfalfa can be grown sucessfully on any good well-drained land that is properly prepared before seeding. This means not only the liming of acid soils but also the addition of borax.

The increased production of livestock and poultry has created a serious protein shortage, and alfalfa is the best protein hay that can be grown. It has about twice the digestible protein of lespedeza and clover hay, five times that of grass hays, and three times the digestible protein of good corn silage. Moreover, alfalfa contains larger quantities of calcium and also Vitamin A. An expanded acreage of this important crop is therefore much to be desired.

There has been increasing use of other improved grasses and legumes. The application of ground limestone secured through the AAA program has been a major factor in achieving this gain. There has been a large increase in the acreage of Crimson Clover, Red Clover, and other clovers and grasses, and away from the rough forages.

Along with better hay has come better ways of handling it. Side delivery rakes are commonplace but hay loaders are already giving place to pick-up hay balers. The 1950 census reported 59 of these in the county. In 1951 three farmers installed hay curing systems in their barns.

Pastures

The shift to or toward a grass economy means improved pastures quite as much as improved meadows. Indeed as the quality of the pastures improves and the length of the grazing season increases, the less is the dependence on forage. Here in the South where the weather is mild eight or nine months in the year, the attainment of more and better pastures is the logical first step toward a better balanced agriculture, and that has been the emphasis of the Extension Service in Orange county. The establishment of pastures has been wonderfully aided by the benefit payments made available since 1933 through the Conservation Program. Each year two or three thousand tons of lime and hundreds of tons of fertilizer have been used in establishing or improving pastures. Now this phase of the program, though not completed, is well advanced. Hence, the management stage, involving careful fertilization, grazing rotations, clipping, and other good managerial practices must be promoted. This is being done. As a part of the educational effort, every high school, both white and colored, participated in 1951 in a grassland oratorical contest. The Hillsboro Branch of the Durham Bank and Trust Company gave $75 in prizes to the winners. The Orange county winners competed with the winners in other counties in a district contest. The Bank of Chapel Hill has also sponsored a pasture improvement contest, the winner in each of ten neighborhoods receiving an attractive farm sign as his reward.

No greater stimulus to pasture improvement in the South could have been conceived than that which has resulted from the introduction of ladino clover. Succulent, rich in protein, hardy, and with a tolerance of almost any kind of soil, it promises to be as great a boon to the South as lespedeza a generation ago. Mixed with other grassess it doubles and trebles the grazing capacity of pastures.

In 1945 there was not an acre of ladino clover in the county. In 1946 half a dozen farmers seeded experimental plots. As a result of these demonstrations, the following year about 200 farmers tried out this amazing new legume, seeding over 1000 acres. Each year since, from 1500 to 2000 acres have been seeded. Experience has shown that ladino clover alone is too rich a diet for livestock, causing bloat, so it is sown with other grasses, most commonly alta fescue or orchard grass. The ease with which excellent pastures can now be developed offers great hope for accelerated progress toward a balanced agriculture even in the tobacco belt. To cite one example, J. R. Whitfield, who converted an old tobacco field to grassland farming, has discontinued the raising of tobacco entirely and now has all his open land seeded to ladino clover grass mixture except about ten acres on which he raises corn. Incidentally, he has averaged over 70 bushels of corn per acre for the past four years. He has his pasture divided into ten lots, grazes 48 beef cattle, and cuts enough hay from these lots to winter the cattle. Several dairymen in the county are now for the first time grazing pastures in December.

Livestock

Dairying—For several years the county has witnessed a steady increase in dairying, and since 1941 the expansion has been pronounced. There are now more than 100 commercial Grade A dairymen marketing milk for consumption in the fluid state. All of them are on an electric line, using water under pressure, electric refrigeration, and other mechanical facilities. At least sixty are using electric milking machines. These dairymen are intelligent and scientific in their production methods. They have not only sought to meet the ever more exacting requirements of the health authorities, but they have stressed economical production through lower feed costs, improved pastures, the elimination of disease, better housing conditions, and more scientific breeding.

Through the years the tested purebred herds of George Watts Hill at Quail Roost Farm in Durham county and of Howard W. Odum at Chapel Hill have done much to improve the quality of dairy cattle and promote the dairy industry. In 1952, there were 1241 dairy cows bred artificially to proven sires, including some of the best in the nation.

In 1944 the Latta Cooperative Dairy was organized and built a small milk plant in Hillsboro. This plant, with a 500 gallon capacity, began operations in June, 1945. For several years it provided a market for the milk produced by thirty farmers located near Hillsboro; it operated milk routes in Hillsboro, Mebane and Durham.

The Farmers Cooperative Dairy, Inc., a larger cooperative organization whose membership included most of the other dairymen of the county as well as many in Chatham and Durham counties, was organized about the same time. Late in 1945 it constructed a large plant in Chapel Hill and early in 1946 this plant got into operation. It is equipped with the most modern machinery not only for handling fluid milk but for the manufacture of butter, ice cream, and condensed milk.

In 1949 these two cooperatives merged and then, in order to have an outlet in Durham, purchased the Long Meadow Dairies plant in Durham county. In effect, the three organizations merged, the new organization taking the Long Meadow name. Processing was discontinued in Hillsboro, but continues in Chapel Hill.

A good local market for Grade A milk has stimulated commercial dairying, and in nearly all parts of the county there are now fine looking dairy farms with gambrel roofed barns, silos, milking parlors and the lush fields and pastures which are the earmarks of a dairy region. The change in the landscape in fifteen years has been truly remarkable.

The sale of dairy products now constitutes the second largest source of income to Orange county farmers, approximating $700,000 a year.

Beef Cattle—The farmers of Orange County have recently developed an interest in beef cattle. In 1942 more than a hundred beef cows and heifers were brought into the county and many pure bred bulls placed. The Farmers Exchange Market bought the Hereford bull which won first place at the State Fair. Fourteen 4-H Club boys bought Hereford heifers. In succeeding years there has been no wild rush into the beef cattle business, but rather a healthy development of several small beef cattle herds. Quite properly farmers gave concurrent attention to pastures and winter feed production. Nevertheless, the high price of beef stimulated a steady expansion and the 1950 Census reported 885 beef cattle two years old and older. Numerous business and professional men have bought farm land and started the raising of beef cattle. All breeds are being used in the county with Hereford and Angus predominating.

In 1951 there were several beef cattle sales and one feeder calf sale in the county at which 182 head sold for an average of 36 cents a pound at the Durham Fat Stock show; 4-H Club members fitted and exhibited 15 fat steers. This was the largest group exhibited by any county. Ten were awarded blue ribbons, four red ribbons, and one a white one. In the fall of 1951 thirty-three 4-H Club members purchased feeder calves, 26 feeding for the first time.

Swine—Until recently the county has been deficient in swine production. With excess corn and a good market provided by a local packing plant and an auction market, the conditions favorable to a profitable enterprise were present. But only within the last six years have the farmers capitalized in any substantial way on these factors. Much of the progress has been achieved by way of 4-H Clubs, which in turn was sparked by the Chapel Hill Rotary Club and the Sears-Roebuck Foundation. The former, led by Dr. W. G. Chrisman, promoted a Spotted Poland China chain among 4-H club members in the southern part of the county, and the latter in the northern part of the county. From these small beginnings, the industry has expanded until now more than 200 farm families own purebred Spotted Poland China hogs. Many families who never kept brood sows before are now keeping from one to four sows. Many others who started with one or two just a few years ago now have ten or twelve brood sows. In the spring of 1951, the demand for good breeding stock was so great that local breeders could not supply the demand.

In 1947, an Orange County Spotted Poland China Breeders Association was organized. Four years later it had 65 members and had become well known and highly regarded throughout North Carolina and nearby states. Its members have shown and sold animals in numerous state shows and sales, at state fairs, and at the Durham Fat Stock Show. They have made an excellent showing in all of these events and on several occasions a member has won the award for showing a grand champion.

In addition to the breeding of purebred swine, much interest is being shown in the commericial feeding of hogs. There is a ready market for top quality hogs. The Piedmont Packing Company uses several hundred hogs each week, and a local hog buying station has been established at the Farmers' Mutual Livestock Market. With plenty of ladino clover pastures, swine grazing and feeding has become a profitable enterprise in the county, and it is a common sight to see thirty or forty shoats grazed out on ladino pastures. Such a sight was seldom seen five years ago.

Poultry and Eggs—In the last decade there has been a tremendous increase in poultry production, the Farmers Mutual Exchange, working with the Extension Service, taking the lead in promoting the expansion. About 1940 the Exchange installed a 30,000-egg all electric incubator and farmers throughout the county with blood tested high producing flocks supplied it with eggs. It not only advanced the baby chicks but furnished a dependable market for eggs and broilers. Several smaller commercial hatcheries were also established. In the last ten years scores of new poultry houses and range shelters have been constructed, the Extension Service usually furnishing the plans. Several commercial egg producers have experimented with hybrid chickens with promising results.

The sale of poultry products now represents the third largest source of farm income, the gross return from poultry and eggs in 1951 reaching one-half million dollars. Orange County producers specialize in laying hens, the number reported in the 1950 Census being 122,000. The trend is toward larger units, and several farmers handle from 2,000 to 4,000 layers.

The members of New Sharon Church, most of whom are poultrymen, built a $50,000 church in 1949 and paid for it in one year.

Although the emphasis has been on layers, there are several broiler producers. In 1951 Jack Kirk of the Orange Grove community built a broiler house 220 by 36 feet and has brooded 10,000 chicks at a time. The house is almost completely automatic in that it is equipped with two endless chain type of feeders, automatic drinking water fountains, and gas heated brooders. It is claimed that with this type of house one man could look after 50,000 chicks. Brooding by means of infra-red electric lights has been tried experimentally. Lantham Latta brooded 2,000 this way, the cost of electric current being only 2.8 cents apiece.

Farmers Exchange

A strong factor in promoting livestock and diversified agriculture in Orange County during the last two decades has been the Farmers Exchange, Inc. This cooperative association was organized in March, 1930 by 400 farmers and farm leaders in Durham and adjoining counties for the purpose of marketing diversified farm products and securing for farmers high quality farm supplies at the lowest practical cost. Today the Exchange has about 4,100 members in Durham, Orange, Chatham, Granville, and Person counties, and does a business in excess of $10,000,000 a year. It pays the farmers the highest price for farm produce and charges the lowest for supplies that is consistent with sound fiscal policy. Earnings have been used to pay interest dividends to stock owned by patron members, to maintain necessary working capital and equipment, to set up reasonable reserves, and to pay patronage dividends to patrons.

The savings that have been enjoyed by its patrons cannot be measured. Of even greater benefit than the immediate financial savings has been the stimulus which the services of the Exchange have given to a balanced agricultural economy. A ready cash market for farm surpluses has been a great encouragement to diversification. So also has been the opportunity to buy approved supplies and equipment at substantial savings. But the Exchange has been more than a buying and selling agency; it has provided facilities for processing some of the things the farmer buys or sells. It operates a feed mill, a seed cleaning plant, grain storage bins, a poultry and egg processing plant, a baby chick hatchery, a live stock market, and a modern slaughterhouse.

Two branch units of the Exchange are operated in Orange County, one at Hillsboro and one at Carrboro. In the year which ended June 30, 1952, these two units purchased $303,096 worth of farm produce and sold $1,149,392 worth of farm supplies. Since many who live near Durham market through that warehouse, these figures do not represent county totals. The unit at Carrboro was not opened until March, 1945.

Although the Farmers Exchange is in a solid financial condition and enjoys the confidence and support of the farmers of five counties, it took faith, courage and patience to establish and nurture this venture in cooperation. As is so often the case, it had a far-seeing and benevolent sponsor in the person of Honorable John Sprunt Hill of Durham. He may rightly be called the father and founder of the Exchange. His deep interest in farm life and farm people and his longing to see this an area of livestock and balanced farming explain his willingness to foster and underwrite the venture. Through the years he has been not only its inspired leader but his financial contributions, his moral support, and his loyal patronage have sustained it in days of adversity. Its roots are now firmly planted in the economic life of the area but no cooperative movement can afford to discontinue its educational work.

Livestock Auction Market

Through the mutual efforts of the Extension Service and the Farmers Exchange there has been established at Hillsboro a modern livestock auction market. The County gave the land, the town of Hillsboro installed an automatic watering system, and the Farmers Exchange built and is operating the livestock barn. The first sale was held November 6, 1941. Each Monday a sale of all kinds of cattle and hogs is held under the strict supervision of the State Department of Agriculture and local veterinarians. It is patronized by farmers for 50 miles around, and it is not unusual for 500 to 700 farmers, stockmen and buyers to be present. The first year $150,000 worth of livestock was sold, and by 1951 the figure had grown to $1,100,000.

Farmers bring their livestock in the forenoon for weighing and tagging. All cattle to be sold for breeders are tested and all hogs sold as breeders or feeders vaccinated to prevent spread of disease on farms. A commission of 4 per cent is charged for selling the livestock through the market. Only half the fee is charged if there is no sale, that is, if the seller is unwilling to accept the best bid. However, the numerous buyers provide wholesome competition and most animals brought to the market are sold. Not only are the farmers able to sell their fat stock and surplus animals advantageously but they can buy selectively to fill their needs.

Buyers with wide experience have complimented the Exchange on the excellent arrangement of the stock pen and auction ring and on the competent manner in which the market is operated. All sales are for cash.

Abattoir

In the summer of 1943 the Farmers Mutual Exchange erected an abattoir on Occoneechee Farm, adjacent to the Livestock Market. Here the farmers may bring for slaughter their cattle and hogs and return the next day and get their meat ready for consumption or preservation. The service is performed at cost. It is estimated that, because of inexperience and inadequate facilities, one-third of the meat from home-slaughtered animals has been lost through waste and spoilage. Centralized slaughtering will prevent much of this waste. Moreover, the abattoir may later have facilities for salvaging most of the by-products of the slaughterhouse.

This new venture in cooperative action is of course made possible by modern transportation and modern refrigeration. Formerly farmers had no choice other than to raise and slaughter their own meat animals or to buy meat at retail in the local markets. Through cooperation they may now be relieved largely of both drawbacks. Farmers with electricity in their homes are not yet utilizing it fully for refrigeration purposes though many have bought standard refrigerators of small capacity.

Farm Forestry

Orange County farmers have generally displayed less foresight and consequently have made less progress in the management of their woodland than in other aspects of the farm enterprise. Since 1942 the part-time services of a state forester have been available and some farmers have made the most of it, but many continue to take the short-run view when it comes to forestry. A few excerpts from the 1947 report of V. G. Watkins, the farm forester in the county that year, reveal a situation which has both hopeful and discouraging aspects.

> Efforts were continued during the past year to get Orange County farmers interested in the rudiments of farm woodland management. The various agricultural workers and agencies in the county cooperated in a fine way...Several thinning demonstrations were held... It is believed that such demonstrations are distinctly worthwhile, even though many of those farmers in attendance will need extra encouragement and personal assistance before doing very much thinning or improvement work in their own woods...Many of them are still ready to reply to the suggestion that a thinning is needed with the statement: 'Pines will thin themselves.' Yes, it is true, pines will thin themselves eventually and to some extent. These farmers must be made to realize, however, that this is the expensive way of growing timber—expensive in time, taxes, and total timber volume produced.
>
> The major portion of the forester's time was spent with individual farmers needing assistance in the measuring and marketing of their timber. A few areas of selectively cut timber have been added this year. In the largest number of cases, however, the farm owner is more interested in finding out the amount of timber which he has than in the best way to cut that area so as to provide for a second harvest in 15 or 20 years.
>
> The sawmill operators...agree that they are now cutting pine timber which averages much smaller in diameter than 15 or 20 years ago. This means that the pine growing stock is gradually being depleted.

Perhaps the most significant advance in farm forestry in Orange County in recent years has been the opening of a new market for farmer-produced forest products. The Farmers Mutual Exchange began operating a wood yard at their Carrboro warehouse in 1947. They began by accepting pulpwood. Farmers were allowed to bring in any amount which they could cut, from a wagon load on up. They received cash on the spot, as it was measured. Since that time several pulpwood buying stations have been developed by the pulpwood industry. Farmers are being advised and encouraged to cut this pulpwood in the form of thinnings and improvement cuttings.

For the last four or five years there has been a market also for white oak timber for barrel staves. Such timber is bought either on the stump or in blocks. Oak is also bought by the Hines Liner Company of Hillsboro to be used in making liners for tobacco hogsheads. There is also a market for cedar poles and each year hundreds of loads are taken from Orange County woodlands. Finally, a limited amount of dogwood is sold to be used in making shuttles.

Farm Mechanization

Although Orange County is characterized by small farms, only 30 per cent of them containing more than 100 acres and only 20 per cent of them harvesting more than 30 acres, the degree of mechanization is striking. According to the 1950 census, 123 farms had grain combines, 21 corn pickers, 59 pick-up hay balers, and 56 milking machines. There were 778 tractors on 659 farms, and 635 motor trucks on 554 farms. Despite the large number of tractors and motor trucks, there were still 1240 farms which had work stock. This can be attributed in part to the usefulness of a horse or mule in cultivating tobacco. Although one is apt to assume that every farmer has an automobile, the census figures disclose that one-third of the farmers of the county do not have one. There are 1750 automobiles on 1314 farms. Probably some farmers without a passenger car do have a truck.

Rural Electrification

The first rural electric line built in the United States with Federal funds was constructed in Orange County. This was in 1933. The line, which extended for three miles from Chapel Hill to Calvander, was erected as a CWA project, Henry S. Hogan, George Lawrence and Don Matheson being the principal sponsors. They worked up the project and when money ran short the Hogan Brothers furnished 30 foot cedar poles on which to string the wires. Success in this project prompted the Calvander

Grange to work up and submit another one which resulted in a ten mile line from Calvander to Orange Grove. Local farmers put up $2,000 to supplement government funds.

Shortly after the construction of these first lines, a survey was made of the entire county and a project submitted requesting federal assistance in the construction of approximately 150 miles of line. The proposal received favorable comment but was not approved as a work relief project. However, after the North Carolina Rural Electrification Authority was organized in 1935, assistance was sought and secured from that quarter. In 1939, an REA cooperative, now known as the Piedmont Electric Membership Corporation, was organized to serve Orange, Person, Caswell and Alamance counties. Later it merged with a cooperative serving Durham and Granville counties, and in the six county area there are now about 1100 miles of line serving over 4,000 rural customers These lines have been built with funds loaned from the Federal REA which are being repaid from service charges. The Piedmont Electric Membership Corporation has its headquarters in Hillsboro in an attractive new building erected in 1949.

Orange county now rates high among rural counties in electrification, The census reports that 1609 farms had electricity in 1950, and some additional farms have obtained current since. The situation is not so good in respect to telephones. In 1945 only 43 farms had telephones and in 1950 the number had increased only to 165. Again, there has been some expansion in the last three years, but the percentage of farms with telephone service is still small.

Agricultural Conservation Program

It has been a national policy since 1933 to give financial assistance to farmers who adopt land use practices conducive to soil improvement. In its early years the program was a part of the effort to discourage price-depressing surpluses of certain crops and the administering agency was known as the Agricultural Adjustment Administration. Since 1945 the agency has been called the Production and Marketing Administration. However the program has always been locally administered.

In Orange County, as elsewhere, there is a county committee and several community committees, each of which has three active members and two alternates. The members of each of Orange County's ten community committees are elected by the eligible farmers of the respective communities, and the county committeemen are elected by delegates to a county convention. James S. Compton has been chairman of the county committee since its formation. Eligible farmers are those who have five or more acres of cropland, either as owner or tenant—a total of about 1400.

The county committee, in collaboration with other agricultural agencies in the county, determines which of the approved conservation practices will qualify for benefit payments, the bases of priority, and other matters of policy. The local committees recommend conservation practices to be encouraged, determine acreage allotments and allocate funds available. They also handle price support operations, including commodity loans and purchases.

Through the years, the program has enabled farmers to secure lime, superphosphate, grass seed, and other materials essential to the improvement of their farms with part of the cost borne by the federal government. Since 1946 the annual allocation to Orange County has averaged at least $50,000. In recent years the program has given a big boost to the efforts of farmers to provide more and better pastures. In 1950 approximately 700 Orange County farmers seeded 3,244 acres of permanent pastures with 50 per cent of the "out of pocket" cost furnished through the PMA. Pasture seed, made available to participating farmers through the program's purchase order system, included 6,489 pounds of ladino clover, 31,212 pounds of orchard grass, and 5,922 pounds of fescue. Moreover, the seed so obtained was of very high quality, meeting the most rigid germination and purity tests.

In 1952 an additional 1,583 acres of permanent pasture were seeded with PMA contributing heavily to the cost of the seed. Other assistance included 2,441 tons of lime spread on 180 farms, superphosphate furnished to 46 farmers, and the distribution of mixed fertilizer to top dress 5,100 acres of crops. A total of 687 farmers received assistance in one form or another to the value of $45,412.

When certain conservation practices become widely established in a county the farm leaders believe that the subsidy should be withdrawn from these particular practices and used to stimulate other practies in the interest of the national welfare which many farmers would not be likely to carry out without some financial assistance. There was a shift toward this policy in Orange County in 1952 and it is being even more emphasized in 1953. Every farm was visited by at least one member of the local committee, and note taken of any conservation plan developed for the farm with the assistance of a State or Federal agency. The farm operator was then given an opportunity to request PMA assistance in carrying out the practice or practices which he and the committee considered most urgent. Conservation practices eligible for PMA assistance in 1953 include the following: (1) applying lime to farmland, (2) applying superphosphate, potash, or basic slag to eligible crops, (3) establishing a winter cover crop of crimson clover, (4) establising a winter cover crop of small grain, (5) establishing or improving a permanent pasture, (6) increasing the acreage of alfalfa, (7) building terraces to control the flow of water on sloping land, (8) establishing sod waterways, (9) planting kudzu or lespedeza sericea on steep slopes or in waterways, (10) planting forest trees, and (11) improving a stand of timber.

The sum of $36,000 was made available for benefit payments in 1953, compared to $46,000 in 1952, and $52,000 in 1951. The theory is that the number of beneficiaries and the amount of assistance should taper off as farmers learn what constitutes sound conservation practices, find that it is to their economic advantage to observe these practices, and accrue enough working capital to make the investment. In a county which a decade ago had many marginal farmers, the financial inducement offered by the program has been a powerful incentive to conservation farming. While a majority of the farmers may no longer need the "crutch", there are still many who do.

Neuse River Soil Conservation District

Another federally sponsored conservation program, using a somewhat different approach and unrelated to crop control, is what was first called the Soil Erosion Service, then the Soil Conservation Service. Since 1952 its work is referred to officially as the Agricultural Resources Conservation program. It considers its program a long range one, and its approach is to plan the long-run use of a whole farm in terms of its inherent capabilities. It operates through Soil Conservation Districts created under state enabling legislation.

The Neuse River Soil Conservation District was established in 1938. The district embraces Durham, Johnston, Orange, Wake and Wilson counties. Work was started in Orange county in 1939. The basic purpose of the program is to assist farmers in bringing about adjustments in the use and treatment of their land that will conserve soil and water and improve fertility. Farmers who desire the technical and engineering advice furnished by the Service enter into an agreement to cooperate with the district in making the land use adjustments and in applying the conservation practices that are mutually agreed upon. The technicians then examine the farm carefully and classify each part of it in terms of its use capabilities, and make a farm plan on the basis of these land resources. The land may be classified into as many as eight different classes. Land classes I to IV are considered suitable for cultivation but with different degrees of intensity and carefulness. Thus, Class I is "very good land that can be cultivated safely with ordinary methods of good farming," while Class IV is "fairly good land that can be cultivated occasionally if handled with great care but is better suited generally to pasture or hay." Classes V to VIII are not suitable for cultivation. Thus, Class VII is land with hazards or limitations so severe that it is best suited generally for forestry. The plan that is worked out does not always represent the ideal in conservation but rather is as advanced a step in that direction as the economic circumstances and limited experience of the farmer will permit. The full plan is not always put into effect the first year; weather factors and other practical considerations sometimes interfere. On the other hand, a cooperator will sometimes go further in making sound land use adjustments than he originally committed himself to do.

As of June, 1953 plans had been prepared for 1265 farms in Orange County covering about 142,000 acres. This represents about 60 per cent of the farms in the county and a much higher percentage of the larger and better ones. The type and extent of the land use adjustments called for in the agreements are summarized below:

Contour farming	9,063	acres
Cover cropping	4,913	,,
Stubble mulching	3,220	,,
Strip cropping	1,825	,,
Pasture improvement	12,685	,,
Seeding permanent pasture	5,984	,,
Woodland management	10,003	,,
Wildlife area improvement	74	,,
Tree planting	599	,,
Terraces built	660	miles
Crop rotation	25,507	acres
Water disposal areas	391	,,
Alfalfa	1,629	,,
Kudzu	373	,,
Sericea	158	,,
Woodland protection	175	,,
Fish ponds	174	,,

Orange county constitutes a work unit within the conservation district, and the Neuse River and the Tar River districts constitute a Conservation Area under the supervision of an area conservationist. The Orange unit has the full-time services of two conservationists. R. L. Mohler was work unit conservationist in Orange from the time the work was started in the county until he was succeeded in March, 1953 by Quentin Patterson. The assistant is C. V. Ferguson, who has been in the county since 1945. These technicians are federal employees but they are administratively responsible to the Neuse River Soil Conservation District supervisors, the policy making body for the district. They are responsible more immediately to the three men who represent Orange County on the district board and constitute the local board. These three men as of 1953 are Henry S. Hogan, J. S. Compton, and C. W. Stanford.

Farmers Home Administration

Another agency of the U. S. Department of Agriculture which has been of service to Orange county farmers is the Farmers Home Administration, earlier known as the Farm Security Administration. It is the function of this agency to assist that group of farmers who cannot get satisfactory credit from any other public or private source to enable them to succeed at farming. In addition to credit, the Farmers Home Administration provides its borrowers with practical guidance, as needed, in planning and carrying out sound and well-balanced farming operations. This combination of credit and supervision is the basis of the Farmers Home Administration Program.

Three types of loans are made to eligible farm families, (1) Farm Ownership Loans, (2) Farm Housing Loans and (3) Operating Loans. Farm ownership loans are made to enlarge or improve inadequate farms, as well as to buy efficient family-type farms. The Bankhead-Jones Farm Tenant Act of 1937 created a program to help farm people who have no land of their own to become owners. This law provides 40 year loans for farm purchase, at low interest rates, to those who cannot obtain suitable credit from other sources.

In 1946 Congress broadened the program by providing loans to farm owners to enlarge and improve farms that are too small or are not sufficiently developed.

By 1952, credit had been extended to 37 farmers in Orange County to purchase or develop farms, and already about half of them had repaid the loans in full and were free of debt. Most of the others were well ahead of schedule with their payments. Farm Ownership loans are made from money appropriated by Congress and also from funds advanced by private lenders and insured by the Farmers Home Administration.

The Housing Act of 1949 authorized the Farmers Home Administration to make loans for construction and repair of farm houses and other necessary farm buildings. Loans for periods up to 33 years at 4 percent interest are made to farm owners who are otherwise unable to finance such improvements for themselves and their tenants. By 1952, credit had been extended to 8 farmers in Orange county for this purpose, and all were current with their payments.

Operating Loans are made by the Farmers Home Administration to help eligible operators of family-type farms get ahead through better farming. These loans are based on farm and home plans developed with each individual family to provide for the best use of land, labor, livestock and equipment. To help borrowers carry out their plans and increase their earnings, the Farmers Home Administration Supervisor makes farm visits, as necessary, to advise and assist them in making planned adjustments in their farming operations and in adopting improved farm and home practices. In 1952 there were 43 Orange county farmers who had Operating Loans with the Farmers Home Administration. These loans are repayable over a period of from one to seven years.

The Farmers Home Administration has an extremely flexible program for creating and maintaining family farms. Whether the small farmer's need is for land, livestock, equipment, or improved managerial ability - or a combination of these essentials for successful farming - the agency has the tools to help him.

Farm Homes

Until recent years a large percentage of the farm homes of the county lacked the conveniences which characterized city homes. This was due in part to limited farm income but perhaps even more to the absence of electric current. The former is still a deterrent in many cases but electric power is now available to most of the rural population. As recently as 1945 only 950 farms had electricity, but by 1950 the number had grown to 1,609 and many additional farmsteads have been wired since. As a result the installation of electrical appliances has been phenomenal. According to the 1950 census, 1,003 farm homes had electric washing machines, 654 electric water pumps, 237 electric hot water heaters, and 103 home freezers. No corresponding census figures are available on the extent of plumbing, though it may be deduced that about one-third of the farm homes have running water at least. In 1940 this was true of only 263 of the 2,507 rural farm dwellings then reported. At that time 2,316 had no private bath, and 2,349 had no toilet.

In 1940 nearly 40 per cent of the farm homes needed major repairs. There is no statistical evidence to indicate how generally these physical deficiencies have been corrected, though one has only to drive over the county to be impressed by the large number of new, remodeled or freshly painted farm houses. On the other hand, the fact that home improvement was selected as one of three things to emphasize in the 1952 Rural Progress Program suggests that there are many rural homes which fall short of attainable standards of comfort.

Much of the credit for the improvement in farm homes which has taken place and the higher standard of living which has come to prevail should go to the Home Demonstration Agents. Orange County has had a home agent for white farm women since 1935 and another for Negro women since 1941. While they welcome office visits from individuals, their principal method of instruction is through neighborhood groups organized as home demonstration clubs. In 1952 there were 16 white clubs and several Negro clubs. Each club took various phases of the Rural Progress Program as its major projects. For example, the St. Mary's Club stressed home improvement, and the tally at the end of the year was two new homes built, three homes remodeled, a bathroom added in another, one new cabinet and sink, two new oil heaters, and 27 electrical appliances bought. The Mt. Carmel Club reported two new homes, three homes remodeled, three rooms added, 18 rooms painted, seven rooms papered, four rooms sheet rocked, four floors laid with tile, seven rooms insulated, one shower bath installed, and five cabinets installed. It also showed many new electrical appliances added. Similar reports came in from all the other clubs.

The clubs teach by demonstration how to can fruits and vegetables, preserve meats, make rugs, upholster furniture, decorate rooms, make garments, trim hats, and many other things that reduce the labor or add to the comfort of farm women. At the same time, they provide another valuable social contact.

According to the 1950 census only 530, or slightly over one-fourth, of Orange County's farms are less than four miles from the trading center visited most frequently, and 609 are more than ten miles from such a center. The average distance is eight miles. While most families have a car, many farm women do not drive and many others are tied pretty closely at home because of small children. Only a small percentage of the farm homes have telephones—a total of only 165 in 1950. Thus the isolation which has characterized the life of farm women has been lessened but by no means universally removed. Radios, and now in some homes, television sets, provide a secondary type of contact with the outside world, but this is not equivalent to a face-to-face contact or even a telephone conversation. A group meeting of farm women where they can discuss practical everyday problems of mutual interest is a refreshing experience. The home demonstration clubs therefore render a valuable service both educationally and socially.

Curb Market

About 25 women in the southern part of the county have found a way to supplement the family income through their curb market in Chapel Hill. The market was promoted by the home demonstration agent and has now been in operation about fifteen years. In the year which ended September 20, 1952 the produce sold at the market brought $27,651. Of this, $7,419 was derived from the sale of poultry, $12,665 from eggs, $6,816 from vegetables, $1,227 from butter, $1,493 from cakes, and the rest from meat, bread, fruit, and miscellaneous products.

Four-H Clubs

The farm youth of the county are provided an excellent channel of expression through the 4-H clubs. There are 12 of these clubs with a normal membership of about 400 boys and 425 girls from 10 to 15 years of age. There is a club at each of the 9 elementary schools and at Chapel Hill, Hillsboro and Aycock high schools. The clubs meet monthly during the school year, with the Assistant County Agent present at the boys' meetings and the Home Demonstration Agent present at the girls' meetings. The first part of each meeting is conducted by the members themselves and the latter part is given over to instruction by the leader. In addition to the discussion of projects, there are often demonstrations of such things as culling poultry, judging cattle, and planting pine seedlings.

Each member is required to undertake and carry through to completion a project, such as raising a calf or pig, growing a garden, constructing a poultry house, or raising a flock of chickens. The girls add sewing and canning projects. In recent years, a favorite project of both boys and girls has been raising a baby beef, and in 1951 fifteen 4-H club members exhibited fat steers at the Durham Fat Stock Show. Ten were awarded blue ribbons. Two 4-H Club boys, Oliver Roberts and Carl Walters, exhibited the Grand Champion and Reserve Champion hogs respectively. Twenty-eight 4-H Club members planted 900 pine seedlings provided by the pulpwood companies. In addition to their projects each member is enrolled in the Health program of the Club. Each year six boy champions and six girl champions are treated to a week's vacation at camp by the merchants of Hillsboro. Other members may join the camping party by paying their own expenses. Each year a number go to the 4-H Club Camp at Camp New Hope where for a week they indulge in swimming, hiking, and other sports as well as receive instruction in woodcraft, nature study and first aid. Others go to State College for a week of 4-H Club activities. Each fall there is an achievement show at which 4-H Club members from all over the county display their handiwork. There is also a county-wide picnic.

Many of the better young farmers of the county got interested in scientific farming, and their wives in better home-making, as youths in 4-H clubs.

Future Farmers of America

In the three white high schools and the two colored high schools of the county there are courses offered in vocational agriculture and home economics. The boys and girls who enroll in these courses and meet certain standards, including the successful completion of a home project, are eligible to membership in the organization known as Future Farmers of America. The national organization sponsors oratorical and essay contests and in other ways stimulates the interest of American youth in the

Nation's conservation problems. Instruction in the practical arts also gives these young people some of the understanding and skill which may later prove so useful.

Community Activities

Agricultural leaders recognize that a satisfying rural life requires a rich community life as well as home conveniences and a comfortable income, and that perhaps progress has not been as great in this respect as in the others.

Automobiles and good roads have undoubtedly destroyed many neighborhood centers and a sense of community in these neighborhoods. While they have dealt a mortal blow to some communities, they have had a rejuvenating effect on others. In general they have reduced the number of centers but have strengthened those which survived. The abandonment of a long-established store, school or church is always painful but the emergence of strong institutions serving a larger area and population is the reward. For many years the pattern of community life in Orange County as elsewhere has been in flux and the outlines of the new and larger communities are not yet fixed. Indeed, it is never possible to draw the exact boundaries of a rural community, for not all of the families go to the same center for all purposes.

For the administration of the agricultural conservation program ten communities are recognized and perhaps they come as near to being the primary communities of the rural population as any that could be outlined. They are Caldwell, Carr, Carrboro, Cedar Grove, Efland, Hillsboro, New Hope, Orange Grove, St. Mary's, and White Cross. While they are not self-contained and the families who compose them have other allegiances, each has a community consciousness and can report noteworthy community achievements.

Similarly, each of the five local Granges in the county tends to develop in the area from which its membership is drawn a community consciousness. In 1948, the Schley Grange won the National Grange Community Service Contest, sponsored by the Sears-Roebuck Company. The prize was a model community house, completely equipped with kitchen, assembly and recreation halls, and library. The cost of the building and equipment has been estimated at $50,000. The Schley community won this national distinction partly as a result of sponsoring a soil conservation field day when 5,000 people saw a complete soil conservation program carried out on Milton Latta's farm. Other community achievments were participation in the construction of 15 miles of rural telephone line, the establishment of a rural youth center, landscaping the grounds of a community church, and carrying on a home beautification contest. In the years since, it has promoted or supported other community activities including the planting of shrubbery and the improvement of farm driveways, a fall festival, a Grange Youth Conference, and the blood donor program.

Not to be outdone, the St. Mary's Grange obtained from the county an abandoned schoolhouse and converted it into a modern community building with kitchen and recreation hall. The grounds have been attractively landscaped with a part of them developed as an athletic field. Facilities have been developed for softball, volley ball, baseball and tennis. In the summer months there is supervised play for children once a week, and for youth one night each week. For adults, one evening each month throughout the year features square dancing and recorded music.

The New Hope Grange has likewise carried out a recreational program with well-planned monthly activities, including square dances, weiner roasts, ice cream parties, and the like. In 1952 it held a series of five educational programs with outstanding speakers present. Members of the community have taken particular pride in its historic Presbyterian church and in keeping the cemetery and church grounds attractive. Since 1947 they have helped liberally in the development of Camp New Hope of Orange Presbytery. In addition to church groups, the camp is available to 4-H clubs, Boy Scouts and other youth groups, and fills a great need in the county and region.

For some time the people of the White Cross community have felt the need of a building in which the activities of the church, school, Grange, home demonstration clubs, and other groups could be held. In 1952 a lot near the school was acquired and several hundred dollars toward the cost of erecting a building was raised. Much material as well as most of the labor will be contributed. The Grange and the Home Demonstration Club jointly sponsored the landscaping of the Antioch Church grounds. White Cross has had a community cannery in operation for several years.

The Calvander Grange has been equally concerned with worthwhile community projects, such as improved telephone service, youth activities, and farmstead beautification. Its membership voted almost unanimously in support of zoning on the outskirts of Chapel Hill to discourage undesirable developments and the disfigurement of the roadsides. Although the zoning has not yet gone into effect, the way has been paved for an early adoption of an ordinance.

Since its organization in 1950 the Cedar Grove Ruritan Club has sponsored many community projects. It has assisted generously in the landscaping of the new Aycock School and in equipping the gymnasium; it has also established and financed a community baseball team, sponsored an interdenominational church picnic at Pullen Park in Raleigh, and obtained group hospital insurance for more than 75 per cent of the club members. In 1952 it won first place among 22 rural organizations competing in the community improvement contest.

There are nine active units of the Parent Teachers Association in the county and also a County Council composed of a representative from each of the local units. Each P.T.A. organization contributes in various ways to school and community betterment. Several have aided in improving the appearance of the school grounds and others in expanding the recreational facilities. Interior improvements have been made, such as providing mirrors in the classrooms or redecorating certain rooms. The Murphy School P.T.A. purchased new office equipment and library books, the Hillsboro P. T. A. a slide projector and screen, and the White Cross P.T.A. paid a public school music teacher and bought records and a record player.

For a long time there has been concern over the lack of rural fire protection, and finally in 1951 something was done about it. Under the stimulus of the Extension Service, 327 rural home owners within a ten-mile radius of Hillsboro cooperated in the purchase of a fire truck. Together they paid over $5,500. The truck is operated by twenty volunteer firemen from Hillsboro under the leadership of fire chief George Gilmore. In one year this fire-fighting equipment fought 15 rural fires and saved property with an estimated value of $25,000 to $30,000. The large number of farm ponds are an almost indispensable element in rural fire protection. Since these ponds are also used for swimming by children and amateur swimmers, they are also a hazard. In view of this, the Hillsboro Lions and Exchange Clubs, cooperating with Orange Rural Fire Department, purchased a respirator as a part of the equipment of the fire truck.

Mention has already been made of the home demonstration clubs in the county, all of which have emphasized community activities as well as home improvements. In 1952 they aided in building community centers, in roadside beautification, in the improvement of church grounds and cemeteries, and in organizing church choirs. On the county level, a choral club was organized, a rural church music school held with 34 churches represented, a recreation school held, and a housing institute sponsored.

Rural Progress Program

Recognizing that rural Orange County has made great progress during the past decade by increasing the cash income of the farms and by improving the living conditions in the homes, the agricultural leaders of the county are agreed that there is still much to be done. The estimated average gross cash income for the family sized farm in 1951 was only $1885, meaning perhaps a net cash income of $1,000. This is inadequate at prevailing prices to maintain a satisfactory standard of living. Many farm homes are attractive and most of them have some of the modern conveniences, but the majority of them could be made more comfortable and more attractive. Finally, the community life of the rural people could be enriched.

In 1952 a concerted effort was made by the farm, civic and religions organizations of the county to speed up progress in these areas. About forty org'anizations and community groups undertook through friendly competition to have their membership excel in the attainment of three goals: (1) to increase farm (family sized) income by $1000 over that of 1951, (2) to make one improvement in every home, and (3) to successfully carry out one or more worthwhile community projects.

On October 30, at a county-wide meeting in Hillsboro reports of the achievements were presented and awards made to those organizations adjudged to be the winners. So successful was the effort in all three respects that it is being repeated in 1953.

Chapter XVI

INDUSTRY, PAST AND PRESENT

By Paul W. Wager

This chapter makes no pretense of being a history of industry in the county. To have written such a history would have required a much longer period of research than was available. Sometime somebody should write that story. All that is attempted here is to illustrate the place occupied by industry at different periods in the history of the county, and to tell a little about those few industries now operating within the county. The chapter is more of a scrapbook than a continuous story.

There were numerous grist-mills, saw-mills, and wool carding machines in the county in the last quarter of the eighteenth and first quarter of the nineteenth centuries, and cotton gins after 1793. Two advertisements in the Hillsboro *Recorder* of 1821 give us an idea of the nature of these establishments:

Fulling Mill

I continue carrying on the Fulling Business, with the assistance of Mr. James Boyle, the well-known northern bred workman, with as great dispatch as possible, and on as reasonable terms as can be afforded.
Orange County, N. C. two miles
east of Hillsborough, June 5, 1821

WILLIAM PRICHETT

The subscriber has just repaired his Grist-Mill, Saw-Mill and Cotton Machine, and has them in full operation; where he will keep on hand, for sale, flour, cotton, plank and lumber. Also wishes to purchase a quantity of WHEAT.
Enoe, Orange Co. Nov. 13, 1821

THOMAS W. HOLDEN

Much of Orange County's early industry was near its western border and hence was lost to the county when Alamance was formed in 1849. It does not seem inappropriate, however, to mention those industries which had their beginning on sites which at the time were in Orange. Indeed it would be a serious omission not to include something about the beginnings of the textile industry in what was then Orange County. Although these cotton mills were not the first to be established in the state, the first one having been established in 1813 by Michael Schenck on the Catawba River near Lincolnton, they were among the first.

For an account of the first textile mills to be established in what was then Orange County, we are indebted to two contributors to the centennial edition (May, 1949) of the Burlington *Daily Times-News*. From the first article, which is unsigned, we learn something about Edwin Michael Holt, the pioneer textile manufacturer of the region. We quote:

> Before 1837 there was no such thing as a cotton mill in the entire county. Edwin Michael Holt, who ran a small store and farm near the home of his father, Michael III, realized that if the raw cotton so abundant in the South could be manufactured into goods in the South, the Southern mill would have the immense advantages of freight exemption, cheap power from the streams of the uplands, raw material at its very doors and abundant and reliable labor. He foresaw that the South was to control the cotton industry of the world, that it had been ordained by the climatic conditions and geography of the southern section.
>
> With this confidence in his own judgment, Edwin Michael erected a cotton mill on the banks of Alamance Creek during one of the most economically unstable times of the century—the panic of 1837. This mill, under the name of Holt and Carrigan, was successful from the start and was destined to be the parent of many similar mills here.
>
> It was Edwin Michael who manufactured the first dyed cloth on power looms south of the Potomac. His story has it that he learned the dyeing process from a Frenchman who taught him how to color cotton yarn for the sum of $100 and his board. In 1853 Edwin Michael took the 80-gallon copper boiler he had been using to boil potatoes and turnips for his hogs and a large cast-iron washpot that he had on sale at his store and constructed his own dyeing implements. Shortly afterward, he built a dye house and installed better dyeing equipment. Then he put in some four-box looms and began the manufacture of what became known as Alamance Plaids.

Edwin Michael Holt lived until 1884 owning at the time of his death many mills and other properties. His sons and grandsons continued for many years to expand the family's textile empire.

The second article deals with the early history of the Saxapahaw community which is not only close to where Holt built his mill but is where John Newlin, in 1844, built the second cotton mill in the county. This is an interesting article by Ben Bulla and a portion of it is reproduced here.

Mr. Bulla states that in 1837 E. M. Holt started a cotton mill on Alamance Creek. He started out with only 528 spindles and in 1861 had only 1200. His operations expanded rapidly, however, during the war and a few years later he was in position to buy a number of smaller mills in the county, including the Newlin mill to be discussed presently. Holt took his two sons-in-law, John L. Williamson and Capt. James W. White, into partnership and operated under the name of Holt, White and Williamson until Holt's death in 1884. With the grandsons becoming more active the partnership adopted the name White-Williamson and Company, and in 1906 incorporated. The mill was again expanded and modernized, and operated successfully until the depression following World War I. With low prices and the severe competition of more up-to-date plants, the company was forced into receivership and in 1927 its assets were purchased by Charles V. Sellars, B. Everett Jordan and other members of the Sellars and Jordan families. Since then it has operated as the Sellars Manufacturing Company, producing fancy combination yarns and "Durene" mercerized yarn. It is considered one of the most modern spinning and mercerizing plants in the United States.

In 1844, seven years after Holt started his mill, John Newlin and his sons started a spinning mill on the east side of Haw River at the site of the present village of Saxapahaw. The Newlins were Quakers and it is surprising that they would use slave labor to build their enterprise. One legend is that they used slaves which were about to be emancipated by a neighbor and then immediately afterward conveyed them to free territory. At any rate, Mr. Bulla states that:

> ... using slave labor, the Newlins dug a race from a three-foot high rock dam across Haw River, the first dam ever erected here, down the side of the river all the way to their cotton mill nearly a mile away. There is some question as to who actually built this first dam. Some contend that the Thompson family operated the grist mill, which was the first mill of any kind at Saxapahaw, be-

fore the Newlins took over, and, therefore the Thompsons had a dam to furnish water power for the water wheel that turned the grist mill machinery. Others maintain that John Newlin was the first to harness the power of the river.

The mill building was constructed of brick made from the red clay along Motes Creek, less than a mile from the mill, and the sand for the mortar was obtained from the opposite side of the river. This building was a brick one-story affair that had fireplaces for heating and was lighted with candles and oil lamps. It measured approximately 200 feet long by 50 feet wide and stood where the present mercerizing end of the mill stands.

It was not until 1848 that the physical properties were completed and the mill was ready to begin production. At first the mill did nothing but spin yarn and it was not a large operation. But some years later two more stories were added to the building and in 1859 looms were installed. In addition to producing small 24 pound bales of coarse cotton yarn which was sold largely to owners of household looms throughout the country, the Newlins began to turn out cotton cloth, which they dyed with their own equipment. Some of their cloth went to clothe the Confederate armies. We quote again from Bulla's article:

It was in 1863, during the Civil war, that Governor Z. B. Vance ordered that a large quantity of baled cotton then stored at Graham, be delivered to "Messrs. John Newland and Sons at Saxapahaw Factory" to be manufactured into cloth and yarn. The cloth was to be delivered to the quartermaster department of the Confederate Army and the yarn was to be sent to Virginia to be exchanged for leather to be made into shoes for the soldiers. North Carolina still boasts that her soldiers were the best dressed troops in the Rebel Army, and Saxapahaw Factory played a conspicuous part in earning that distinction.

John Newlin died in 1867. A few years later his sons, James and Jonathan, and George Guthrie, a minor stockholder, laboring under the difficulties of the post war reconstruction era, decided to sell out to the eminently successful Edwin M. Holt, who by then was the owner of several cotton mills throughout the county. The sale of the mill was made in 1873. and thereafter its history is entwined with that of the Holt mills. In one of the modernization programs, in 1937, all of the original buildings, including the Newlin mill, were torn down and replaced with sturdier structures of brick and steel.

We are also indebted to Mr. Bulla for some light on the earliest grist mills, at least in the Saxapahaw section of the county. We quote:

> All existing records indicate that the first grist mill in this section of the county was put into operation by Hugh Laughlin and Thomas Lindley in 1756 on the banks of Cane Creek. This location is now known as Sutphin Mill, but it was known as Lindley's Mill for over 100 years.
>
> When the first grist mill was erected on the east side of Haw River at Saxapahaw, apparently remains unknown. However, it is generally believed that the grist mill here had been grinding grain for a number of years prior to the date of the establishment of John Newlin's first cotton mill here in 1844-48.

It is fortunate for the county historian that the Hillsborough *Recorder*, in its issue of February 7, 1852, made an inventory of the manufacturing establishments in Orange County at that time. We quote from the article:

> While on the subject of improvements we propose to notice some which have recently taken place in the county, and which promise, at no distant day, greatly to advance the business and interests of the people.
>
> Messrs. Webb and Douglass have just completed a Cotton Factory, on Little River, about thirteen miles east of Hillsborough, and are now receiving their Machinery from the North. They expect to commence operations during the summer, and will run 1000 spindles.
>
> Messrs. Robert and John Shields have also erected a Woollen Factory on Enoe, about seven miles East of Hillsborough. The machinery has all been received; and it is expected that they will commence operations in a few days. This we think is the third or fourth Woollen Factory in the State; and we look upon their introduction as of more importance, because, if we are not much mistaken, if proper facilities are afforded, Western North Carolina will eventually become a great wool growing country. We hope the location of the factory in Orange will induce our people to pay more attention to the raising of sheep; for it is generally considered to be the most profitable animal we can raise.
>
> Eagle Foundery, owned by Messrs. Brown and Wilkinson, is situated on Enoe, about three miles east of Hillsborough. It has been in operation only a short time, and its ingenious and enter-

prising proprietors are constantly adding improvements. We are gratified to learn that the demand for their work is quite equal to their ability at present to meet it.

Messrs. Dickson and Brown's establishment for manufacturing wool carding machines, wheat fans, etc. is situated on Enoe River about six miles east of Hillsborough. (This company's ad in the same issue also lists wagons, ploughs, and bedsteads among the articles manufactured.)

To these we may add Mr. R. F. Webb's establishment for manufacturing Window Blinds, a handsome article of which we have before spoken; and the Rev. John A. McMannen's establishment at South Lowell, at which are manufactured smut machines, which we see by frequent mention in our exchanges are obtaining considerable celebrity in the State on account of their excellence. He also manufactures Patent Corn Shellers, etc. which are in good repute.

There may be other manufacturers in the county which have recently been commenced, but they do not occur to us now. These, though few in number, form quite a respectable beginning, and furnish sufficient data upon which to build a reasonable calculation of the prosperity that must attend a well-directed energy when our Rail Road is put in operation.

We do not know the subsequent history of all of these plants, though it is known that some of them were successful and continued to operate for many years. The one started by Webb and Douglass continued under a succession of owners and under various names until perhaps 25 years ago. At one time it manufactured rope. The Shields factory, later called the Alpha Woolen Mills, continued for many years. The Eagle Foundry, located near what was called Berry's mill, also had a long history. Dickson and Brown's establishment was probably about where the Eno steam power plant is now located. It operated for many years.

There was quite a surge of industrial activity about the middle of the nineteenth century. It is probable that many of these plants succumbed during the Civil War or the Reconstruction period. If there were others brought into being by the coming of the railroad in 1855 some of them too went under. Yet the demands of the war itself certainly kept some of them alive. This advertisement appearing in the Hillsboro *Recorder* in 1862 is evidence of that.

WOOL CARDING

> The Subscriber, living eight and a half miles north of Hillsborough, will have his Steam Carding Machine in first rate order by the 10th of June. Thankful for the former patronage which has been bestowed upon him, he hopes still to receive the custom of all who want good work done. Carding will be done for 12 cents per pound, for white wool, or one-fifth part of the wool. Mixed, if the different colors are pulled together before they are brought, will be carded for 15 cents per pound; if not pulled together, an extra charge will be made. He expects to have a good Picker or Buring Machine in operation. Bring your wool in good order, and put one pound of grease to twelve pounds of wool, and you will get good work.
>
> June 4, 1862   LEMUEL WILKINSON

There must have been something of an industrial revival about 1880, for some of the county's oldest citizens speak of there being mills every few miles on the Eno and Little rivers in their childhood. It may surprise many people to know that there were also tobacco factories in the county in the last quarter of the nineteenth century. There were no less than three in Hillsboro. E. J. Pogue manufactured plug tobacco about 1885, as did also a man by the name of Whitted. Col. H. B. Jones had a factory, which stood just west of the Hillsboro depot, where he manufactured smoking tobacco before Washington Duke got started in the business. Walker Brothers' grist mill adjacent to the courthouse was once a tobacco factory. However, all of Orange's tobacco factories closed prior to 1900, probably forced out of business by the severe competition of the rapidly growing Durham industry.

Even prior to the American Revolution, Hillsboro was an important center of trade and supported big mercantile houses, such as those of Nathaniel Rochester and Ralph McNair, but if they advertised, none of their advertisements have been found for inclusion here. We can, however, reproduce an advertisement of a prominent Hillsboro merchant of a half century later. In the Hillsboro *Recorder* of March 15, 1820 appears an announcement which not only indicates a large trade but throws light on the demands of the people.

CASH STORE

The subscriber has lately opened a store in Hillsborough, in the house formerly occupied by him, where he offers for sale on very low terms for cash, a very considerable assortment of

FRESH GOODS

Among which are,

A large assortment of superfine, fine, and coarse broad cloths, superfine and fine cassimeres, bed, duple and Dutch blankets, coatings vestings, white and coloured plains, flannels and baises, cassimere and Canton crape shawls, collicos, bombazettes, cotton hose, black silk handkerchiefs, an assortment of guns, some of which are of a very superior quality; trace chains, weeding hoes, frying pans, anvils, vises, sledge and hand hammers, bellows pipes and bands, crawley and blistered steel, carpenter's planes, imported wagon boxes, patent cutting knives, and scythe blades, and a very large assortment of Hardware and Cutlery.

Kirkland, Webb and Co. have always on hand a considerable quantity of skirting, bridle, bag, upper and soal leather.

I wish to employ a sober, steady young man, who can come well recommended, and who has been brought up to the mercantile business, and is a good accountant.

Hillsborough, February 23, 1820   WM. KIRKLAND

Another of the same period, though listed as a grocery store, seems to have been a liquor store and general emporium as well. This is the advertisement.

GROCERY STORE

The subscriber has opened a Grocery Store, in the house formerly occupied by Mr. Bacon, as a shoe shop, where, among other articles, may be had for cash,

Coffee, first and second quality
Brown and loaf Sugar
Molasses
Good old Rum
New England ditto
French Brandy
Sherry and Malaga Wine
Porter and Cordial
Imperial Tea
Ditto in canisters of two pounds each, superior quality
China, in boxes of forty-eight pieces
Liverpool, Queen, Glass and Stone Ware
Muscatel Raisins, Figs, Prunes, Palm Nuts and Almonds
Nails, 4, 6, 8, 10, 20d

Window Glass 8 by 10, and 10 by 12
Putty, White Lead, Red Lead, and Spanish Brown
Pepper and Spice
Writing and Letter Paper
Pots and Ovans
Best Rifle Powder, and Shot of all sizes
    No credit can or will be given
Hillsborough, May 22, 1820   D. YARBROUGH

Since there was a good deal of travel by salesmen, always of course on horseback or by horse drawn carriage, there was a need for hostelries. Advertisements of two of them—one in Hillsboro and one in Chapel Hill—may be of interest.

          Mason Hall Eagle Hotel
               A. Mason

    Wishes to inform his former customers and the public generally, that he has nearly finished his house, so that he is now able to accommodate as many as may honor him with their company. His house is large, having seven comfortable rooms, which have fireplaces in them, suitable for families or traveling gentlemen wishing such. He has provided good beds, liquors, etc and will keep as good a table as the neighborhood will afford. He is also provided with good stables, and will always keep the best provender. The situation of the place is pleasant and very healthy. Gentlemen wishing to visit him with their families, during the summer season, can be accommodated on moderate terms.

    The keeper of this establishment pledges himself to the public to do all in his power to please and give entire satisfaction. Gentlemen who call can amuse themselves in reading the newspapers in his hallroom, where he keeps files of papers from almost every part of the United States.

Feb. 28, 1820   Mason Hall, Orange County, N. C.

              University Hotel
                Chapel Hill

    The subscriber informs the public that he has opened a House of Entertainment at Chapel Hill, the scite of the University of N. C. He has taken the buildings and lots immediately opposite Mr. Watts' Hotel, and has erected large and commodious stables, which will be attended by a faithful ostler, and plentifully supplied with provender. He hopes that the travelling public will give him a call, and assures them that every exertion will be made by him to please as well as accommodate.

December 30, 1834   I. C. PATRIDGE

Banking

There was a branch of the Bank of Cape Fear in Hillsboro as early as 1816. It is not known how long it operated but in 1854 it was not listed in state banking reports. There must have been another bank in Hillsboro, however, for in the Hillsboro *Recorder* of August 27, 1862 appears this notice:

> At a called meeting of the stockholders of the Hillsboro Savings Institution held on the 9th of August, 1862—Stockholders represented 512 shares—it was
>
> Resolved, that from and after the 16th day of September next, no interest will be paid on certificates of deposit heretofore issued by this institution, and the holders of such certificates are required to present the same on or before that day for settlement, and that the cashier be required to give special notice of this resolution.
>
> August 13, 1862   JOHN U. KIRKLAND, *Cashier*

Following the Civil War, there was no bank in Hillsboro until 1904, the next bank in Orange County being the Bank of Chapel Hill, established in 1899. It started with an authorized capital of $10,000, and with $2,500 paid in. Today it has $100,000 capital and assets of $8,500,000. The presidents, in order, have been General Julian S. Carr, James C. Taylor, J. W. Gore, C. H. Herty, M. C. S. Noble, and since 1942 Clyde Eubanks. The cashiers, in order, have been A. W. Peace, W. D. Wildman, C. T. Beasley, Robert C. Shaw, James C. Taylor, M. E. Hogan, W. E. Thompson and J. T Gobbel.

There was another bank in Chapel Hill, the Peoples Bank, from about 1912 to 1925. Vernon Howell was the first president and he was followed by J. D. Webb. The assets of the bank were purchased by the Bank of Chapel Hill in 1925.

In May, 1904 the Bank of Orange was started in Hillsboro with an initial capitalization of $5,000. It operated as an independent bank until 1936 when it was bought by the Durham Bank and Trust Company. Its assets at the time of its sale were about $750,000. Throughout its entire history, Dr. J. S. Spurgeon was president and Paul C. Collins was cashier.

A second bank in Hillsboro, the Farmers and Merchants Bank, was acquired by the Durham Bank and Trust Company in

1939. Since that date the Durham bank has operated a single branch in Hillsboro.

For some years there was a small bank in Efland, with John L. Efland as its president. It closed down in 1931 or 1932.

Hillsboro and its Industries

The Belle-Vue Manufacturing Company has been in operation in Hillsboro since 1904. Shepherd Strudwick, Sr. was its first president, continuing in that capacity until 1929. For many years T. Norfleet Webb was secretary and treasurer. Since 1929 L. E. Beard has been president and treasurer. Local ownership and control of the mill ended in 1945, when it was purchased by Hesslein and Company.

During its long history the mill has had its ups and downs, but most of the time it has provided steady employment to an increasing number of workers and a fair margin of profit to its owners. Since its purchase by the Hesslein Company more than a half million dollars has been spent in improvements. These have included new opening and picking machines, new carding machines, new drawing and spinning frames, a new boiler plant, a splendid new lighting system, and the installation of white tiled washrooms. Other improvements which are contemplated are new spooling and warping equipment, new equipment in the dye-house, a first aid room at the mill, and modernization of the company-owned houses. Already hot and cold water and bathrooms have been put in every one of the village houses.

The plant manufacturers ginghams and related fabrics. At the present time it employs 355 workers, 225 of whom are men. Currently the mill is running two shifts, and a few of the looms operate a third shift.

Some idea of the important place which the mill occupies in the life of the community can be gained from the employees record of employment. On June 12, 1948 the company gave service pins to 220 employees who had worked at the mill for periods of from five to 40 years. There were 38 who had been employed 25 years or more.

The Eno cotton mill in Hillsboro was established in 1896 by Allen J. Ruffin and James Webb. It began as a yarn mill with about 10,000 spindles. In 1904 looms were added as well as more spindles, and the company began the manufacture of chambray and plaid cloth. In 1909 the mill was further enlarged and gingham was added to the list of products. It might be stated that some of the yarn continued to be sold rather than woven into cloth until the first World War.

In 1929 new machinery was installed and the use of combed yarn substituted for coarse carded yarn. Since then the major products of the mill have been broadcloth shirting and corduroy, though during World War II a heavier cloth was made for the Army. The mill does no bleaching or dyeing, its product being what is known as grey goods.

Today the plant has 30,000 spindles and 676 looms. When operating at capacity, three shifts a day, as it has since 1939, about 600 persons are employed. Approximately half of the employees are women. The company provides 148 houses for its workers; employees not accommodated in the mill village live in Hillsboro and the surrounding country. The wage paid is that which prevails generally in the Carolinas. With good wages many young people have been able to save a sizable nest egg for investment in a farm or business for their maturer years.

On January 1, 1952 the Eno mill became a part of Cone Mills, Incorporated, of Greensboro. Sydney Green, who has been with the Eno plant since 1933 and was Vice President of the local company, is the resident manager. James E. Webb, who was President of the local company, became a vice president of the Cone organization.

Located about five miles north of Hillsboro on Highway 86 is one of the most complete and up-to-date meat packing plants in the state. It is owned and operated by G. C. Kennedy and Sons and chartered as the Piedmont Packing Company.

The daily capacity of the plant is about 30 cattle, 25 calves, and 5000 pounds of wieners. Retail markets in Hillsboro, Chapel Hill, Roxboro, Durham, Mebane, and Raleigh are supplied with this fully inspected meat. Permit No. 18 was issued to this packing plant by the State Department of Agriculture, and meat so stamped can be sold anywhere in the state. Inspection is by a graduate licensed veterinarian, approved by the state department of health, the state department of agriculture, the U. S. Government and the county health department. He is selected by the Orange County board of commissioners.

The original plant was built in 1937 and there have been several additions since. Employment is given to about 40 persons including about 20 girls who work in the sausage and wiener department. The exterior of the plant and the surrounding grounds are as neat and attractive as the interior is sanitary.

At Hillsboro there is a branch of the White Furniture Company which employs 125 workmen. It makes high quality dining room furniture, mainly reproductions of Eighteenth Century furniture. This plant was started in 1925 by the four Bivins brothers and for some years manufactured tobacco baskets. Later the company, designating itself Orange Furniture Craftsmen, made some upholstered furniture. In 1940 the plant was acquired by the White Furniture Company. It soon discontinued making upholstered furniture and concentrated on dining room buffets and cabinets. Mr. H. Ted Smith is superintendent of the Hillsboro unit.

Another small industry in Hillsboro is the Hines Liner Company. This company, which had its beginning in 1918 as the Bivins Liner Company, makes liners for tobacco hogsheads. Liners are the inside hoops which hold the heads in place. Another division of the industry is a lumber and planing mill a few hundred yards away which not only furnishes oak timber for the liners but produces finished lumber for the market. It ships three or four carloads a week. The lumber yard and mill employ 16 people and the liner factory 9 persons. Frank Ray is manager of the liner factory, while E. M. Hines, himself, is superintendent of the lumber mill.

Efland and its Industries

The little village of Efland on the railroad midway between Hillsboro and Mebane is both one of the oldest and one of the youngest industrial locations in the county. Until it burned in 1949, and was almost immediately rebuilt, there was a flour mill at Efland which had been in continuous use for more than 150 years. It is not known who built and first operated it. For fifty years or more, it has been operated by John L. Efland, before that his father Madison L. Efland operated it, and before that Tom Johnson. The mill is on or near what was once the Thomas Hart place, where Senator Thomas Hart Benton was born. Old maps show a Hart's mill near here, so conceivably Thomas Hart was the original operator.

In 1906 Mack P. Efland, a brother of John L., established the first excelsior plant to be established in this part of the state and one of the first to be established anywhere. It has been in continuous operation since. The product, made from pine wood, is sold in bales and also in paper-covered pads of various sizes. It is shipped all over the United States and is used in upholstered furniture and for packing lamps, dishes, and many other things. The little industry normally employs 22 people; it gets its pine logs mostly from the woodlands of Orange and Alamance counties.

Efland also has an expanding hosiery industry, all operated by Efland brothers and cousins. The oldest factory, from which the others are offshoots, was started by John L. Efland in 1912. It has been in almost continuous operation since. It first made half hose but later shifted to full-fashioned hosiery. The newer factories are the Efland Knitting Company started about 1940, the Orange Hosiery Mill which started in 1947, and the Tar Heel Hosiery Mill which started in 1952. Only the Orange Hosiery Mill is in corporate ownership. The four plants all make full-fashioned hosiery and employ a total of about 100 operatives.

Mebane and its Industries

The village of Mebane is partly in Orange county and partly in Alamance. Most of its industry is on the Alamance side of town but it draws its employees in considerable numbers from Orange county and thus is a factor in the economy of the county.

Mebane came into existence as a cluster of houses along the new North Carolina Railroad in 1854. It was named for the Mebane family, whose members have played prominent roles in public affairs since before the Revolution. With the coming of the railroad, families from the surrounding region began to seek home sites near the tracks, and formed a little settlement called Mebaneville. A large number of these came from the Hawfields section to settle in the new village. Stephen A. White was the first settler, and he was soon followed by Frank Mebane and Thomas B. Thompson. The town grew rapidly and in 1881 was incorporated, and in 1883 the name was shortened to Mebane.

In a hundred years Mebane has grown into a thriving town of 2,000 people, with a half dozen important industries. They include both furniture and textile plants.

The White Furniture Company, which makes high quality bedroom and living room furniture, is one of the oldest manufacturers of fine furniture in the South. The company was founded in 1881 by two brothers, Will and Dave White. The Whites were descendants of one of the oldest families of the region, their forebears having settled there in 1775. The two brothers were related through their mother to the Mebanes. Starting with a few hundred dollars which they had saved and a small loan from a family friend, the two young men purchased a carload of lumber and a second-hand planer and set up a plant to manufacture wood products. Within a short time they began to make bedroom furniture, and it was not long before dining room furniture was added. From the very beginning the two brothers endeavored to make good products, and throughout its history the company has adhered steadfastly to this policy.

After operating 15 years as a partnership, the company was incorporated in 1896. Mr. Will White became president; Mr. Dave White was made general manager; and a younger brother, J. Sam White, was brought into the organization as secretary and treasurer. After the death of Will White in 1935, J. Sam White became president. Though still active at 74, executive responsibility is now shared with his son, Stephen A. White.

On December 22, 1923 the company's plant was completely destroyed by fire. It was rebuilt the next year, with what was at that time the most modern machinery. Since 1947 more than a quarter of a million dollars has been spent to effect another modernization program. In 1939 the White Furniture Company purchased the Orange Furniture Craftsmen, a small furniture plant in Hillsboro, already mentioned.

At its Mebane plant, the White Furniture Company has

about 300 employees, practically all men. About 25 per cent of them are Negroes. The company has always enjoyed excellent relations with its labor. The plant is small enough so that there is easy personal contact between management and labor. Many of the workmen have been employed there for years; in the summer of 1948 service buttons were presented to 68 who had been there 20 years or more. A few have been employed there more than 50 years. Mr. Sam White and 'Steve' know most of the men by their first names, and their doors are always open to them to come in and discuss their personal problems. Although assembly line methods leave less opportunity for the craftsmen, the workmen generally take pride in their work and in the finished product.

It is pertinent to close this sketch with the statement which appears at the beginning of one of the company's recent brochures:

> Good furniture was a tradition in the famous little town of Mebane, North Carolina, long before the year 1881, when the first piece of White furniture was made.
> The White boys, Will and Dave, had watched journeymen craftsmen fashion pieces of rich and lasting beauty. In the homes of the Pages, the Mebanes, and other old Haw River Valley families dating back to Colonial days. . .They had lived familiarly with furniture that had enriched, and been enriched by, the good life of many generations.
> On the exact site of the first White Furniture shop. . . . descendants of the founders and the early craftsmen are still building furniture of enduring usefulness and beauty. . . .until the town that General Alexander Mebane founded. . . .and made famous as a stronghold of patriotism in Revolutionary days. . . . has become, in our time, synonomous with the finest in furniture.

Another old established industry at Mebane which has always drawn a part of its labor supply from Orange county is one which makes mattresses and springs, cots, Hollywood beds, and studio couches. It was organized in 1904 as the Mebane Bedding Company. In 1929 it merged with the Royal-Borden Manufacturing Company and took the name Mebane-Royal Company. It operated under this name until May, 1947 when it became The Mebane Company. It employs 150 persons, mostly men, about 25 per cent of whom are Negroes. At least 30 or 35 of its workmen live in Orange county.

The youngest of the furniture companies is Craftique, Inc., established in 1945. This rapidly growing company, now employing about 150 workmen, makes solid furniture exclusively, much of it of mahogany, Honduras, and other Central American woods.

Largest of the textile mills is the Rockfish-Mebane Yarn Mills, Inc. This company was organized as the Mebane Yarn Mill in 1936, taking its present name after a reorganization in 1946. It makes cotton yarn which it sells mainly to hosiery mills. It employs about 230 people.

Kale Knitting Mill, Inc., established in 1939, has two small plants. One is a knitting plant, the other a finishng plant. The company makes both full-fashioned hose for women and half hose for men and boys. It has its own dyeing equipment, and is thus prepared to produce a varied as well as a quality product.

The Baker-Mebane Hosiery Mill, a subsidiary of Baker-Cammack of Burlington, manufactures half hose. It employs about 75 persons.

The Southerland Dyeing and Finishing Mills, established in 1948, are also engaged in the manufacture of men's hosiery. This company employs about 40 workers.

Apparel, Inc., in operation since 1946, makes women's and children's dresses. It employs about 75 white women, having witnessed a steady growth since its establishment.

The Mebane Lumber Company makes or handles all kinds of home building supplies. It buys rough lumber and processes it for the building trade. It also does some custom work. The company presently employs 20 people. Unlike the other Mebane establishments included in this enumeration, this one is located in Orange county. Another small concern on the Orange county side of the line is the Walton Lumber Company. It buys small lots of hardwoods from loggers and sorts and assembles for the trade.

Carrboro and its Industries

The villages of Chapel Hill and Carrboro are contiguous, the western boundary of Chapel Hill being Carrboro's eastern boundary. Chapel Hill is a much older town, being laid out in 1793 at the same time that the University laid the cornerstone of its first building. Carrboro's history begins with the extension of the railroad, or more precisely a 10 mile spur of the railroad, in 1882 from what was thereafter called University Station to a point about a mile west of the University. In the Chapel Hill *Weekly*, March 21, 1947, Louis Graves has told how Carrboro began and how it grew, and we quote from this interesting article:

> My Memory extends to the early 1890's when there were no buildings on the site of the present Carrboro but the railway station,—which everybody called "the depot,"— a cotton gin, a flour mill, a blacksmith shop, and one or two dwellings. Hacks with Negro drivers met every train and brought the passengers into Chapel Hill. Sometimes the drivers would whip up their horses and race with each other down the main street, raising clouds of dust in dry weather or sprays of mud in wet weather.
>
> . . . . .
>
> Automobiles finally put this branch railway line out of business for passenger service. When the last train ran, a dozen or so years ago, Bruce Strowd issued an invitation to the children of Chapel Hill to make the trip over to the junction and back. Many of them found it an exciting adventure because they had never been on a railway train before. . . . .Captain Fred Smith was conductor on the train from 1889 for about fifty years. . . .
>
> Carrboro's growth into a real town began when Tom Lloyd built his cotton mill in 1898. His remarkably keen mind, and his natural-born gift for trading, enabled him to become the richest man in Chapel Hill despite the handicap of having had no schooling. He could neither read nor write until he was well along in years. Then he learned to write his name so that he could sign checks and business documents. That was all the learning he needed for his purposes and all he wanted.
>
> Tom Lloyd's red brick house, up on West Cameron avenue, is one of the few pre-Civil War houses still standing in Chapel Hill. It was bought by the Leon Wileys several years ago and is now their home. They have made interior alterations, but the house is practically unchanged on the outside.
>
> The little settlement clustered around the depot and the

cotton mill grew steadily. It was named Venable, for Francis P. Venable, President of the University, for several years. When the Carrs bought the Lloyd cotton mill the name was changed to Carrboro.

The mill became part of the Durham Hosiery Mills, being known as No. 4. Another mill, which had been built by Lueco Lloyd, Isaac Pritchard, and others was bought by the Durham concern and became No. 7. The business of the Durham Hosiery Mills began to contract even before the depression. No. 4 closed in 1930 and No. 7 later.

Carrboro was in the grip of hard times in the 1930's, but its distress was alleviated to a great extent by the successful effort of the University administration to provide jobs for its citizens in building operations and other University activities. The town had a come-back in 1942 when the former No. 7 mill was converted into a munitions plant. The plant stayed in operation 3 years and paid out several thousand dollars a week in wages. This was a real boom time for Carrboro. . . .

About two years ago came the cheering news that the Pacific Mills, one of the country's greatest wool-manufacturing companies, had bought the former No. 4 mill and would open a branch factory in Carrboro. Later the company bought the munitions plant building which had been stripped of its contents and left idle after the end of the war.

The Pacific Mills' Carrboro branch, which is named the Carrboro Woolen Mills, began operations in April, 1945 after the first unit had been thoroughly modernized with air-conditioning, fluorescent lighting, and the latest spinning and weaving equipment. Not only was the interior of the building renovated and modernized but the grounds were attractively landscaped. After the second building was purchased, it was similarly modernized. The first bolt of woolen military cloth, made on contract for the government, came from the looms April 27, 1945. Within a few months, however, Pacific Mills was manufacturing its pre-war type of products—high grade worsteds for men's and ladies' suits, dress material, auto fabrics, and the like. The mills regularly employ about 525 persons, and have an annual payroll of $1,100,000. Except for a few key men, all are local people who had to learn the processes after they were employed. The resident manager is David E. Arthur, who came to Carrboro from Lawrence, Massachusetts.

The industry is a great asset to the county, giving it a vastly improved agricultural-industrial balance. Of course, it has given a tremendous fillip to the village of Carrboro. This is reflected in new houses, new stores, paved streets, and a general evidence of prosperity. The Bank of Chapel Hill reopened a branch there.

Although the woolen mills are the town's largest industry, there are several small but important concerns. The oldest is the Fitch Lumber Company. When R. B. Fitch bought the business of Andrews and Lloyd in 1923 he acquired one employee and a handful of lumber. Now the company employs 20 men to operate a planing mill, a coal yard, and five trucks. It owns and cuts much of its own timber which it converts into all kinds of building material.

Another business, established only in 1947, but now employing 20 persons, is the Colonial Press, Inc. With seven modern presses, it does all kinds of commercial printing including a great amount of work for the University of North Carolina and other institutions and departments of the state government. Its proprietor, Orville Campbell, has won distinction as the composer of the popular football song, "All the Way Choo-Choo."

Chapel Hill

Chapel Hill is the site of the county's largest employer, the University of North Carolina. The University owns and operates a waterworks, a telephone system, a power plant, a laundry, and a hotel, namely the Carolina Inn. It also owns and operates a second dining room which serves the public—the Monogram Club. The operation of these utilities and service plants together with the maintenance of the campus with its 60-odd buildings provides employment to many people. The laundry employs 110 at the present time, the hotel and eating establishments 100, the utilities 100, and the buildings and grounds 225. Another 75 work at the gymnasium or in caring for the swimming pools and athletic fields. The service and maintenance people at the hospital number about 200. Thus it may be seen that the University gives employment to more than 1,000 persons outside of the academic and professional personnel. Some live in Chapel Hill, some live in Carrboro, many live out in the country in all directions. Many are skilled workmen—carpenters, painters, telephone linesmen, cooks. Many Negroes are employed, as janitors, waiters and waitresses, laundresses, as well as in skilled occupations.

The academic and professional personnel—teachers, doctors, nurses, accountants, secretaries, and the like—amounts to another 1,000. Thus in normal times when there is no construction going on the University has about 2,000 employees, with an annual payroll of at least $8,500,000. The impact of this flow of income into the county, to say nothing of what is spent by students, visitors and attendants at athletic events cannot be measured, but the evidence of it is visible in the homes, churches, schools, and places of business throughout the southern end of the county.

In the usual meaning of the term, Chapel Hill has only two industries, The Orange Printshop and the Hill Bakery. The Orange Printshop was founded in 1923 by Louis Graves as an addition to his newspaper, *The Chapel Hill Weekly*, and was leased to W. M. Pugh in 1940. It now employs between 30 and 40 people and does all kinds of commercial printing, books and magazines. During and immediately following World War II, it did work for Chas. Scribner's Sons of New York and the U. S. Government. It holds the record for delivery of the Session Laws of the North Carolina Legislature, 22 days after adjournment of the session.

The Hill Bakery was established in 1921 by William B. Neal and first located on the lot which was soon to be occupied by the Strowd Motor Company. After Mr. Neal's death the bakery continued to be operated for some years by Mrs. Neal, but in 1945 she relinquished the management to R. A. Reinhardt, retaining only the building. For more than thirty years the University community has depended on this local bake shop for most of its bread and much of its pastry, and it in turn has enjoyed the high praise of its patrons.

Distribution of Employment

According to the 1950 Census there were 25,713 persons in Orange county over 14 years of age. Since this number includes children in school, unemployed housewives, the aged, sick and infirm, only 12,447 persons, or slightly less than half of the total group are considered in the county's civilian labor force. All were employed at the time the Census was taken except 192 men and 141 women. An occupational breakdown of those employed follows:

	Men	Women
Professional and technical	1019	593
Farmers	1410	21
Managers, officials and proprietors, other than farmers	580	124
Clerical workers	315	708
Sales workers	296	152
Craftsmen and foremen	1141	21
Operatives	1581	966
Private household workers	17	502
Other service workers	803	340
Farm laborers, unpaid	310	136
Farm laborers, paid	353	22
Laborers, other than farm	567	17
Occupation not reported	91	29
Total employed	8483	3631

This body of workers is also classified by the Census according to the type of industry providing the employment. The classification follows:

	Men	Women
Agriculture	2084	181
Forestry	3	....
Mining	2	....
Construction	771	10
Manufacturing		
Furniture, lumber and wood products	592	22
Textiles	871	750
Food and kindred products	59	17
Printing and publishing	83	24
All others	174	67
Railroads and railway express	37	1
Trucking and warehousing	68	3
Other transportation	62	6
Utilities and sanitary services	133	9
Communications	17	24

Wholesale trade	84	17
Food and dairy stores, milk retailing	223	73
Eating and drinking places	180	132
Other retail trade	556	170
Finance, insurance and real estate	111	130
Repair services	94	2
Private households	77	519
Hotels and lodging places	98	43
Other personal services	135	169
Business services	20	23
Medical and health services	59	105
Entertainment and recreation	67	22
Education services	1463	934
Other professional services	110	67
Public administration	157	70
Not reported	93	41
Total	8483	3631

Although many of Orange county's industrial workers are employed in Durham and Alamance counties and are credited to those counties, the Employment Security Commission of North Carolina credited Orange county in 1951 with 94 employers whose workers were covered by unemployment insurance. The number of workers covered was 3,242, and their average weekly wage was $43.81.

These figures indicate that Orange is no longer an unbalanced county. Not only are its farms better and more prosperous than ever before but there are many opportunities for off the farm employment. This is provided across the line in Durham, across the line in Alamance, at the University at Chapel Hill, in several factories within the county, and in garages, stores, and repair shops everywhere. This means more universally a respectable standard of living and a general increase in wealth.

CHAPTER XVII

THE CHURCHES OF ORANGE COUNTY

BY L. J. PHIPPS

Chairman, Bi-Centennial Committee

The people who settled the country covered by the original thirteen colonies were very different in their political and religious sentiments, in their pecuniary circumstances and habits of living and were influenced by different motives in exchanging a civilized for a savage country. Those who settled New England and most of the country north of the Potomac were actuated by religious motives and sought the wilds of America as an asylum from religious intolerance and persecution in the Old World. The country south of the Potomac was largely settled under the auspices of men who belonged to the ranks of the nobility, the wealthy and influential, whose object was to increase their wealth or fame, and hence their efforts from the first were to introduce into their colonies orders of nobility and the established church.

William Warren Sweet in *Religion in the Development of American Culture* suggests that the person who would learn the background for the historical events of any society must first comprehend the spiritual motivation of the people concerned. An understanding of some of the racial characteristics and culture of the colonists of early America is a prerequisite to the appreciation of the magnitude of their various accomplishments.

In Virginia Sir William Berkeley, who entered upon his duties as Governor in 1642, was popular as a man and as a Governor, but he was a zealous high churchman and exerted himself to have the Church of England fully established. In 1643 "it was especially ordered that no minister should preach or teach publicly or privately except in conformity to the constitution of the Church of England and non-conformists were banished from the colony." Some of those who were thus banished came over into North Carolina.

The Earl of Granville, a zealous member of the Church of

England, exercised all of his influence to get the church established. The Province of North Carolina was early divided into parishes and provision was therein made for the support of ministers, the purchase of glebes, erection of churches, etc., and for these purposes the vestry was empowered to levy a tax of five shillings per poll. An act was passed requiring the members of the Assembly to conform to the religious worship in the Province according to the Church of England, and to qualify for office by receiving the Sacrament of the Lord's Supper according to the rights and usages of that church.

In searching out the origins of the churches of Orange county one will see that the early settlers, zealous for their freedom of body, mind and spirit and finding the old regimes of their homelands encroaching upon their religious principles, came not only from Europe but from other American colonies as well in their search for new lands where they might work out their own salvation with fear and trembling in the sight of God, but without fear of any man.

Chapter VI of the Laws of 1752 which created Orange county also established the Parish of St. Matthews and named as vestrymen for the parish the following: Alexander Maben, James Watson, Mark Morgan, John Patterson, Andrew Mitchell, Thomas Loveletter, Lawrence Bankston, James Ellison, William Bolling, John Gray, John Pitman and Joseph Tate.

In 1754, two years after the formation of Orange county, Governor Arthur Dobbs secured the passage of a Vestry Act, but King George II disallowed the law because it conferred the right of presentation upon the vestries. The crown also disallowed church laws passed in 1758, 1760, 1761, and 1762 on the same grounds. As a result Anglican clergy were left without support and the number of clergymen in North Carolina began to decrease. In 1764, Dobbs reported that there were only six Anglican clergymen in the whole colony. Under the encouragement of Governors William Tryon and Josiah Martin and supported by the Vestry Act of 1764, renewed in 1768 and again in 1774, the number of clergymen increased from six to eighteen.

Though no dates have been established it is known that in addition to St. Matthews Church in Hillsboro at least two other

Chapels of the Church of England, the established church, were organized in Orange county prior to the Revolution. St. Mary's in the Eastern part of the county and New Hope Chapel in the Southern part of the county on the hill that is now Chapel Hill were in existence prior to the war. The Rev. George Micklejohn, rector in the parish, probably preached at all three places until the outbreak of the Revolution, when he, like most of the other ministers of the Church of England, was compelled to resign his position because he remained loyal to the crown.

The Revolution had the effect of disestablishing the Church of England in the colonies. The tie between church and state was completely severed with the adoption of the Federal Constitution which declared "Congress shall make no law respecting an establishment of religion." At the close of the war only five of its clergy remained in North Carolina.

The various denominations will be treated, as nearly as possible, in the order of the establishment of the first church of the particular denomination in the area which was first created into Orange county.

QUAKERS

The Quakers, who in 1752 found themselves within the limits of the newly created Orange county, began coming into that area in 1748 on a wave of migrations which penetrated the whole of the Carolina Piedmont, but these Quaker settlements were also a product of a great chain of migrations of their own which broke out from Pennsylvania two decades earlier. It had already resulted in the establishment of Quaker communities and Meetings in Maryland and Piedmont Virginia. When this movement reached the Cane creek watershed to the west of Haw river that area was still a part of the great hinterland of Bladen county. During the next two decades this expansion spread into the hills of South Carolina, and dwindled out in Georgia. In the Quaker settlements in the interior of the Carolinas the Cane Creek Monthly Meeting occupied the pivotal position. Every Meeting in Western North Carolina traces its constitutional ancestry back to Cane creek.

By 1751, the Cane creek community contained 30 Quaker families—enough to warrant the establishment of a Monthly Meeting for business under North Carolina Yearly Meeting of Friends. During the next three years the number grew to 100 families, and subordinate Meetings were being set up by Cane creek in different parts of Orange county — one in the Eno river valley northeast of Hillsboro — most of them in the area later included in Chatham county, and one in Rowan county. These Quaker pioneers in Orange county were nearly all from other colonies: most of them from Pennsylvania, some from Maryland, a considerable number from Virginia, and a few from Eastern North Carolina, where they had held their first Monthly Meeting in Albemarle in 1672, and some straight from Ireland. Many of these settlers were young men without families. Their thrift, social standards, loyalty to peaceful living, and interest in education caused the Quakers to exercise a wholesome influence on the areas in which they settled.

Until the outbreak of the Revolution, the flow of Quaker immigrants into the Piedmont section continued as a steady stream. The number of subordinate meetings set up by Cane creek eventually reached a total of ten.

The Society of Friends has always maintained a strong testimony against resort to war. The Cane Creek Meeting was put to a severe test during the period of the Regulator movement and the succeeding period of the Revolution. The geographic limits of the Orange county Quaker Meetings were torn by the activities in each of these great movements. While Cane Creek Meeting stuck rigidly to its testimony for peace many of its members joined the Regulator movement and others later joined the forces fighting for independence. By the end of the Revolution, Cane Creek Meeting had disowned between 40 and 50 of the men of its membership for joining the Regulators or for participation in the Revolution. Herman Husbands, the leader of the Regulators, was not among those disowned during the Regulator Movement. He was disowned for severe criticism of the Meeting before the beginning of this movement.

With the beginning of the Revolution, the Quaker immigration to the area slowed down to a trickle and a stream of emigration began to get under way. The establishment of Guilford, Chatham and Alamance Counties removed most of the Quakers from Orange county — leaving only the Eno Meeting, which came to an end approximately 100 years after the founding of Orange county. A large cemetery surrounded by a rock wall is all that now marks the spot of this Meeting. The location is just off the Hillsboro-Schley road and about one-quarter of a mile east of Mars Hill Baptist Church. After Eno Meeting was laid down there was no organized Friends Meeting in Orange county until the Chapel Hill Meeting was established in 1944.

During the reconstruction period the Friends from Philadelphia operated a school for ex-slaves in Chapel Hill on West Franklin street for many years and then transferred the property to the local school board when schools were provided for Negroes at public expense. They also transferred a lot in Hillsboro to Dickerson's African Methodist Episcopal church.

PRESENT CHURCH: CHAPEL HILL MONTHLY MEETING OF FRIENDS; organized: May 21, 1944; leaders in organization: A. W. Hobbs, R. J. M. Hobbs, and D. D. Carroll. No building. The Meeting has purchased a lot on Highway 54 in Chapel Hill for a building in the future. Membership July 1, 1953: 30.

PROTESTANT EPISCOPAL

The Revolution almost destroyed the colonial Church of England. Under special oath of allegiance to the King the clergy either fled to England or Canada, or remained as Loyalists in the colonies. At the war's end there was no episcopacy, no association of churches, not even the semblance of an establishment. Few thought of any future for this church, which suffered more than any other in the colonies. It was slow in becoming reestablished as the Protestant Episcopal Church. As late as 1817 when the Diocese of North Carolina was established, it contained only three clergymen and less than 200 communicants.

It is stated in the preface of the Book of Common Prayer of the Protestant Episcopal Church that "this church is far from intending to depart from the Church of England in any essential point of doctrine, discipline or worship". Therein lies the hint of its origin; the Protestant Episcopal Church constitutes "the self-governing American branch of the Anglican Communion"; for a century and a half in this country it bore the name of the Church of England.

With the outbreak of the Civil War disruption again threatened the Protestant Episcopal Church, but unlike the Baptist and Methodist Churches, it survived this threat.

The Episcopal form of government closely parallels that of the Federal government. The basic unit is the parish, governed by the rector, or priest; wardens, who have charge of the church records and the collection of alms; and vestrymen who have charge of all church property. Parishes are grouped into dioceses.

PRESENT CHURCHES: ST. MARY'S CHAPEL (23)* was admitted to the Episcopal Convention in 1819 and the building was consecrated on November 25, 1859, by the Rev. Dr. Curtis and Bishop Atkinson. This church was, on account of decline in membership, discontinued about 20 years ago. Now on the 3rd Sunday in August each year the former members observe a homecoming.

ST. MATTHEWS of HILLSBORO as a branch of the established church of England dates its organization from the founding of the county in 1752. The original church was inactive during the Revolution and for several decades thereafter. The present church was reorganized in 1824 under the leadership of William Norwood, Jonathan Sneed, Thomas Ruffin, Francis L. Hawks, and Walker Anderson; first rector of the original church was the Rev. George H. Micklejohn and of the reorganized church the Rev. William Mercer Green, who was afterwards Bishop of Mississippi; the building was erected in 1824 and seats 150; membership 86; last rector: The Rev. R. C. Masterton.

CHAPEL OF THE CROSS of CHAPEL HILL: organized in 1842; leader and first pastor was The Rev. William Mercer Green; first Chapel erected in 1848 seats 132 and present building erected in 1925 seats 376; membership: 391; present rector, Rev. David W. Yates.

THE CHURCH OF THE HOLY FAMILY of CHAPEL HILL: organized January 27, 1952; leaders: George D. Penick, John B. Saunders, W. Robert Mann, John Clayton, U. T. Holmes Jr.; first pastor: Maurice Arthur Kidder; ground breaking for new building to seat 150 on June 7, 1953; membership: 172; present pastor: Rev. Maurice Arthur Kidder.

---

* Location on map on page 314.

PRESBYTERIAN

The pioneers who settled Piedmont North Carolina about the middle of the 18th century, in addition to the Quakers, were largely Scotch and Scotch-Irish and were of the Presbyterian faith. Presbyterianism had its origin in the struggle to prevent the state from exercising control of church government. It is a form of church government developed in the 16th century by Calvin and other reformers. The Presbyterian form of government had long been characteristic of the established church of Scotland and with some doctrinal variations the pioneers adapted this religion to the needs of the frontier people.

Presbyterians migrated by the thousands to Pennsylvania where the principles of civil and religious liberty were fully entertained; but, partly from the difficulty of obtaining land, and partly for other reasons, they found it expedient to move further South. In Virginia, land could be obtained in abundance and upon easy terms, but the government there was in constant hostility with religious freedom, and the greater part of the people came to North Carolina and settled on the lands of the Earl of Granville. They have been staunch friends of liberty and of everything else that can elevate the character or promote the general welfare. Combining the intelligence, orthodoxy, and piety of the Scotch with the ardor and love of liberty peculiar to the Irish, they were the most efficient supporters of the American cause during the Revolution and have done much for the support of learning, morality and religion.

The first church established by this sect in the newly created Orange County was Grier's Presbyterian Church at High Towers, now in Caswell County, in 1753, followed by Hawfield's in the attractive rural environment of what is now eastern Alamance in 1755 and Eno, now located at Cedar Grove, in 1755 and New Hope in 1756.

The pastors of these churches together with several other Presbyterian ministers constituted in 1770 the first Presbytery for North Carolina, then and now known as the Orange Presbytery. The leaders in the organization of these churches and the presbytery were Hugh McAden, a Presbyterian missionary, Henry Patillo, who was for a number of years pastor of Hawfield's, Eno, Little River and New Hope, and David Caldwell, who was for several years pastor of Alamance and Buffalo Churches. These names are distinguished for dissent in politics as well as in religion and David Caldwell particularly was a most sympathetic adviser of the Regulators in 1770-1771 and voiced the sentiments of pure democracy in the Halifax convention which framed the constitution of 1776.

PRESENT CHURCHES: ENO PRESBYTERIAN CHURCH (13); organized in 1755; leader: Hugh McAden; first pastor: Henry Patillo; originally located on Eno River about 2 miles Southeast of Cedar Grove; after its building was destroyed by the big fire of 1890 the church moved to Cedar Grove; building seats 300; membership: 101; present pastor: Rev. K. M. Misenheimer.

NEW HOPE PRESBYTERIAN (41); organized in 1756; leaders: Gilbert Strayhorn and John Craig; first pastor: Henry Patillo; first building erected in 1756; fourth and present building erected in 1863, seats 175; membership: 104; present pastor: Rev. John E. Ensign.

LITTLE RIVER PRESBYTERIAN CHURCH (14); organized in 1761; leader: Hugh McAden; first pastor: Henry Patillo; building seats 250; membership: 135; present pastor: Rev. K. M. Misenheimer.

HILLSBORO PRESBYTERIAN CHURCH, organized in 1816; leaders: Rev. John Witherspoon, Susan D. Witherspoon, Frank Nash, Mary G. Nash, James Phillips, Mary Phillips, Anne A. Webb, Mary Burk, Henry Thompson, Sr., and John Allison; first pastor: Rev. John Witherspoon; building erected in 1816 seats 185; membership: 199; present pastor: Rev. Charles H. Reckard.

BETHLEHEM PRESBYTERIAN CHURCH, (50); organized in 1822; leaders: Rev. Elisha Mitchell, Rev. Elijah Graves and Col. Samuel Child; first pastor: Rev. John Witherspoon; first building erected in 1823; seats 250; membership: 88; no regular pastor; Rev. Max Polly of Duke University supply.

FAIRFIELD PRESBYTERIAN CHURCH (19); organized in 1834; first pastor: Samuel Paisley; building seats 100; membership: 82; present pastor: Rev. K. M. Misenheimer.

THE PRESBYTERIAN CHURCH of CHAPEL HILL, organized on June 8, 1845; leaders: James Phillips, Rev. Elisha Mitchell, Charles Phillips and David Swain; first pastor: Rev. John B. Shearer; building erected in 1849; remodeled in 1919 seats 424; membership: 413; acting pastor: Rev. Robert J. McMullen.

EFLAND PRESBYTERIAN CHURCH; organized Nov. 1, 1908; leaders in organization: D. C. McAdams, M. L. Efland, D. E. Forrest, Rev. S. M. Rankin, Rev. M. C. Arrowood and John Efland, Sr.; first pastor:

Rev. S. M. Wilhelm; building erected in 1910 seats 150; membership: 31; present pastor: Rev. John E. Ensign.

COVENANT PRESBYTERIAN CHURCH of CHAPEL HILL, organized January 25, 1953; leaders: T. D. Rose, C. Hugh Holman, Carl F. Brown, John H. Hinson, Miles M. Fitch; no building; membership: 33; present pastor: Rev. Wm. R. Thurman.

METHODIST

England's famed old Oxford University has been called "the cradle of lost causes", but at least one cause was born there which was not lost. This was Methodism, formed in 1729 chiefly by John and Charles Wesley, sons of a clergyman of the Church of England.

Methodism was from the outset frankly evangelical and the Methodists were not restrained by doctrinal obstacles from carrying the message of the gospel to rich or poor wherever and whenever they could be found. The founder of Methodism, John Wesley, while a missionary in Georgia in 1736, did not step out of his character as an ordained minister of the Church of England, and his successor, George Whitefield, also regarded as one of the patriarchs of the Methodist Church, was a steadfast Anglican communicant. Whitefield was "a flame of fire" from Georgia to Maine, visiting North Carolina in 1739 and several times thereafter, and like other evangelists of the period he was at no time circumscribed by denominational lines; his great work was the breaking down of the barriers to the direct relationship of man to God. This was essentially a democratic process and these early preachers were more or less unconsciously aiding the political revolution at the time they were preparing the ground for the religious awakening in the colonies.

Wesley did his best to keep the movement within the Church of England, an evangelical party within the church, but the great numbers recruited among the unchurched made a separate organization imperative. The separate movement invaded the American colonies and in 1769 the New York Methodists had built Wesley Chapel. The Methodist ministers prior to the Revolution were nearly all from England and were so roughly treated during the Revolution that nearly every one of them had fled either to Canada or home to England by 1779.

Joseph Pilmore is credited with having preached the first Methodist sermon in North Carolina at Currituck court house on September 28, 1772, and the next year saw the first Methodist society in the province. After the Revolution, Francis Asbury worked almost single handed and a miracle seemed to happen. Of all the religious groups in the colonies the Methodists alone actually seemed to prosper during the Revolution. Methodism not only swept through the cities; it developed an amazing strength in small towns and in the rural areas. Everywhere there were circuit riders—ministers on horseback riding the expanding frontier. The "multitudes" found a satisfaction in the creeds and practices of Methodism which explains the rapid growth of the church. The circuit-riders in North Carolina increased from 18 in 1783 to 27 in 1800, and these, with the co-operation of the "local" ministers, brought the influence of this denomination to nearly every section of the state.

Divisions came to the Methodists when several bodies broke off: Republican Methodists in 1792; Methodist Protestants in 1830. In 1844 came the most devastating split of all, the bisecting of the Methodist Episcopal Church into two churches, the Methodist Episcopal Church, the Northern body, and the Methodist Episcopal Church, South. The cause of this major split was, of course, slavery. It was a split that concerned neither doctrine nor polity; it was purely political and social, and it was a wound that waited until 1939 for healing.

PRESENT CHURCHES: NEW SHARON METHODIST CHURCH (22); organized in 1768; building erected in 1948, seats 250; membership: 265; present pastor: Rev. A. Morris Williams.

HILLSBORO METHODIST CHURCH: organized about 1807; building erected in 1867, seats 200; membership: 300; present pastor: Rev. A. Morris Williams.

LEBANON METHODIST CHURCH (18); organized in 1820; building erected in 1937, seats 250; membership: 145; present pastor: Rev. James R. Hailey.

CEDAR GROVE METHODIST CHURCH (12); organized about 1830; present building erected in 1937, seats 200; membership: 225; present pastor: Rev. Henry B. Lewis.

ORANGE METHODIST CHURCH (53); organized in Davis School House near the Wash Fowler home about 1830; leaders in organization: Rev. Alexander Gattis, Jones Watson, Wm. Robson, Isaac J. Collier, Elijah Hatch, James Gattis, Daniel Hogan, Wesley Snipes, Jacob Potts and William Gattis; first pastor: Rev. Alexander Gattis; first building about 1838; present building erected in 1924, seats 200; membership: 128; present pastor: Rev. Clifford Shoaf.

PLEASANT GREEN METHODIST CHURCH (32); organized about 1832; leaders in organization: William Harris, William Piper, Samuel Piper, Jacob Pealor, Abel G. Jackson, Francis F. Workman, Thomas W. Holden; membership: 162; present pastor: Rev. K. B. Sexton.

CLOVER GARDEN METHODIST CHURCH (54); organized before 1836; building erected in 1836 seats 150; present pastor: Rev. C. C. Wiggers.

UNION GROVE METHODIST CHURCH (46); organized September 23, 1846; leaders: Thomas Long, Lemuel Carroll, Thomas C. Hayes, Calvin Bishop and Daniel Thompson; first pastor: possibly Alson Gray; cornerstone present building laid September 23, 1946, seats 200; membership: 100; present pastor: Rev. James R. Hailey.

WALNUT GROVE METHODIST CHURCH (7); organized about 1850; building erected in 1939, seats 400; membership: 400; present pastor: Rev. Henry B. Lewis.

ORANGE CHAPEL METHODIST CHURCH (55); organized in 1850; leader in organization: Alson Gray; first pastor: Alson Gray (circuit-rider); first building erected in 1850; a new building being erected in 1953 to seat 225; present pastor: Rev. C. C. Wiggers.

UNIVERSITY METHODIST CHURCH of CHAPEL HILL; organized in July, 1853; leaders: Charles F. Deems and Rev. J. Milton Frost. first pastor; Rev. J. Milton Frost; building erected in 1925, seats 866; membership: 580; present pastor: Rev. W. M. Howard, Jr.

NEW BETHEL METHODIST CHURCH (5); organized in 1859; leaders: John R. McMannan, Jonathan Nichols, Wm. H. Pass; Wm. Carrington, Wm. Harris, Robert N. Hall and Jackson Latta; building erected in 1925, seats 250; membership: 209; present pastor: Rev. Walton N. Bass.

CHESTNUT RIDGE METHODIST CHURCH (36); organized about 1890; membership: 270; present pastor: Rev. J. R. Hailey.

EFLAND METHODIST CHURCH; organized May 14, 1905; leaders: Mrs. M. P. Efland, Mr. and Mrs. O. E. Bivins and Mr. and Mrs. C. A. Bivins; first pastor: Rev. W. D. Fogleman; building erected in 1905, seats 250; membership: 242; present pastor: Rev. James R. Hailey.

CARRBORO METHODIST CHURCH; organized in 1910; leaders: T. H. Raney, Mr. and Mrs. W. H. Parker, Mr. and Mrs. T. N. Mann, Mrs. Nannie Thrift; first pastor: Rev. W. A. Stanbury; present building erected in 1953, seats about 300; membership: 314; present pastor: Rev. M. E. Tyson.

CARR METHODIST CHURCH (4); organized in 1913; leader: G. T. Pentecost; first pastor: J. M. Ormond; building erected in 1915, seats 150; membership: 55; present pastor: Rev. Henry B. Lewis.

ENO METHODIST CHURCH of WEST HILLSBORO; organized about 1913; membership: 147; present pastor: Rev. M. D. Tyson.

PALMER GROVE METHODIST CHURCH (34); organized about 1938; leaders in organization: E. T. Blakely, R. T. Murdock, and T. H. Yates; membership: 106; present pastor: Rev. M. D. Tyson.

BAPTISTS

When the Reformation set the Bible and men free early in the 16th century, scattered groups appeared advocating the convictions of faith which are today the warp and woof of Baptist theology and ideology. The early British Baptists wielded a tremendous influence in their times and upon the future; it is claimed for them that "more than any king or Parliament, they set the heart and mind of England free." In 1631 Roger Williams came to America and he was to be the first great champion for faith and conscience on this side of the Atlantic.

Williams was not a Baptist but a Separatist minister when he arrived. Preaching "new and dangerous opinions against the authority of the magistrates," he fled their courtly wrath and organized a Baptist Church at Providence, R.I., in 1639.

The Baptists became strongly rooted in Massachusetts and Pennsylvania during the 17th century and a group of the sect had also established themselves in South Carolina. A congregation of Baptists was in existence near Perquimans river as early as 1727. Except in holding office, Baptists and other dissenters suffered little disadvantage as residents of North Carolina. On the other hand, many instances occurred in Virginia involving actual persecution of dissenters. Thus North Carolina offered a relatively safe haven to members of faiths which officially were not tolerated in Virginia. This was a factor inducing a diversified religious affiliation among the peoples of this state.

In the matter of church government the Baptists do not submit to any central oversight. Each congregation stands on its own but at an early time the Baptists recognized the value of voluntary association and both local and state associations now exist. The Baptist denomination had ministers and churches in the newly created Orange county about as early as the Presbyterians and other dissenters. Shubael Stearns came into what is now Randolph county about the year 1755 and in a few years had a church on Sandy creek of more than 600 members. In this section other Baptist churches were established prior to the Revolution as follows: Deep River, now in Chatham county, in 1757; Haw River, and Rock Spring, now in Chatham county, in 1764; County Line, now in Caswell county, in 1772; and Rocky River in Chatham county in 1776.

The churches in the Sandy creek area were early organized into the Sandy Creek Association and for a number of years most of the churches in Orange county were members of this association. The Mount Zion Association was formed in 1870 and now practically all of the Baptist churches in the county are members of this association; a few are members of the Yates (Durham) Association.

The Baptist convention of 1814 marked the first real denominational consciousness in the state. The great division of the Baptists came in 1845 and, like the division in the Methodist Episcopal Church, was over the question of slavery. The Southerners "seceded" and formed their own Southern Baptist Convention in order to carry on more effectively the work of the Southern Baptist churches. This breach has not yet been mended.

Baptists have insisted upon freedom of thought and expression in pulpit and pew; this has made this denomination one of the most democratic religious bodies in America, and one in which liberal and conservative doctrines are preached freely. They have insisted too upon the absolute autonomy of the local congregation. Today they constitute the largest Protestant group in in the United States and the largest religious group in the State of North Carolina.

PRESENT CHURCHES: CANE CREEK BAPTIST CHURCH (45); organized in 1789; leaders in organization: Rev. Thomas Cates, Richard Cates, Joseph Cates, Bernard Cates, Robert Cates, John Workman, John Strader, and Mary Christmas; first pastor: Rev. Thomas Cates; membership: 182; present pastor: Rev. Harry Bird.
MOUNT CARMEL BAPTIST CHURCH (60); organized in 1803 at Pritchard's Mill and moved to present location in 1873; first pastor

ORANGE COUNTY—1752-1952   301

was probably Elder Robert T. Daniel; present building erected in 1873 seats 300; membership: 353; present pastor: Rev. Henry A. Morgan.

ANTIOCH BAPTIST CHURCH (56); organized by Cane Creek in 1806 as Haw River Mountain Church and moved to present location in 1830; leaders: Jesse Buckner, George Pope and Thomas Cates: first pastor: Elder Mark Andrews; membership: 247; present pastor: George Pirtle.

MOUNT MORIAH BAPTIST CHURCH (49); organized in 1823; present pastor: Rev. Joe Bridgers.

MARS HILL BAPTIST CHURCH (27); organized in June 1834 by members of Cane Creek Baptist Church; leaders in organization: Levi Andrews and Stephen Pleasants; building erected in   ; seats 150; membership: 165; present pastor: Rev. W. R. Eaton.

MOUNT HERMON BAPTIST CHURCH (40); organized on June 24, 1848; first pastor: Rev. Jesse Howell; building erected about 1913 seats 300; membership: 250; present pastor: Rev. Mr. Eddington.

BETHEL BAPTIST CHURCH (51); organized in 1851; present building erected about 1900, seats 250; membership: 196; present pastor: Rev. L. C. Cheek.

FIRST BAPTIST CHURCH of HILLSBORO; organized Nov. 19, 1853; leaders in organization: Mrs. Wm. A. Graham and Rev. A. Jones, Jr.; first pastor: Rev. A. Jones, Jr.; building erected in 1860 seats 300, remodeled in 1953; membership: 215; present pastor: Rev. Charles E. Maddry.

THE BAPTIST CHURCH of CHAPEL HILL; organized April 14, 1854; leaders in organization: William Henry Merritt, George W. Purefoy and Brantley J. Hackney; first pastor: Elder J. P. Mason; original building erected 1854-55 now the Chapel Hill Masonic Temple, present building erected in 1922-23 seats 900; membership: 769; present pastor: Dr. Samuel Tilden Habel.

CROSS ROADS BAPTIST CHURCH (38); organized in 1883 as Betheden Baptist Church; leaders in organization: W. P. Roberts and S. S. Cates; first pastor: Rev. R. A. Patterson; building erected in 1910 seats 300; membership: 125; present pastor: Rev. Robert Gaines.

BERRY'S GROVE BAPTIST CHURCH (2); organized in 1887; leaders Rev. J. H. Lambreth, A. T. Hord, R. H. Hall, J. E. Harris; first pastor: Rev. A. T. Hord; building erected in 1888 seats 400; membership: 295; present pastor: Rev. E. B. Booker.

MOUNT ADAR BAPTIST CHURCH (3); organized in 1889; leaders in organization: W. H. Whitted and A. J. Compton; first pastor: Rev. A. T. Hord; membership: 69.

EBENEZER BAPTIST CHURCH (29); organized in 1896; leaders in organization: A. O. Cates, J. M. Martin and W. J. Dollar; first pastor: Dalphus Crabtree; first building erected in 1896 and present building in 1952 seats 300; membership: 117; present pastor: Rev. R. E. Scarlett.

CARRBORO BAPTIST CHURCH; organized October 30, 1902; leaders in organization: Rev. J. C. Hocutt and Dr. J. William Jones; first pastor: Rev. J. C. Hocutt; building erected in 1924 seats 600; membership: 700; present pastor: Rev. Troy E. Jones.

EFLAND BAPTIST CHURCH; organized in 1904; membership: 55.

WEST HILL BAPTIST CHURCH of WEST HILLSBORO; organized April 27, 1917; leaders in organization: Rev. J. F. McDuffie and Rev. S. W. Oldham; first pastor: Rev. S. W. Oldham; building erected May 1, 1920, seats 350; membership: 183; present pastor: Rev. H. D. Booth.

McDUFFIE MEMORIAL BAPTIST CHURCH (48); organized in 1922; leaders in organization: Mr. and Mrs. J. O. Franklin and Rev. J. F. McDuffie; first pastor: Rev. J. F. McDuffie; building erected in 1922 seats 130; membership: 53; present pastor: Rev. O. K. Webb, Jr.

OAK GROVE BAPTIST CHURCH (43); organized in 1936; leaders in organization: Robert A. Thompson, Jesse E. Sykes, Woody Thompson and M. E. Thompson.

GOSPEL BAPTIST TABERNACLE (39); organized in 1946; leaders in organization: Willie Thompson, S. E. Elmore and W. J. Johnson; building erected in 1946 seats 250; first pastor: Rev. S. E. Elmore; membership: 125; present pastor: Rev. W. I. Conway.

FAIRVIEW BAPTIST CHURCH of HILLSBORO; organized in October, 1952; leaders in organization: W. P. Berry, Jr., A. L. Hinson, E. L. Hardee, James J. Freeland and Mrs. C. W. Sharpe; first pastor: Rev. James Clegg; building erected in 1952, seats 250; membership: 50; present pastor: Rev. James Clegg.

CONGREGATIONAL CHRISTIAN

The Christian Church was born in protest against ecclesiasticism and the denial of individual freedom in the Methodist Episcopal Church. In 1792, James O'Kelly, Methodist minister in Virginia, withdrew from that church in protest against the development of the superintendency especially in so far as it gave the Methodist Bishops absolute power in appointing ministers to their charge. O'Kelly and his followers organized under the name of Republican Methodists which name was later changed to Christian. James O'Kelly migrated to North Carolina, purchased a farm in Chatham County, and is buried on that farm near the Orange, Durham and Chatham county lines. He organized and was the first pastor of the Damascus Christian church in the year 1797. A Christian Church was organized in the 19th century in the Town of Hillsboro but did not flourish and was later absorbed by the Methodist Episcopal Church of Hillsboro.

Merged in 1931, the Christian Church and the Congregational Church, separated by many years in their establishments, were nevertheless almost identical in their ideals and principles. After the merger the Christian churches in the county took the names as indicated below.

PRESENT CHURCHES: DAMASCUS CONGREGATIONAL CHRISTIAN CHURCH (58); organized 1797; leaders in organization: Col. Matthew McCauley, John Wilson and Jesse Neville; first pastor: James O'Kelley; present building erected in 1892, seats 350; membership: 70; present pastor: Rev. E. M. Powell.
MOUNT ZION CONGREGATIONAL CHRISTIAN CHURCH (10); organized in 1832; leaders: Rev. Thomas Reeves, Thomas Lynch and John Walker; first pastor: Rev. Thomas Reeves; buildings erected in 1833 and 1899, remodeled in 1949, seats 300; membership: 152; present pastor: Rev. Thomas D. Sutton.
UNITED CONGREGATIONAL CHRISTIAN CHURCH of CHAPEL HILL: organized on May 10, 1910; leaders: Rev. W. C. Clements, W. E. Lindsay, D. S. Long, Rev. T. W. Strowd, E. W. Neville, I. W. Pritchard, R. W. Foister; first pastor: Rev. W. C. Clements; building erected in 1914, seats 135; membership: 154; present pastor: Rev. Richard L. Jackson.
MEBANE CONGREGATIONAL CHRISTIAN CHURCH (25); organized on May 16, 1915; leaders: J. W. Fowler, R. H. W. Jones, Mrs. H. L. Jones, Mr. and Mrs. A. A. Lynch; first pastor: Rev. W. C. Clements; building completed in 1931, seats 200; membership: 26; present pastor: Rev. Randall C. Mason, Jr.

PRIMITIVE BAPTISTS

The Primitive Baptists have the reputation of being the most strictly orthodox and exclusive of all Baptists. Unique in that they have never been organized as a denomination and have no associations or administrative bodies of any kind, they represent a protest movement against missions and Sunday schools. A strong Calvinism runs through their doctrine. Their two biblically authorized ordinances are the Lord's Supper and baptism of believers by immersion.

PRESENT CHURCH: HARMONY PRIMITIVE BAPTIST CHURCH (15); organized about 1835; present building seats about 75; membership: 3; present pastor: Rev. Ernest Oakley.

AFRICAN METHODIST EPISCOPAL

The African Methodist Episcopal Church began with the withdrawal in 1787 of a group of Negro Methodists from the Methodist Episcopal Church in Philadelphia; their objection was directed largely against practices of discrimination. It was a church confined in the years preceding the Civil War largely to the northern states; following the war its membership increased rapidly in the South. Next to the Negro Baptist churches, this sect has organized more churches in Orange county than any other Negro denomination.

PRESENT CHURCHES: WHITE CROSS A. M. E. CHURCH (26): organized in May, 1832; leaders: Alexander Faucette, George McAdoo, Harper Allison; first pastor: Rev. Jobe Waddell; building erected in May, 1832 and rebuilt in April, 1921, seats 200; membership: 73; present pastor: Rev. S. G. Tompkins.

ST. PAUL A. M. E. CHURCH of CHAPEL HILL; organized in 1864; leaders: Jerry Hargraves and Edwin Allen; first pastor: Rev. Green Cordal; building erected 1892, seats 500; membership: 255; present pastor: Rev. R. L. Upshaw.

DICKERSON'S A. M. E. CHURCH of HILLSBORO; organized 1873; leaders: Charles Day, Jordan Hooker, Franklin Turrentine, George Washington Day, Joseph Thomas Wallace; first pastor: Rev. Joseph Berry; building seats 300; membership: 65; present pastor: Rev. J. R. Bridgers.

MOUNT ZION A. M. E. CHURCH (16); organized about 1878 at Martinsville by Jack Horner, Bedford Corbett, Richard Jordan, Sam McBroom and Richard Thompson; moved to Poplar Spring and about 1927 when present building erected moved to present location; building remodeled in 1947 seats 300; membership: 230; present pastor: Rev. J. R. Bridgers.

GAINS CHAPEL A. M. E. CHURCH of EFLAND; organized about 1906; leaders: Robert Watson, Shurman Morrow, Brown Wright;

FLAT ROCK A. M. E. CHURCH (21); organized about 1915; leaders: Guthrie Thompson, B. F. Moore, Thomas Holeman; building erected in 1952 seats 300; membership: 25; present pastor: Rev. J. S. T. Decker.

HARRIS GROVE A. M. E. CHURCH (9);
HUNTER'S CHAPEL A. M. E. CHURCH (30);
PAYNES CHAPEL A. M. E. CHURCH (17);

NEGRO BAPTISTS

The first Negro Baptist Church in America was organized at Silver Bluff, across the Savannah River from Augusta, Georgia, in 1773. It is interesting that Andrew Bryan, a slave, was the first pastor of the First African Baptist Church of Savannah, Georgia, and that it came about through the efforts of Rev. Abraham Marshall (white) and the Rev. Jesse Peter (Negro).

As early as 1700 white slaveholders in the South were providing religious teaching and places of worship for their slaves. Usually, however, the Negro slave sat in the gallery of the white church identified with the faith of his owner. The great majority of the Negroes in pre-Civil War days were either Baptists or Methodists.

The lack of formality in the Baptist church, together with absence of ritual and with the freedom and democracy of the local congregation, appealed to the Negro more than the episcopal structure of the Methodist.

Negro Baptist doctrine runs quite parallel to that of the doctrine of white Baptist churches though it is slightly more Calvinistic.

PRESENT CHURCHES: FIRST BAPTIST CHURCH of CHAPEL HILL (formerly ROCK HILL); organized in 1865; leaders: Haywood Purefoy, Tony Strayhorn, George Trice, Bill Peace, Jordan Weaver. Ben Craig, Jordan Swain, Tom Kerby, George Hargraves and John Jones; first pastor: Rev. E. D. Cole; building erected in 1953, seats 600; membership: 400; present pastor: Rev. J. R. Manley.

TERRELL CREEK BAPTIST CHURCH (57); organized in 1868 by Ned Strowd on Atwater road about 2 miles south of present location; building erected about 1914 seats 250; membership: 200; present pastor: Rev. L. S. Thompson.

MOUNT SINAI BAPTIST CHURCH (44); organized in 1870; leaders in organization: Alex Craig, Jessie Barbee, Abel Maddry and Bettie Trice; first pastor: Rev. E. H. Cole; building seats 375; membership: 230; present pastor: Rev. James A. Stewart.

MOUNT BRIGHT BAPTIST CHURCH of HILLSBORO; organized in 1872; leaders: Rev. Alfred Bright, M. Henderson, Ned Horabout, F. Bolden, G. Craig, M. Long, N. Wheaton, A. Alston; first pastor: Rev. Alfred Bright; building erected in 1875, seats 300; membership 230; present pastor: Rev. A. B. Johnson.

HICKORY GROVE BAPTIST CHURCH (52); organized on September 28, 1877; leaders: Jesse Hopson, Robert Davis, Charles Minor, Ned Strowd, Zack Hogan and Mrs. Susan Hopson; first pastor: Rev. C. D. Hackney; building erected about 1905 seats 250; membership: 300; present pastor: Rev. J. R. Manley.

LATTA GROVE BAPTIST CHURCH (1); organized about 1879; leaders in organization: Jerry M. Latta, Marshall Walker, Henry Jones and Major Cooper.

ORANGE CROSS ROADS BAPTIST CHURCH (20); organized about 1880; building erected in 1923, seats 200; membership: 35; present pastor: W. N. White.

GLENN'S GROVE BAPTIST CHURCH (8); organized about 1880; leaders: John Bonnet, Dee Bass, Daniel Daye; first pastor: Rev. Henry Fuller; building erected in 1927 seats 100; membership: 49; present pastor: Rev. J. B. Brooks.

PINEY GROVE BAPTIST CHURCH (33); organized in 1888; leaders in organization: Rev. W. M. Ray, Alfred Pratt and George Pratt; first pastor: Rev. W. M. Ray; building erected in 1930 seats 200; membership: 95; present pastor: Rev. H. G. Walker.

LEE'S CHAPEL BAPTIST CHURCH (11); organized in 1893; leader in organization and first pastor: Rev. William H. Standfield; building erected in 1918, seats 250; membership: 150; present pastor: Rev. James Corbett.

WHITE OAK GROVE BAPTIST CHURCH (6); organized about 1914; leaders: Charles Wells, William Thompson,

MOUNT OLIVE BAPTIST CHURCH of EFLAND; organized April 18, 1920; leaders: Robby Bryant, Walter Turner, W. M. Walker, Albert Wilson; first pastor: Rev. C. P. Harris; building erected in 1920, seats 200; membership: 25; present pastor: Rev. A. A. Chavis.

SECOND BAPTIST CHURCH of CHAPEL HILL; organized October, 1937; leaders: Alex Washington, Ed Jones, Rev. J. H. Jones, Malley Jones, and Thomas Booth, Sr.; first pastor: Rev. J. H. Jones; building erected in April, 1938, seats 200; membership: 104; present pastor: Rev. L. E. Day.

NUNN'S CHAPEL BAPTIST CHURCH (47); organized October 30, 1938; leaders: Rev. W. N. Nunn, Rev. J. H. Smith, Rev. W. H. Williams, William McCauley and George Jones; first and present pastor: Rev. M. N. Nunn; building erected in 1946, seats about 150.

LIPSCOMBE GROVE BAPTIST CHURCH (24);
MOUNT GILEAD BAPTIST CHURCH (35);
present pastor: Rev. T. M. Mosby.
MOUNT MORIAH BAPTIST CHURCH (31);
BETHSADA BAPTIST CHURCH (42); leaders: Jesse Morrow, Rudy Whitmore; first pastor: Rev. L. C. Hackney; building erected in 1947 seats 500; membership: 42; present pastor: Rev. E. U. Chavis.

COLORED METHODIST EPISCOPAL

The Colored Methodist Episcopal Church was established in 1870 in the South in an amicable agreement between white and Negro members of the Methodist Episcopal Church, South, and parallels the Methodist Church in doctrine and polity.

PRESENT CHURCHES: ST. JOSEPH C. M. E. CHURCH of CHAPEL HILL; organized as Cotton Chapel on January 22, 1896; leaders: John W. Roberts, Rev. J. M. Roundtree, Kenneth Cheek; first pastor: Rev. J. M. Roundtree; first building erected in 1904 and present building erected in 1935 seats 350; membership: 181; present pastor: Rev. David W. Roston.

HARVEY'S CHAPEL C. M. E. CHURCH (37); organized about 1903 by Avery Harvey and Harpy Elkins; first pastor: Rev. Sandy Aiken; building erected about 1946 seats 100; membership: 21; present pastor: Rev. S. G. Tompkins.

AFRICAN METHODIST EPISCOPAL ZION

The African Methodist Episcopal Zion Church dates from 1796 when its first organization was instituted by a group of Negro members protesting discrimination in the John Street Church in New York City. This church spread quickly over the Northern states, and by 1880, there were 15 annual conferences in the South.

PRESENT CHURCH: O'Bryant's A. M. E. Zion Church of Chapel Hill.

PILGRIM HOLINESS

The Pilgrim Holiness Church is conservative, stressing the Trinity, the new birth, entire sanctification, divine healing and the inspiration of the Scriptures. Local churches are governed by a church board composed of the pastor, elders, deacons and other church officers.

PRESENT CHURCH: PILGRIM HOLINESS of WEST HILLSBORO;
organized in 1902; building seats 250; membership: 27; present pastor:
Rev. J. F. Kernodle.

PENTECOSTAL HOLINESS

This church was organized in 1898 at Anderson, S. C. by a number of Pentecostal associations. The theological standards of Methodism prevail with certain modifications. Three works of grace are stressed by this church as all-important: justification by faith, sanctification, and Spirit baptism attested by speaking in other tongues. Polity is also Methodistic.

PRESENT CHURCH: FIRST PENTECOSTAL HOLINESS CHURCH
of WEST HILLSBORO; organized in 1910; leaders in organization: Rev. A. G. Cannady, Rev. Chas. Martin, R. S. Andrews, Ed Cannady and W. J. Andrews; first pastor: Rev. A. G. Cannady; building erected in 1948 seats 234; membership: 50; present pastor: Rev. R. C. Frazier.

UNITED HOLY CHURCH OF AMERICA

Originating at Method, North Carolina, in a meeting held by the Rev. Isaac Cheshier, I. M. Mason, G. A. Mials and H. C. Snipes, all of Raleigh, in 1886, this body was successively called the Holy Church of North Carolina, the Holy Church of North Carolina and Virginia, and finally in 1918 the United Holy Church of America. Its purpose officially is to establish and maintain "holy convocation, assemblies, conventions, conferences, public worship, missionary and school work, orphans' homes, manual and trades training."

Articles of faith contain statements of belief in the Trinity; the record of God's revelation of himself in the Bible, redemption, resurrection, justification, instantaneous sanctification following justification; the baptism of the Holy Spirit and the ultimate reign of Christ over the earth.

PRESENT CHURCHES: WADE'S TEMPLE at EFLAND; organized in 1912; first pastor: Rev. George Wade; building erected in 1915, seats 200; membership: 42; present pastor: Rev. S. G. McCoy.
MEBANE CHAPEL of HILLSBORO; organized in 1913; leaders in organization: Samuel Wade, James Obie, Mac Clark, Grace Obie, Janie Grady, Rev. P. H. Wiley; first pastor: Rev. A. Alston; church

erected in 1914, seats 250; membership: 45; present pastor: Rev. P. H. Wiley.

TEMPLE OF TRUTH (28); organized in 1918; leaders: Henry Thompson, Alex Mitchell, James Thompson, Guther Thompson, Roy Lee Thompson, Rev. R. C. Turner; building erected in 1918, seats 175; membership: 27; present pastor: Rev. R. C. Turner.

WHITE ROCK CHURCH (59); organized March 10, 1928; leaders: Laura Atwater, Henry Thompson, Roy Thompson, Clyde Thompson; first pastor: Rev. R. C. Turner; building erected in 1928 seats 250; membership: 63; present pastor: Rev. R. C. Turner.

OAK GROVE HOLINESS CHURCH of HILLSBORO.

CHURCHES OF GOD

Several independent religious bodies bear the name of Church of God in one form or another. There are minor differences in doctrine between these groups but generally they emphasize justification by faith, sanctification, baptism of the Holy Spirit, speaking in other tongues, being "born again", fruitfulness in Christian living, and a strong interest in the second coming of Christ.

PRESENT CHURCHES: CHURCH OF GOD of CARRBORO; organized on December 27, 1927, by Rev. C. T. Boyd, Mrs. Celia Boyd, Mrs. A. V. Goins, T. M. Miller and Bertha Miller; first and present pastor: Rev. C. T. Boyd; building erected in 1928, seats 450; membership: 150.

CHURCH OF GOD of WEST HILLSBORO; organized 1935; leaders: Garland Crabtree and T. E. Boman; first pastor: Edd Mize; building erected in 1945 seats 250; membership: 64; present pastor: Rev. W. P. Gosnell, Jr.

CARRBORO CHURCH OF GOD; organized July, 1950; leaders: Clyde Maynor, Frank King, Robert Hill; first pastor: Rev. T. W. Choplin; building erected in 1952, seats 300; membership: 15; present pastor: Rev. Willie Bowman.

CATHOLICS

For the first fifteen hundred years of Christendom, up to the time of the Protestant Reformation and the break of Henry VIII of England with the Church, the Western world was almost solidly Roman Catholic. The Roman Catholic Church dates its beginning from the moment the apostle Peter was selected by Christ as guardian of the keys of heaven and earth and as chief of the apostles; that Peter then became the first pope of this church. It gained real authority and power when it arose as the only body strong enough to rule after the fall of the city of Rome.

Long before the time of Martin Luther, the first permanent parish in America was established at St. Augustine, Florida, in 1565. In 1632 the Roman Catholics founded Maryland; later they were restricted by law in Maryland and the other colonies and these restrictions were not removed until after the Revolution. In the face of these restrictions and in the face of the fact that most colonial immigrants were Protestants this church grew slowly in colonial times. However, Catholics in large numbers were in the Continential Army during the Revolution; among the signatures on the article of Confederation, the Declaration of Independence, and the Constitution are found those of Thomas Fitzsimmons, Daniel Carroll and Charles Carroll; and Thomas Burke of Hillsboro was elected Governor of North Carolina in 1781. The Revolution brought to the Catholics freedom, religious as well as political; religious equality became law with the adoption of the Constitution in 1787.

At the head of the government of the church stands the Pope. His authority is supreme in all matters of faith and discipline; no layman may have any voice in the church government; parishes cannot call their priests, but the parish laymen are often consulted on certain phases of parish work.

No church was organized in Orange county until recent years; though there is on record in the Orange County Registry a deed from John C. Blake to the Roman Catholic Diocese of Raleigh for 15 acres of land on Eno River which bears the date of April 1, 1879.

PRESENT CHURCH: CATHOLIC CHURCH of CHAPEL HILL; organized Sept. 8, 1934; leaders in organization: Dr. Frank Cameron, Mrs. Robert Wettach, Mr. and Mrs. J. J. Keller, William D. Carmichael, Giles Horney; first priest: Rev. Francis J. Morrissey, D.D.; no building, the services are held in Gerrard Hall on the campus of the University of N. C.; membership: about 500; present priest: Rev. John A. Weidinger.

JEWS

Throughout the centuries one reaction of Jewish persecution has been migration; they have spread all over the Western world. Jews arrived early in American colonies and like the dissenters they were fleeing persecution in Europe. They were in New Amsterdam, Rhode Island and Georgia with the early settlers and established their first congregation in New Amsterdam in 1655; they organized a synagogue in Savannah as early as 1733, but the bulk of the Jewish immigrants arrived in this country between 1880 and 1914. A few families have settled in Orange county.

The historic sense of unity among the Jewish people soon demonstrated itself here as it had abroad. That unity had defied centuries of persecution and it has now welded the Jews into one of the most influential religious groups in America. Within the local congregations there is full independence. There are no synods, assemblies, or hierarchies of leaders whatever to control the synagogue. At the head of the congregation is the rabbi. He is the preacher and pastor and performs the rites of the Jewish faith.

The Jews, probably because of the small number of residents in Orange county today, have never established a synagogue in the county; they worship at synagogues in nearby cities, principally in Durham. In recent years a number of Jews have been in attendance at the University of North Carolina at Chapel Hill as students and in order to minister to the needs of these the North Carolina B'nai B'rith Hillel Foundation in 1944 purchased on Cameron Avenue in Chapel Hill a lot on which in recent years a building has been erected where the rabbi conducts services for both the students and the townspeople. Present rabbi: Efraim M. Rosenzweig.

LUTHERAN

Lutheran was a name fastened upon the followers of Martin Luther by their enemies in the days of the Protestant Reformation; today it stands for something far more comprehensive. Luther's teachings of justification by faith and of the universal priesthood of believers might be called the cornerstone of

Protestantism. The story of Luther's rebellion against the Roman Catholic Church is well-known history. Men were forgiven and absolved of their sins, he believed, not by good works or imposed church rites, nor through the purchase of indulgences offered for sale by the Roman Catholic Church, but by man's action in turning from sin directly to God. Some few Lutherans came into Orange County about the middle of the 18th century but pushed on further west without organizing a church in the county. The first synod in North Carolina was organized in 1803. The church in Chapel Hill was organized in 1946, though work with the students at the University of North Carolina proceeded the organization of the church by many years.

PRESENT CHURCH: HOLY TRINITY LUTHERAN CHURCH of CHAPEL HILL: organized on July 21, 1946; leaders: Rev. D. P. Rudisill, Dr. J. L. Morgan, R. W. Bost, George F. Horner, J. C. Earnhardt, V. G. Thompson and 28 other charter members; first pastor: Rev. D. P. Rudisill: building erected in 1951 and consecrated on January 6, 1952, seats 300; membership 65; last pastor Rev. E. C. Cooper who retired on Easter Sunday of 1953.

UNITARIAN

Unitarian thought was prevalent in the early Christian centuries before the concept of Trinitarianism was developed; but Unitarianism as we know it today began with the Protestant Reformation. American Unitarianism developed independently out of New England Congregationalism. They asked only to join a covenant in that church and never to subscribe to a creed. Cardinal points in their belief are those of the oneness of God, the strict humanity of Jesus, the perfectability of human character, the natural character of the Bible, and the ultimate salvation of all souls.

PRESENT GROUP: UNITARIAN FELLOWSHIP of CHAPEL HILL: organized in 1951 by Harriet Doar, John Gillin, Raymond Adams, Mrs. Alex Heard, and Mr. and Mrs. Roger Guthrie. A Unitarian Fellowship is a lay group that holds Unitarian religious meetings. It is not a full-fledged church, though it is an organized religious body; membership: 25.

The early settlers, pioneers of Piedmont North Carolina, farmers, hunters, trappers and planters of Orange county, zealous for their freedom of body, mind and spirit, in search for new homes where they might work out their own salvation with fear and trembling in the sight of God, but without fear of any man, worked out that salvation through the various beliefs of the established church and of various dissenter groups, moulded a civilization and love of country which has stood the test of two centuries; and the present citizens, direct descendants of these sturdy pioneers, and others who have steadily come into Orange county, can point with pride to the religious, social and political achievements of their forefathers and can now face the future in a land where they may worship God in fear and trembling and without fear of any man, whether that form of worship be Protestant, Catholic or Jewish.

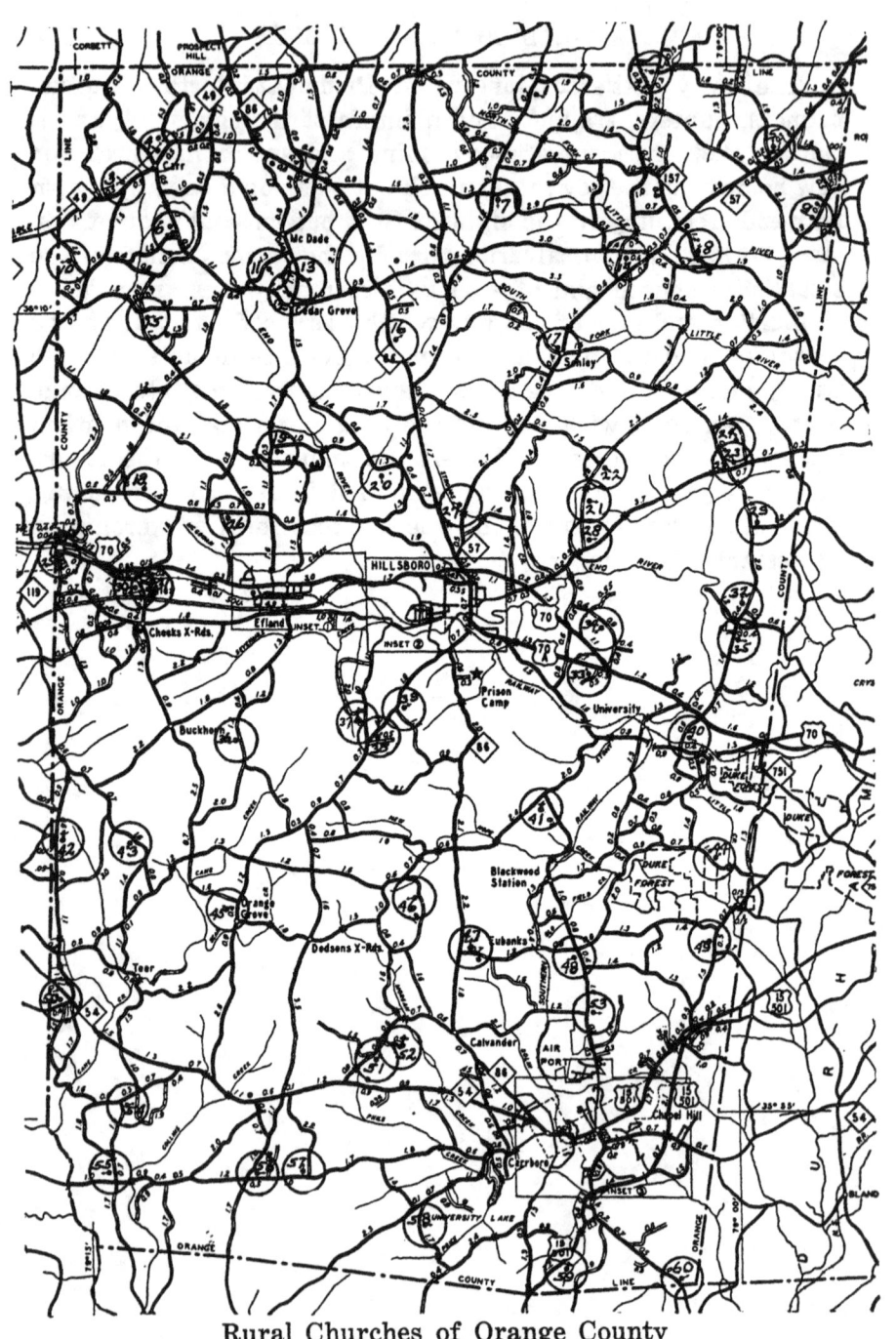

Rural Churches of Orange County

LEGEND FOR RURAL CHURCHES

1. Latta Grove Baptist Church
2. Berry's Grove Baptist Church
3. Mount Adar Baptist Church
4. Carr Methodist Church
5. New Bethel Methodist Church
6. White Oak Grove Baptist Church
7. Walnut Grove Methodist Church
8. Glenn's Grove Baptist Church
9. Harris Grove A. M. E. Church
10. Mount Zion Congregational Christian Church
11. Lee's Chapel Baptist Church
12. Cedar Grove Methodist Church
13. Eno Presbyterian Church
14. Little River Presbyterian Church
15. Harmony Primitive Baptist Church
16. Mount Zion A. M. E. Church
17. Paynes Chapel A. M. E. Church
18. Lebanon Methodist Church
19. Fairfield Presbyterian Church
20. Orange Cross Roads Baptist Church
21. Flat Rock A. M. E. Church
22. New Sharon Methodist Church
23. St. Mary's Episcopal Church
24. Lipscombe Grove Baptist Church
25. Mebane Congregational Christian Church
26. White Cross A. M. E. Church
27. Mars Hill Baptist Church
28. Temple of Truth
29. Ebenezer Baptist Church
30. Hunter's Chapel A. M. E. Church
31. Mount Moriah Baptist Church, col.
32. Pleasant Green Methodist Church
33. Piney Grove Baptist Church
34. Palmer Grove Methodist Church
35. Mount Gilead Baptist Church
36. Chestnut Ridge Methodist Church
37. Harvey's Chapel C. M. E. Church
38. Cross Road Baptist Church
39. Gospel Baptist Tabernacle
40. Mount Hermon Baptist Church
41. New Hope Presbyterian Church
42. Bethsada Baptist Church
43. Oak Grove Baptist Church
44. Mount Sinai Baptist Church
45. Cane Creek Baptist Church
46. Union Grove Methodist Church
47. Nunn's Chapel Baptist Church
48. McDuffie Memorial Baptist Church
49. Mount Moriah Baptist Church, white
50. Bethlehem Presbyterian Church
51. Bethel Baptist Church
52. Hickory Grove Baptist Church
53. Orange Methodist Church
54. Clover Garden Methodist Church
55. Orange Chapel Methodist Church
56. Antioch Baptist Church
57. Terrell Creek Baptist Church
58. Damascus Congregational Christian Church
59. White Rock Church
60. Mount Carmel Baptist Church

ALPHABETICAL LIST OF RURAL CHURCHES

Antioch Baptist Church, 56
Berry's Grove Baptist Church, 2
Bethel Baptist Church, 51
Bethlehem Presbyterian Church, 50
Bethsada Baptist Church, 42
Cane Creek Baptist Church, 45
Carr Methodist Church, 4
Cedar Grove Methodist Church, 12
Chestnut Ridge Methodist Church, 36
Clover Garden Methodist Church, 54
Cross Road Baptist Church, 38
Damascus Congregational Christian Church, 58
Ebenezer Baptist Church, 29
Eno Presbyterian Church, 13
Fairfield Presbyterian Church, 19
Flat Rock A. M. E. Church, 21
Glenn's Grove Baptist Church, 8
Gospel Baptist Tabernacle, 39
Harmony Primitive Baptist Church, 15
Harris Grove A. M. E. Church, 9
Harvey's Chapel C. M. E. Church, 37
Hickory Grove Baptist Church, 52
Hunter's Chapel A. M. E. Church, 30
Latta Grove Baptist Church, 1
Lebanon Methodist Church, 18
Lee's Chapel Baptist Church, 11
Lipscombe Grove Baptist Church, 24
Little River Presbyterian Church, 14
McDuffie Memorial Baptist Church, 48
Mars Hill Baptist Church, 27
Mebane Congregational Christian Church, 25
Mount Adar Baptist Church, 3
Mount Carmel Baptist Church, 60
Mount Gilead Baptist Church, 35
Mount Hermon Baptist Church, 40
Mount Moriah Baptist Church, Col., 31
Mount Moriah Baptist Church, W., 49
Mount Sinai Baptist Church, 44
Mount Zion A. M. E. Church, 16
Mount Zion Congregational Christian Church, 10
New Bethel Methodist Church, 5
New Hope Presbyterian Church, 41
New Sharon Methodist Church, 22
Nunn's Chapel Baptist Church, 47
Oak Grove Baptist Church, 43
Orange Chapel Methodist Church, 55
Orange Cross Roads Baptist Church, 20
Orange Methodist Church, 53
Palmer Grove Methodist Church, 34
Paynes Chapel A. M. E. Church, 17
Piney Grove Baptist Church, 33
Pleasant Green Methodist Church, 32
St. Mary's Episcopal Church, 23
Temple of Truth, 28
Terrell Creek Baptist Church, 57
Union Grove Methodist Church, 46
Walnut Grove Methodist Church, 7
White Cross A. M. E. Church, 26
White Oak Grove Baptist Church, 6
White Rock Church, 59

URBAN CHURCHES

CARRBORO
- Carrboro Baptist Church
- Carrboro Church of God, W.
- Carrboro Methodist Church
- Church of God, Col.
- St. Paul A. M. E. Church

CHAPEL HILL
- Baptist Church of Chapel Hill
- B'Nai B'Rith Hillel Foundation
- Catholic Church of Chapel Hill
- Chapel Hill Monthly Meeting of Friends
- Chapel of the Cross
- Church of the Holy Family
- Covenant Presbyterian Church
- First Baptist Church
- Holy Trinity Lutheran Church
- O'Bryant's A. M. E. Zion Church
- Presbyterian Church of Chapel Hill
- St. Joseph C. M. E. Church
- Second Baptist Church
- Unitarian Fellowship
- United Congregational Christian Church
- University Methodist Church

EFLAND
- Efland Baptist Church
- Efland Methodist Church
- Efland Presbyterian Church
- Gains Chapel A. M. E. Church
- Mount Olive Baptist Church
- Wade Temple Holiness Church

HILLSBORO
- Dickerson's A. M. E. Church
- Fairview Baptist Church
- First Baptist Church
- Hillsboro Methodist Church
- Hillsboro Presbyterian Church
- Mebane Chapel Holiness Church
- Mount Bright Baptist Church
- Oak Grove Holiness Church
- St. Matthews Episcopal Church

WEST HILLSBORO
- Church of God
- Eno Methodist Church
- First Pentecostal Holiness Church
- Pilgrim Holiness Church
- West Hill Baptist Church

CHAPTER XVIII

FRATERNAL ORDERS IN ORANGE COUNTY

BY WALLACE E. CALDWELL

Professor of History, University of North Carolina

Many fraternal orders have had a share in the life and work of the citizens of Orange County. Of these, the oldest and the best documented is the Masonic fraternity. Masonry came to North Carolina during the colonial period. Individual Masons probably moved into the colony soon after the establishment of the Grand Lodge of England in 1717. Solomon Lodge in New Hanover County is said to have been chartered in 1735; but no records of it exist today in North Carolina. The first lodge of record was St. John's Lodge No. 1 of Wilmington chartered in 1755 followed in 1767 by Royal White Hart Lodge at Halifax, and these by nine others prior to the Revolution. While some members remained loyal to the King most became active in the Revolutionary cause and some played prominent parts. After the Revolution steps were taken to reorganize the fraternity. Delegates from the surviving lodges met in Tarboro in December, 1787 and organized the Grand Lodge of North Carolina. Its first regular meeting was held in Hillsboro, July 23, 1788. No records exist of any Masonic organization in Orange County prior to this time. Doubtless some citizens of the town were Masons. Accordingly in 1791 a group applied to the Grand Lodge for a charter which was granted in December of that year with the name and number of Eagle Lodge No. 19.

This lodge took part in the ceremonies of the Grand Lodge when cornerstones were laid for Old East (1793) and South Building (1798) at the University of North Carolina. In 1798 by special dispensation of the Grand Master it met in Chapel Hill and initiated Joseph Caldwell, then Presiding Professor, later first President of the University, and three members of the faculty.

The old minutes cease in 1799 and for twenty years the lodge was dormant. It was revived in 1819 with a new number, 71.

(The original number was restored to the lodge by action of the Grand Lodge in 1932.) It at once began to play an active part in the life of Hillsboro and, following the customs of the time, it held a lottery (1821-1832) from the proceeds of which it erected the Masonic Hall which is still standing and in use. The cornerstone was laid by one of its own members, James Strudwick Smith, who was Grand Master in 1822. Joseph Caldwell was elected a life member of the lodge and his name appears frequently in the minutes as he preached sermons or delivered addresses before the lodge.

The lodge took an active part in promoting education by voting to contribute funds to assist in the building of a Male Academy in the village (1820). Again in 1843 it supported with a resolution and funds the plan of the Grand Lodge to erect a seminary for the children of deceased brothers in the State. In the same year a delegation took part in the laying of the cornerstone of Greensboro Female College in that city, and in 1855 another delegation shared in a similar ceremony at St. John's College in Oxford and again at Hillsboro Military Academy in 1859.

Lodge activities speeded up with the outbreak of the War Between the States. Many new members were admitted and the minute book contains the names of visitors from many states in the Confederacy. A member of the lodge, Eli F. Watson, served as Grand Master in the state for the years 1862 and 1863. In spite of the difficult times that followed, the lodge continued quietly at work though for a period annual dues had to be set at fifty cents.

The record reports the transformation of St. John's College in Oxford into the Masonic Orphanage in 1873 and Eagle Lodge has maintained active interest and support of this institution. One of its distinguished members, Samuel M. Gattis, was elected Grand Master in 1908 and another, James H. Webb, came to this office in 1922. Continuing its interest in education, it took part in laying several cornerstones at the University, notably that of Grimes Dormitory in 1921 when **Past Grand Master** Samuel M. Gattis, acting as Master of Ceremonies, delivered the address. The lodge continues today in flourishing and active condition with many prominent and influential citizens on its roll. Among them might be mentioned the beloved Shepherd Strudwick, who has been a member of Eagle Lodge for fifty-three years.

Masonry has been active in Chapel Hill though with a less continuous record. University Lodge No. 80 was chartered in 1824. Names still familiar in the area appear on its rolls—McDade, Lloyd, Cheek, Barbee, McCauley, Freeland, Neville, and Henderson. It failed to add new members and the scant records state that its older members died, moved to other towns or traveled west. The lodge ceased to function in 1849. A group of its loyal members secured a new charter in 1855 as Caldwell Lodge No. 180, named for the late President of the University. This lodge like Eagle in Hillsboro increased in membership with the war years and functioned with some difficulty under Reconstruction. Among its officers are listed Professors Fetter and A. W. Mangum of the University and Solomon Pool, its President during those troubled times. With the closing of the University the lodge suffered as many of its members withdrew. It survived, however, until 1880. In that year a disastrous fire destroyed all the old records and the lodge surrendered its charter.

Again a few faithful members went to work and secured a new charter in 1888 as University Lodge No. 408. The leading spirit in this revival was W. N. Pritchard, its first Master. It met for many years above a store on Franklin Street. In 1931 it purchased the old Baptist Church which it converted into a lodge hall of which it is justly proud. The electric insignia which stands in front of it was erected in 1941 in memory of its distinguished Past Master, Dr. E. A. Abernethy. It has played a quiet yet active part in the affairs of the town and University. It shared in the laying of cornerstones for Alumni Building in 1898, for Grimes Dormitory in 1921, and for the Memorial Hospital in 1951. One of its members, W. E. Caldwell, was Grand Master for 1950-51 and the Grand Lodge held its annual meeting in Chapel Hill under his direction in April, 1951.

The Order of the Eastern Star is represented in both Hillsboro and Chapel Hill. The chapter in Hillsboro was established in

Presbyterian Church, Chapel Hill.

Top: Gilbert Strayhorn House, New Hope Section, about 1750.
Bottom: Chapel Hill Graded School about 1910.

Top: Chapel of the Cross, old and new, Chapel Hill.
Bottom: New Hope Presbyterian Church, erected in 1863.

Top: Walnut Grove Methodist Church.
Bottom: Old Baptist Church, Chapel Hill, erected in 1853, now Masonic Temple of University Lodge.

Top: Eno Presbyterian Church.
Bottom: St. Mary's Episcopal Church.

Top: Arboretum, U.N.C.
Bottom: Little River Presbyterian Church.

Top: Morehead Planetarium, U.N.C.
Bottom: Memorial Hospital, U.N.C.

Top: Home Office Hospital Saving Association, Chapel Hill.
Bottom: Franklin Street, Chapel Hill, about 1945. Colonial architecture required by Chapel Hill Planning Board.

1925 and that in Chapel Hill in 1947. The Rainbow Girls were active for some years among the young people of Hillsboro.

The Knights of Pythias flourished for some years in Chapel Hill. Moody Durham was for a time District Deputy and Claude Best held the highest state office, Grand Chancellor. Among its members were S. W. Andrews, Zeb Council and Frank P. Graham. A lodge was established in Hillsboro which is still in existence.

The Independent Order of Odd Fellows found adherents in Hillsboro in the late nineteenth century but lasted only a few years. Another lodge, Occoneechee No. 299, received its charter in 1907 and lasted until 1921.

The Junior Order of United American Mechanics established a lodge in Hillsboro in 1897. This moved to Carrboro and later to Chapel Hill. It exists and works today as Davie Council No. 52.

The Woodmen likewise had a fine group in Carrboro early in the twentieth century. This group suffered from the depression and disbanded.

Among the forgotten orders was the League of Good Templars. This was an order founded in the nineteenth century to promote temperance. It is mentioned in the records of Eagle Lodge in Hillsboro, whose building it was allowed to use.

Various fraternal orders have played an important part in the life of the Negro citizens of Orange County. Mention is made of the Knights of King David and the Knights of King Solomon. The latter seems to have originated in Chapel Hill. More prominent have been the Odd Fellows who have a good lodge in Chapel Hill and associated with it a sister organization, the House of Ruth. The Elks likewise have a club in Chapel Hill. Prince Hall Masonry (as Negro Masonry is designated) has been active in Chapel Hill and Carrboro. Mt. Olive Lodge No. 86 was established in 1880 and is strong and active. Many of the prominent Negroes of the community are listed among its members. Associated with it is Randolph Chapter No. 185, Order of the Eastern Star. Similar organizations have existed in Hillsboro but are now dormant.

CHAPTER XIX
DICTIONARY OF ORANGE COUNTY BIOGRAPHY
BY WILLIAM S. POWELL

First Assistant, North Carolina Historical Collection, University of North Carolina Library

THOMAS WINGATE ANDREWS (1882-1937) *Educator.* Born Orange county. Graduate U.N.C., 1908; doctor of education (1933), High Point college. Superintendent Orange County Schools, 1908-11; of Reidsville City Schools, 1911-17; Salisbury, 1917-24; High Point, 1924-37. Expanded school plants and built up progressive units. Vigorously opposed retrenchment imposed by 1933 general assembly on schools of state. Member N. C. Textbook Commission; president N. C. Education Association.

GEORGE EDMUND BADGER (1795-1866) *Secretary of Navy, Senator.* Born New Bern. Attended Yale. Studied law; admitted to bar 1814. Member N. C. House of Commons; judge superior court; Secretary of Navy in cabinets of President William H. Harrison and John Tyler; U. S. Senator 1846-53; member Convention of 1861. Practiced law for a time in Hillsboro.

KEMP PLUMMER BATTLE (1831-1919) *Educator.* Born Franklin county. Graduate U. N. C., 1849. Tutor in mathematics, 1850-54. Practiced law Raleigh, 1854-76. Member Convention of 1861. President Chatham Railway Company, 1861-65. State Treasurer, 1865-68. President State Agricultural Society, 1867-70. Took lead in reorganizing University, 1875; president U.N.C., 1876-91. Alumni professor of history, 1891-1919. Trustee, 1862-68, 1874-1919. Author of two-volume *History of the University of North Carolina.*

WILLIAM HORN BATTLE (1802-1879) *Lawyer.* Born Edgecombe county. Graduate U. N. C., 1820. Practiced law in Louisburg, 1825-39; in Raleigh, 1839-43, when he moved to Chapel Hill. Appointed professor of law at U.N.C. 1845 (beginning of law school) and served until University closed in 1871. Reporter to supreme court, 1834-40; judge superior court, 1840-48; judge supreme court, 1848-68. Served on commission with Nash and Iredell to revise public laws of state; 1872 appointed as sole reviser of statutes and in 1873 "Battle's Revisal" appeared.

RICHARD BENNEHAN (1747-1825) *Planter, Merchant.* Lived at Stagville, now Durham county. In partnership with William Johnston operated Little River Store, Snow Hill, in Orange county from 1769 to at least as late as 1788. Trustee U. N. C., 1799-1804; early donor to university, giving 32 volumes to library (some of which are still there) and "apparatus" for instruction.

JESSE BENTON (? -1790) *Lawyer.* Moved to Orange county from Granville. Opponent of Regulators. Practiced law in Hillsboro. Speculated in western lands. Representative from Orange county in general assembly of 1781. Owned Eno plantation, Orange county, and over a thousand acres elsewhere in the state. Active briefly against Tories during Revolution. Father of Thomas Hart Benton.

THOMAS HART BENTON (1782-1858) *Senator.* Born near Efland, Orange county. Attended U. N. C., 1799. Moved to Tennessee and served in general assembly. U. S. senator from Missouri, 1821-51; member of congress, 1853-55. Author, newspaper editor.

HARRIET MOREHEAD BERRY (1877-1940) *Leader in Good Roads Movement.* Born Hillsboro; graduate Woman's College, U.N.C.; student U.N.C., 1905. Writer for *Greensboro Daily News*, editor *Cherokee Scout*. Secretary State Drainage Association, the Fisheries Association, the American Association of State Highway Officials, and the Legislative Council of Women. Her leading work was done as secretary of the North Carolina Good Roads Association, a position she held for fifteen years. She was chiefly instrumental in securing the passage of the first $50,000,000 highway bond issue and was co-author of the bill establishing the North Carolina highway system passed in 1921. For some sixteen years Miss Berry was with the N. C. Geological and Economic Survey and during World War I, while acting as director, was called into consultation by President Wilson. During the final ten years of her public life she was superintendent of the State Credit Union.

JOHN BERRY (1798-1870) *Builder, Architect.* Born Hillsboro. Received training under Samuel Hancock, brickmason. First native brickmason of sufficient skill to attempt an entire building of brick. Built Orange county courthouse (1846); Baptist and Methodist churches in Hillsboro and perhaps also the Episcopal and Presbyterian churches; Smith Hall (Playmakers Theatre), Chapel Hill; St. Luke's Church, Salisbury; a number of houses; and a courthouse at Yanceyville, now destroyed. He also worked in Wake Forest and Oxford.

ROBERT BINGHAM (1838-1927) *Educator.* Born Hillsboro, son of William James Bingham. Graduate U. N. C., 1857. Joined father and brother as junior partner in the Bingham School with which he continued the remainder of his life. Served as captain during Civil War. Became headmaster of Bingham School, 1873. Said to have built first school gymnasium in South.

WILLIAM BINGHAM (1754-1826) *Educator.* Born Northern Ireland. Graduate University of Glasgow. Settled in Wilmington, 1789, as a teacher. In 1793 moved to Pittsboro and established his own school. Taught Latin and Greek at U. N. C. for a short time after 1801, but soon returned to his own school which he relocated, first in Hillsboro and later at Mount Repose, eleven miles northwest.

WILLIAM BINGHAM (1835-1873) *Educator.* Born Hillsboro. Educated at Bingham School. Graduate U. N. C., 1856. Joined his father, William J. Bingham, as a partner in operating Bingham School. Wrote and published a number of textbooks. Was physically unable to serve in Civil War, but operated his school as a military academy.

WILLIAM JAMES BINGHAM (1802-1866) *Educator.* Born Chapel Hill. Studied at Bingham School and taught for several years at Williamsboro, Granville county, before entering U. N. C. from which he was graduated, 1825. Headed Bingham School, 1826-1866. Interested in anti-slavery and colonization movements and opposed secession until South was invaded after which he supported Confederacy.

THOMAS BURKE (*c.* 1747-1783) *Governor.* Born Ireland. Settled in Virginia, 1764, and practiced medicine. Studied law.

Moved to Hillsboro in 1771. Delegate to conventions at New Bern and Hillsboro, 1775, and Halifax, 1776; member House of Commons, 1777; Continental Congress, 1776-81; governor, 1781-1782. Died at his home, "Tyaquin," near Hillsboro.

JOHN BUTLER (? -1786) *Revolutionary Leader.* Lived in Hawfields. Sheriff in 1770 at time Regulator disturbances. Colonel of Orange county militia and later brigadier general for Hillsboro District during Revolution. Led troops at battles of Camden and Guilford Court House. Member of general assembly at various times between 1777 and 1786. Councillor of State.

JOSEPH CALDWELL (1773-1835) *First University President.* Born New Jersey. Graduate Princeton, 1791. Taught in small local school; accepted tutorship at Princeton, 1795; became professor of mathematics and Presiding Professor at U. N. C., 1796. In 1804 he was chosen first president of the University and elected a trustee, a post which he held thirty-one years until his death. He resigned as president in 1812, but continued to hold the chair of mathematics. At his successor's resignation in 1816 he again became president and remained in office until his death. In 1831 he was authorized to build an observatory, the first college building of its kind in the United States. Caldwell County was named for him when it was formed in 1841.

BENNEHAN CAMERON (1854-1925) *Planter, Railroad Official.* Born Stagville (now Durham county). Graduate Virginia Military Institute. Managed large agricultural interests. President N. C. State Fair Association. Director N. C. Railroad and promoter of other railroads. Influenced consolidation of small lines into Seaboard Air Line system. State Guard officer.

DUNCAN CAMERON (1777-1853) *Lawyer, Banker.* Born Mecklenburg county, Va Studied law. Moved to N. C. and admitted to bar 1798. Located first at Martinsville, seat of Guilford county, but soon moved to Hillsboro. Served a number of terms in both houses of general assembly. Judge of superior court. In 1829 became president of the State Bank of N. C., a position he held for twenty years. Chairman of committee to build present state capitol, and to build Christ Church, Raleigh.

PAUL CARRINGTON CAMERON (1808-1891) *Planter.* Born Stagville (now Durham county). Attended U. N. C., 1824-1825, graduate Washington College (now Trinity), Hartford, Conn. Managed large agricultural interests. President agricultural society. Director Raleigh and Gaston and other railroads. State senator. U. N. C. trustee for twenty-six years.

RICHARD CASWELL (1729-1789) *Governor.* Born Maryland. Moved to N. C., 1746. Clerk of Court, Orange County, 1752-1754; admitted to bar and began practice in Hillsboro, 1754. Commanded part of Tryon's forces at Battle of Alamance, 1771. Served in Revolutionary Army. Member Continental Congress, 1774-1776. Delegate to and president of state constitutional convention, 1776. First governor of N. C. after statehood, serving 1776-1780, 1785-1788. Member state convention adopting Federal constitution. Buried family cemetery, Kinston.

THOMAS CHILD (*fl.* 1747-1766) *Colonial Official.* Son of Richard Child of Lavenham, Suffolk, England. Doctor of Medicine. Attorney general of N. C., 1747-1755, 1759-1766. As attorney, agent, commissioner, and auditor for the Earl of Granville, one of the Lords Proprietor, he was guilty of corruption and extortion both from Granville and his tenants. The county seat of Orange county was incorporated in 1759 as Childsburg in his honor; changed to Hillsborough in 1766.

WILLIAM CHURTON (? - d. 1767) *Surveyor, Mapmaker.* In October, 1749, Churton was one of four men appointed from North Carolina and Virginia to establish a portion of the boundary between the two colonies. He surveyed large areas of land for the Moravians in the Piedmont and in 1753 Bishop Spangenberg reported some land surveyed by him west of the mountains in North Carolina was believed to be the first actual survey made there. Between 1754 and 1762 Churton represented Orange county in the General Assembly and also served as Register of Deeds. Grants of land to Churton totaled between 11,000 and 12,000 acres and both the towns of Hillsboro and Salisbury were established on land which he originally owned. For nearly 20 years Churton was surveyor for the Earl of Granville and during more than 10 years of that time he worked on a map of North Carolina. It was nearly finished at the time of his death and in 1766 the Assembly appropriated 1155 Proc. to Churton to enable him to have his map "of the inhabited part of this Province" published in England. Churton died in December of the following year, however, and the map was left in the care of Governor Tryon. Of Churton's map Tryon said, "I am enclined to believe there is not so perfect a draft of so extensive an interior country in any other colony in America." Tryon turned Churton's map over to Captain John Collet to be finished. It was published in London in May, 1770.

FRANCIS CORBIN (*fl.* 1744-1760; *d. c.* 1766 or 1767) *Colonial Official.* Believed to have come to N. C. from London in November, 1744. Served as agent for Earl of Granville during the surveying of his lands. Member of governor's council, 1751-1760. In 1758 built the Cupola House, Edenton. One of early victims of Regulator attacks. Moravian Bishop Spangenburg called him "a walking encyclopedia concerning North Carolina affairs." For a time the seat of Orange county was called Corbinton in his honor.

MOSES ASHLEY CURTIS (1808-1872) *Scientist, Clergyman.* Native of Massachusetts. Rector of St. Matthew's Church, 1841-1847, 1856-1872. Head of Episcopal School for Boys, Raleigh, 1837-1839. Made scientific study of fungi, shrubs, woody vines, and other plants. Discovered and named number of new plants. First to understand and describe process by which Venus Fly Trap "eats" insects.

JAMES BUCHANAN DUKE (1856-1925) *Manufacturer.* Born in Orange county near present site of Durham. At an early age began work with his brothers and father in manufacturing smoking tobacco on his father's farm. Business expanded into a wooden factory in Durham early in the 1870's. Headed firm of W. Duke and Sons. Travelled as salesman. Expanded business. Formed American Tobacco Company and became its president. Established Duke Endowments; provided funds for Duke and other universities and colleges and for hospitals.

WASHINGTON DUKE (1820-1905) *Manufacturer.* Born Orange county. Served in Confederate Army and Navy. Began manufacturing smoking tobacco on his farm soon after Civil War. Business expanded largely through interest and efforts of his sons. Contributed freely to Trinity College when it was moved to Durham at his behest.

DAVID FANNING (1756?-1825) *Loyalist Leader.* Born in Johnston county (now Wake). About 1772 lived at Hawfields, Orange county, and later moved to S. C. During Revolution commanded Loyalist forces in N. C., conducting raids to burn homes, plunder the countryside, and murder any who attempted to stop him. After the war lived for a time in St. Augustine, Fla., but in 1784 moved to Canada.

EDMUND FANNING (1737-1818) *Colonial Official.* Born Long Island, New York. Graduate Yale, 1757. Moved to N. C. 1761, and located at Hillsboro to practice law. Represented Orange county in assemblies of 1762, 1766, 1767, and 1768; borough of Hillsboro in 1770 and 1771. Register of deeds, 1763-1768. Also judge of superior court and colonel of militia. Object of anger and hatred of Regulators. Returned to New York, 1771. Commanded Tories during Revolution. After war became a general in the British Army. Died in London.

WILLIAM FEW (1748-1828) *Senator.* Born near Baltimore. Moved with parents to Orange county, 1758. Member Continental Congress from Georgia, 1780-1782 and 1785-1788. Original trustee for establishing University of Georgia. U. S. Senator. Moved to N. Y., 1799, and held various state offices.

SAMUEL MALLETTE GATTIS (1863-1931) *Lawyer.* Born Orange county. Graduate U. N. C., 1884. School principal, 1884-1887. Clerk Orange county superior court, 1888-1894. Practiced law in Hillsboro. Member general assembly for several terms and speaker of House in 1903.

JOHN WASHINGTON GRAHAM (1838-1928) *Lawyer.* Born Hillsboro. Graduate U. N. C., 1857. Major in Confederate Army. Teacher, 1858-60; began practice of law in 1860. Member constitutional convention of 1868. Served a number of terms in state Senate.

WILLIAM ALEXANDER GRAHAM (1804-1875) *Governor, Secretary of Navy.* Born Lincoln county. Graduate U. N. C., 1824. Began practice of law in Hillsboro, 1825. Member general assembly (speaker of House for two terms). United States Senator. Governor, 1845-1849. Secretary of Navy under Fillmore (1850-

1853). Whig nominee for vice president, 1852. Confederate Senator.

WILLIAM MERCER GREEN (1798-1889) *Bishop.* Born Wilmington. Graduate U. N. C., 1818. Rector St. Matthew's Church, 1825-1837. Professor U. N C, 1838-1849. Elected first Bishop of Mississippi, 1849. Active in establishing University of the South, Sewanee, Tenn., and its chancellor from 1867.

GEORGE EMRICK HARRIS (1827-1911) *Congressman.* Born Orange county. Moved to Tennessee and thence to Mississippi. Lieutenant colonel in Confederate Army. Member Congress, 1870-1873. Lieutenant governor of Miss.

HENRI HARRISSE (c. 1829-1910) *Bibliographer.* Born in France. Came to Charleston, S. C., as a youth. Studied law. Instructor in French, U. N. C., 1853-1857. Removed to Chicago and finally to New York to practice law. About 1865 began work as bibliographer in library of Samuel L. M. Barlow. Author of a number of outstanding bibliographical works.

THOMAS HART (1730-1808) *Merchant, Land Speculator.* Born in Virginia; moved to Orange county about 1757. Justice of the peace and sheriff of Orange county. Lieutenant colonel of militia; fought against Regulators. Had an interest in a store in Hillsboro and owned Hart's Mill, two miles from town. Member general assembly. Commissary officer for troops during Revolution. Moving spirit in establishing Transylvania Land Co. Operated a number of stores; moved to Kentucky.

FRANCIS LISTER HAWKS (1798-1866) *Clergyman, Historian.* Born New Bern. Graduate U. N. C., 1815. Studied law under William Gaston and practiced briefly. Took up study of theology and ordained (Episcopalian) 1827. Served churches in Conn., Penna., and N. Y. Three times declined election as Bishop. In 1846 became professor of history, U. N. C. Three years later returned to Louisiana where he had earlier been first president of University of La. Wrote widely in field of church history, general history, and biography. Author of two-volume *History of North Carolina,* published 1857-1858.

DENNIS HEARTT (1783-1870) *Newspaper Editor.* Born in Conn. Served apprenticeship in New Haven, 1798-1802. Moved to Philadelphia and began publishing his own paper. Was one of the invited guests of Robert Fulton on the trial trip of the *Clermont*. Moved to Hillsboro and on February 20, 1820, began to publish the *Hillsborough Recorder* which he continued for nearly half a century. It came to be the best known paper in central N. C. Sold his paper in 1869.

RICHARD HENDERSON (1735-1785) *Judge, Land Speculator*. Born in Va. Living in Hillsboro in 1769 when appointed judge of superior court by Gov. Tryon. Was driven from the bench in 1770 by Regulators. One of the backers of the ill-fated State of Transylvania. Member N. C. council of state and of House of Commons.

JAMES HOGG (1729-1805) *Merchant*. Born in Scotland. Arrived in Wilmington, 1774, and settled in Fayetteville as a merchant. Served on committee of safety during Revolution and on one occasion travelled to Connecticut on public business. Moved to Orange county after the Revolution. One of first trustees of U. N. C. and early benefactor. Member Transylvania Land Co.

WILLIAM WOOD HOLDEN (1818-1892) *Journalist, Governor*. Born Orange county. Apprenticed to Dennis Heartt and worked on *Hillsboro Recorder* for six years. Went to Raleigh, 1837, and worked on the *Star;* editor *North Carolina Standard*. During Civil War became leader in peace movement. Made provisional governor by Pres. Johnson, May 1865; elected 1868. Postmaster in Raleigh, 1873-1881.

EDWIN MICHAEL HOLT (1807-1884) *Manufacturer*. Born Orange (now Alamance) county. Operated small farm and store. In 1837 began operation of cotton factory on Great Alamance creek. Began dyeing operations in 1853 and wove first colored cotton goods in South. Supported N. C. Railroad. Greatly expanded his cotton manufacturing before his retirement in 1866.

MICHAEL HOLT (1723-1799) *Revolutionary Character*. Born in Va. Moved to Orange county about 1740. Captain of county militia against Regulators. In 1776 answered Gov. Martin's call for Loyalist support, but after reaching Cross Creek en route to Brunswick returned home. Arrested at home and imprisoned in Philadelphia. Released and returned to Orange county. Aided American cause by donating supplies.

THOMAS MICHAEL HOLT (1831-1896) *Governor.* Born Orange (now Alamance) county on site of Battle of Alamance. Student U. N. C., 1849-1850. Cotton manufacturer. President N. C. Railroad. Frequent member of general assembly. Lieutenant governor, 1889-1891; governor 1891-1893.

WILLIAM HOOPER (1742-1790) *Signer Declaration of Independence.* Born Boston, Mass. Graduate Harvard. Moved to Wilmington, 1767, and practiced law. Member Continental Congress. Signer of Declaration of Independence. Revolutionary leader. Moved to Hillsboro, 1781, where he died.

GEORGE MOSES HORTON (1797-1883). *Negro Poet.* Born of pure African parentage on the plantation of William Horton, Northampton county. Remained in slavery until the end of the Civil War. When he was about six his master moved to a new farm in Chatham county, ten miles from Chapel Hill. About 1815 he began to peddle fruit and farm products in Chapel Hill and came to the attention of students and teachers in the University. His ability at rhyming and composing was such that his friends in Chapel Hill started teaching him. Horton soon was composing love poems for the students who paid him small sums for them. In 1829 his first book of poems, *The Hope of Liberty,* was published in Raleigh by Joseph Gales. Contributions to a number of periodicals followed and in 1845 his *Poetical Works* were printed in Hillsboro. In 1865 *Naked Genius* was published in Raleigh. Towards the end of the war Horton became attached to the Union Army and afterwards went with Captain Will H. S. Banks to Philadelphia where he spent the remainder of his life.

REDNAP HOWELL (? -1787)*Regulator.* Probably a native of New Jersey. Schoolmaster, first in lower Orange (now Chatham) county, but by 1768 had moved to that part of the county which is now Randolph. Leader of Regulators. Drew up statement of grievances presented to Gov. Tryon. Wrote ballads popular at the time concerning complaints of Regulators and he may have been the author of the pamphlet *A Fan for Fanning and a Touchstone to Tryon.* Active in Hillsboro riot, 1770. Fought at Alamance, 1771, and afterwards took refuge in Maryland. Died in N. J.

FORDYCE MITCHELL HUBBARD (1809-1888) *Professor.* Born Massachusetts. Rector Christ Church, New Bern, 1842-47. In charge of Episcopal School near Raleigh, 1847-49. Professor of Latin Language and Literature, U. N. C., 1849-1868. Author of life of Davie, a number of textbooks, and articles in magazines. Died in Raleigh.

ROSWELL HUNTINGTON (1763-1836) *Silversmith, Engraver.* Born Norwich, Conn. Revolutionary soldier. Moved to Hillsboro about 1786. In 1789 was one of nine members of the Orange County Horse employed to guard the removal of state funds from Hillsboro to Fayetteville. In 1793 he engraved the brass plate deposited in the cornerstone of Old East building at U. N. C. Moved to Alabama, 1833.

WILLIAM HUNTINGTON (1792-1874) *Merchant, Silversmith.* Born Hillsboro. Learned trade from his father, Roswell Huntington, and established his own business in 1815, selling, in addition to silverware, such things as grave stones, flour, and medicine. He also operated a blacksmith shop. Moved to Alabama, 1833.

HERMON (HERMAN, HARMON) HUSBAND (1724-1795) *Regulator.* Born probably in Cecil county, Md., of Quaker parentage. Settled at Corbinton (now Hillsboro) in 1755. Engaged extensively in local land speculation. Leader of Regulators. In April, 1768, he converted unorganized mob into oathbound organization (Regulators). He took no part in violence, but was arrested after an outbreak. Represented Orange county in general assembly, 1769, 1770-1771. Left field at Battle of Alamance before fighting started. Fled to Maryland and later lived in Pennsylvania where he was active in the Whiskey Rebellion.

WILLIAM JOHNSTON (*fl.* 1769 - *d. c.* 1791) *Merchant, Land Speculator.* Born in Scotland, settled in Hillsboro about 1767 or 1768. In 1769 joined Richard Bennehan in operating Little River Store. Owned farm, mill, and other property in Orange county. One of members of Louisa Company, 1774, to develop western territory. Treasurer of Transylvania Company. Represented Orange county in provincial congresses of April and November, 1776.

PRIDE JONES (1815-1889) *Physician.* Born Hillsboro. Graduate U. N. C., 1834. Clerk of superior court; member general assembly, 1858, 1872; captain Orange Guards, later Lieutenant colonel, in Civil War.

GEORGE LAWS (1801-1881) *County Official.* In early life a carpenter. Deputy sheriff, 1829. Clerk of court for more than thirty years.

JOHN LAWS (1824-1913) *County Official.* Register of deeds for Orange county for more than sixty years.

BRAXTON BYNUM LLOYD (1886-1947) *Physician.* Born Chapel Hill. Student U. N. C., graduate of the University medical school in Raleigh, 1906. Engaged in general practice in Carrboro, 1912-1947. Widely loved as typical family doctor. Mayor of Carrboro, 1920-1921.

THOMAS F. LLOYD (1736-1792) *Colonial Official.* Born in Pennsylvania. Came to N. C. about 1758 and settled about three miles west of the site of Chapel Hill. Between 1760 and 1770 he was coronor, justice of the peace, chairman of the county court, member of the vestry of the parish, and an officer of the militia; from 1761 to 1768 he represented the county in the general assembly. In 1768 he was appointed major general by Gov. Tryon.

LEMUEL LYNCH (1808-1893) *Silversmith, Jeweler.* Born Back Creek, Orange county. Apprenticed to William Huntington. In 1828 opened his own shop in Greensboro and in 1832 in Concord. Began work in Hillsboro in 1834 where he remained the rest of his life. Appointed justice of the peace, 1841.

PRIESTLY HINTON MANGUM (1795-1850) *Lawyer.* Born Orange county. Graduate U. N. C., 1815. Tutor at University following graduation. Practiced law in Hillsboro. Representative in general assembly, 1832. County solicitor. Brother of Willie P. Maugum.

WILLIE PERSON MANGUM (1792-1861) *Senator.* Born Orange county. Graduate U. N. C., 1815. Admitted to bar, 1817. Represented Orange county in general assembly, 1818-1819. Member congress, 1823-1826; senator, 1831-1836, 1840-1853. President pro tempore of senate 1842-1845. Received eleven electoral votes for president in 1836.

WILLIAM JOSEPH MARTIN (1830-1896) *Military Officer, Professor.* Born Richmond, Va. Educated University of Va. Elected to chair of chemistry, U. N. C., 1858. In 1861 raised a company of volunteers in Orange county which became Co. G, 28th Regt. Martin afterwards became colonel of 11th Regt. After the war returned to Chapel Hill for two years. Went to Davidson college in 1870. Became acting president of college in 1887. Declined nomination as president, but was made vice president.

ALEXANDER MEBANE (1744-1795) *Congressman.* Born Hawfields. Delegate to Provincial Congress, 1776. Justice of peace and sheriff of Orange county. Auditor Hillsboro district, 1783-1784. Member Hillsboro and Fayetteville conventions, 1789; of general assembly, 1787-1792; and of congress, 1793-1795.

JAMES MEBANE (1774-1857) *Legislator.* Born Orange county. Student, U. N. C., 1795. First president Dialectic Society. Member general assembly, 1798, 1801-1803, 1808-1811, 1821-1823, and 1828; speaker of house, 1821.

GEORGE MICKLEJOHN (c 1717-c 1817) *Clergyman.* Born probably in Scotland. Said to have been educated at Cambridge, to have served as a chaplain under Frederick the Great, and to have been with the Duke of Cumberland at the Battle of Culloden. The title page of a sermon by Micklejohn published in New Bern in 1768 indicates that he held the degree of Doctor of Sacred Theology. March 12, 1766, licensed by Bishop of London for work in North Carolina. He went first to Rowan county, but shortly afterwards became rector of St. Matthew's, Hillsboro. Opposed Regulators. Inclined at first, during Revolution, to be Loyalist. Captured at Moore's Creek but paroled. Took oath of loyalty at Halifax convention. Moved to Granville county. In 1790 was president of first Episcopal convention in N. C. In early 1800's removed to Virginia.

ELISHA MITCHELL (1793-1857) *Professor, Explorer.* Born Connecticut. Graduate Yale, 1813. In 1817 appointed to chair of mathematics, U. N. C., and to chemistry in 1825. Conducted botanical and geological expeditions throughout the state. Made many scientific studies and explorations of N. C., particularly in the mountains. Measured highest peaks. Killed on Mount Mitchell, named for him.

WILLIAM MONTGOMERY (1789-1844) *Physician, Congressman.* Born Guilford county. Studied medicine and practiced in Albrights, Orange county. Represented the county in state senate 1824-1827, 1829-1834. Member congress, 1835-1841.

STEPHEN MOORE (c 1740-1800) *Revolutionary Leader.* Born New York City. Served in French and Indian War (1758-1760). From 1765 to 1775 he lived at West Point, which he owned. Shortly before Revolution bought land in Caswell (now Person) county and built "Mt. Tirzah," his home. Appointed lieutenant colonel of Hillsboro district. In 1781 stationed in Hillsboro by Gov. Burke as deputy quartermaster general.

ARCHIBALD DeBOW MURPHEY (1777-1832) *Jurist.* Born Caswell county. Graduate U. N. C., 1799. Began practice of law in 1802. Member state senate from Orange county, 1812-1818. Strong advocate of internal improvements, canals, roads, schools. Judge superior court, 1818-1820.

FRANCIS NASH (*c.* 1742-1777) *Revolutionary Officer.* Born Virginia. Moved to Hillsboro about 1763. Justice of the peace and clerk of county court. Represented Orange county in general assembly, 1764-1765, and Hillsboro in 1773-1775. One of victims of abuse by Regulators. Captain and later colonel of militia. At Battle of Alamance. Member of provincial congress, April and August, 1775. Appointed lieutenant colonel of First Regiment, Continental Line, September, 1775; brigadier general, February, 1777. Fatally wounded at Battle of Germantown, October 4, 1777.

FRANCIS NASH (1855-1932) *Lawyer.* Born Robeson county. Grew up and educated in Hillsboro. Began practice of law in Tarboro, 1877, where he became mayor in 1881 and served as county judge from 1881 to 1885. Returned to Hillsboro to practice law and served as mayor, 1908-1912; county attorney, 1910-1915; state senator, 1915. Assistant attorney and clerk of N. C. supreme court. Author of a number of historical and biographical works.

FREDERICK NASH (1781-1858) *Chief Justice.* Born Tryon's Palace, New Bern, which his father occupied while governor.

Graduate Princeton, 1799. Admitted to bar, 1801. Moved to Hillsboro, 1807. Represented Orange county in general assembly, 1814-1817, and Hillsboro in 1828-1829; speaker in 1814. Judge of superior court, 1818-1826, 1836-1844. Succeeded Gaston on supreme court, 1844, and continued until his death. Chief Justice after 1852.

JOHN WALL NORWOOD (1802-1885) *Lawyer.* Born Hillsboro. Graduate U. N. C., 1824. Practiced law in Hillsboro. Member general assembly for Orange county, 1858; of state senate, 1872. Advocated and practiced scientific farming.

WILLIAM NORWOOD (1766-1842) *Lawyer, Judge.* Born probably in Scotland. Represented Hillsboro in general assembly, 1806-1807; was practicing law in Hillsboro as early as 1818; judge superior court, 1820-1836. Early benefactor of University and later contributed towards completion of South Building.

DENISON OLMSTED (1791-1859) *Professor.* Born Connectticut. Graduate Yale, 1813. Professor of chemistry, U. N. C., 1817-1825. Undertook geological survey of N. C. for the general assembly. Strong advocate of teacher training and improvement of common schools.

HENRY PATILLO (1726-1801) *Clergyman.* Born in Scotland. Settled in Virginia; clerked in a store and taught school. In 1751 began to study with view to ordination in Presbyterian church. Ordained and preached in Va. Moved to Hawfields, 1765. Chaplain to provincial congress in Hillsboro in August and September, 1775. In 1780 removed to Granville county.

CHARLES PHILLIPS (1822-1889) *Professor.* Born Harlem, N. Y. Graduate U. N. C., 1841. Tutor, 1844-1854; professor of engineering, 1854-1860; of mathematics, 1861-1868, and 1875-1879. Professor at Davidson College, 1869-1875. Author of textbooks and other works.

JAMES PHILLIPS (1792-1867) *Professor.* Born England. Settled in Harlem, N. Y., as a teacher in 1818. In 1826 he became professor of mathematics and natural philosophy, U. N. C., where he remained for forty years. Licensed by the Orange Presbytery, 1833, and preached more or less regularly until about 1863.

SAMUEL FIELD PHILLIPS (1824-1903) *Lawyer*. Born Harlem, N. Y. Graduate U. N. C., 1841. assistant professor of law, 1854-1859; represented Orange county in general assembly, 1852-1854, 1864-1865 (speaker of house, 1865); member constitutional convention of 1865; state auditor; U. S. solicitor general, 1873-1885.

SOLOMON POOL (1832-1901) *University President*. Born Elizabeth City. Graduate U. N. C., 1853. Tutor and professor, 1853-1868. President U. N. C., 1868-1874. Methodist minister.

NATHANIEL ROCHESTER (1752-1831) *Merchant, County Official*. Born Virginia. Educated at school conducted by the Rev. Henry Patillo. Settled in Hillsboro, 1773, and joined Thomas Hart in operating a store. Delegate to provincial congresses in 1775 and 1776. Lieutenant colonel of an Orange county regiment of militia. Member general assembly, 1777. Clerk of court, 1777-1782. Left N. C. in 1782. Founder of Rochester, N. Y.

THOMAS RUFFIN, Sr. (1787-1870) *Chief Justice*. Born Virginia. Educated Warrenton, N. C., academy. Graduate Princeton, 1805. Studied law. Settled in Hillsboro, 1809. Represented Hillsboro in general assembly, 1813, 1815, 1816. Judge of superior court. Justice of supreme court, 1829-1833; chief justice, 1833-1852. Retired 1852, but served again as justice, 1858-1860. Delegate to secession convention.

THOMAS RUFFIN, Jr. (1824-1889) *Lawyer*. Born Hillsboro. Graduate U. N. C., 1844. Licensed to practice law. In Civil War, lieutenant colonel, 13th regiment. Justice of the state supreme court, 1881-1885.

JAMES STRUDWICK SMITH (1790-1859) *Physician, Congressman*. Born near Hillsboro. Graduate Hillsboro Academy and Jefferson Medical College, Philadelphia, 1818. Practiced medicine near Hillsboro at first and later near Chapel Hill. Member of congress 1817-1821; general assembly 1821-1822; and delegate to state constitutional convention in 1835.

CORNELIA PHILLIPS SPENCER (1825-1908) *Writer*. Born in Harlem, N. Y., daughter of Prof. James Phillips. Moved to Chapel Hill as a child where she lived until 1894 when she went to Cambridge, Mass., to live with her daughter. Mrs. Spencer gave long years of service to North Carolina in many fields — political, religious, educational, and literary. Her letters and personal pleas were largely responsible for the re-opening of the University in 1875 at the end of the carpetbag regime. She was the author of a popular school history of North Carolina and her *Last Ninety Days of the War in North Carolina* has long been regarded as a vivid and strong account of the end of the Civil War in the state. Mrs. Spencer wrote frequently for magazines and newspapers and was the author of a number of songs and hymns.

RICHARD STANFORD (1767-1816) *Congressman*. Born near Vienna, Maryland. Educated locally. Moved to Hawfields, Orange county, about 1793 and established an academy. Elected as a Democrat to the Fifth and to the nine succeeding Congresses, serving from 1797 until his death nearly twenty years later. In Congress he advocated economy and opposed the Alien and Sedition Laws; during the difficult times preceding the War of 1812, he spoke strongly against war. Stanford was a close personal friend of Nathaniel Macon, John Randolph of Roanoke, and William Gaston. He was a firm supporter of Thomas Jefferson.

WILLIAM FRANKLIN STROWD (1832-1911) *Congressman*. Born near Chapel Hill. Attended Bingham School and Graham Institute. Moved to Chatham county in 1861. Served as private in Civil War. Served as a Populist in congress, 1895-1899. Resumed agricultural pursuits.

EDMUND STRUDWICK (1802-1879) *Physician*. Born Orange county. Educated Bingham School. Graduate U. of Penna., 1824. Began practice of medicine in Hillsboro, 1826. First president (1849) N. C. State Medical Society. Gained reputation as a surgeon and operated in Raleigh, Wilmington, Charlotte, and Greensboro.

WILLIAM FRANCIS STRUDWICK (? -1812) *Congressman*. Born "Stag Park," New Hanover county. Limited education. Engaged in agriculture. Delegate from Orange county to state convention of 1789; member state senate from Orange county, 1792, 1797. Member congress, 1796-1797; of general assembly, 1801-1803. Died at his home, Hawfields.

DAVID LOWRIE SWAIN (1801-1868) *Governor, University President*. Born Buncombe county. Attended Newton Academy and U. N. C. Licensed to practice law, 1822. Member general assembly; judge superior court. Governor, 1832-1835. President U. N. C., 1835-1867. Improved and enlarged University.

ABSOLOM TATOM (TATUM) (1742-1802) *Congressman*. Native North Carolinian. Sergeant in militia, 1763. Lieutenant in 1st N. C. Continental Regt., 1775, promoted captain, 1776. Assistant quartermaster and keeper of arsenal, Hillsboro, 1778. Major, N. C. Light Horse, 1779. District auditor for Hillsboro, 1781. Private secretary to Gov. Burke. Delegate from Hillsboro to constitutional convention, 1788. Member congress, 1795-1796; general assembly, 1797-1802, from Hillsboro.

CHARLES COURTENEY TEW (1824-1862) *Confederate Officer*. Born South Carolina. First graduate of the Citadel; superintendent of the arsenal, Columbia, S. C. Moved to Hillsboro several years before the Civil War. Formed Hillsboro Military Academy. Colonel, 2nd N. C. Regt.; killed Sept. 17, 1862, at Sharpsburg.

JAMES THACKSTON (*fl.* 1770-1781; *d. after* 1790) *Revolutionary Leader*. Opponent of Regulators. Colonel Orange county troops at Battle of Moore's Creek Bridge, February 27, 1776. Lieutenant colonel, 4th N. C. Regt., Continental Line, April 15, 1776 to January 1, 1781, when he retired. Presumably moved to Cumberland county which he represented in the general assembly in 1787. Living there at time of 1790 census.

JOSIAH TURNER, JR. (1821-1901) *Lawyer, Confederate Congressman*. Born Hillsboro. Student U. N. C., 1842-1843. Licensed to practice law, 1845. Member general assembly, 1852, 1854, 1856, 1858, 1860, 1868. Captain, Confederate Army; wounded and forced to retire. Confederate congressman, 1864. Publisher Raleigh *Sentinel*. Elected to congress, 1865, but denied seat.

FRANCIS PRESTON VENABLE (1856-1934) *Chemist, University President*. Born Virginia. Graduate U. of Va., 1879. Professor U. N. C., 1880-1900; president, 1900-1914. Outstanding chemist who "made the natural sciences as respectable and respected as the humanities, law, medicine, and theology."

ALFRED MOORE WADDELL (1834-1912) *Congressman*. Born Hillsboro. Graduate U. N. C., 1853. Admitted to bar, 1855, and began practice in Wilmington. Newspaper editor; lieutenant colonel in Civil War. Member congress, 1871-1879. Mayor of Wilmington, 1898-1904.

HUGH WADDELL (1799-1879) *Lawyer.* Born Orange county. Graduate U. N. C., 1818. Represented Orange county in general assembly, 1828; state senator, 1836, 1844-1846; lieutenant governor, 1836.

JAMES WATSON (*fl.* 1752-1770) *County Official.* Pioneer settler of Orange county. In 1752 was one of the commissioners to establish the boundaries of the county. Vestryman of the Parish of St. Matthew. The site selected for a courthouse in 1754 was on property owned by Watson and in 1759 he was one of the commissioners appointed to establish the town of Childsburg. During the French and Indian War he assisted in raising supplies for the Indian allies of North Carolina. At the time of the Regulator violence Watson sided with Tryon and reported to him on the disturbance at the September, 1770, session of Orange court. He was Clerk of Court for several years.

CHAPTER XX

APPENDICES

The Act Creating Orange County

LAWS OF NORTH CAROLINA—1752

CHAPTER VI

An Act for dividing Part of Granville, Johnston, and Bladen Counties, into a County and Parish, by the Name of Orange County, and the Parish of St. Matthew, and for appointing Vestrymen for the said Parish, and other Purposes therein mentioned.

I. Whereas the Counties of Johnston, Granville, and Bladen, are now become so very extensive, that many of the Inhabitants thereof live very remote from the Places where the Courts of the said Counties are held; whereby a great many Difficulties and Hardships arise to the upper Inhabitants thereof, not only in attending their Ordinary Business in the said Courts, but as also by being compelled to serve as Jurymen, and often Times as Evidences, at the said Courts: for Remedy Whereof,

II. We pray that it may be Enacted, And be it Enacted, by his Excellency Gabriel Johnston, Esq., Governor, by and with the Advice and Consent of his Majesty's Council, and the General Assembly of this Province, and it is hereby Enacted, by the Authority of the same, That the upper Part of Granville, Johnston, and Bladen Counties, be erected into a County and Parish by the Name of Orange County, and the Parish of St. Matthew, and be divided by a Line, beginning on the nearest Part of the Virginia Line to Hico Creek, thence a direct line to the Bent of Eno River, below the Occanechas, near to the Plantation where John Williams now dwelleth; thence down the South side of Eno River, to Neuse River; thence down Neuse River, to the Mouth of Horse Creek; thence a direct line to the Place where Earl Granville's Line crosses Cape Fear River; thence along the said Line, to the Eastern Bounds of Anson County; thence along the dividing Line of Anson County to the End there of: And that the upper Parts of the said Counties be divided and run accordingly, by the Commissioners hereinafter appointed: And that the said County and Parish shall enjoy all and every the Privileges which any other County or Parish in the Province holds or enjoys.

III. And be it further Enacted, by the Authority aforesaid, That it shall and may be lawful, for the Justices of the said

County, to lay a Tax on all the Tithables in the said County, not exceeding One Shilling, Proclamation Money, per Annum, for the Term of Four Years, for running the Boundary Lines, and for building a Court-house, Prison, and Stocks, in the said County, at such Places as the Justices shall agree upon and appoint at the County Court to be held at the House of John Greys, on the Second Tuesday in June next, after the passing of this Act, or the then next succeeding Court; and shall further divide the said County into Districts, and shall appoint Commissioners of the Roads for the same; Which said Tax shall be collected by the Sheriff of the said County, at such Times, and in the same Manner, as other Taxes are collected.

IV. And be it further Enacted by the Authority aforesaid, That the Courts of the said County shall be held on the second Tuesdays in June, September, December, and March, Yearly.

V. And be it further Enacted, That Alexander Maben, be, and is hereby appointed Sheriff of the said County of Orange, until the Time prescribed by Law for appointing Sheriffs for this Province; and shall be commissioned by his Excellency the Governor and vested with the same Powers and Authorities as any other Sheriff of any other County in this Province is vested with.

VI. And be it further Enacted, by the Authority aforesaid, That Alexander Maben, James Watson, Mark Morgan, John Pattison, Andrew Mitchell, Thomas Loveletter, Lawrence Bankston, James Ellison, William Bolling, John Gray, John Pitman, and Joseph Tate, be, and they are hereby appointed Vestrymen of the said Parish of St. Matthew, until the General Election of Vestrymen according to Law, and that the said Vestrymen shall be summoned, by the Sheriff of the said County to meet at such Time and Place, as the Majority of the said Vestrymen shall appoint; and shall be qualified as a Vestry, and proceed to Parish Business.

VII. And be it further Enacted, That all County and Parish Taxes, already laid on any of the Inhabitants of the several Counties of Granville, Johnston, and Bladen, shall be collected by the respective Sheriffs of the said Counties of Granville, Johnston, and Bladen, and account for in the same Manner as tho' this Act had not been made.

VIII. And to the End, that no Action commenced in Granville, Johnston, and Bladen Counties be defeated, by the Division aforesaid, Be it Enacted, by the Authority aforesaid, That where any Action is already commenced in any of the said Counties of Granville, Johnston, and Bladen, and the Parties or Evidences shall be the Inhabitants of Orange County, all subsequent Process against such Parties or Evidences, shall be directed to be executed by the Sheriffs of Granville, Johnston, and Bladen Counties, to the End and final Determination of the said Causes; any Law Usage or Custom, to the Contrary, notwithstanding.

IX. And be it further Enacted, by the Authority aforesaid, That the County of Orange be, and is hereby obliged to send Jurors to the General Court, at New Bern, and the Sheriff of the said County shall account with the Treasurer of the Southern District of this Province, at New Bern, at the same Time, and in the same Manner, as other Sheriffs of Counties in the Southern District aforesaid are obliged to account.

X. And be it further Enacted, by the Authority aforesaid, That Mr. James Pain, Mr. William Pugh, and Mr. James Watson, be appointed Commissioners, and are hereby impowered and directed, to run a dividing Line between the Counties of Granville, Johnston, Bladen and Orange agreeable to the Directions in this Act beforementioned.

POPULATION OF ORANGE COUNTY, 1790-1950

1790—12,216
1800—16,362
1810—20,135
1820—23,492
1830—23,908
1840—24,356
1850—17,055 (Alamance County was formed from Orange in 1849)
1860—16,497
1870—17,507
1880—23,698
1890—14,948 (Durham County was formed from Orange, Wake, and Granville Counties in 1881)
1900—14,690
1910—15,064
1920—17,895
1930—21,171
1940—23,072
1950—34,435

ORANGE COUNTY—1752-1952 345

REGISTER OF OFFICIALS FROM ORANGE COUNTY, 1753-1953

I. Members of the Colonial Legislature

County Members

1753	Josiah Dickson, Mark Morgan
1754-1760	William Churton, John Gray
1760	Tyree Harris, John Gray
1761	William Churton, Thomas Loyd [Lloyd]
1762 [April]	William Churton, Thomas Lloyd
1762 [November]	Thomas Lloyd, Edmund Fanning
1764-1765	Thomas Lloyd, Francis Nash
1766-1768	Edmund Fanning, Thomas Lloyd
1769	Hermon Husband, John Pryor
1770-1771	Hermon Husband, John Pryor, Ralph McNair, Francis Nash
1773 [January]	John Gray, Ralph McNair
1773-1774	Ralph McNair, Thomas Hart
1775-	Ralph McNair, Thomas Hart

Borough Members from Hillsboro

1770-1771	Edmund Fanning
1773 [January]	Francis Nash
1773-1774	Francis Nash
1775	Francis Nash

II. Delegates to Provincial Congresses

County Members

August, 1774	Thomas Hart
April, 1775	Thomas Hart, Thomas Burke, John Kinchen, Francis Nash
August, 1775	Thomas Burke, John Kinchen, Thomas Hart, John Atkinson, John Williams
April, 1776	James Saunders, William Moore, John McCabe, John Atkinson, John Paine — Seats were declared vacant because of disorders at the polls.
	Thomas Burke
	Nathaniel Rochester
	Alexander Mebane
	John Butler
	John McCabe

Borough Members from Hillsboro

August, 1774	
April, 1775	
August, 1775	William Armstrong, Nathaniel Rochester
April, 1776	William Johnston
November, 1776	William Johnston

ORANGE COUNTY—1752-1952

Member of Provincial Council

Elected by the Provincial Congress, September 10, 1775 .... John Kinchen

III. Councilors of State

Elected by the General Assembly of North Carolina

June 26, 1781	John Butler
December 13, 1787	John Kinchen
November 11, 1788	John Kinchen
December 28, 1793	John Umstead
December 2, 1807	James Mebane
December 15, 1808	John Umstead
December 5, 1809	John Umstead
December 4, 1810	John Umstead
December 14, 1813	John Umstead
December 8, 1815	John Umstead
December 6, 1817	John Umstead
November 26, 1818	John Umstead
November 29, 1819	John Umstead
December 18, 1820	John Umstead
January 6, 1851	J. U. Kirkland

IV. Officials of the General Assembly

Speaker of House of Commons

Frederick Nash	1814
John Craige	1815
Thomas Ruffin	1816
James Mebane	1821-1822
William A. Graham	1838-1839
William A. Graham	1840-1841
Samuel F. Phillips	1865-1866

Speaker of the House of Representatives

John D. Cameron	1874-1875
John D. Cameron	1879-1880
John D. Cameron	1881-1883
S. M. Gattis	1903-1905
A. H. Graham	1929-1931

Speaker of Senate

Hugh Waddell 1836-1837

V. Other State Officials

Auditor of Public Accounts

1862-1864 .... Samuel F. Phillips

Solicitor General

1827-1828 .... John Scott

ORANGE COUNTY—1752-1952 347

Chief Justices
Justices of the Supreme Court

Thomas Ruffin	1833-1852
Frederick Nash	1852-1858

Associate Justices

Thomas Ruffin	1829-1833
Frederick Nash	1844-1852
Thomas Ruffin	1858-1860
Thomas Ruffin, Jr.	1881-1885

Judges of the Superior Court

Duncan Cameron	1814-1816
Thomas Ruffin	1816-1818
Frederick Nash	1818-1826
Archibald D. Murphey	1818-1820
Willie P. Mangum	1819-1820
William Norwood	1820-1836
Thomas Ruffin	1825-1828
Willie P. Mangum	1827; 1828-1830
Frederick Nash	1836-1844

Members of the House of Commons, 1777-1835, from Hillsboro

Year	Member	Year	Member
1777	William Courtney	1791	David Ray
1778	William Courtney	1792	Samuel Benton
1779	Thomas Tullock	1793	Alexander D. Moore
1780	Thomas Tullock[?]	1794	John Hogg
1781	Thomas Tullock	1795	Samuel Benton
1782	Thomas Farmer	1796	John Hogg
1783	Thomas Farmer	1797	Absalom Tatom
1784, Apr.	Archibald Lytle	1798	Absalom Tatom
1784, Oct.	Archibald Lytle	1799	Absalom Tatom
1785	John Taylor	1800	Absalom Tatom
1786	John Taylor	1801	Absalom Tatom
1787	John Taylor	1802	Absalom Tatom
1788	Absalom Tatom	1803	Barnaby O'Farrel
1789	William Nash		Catlett Campbell
1790	William Nash	1804	Catlett Campbell
1805	Catlett Campbell	1816	Thomas Ruffin
1806	William Norwood	1817	William Lockhart
1807	William Norwood	1818	John Scott
1808	Catlett Campbell	1819	John Scott
1809	Catlett Campbell	1820	John Scott

1810	Henry Thompson	1821	James S. Smith
1811	Henry Thompson	1822	Thomas Clancy
1812	John Street	1823	Thomas Clancy
1813	Thomas Ruffin	1824	John Scott
1814	James Child	1825	John Scott
1815	Thomas Ruffin	1826	John Scott
1827	John Scott	1831	Thomas J. Faddis
1828	Frederick Nash	1832	Thomas J. Faddis
1829	Frederick Nash	1833	William A. Graham
1830	William H. Phillips	1834	William A. Graham
		1835	William A. Graham

County Members of the General Assembly, 1777-1953

Year	Senators	Representatives
1777	Thomas Hart	Nathaniel Rochester (resigned)
		Thomas Burke
		John Butler
1778	John Kinchen	John Butler (resigned)
		Thomas Burke (resigned)
		William McCauley
		Mark Patterson
1779	John Hogan	William McCauley
		Mark Patterson
1780	William Courtney	William McCauley
		Mark Patterson
1781	John Butler	Jesse Benton
		Robert Campbell
1782	William Mebane	William McCauley
		Mark Patterson
1783	William McCauley	Alexander Mebane
		Thomas Burke
1784	William McCauley	William Hooper
		John Butler
1784, Oct.	William McCauley	Alexander Mebane
		John Butler
1785	William McCauley	William Courtney
		William Cain
1786	William McCauley	Jonathan Lindley
		John Butler
		William Hooper
1787	William McCauley	Alexander Mebane
		Jonathan Lindley
1788	William McCauley	Alexander Mebane
		Jonathan Lindley

ORANGE COUNTY—1752-1952 349

1789	Joseph Hodge	Alexander Mebane
		Jonathan Lindley
1790	William Courtney	Alexander Mebane
		John Carrington
1791	Joseph Hodge	Alexander Mebane
		Jonathan Lindley
1792	William F. Strudwick	Alexander Mebane
		William Nash
1793	William Sheppard	Walter Alves
		William Nash
1794	William Cain	William Lytle
		Walter Alves
1795	William Cain	Walter Alves
		William Lytle
1796	William Cain	Samuel Benton
		John Cabe
1797	William F. Strudwick	Samuel Benton
		John Cabe
1798	David Ray	James Mebane
		John Cabe
1799	David Ray	Samuel Benton
		William F. Strudwick
1800	David Ray	Samuel Benton
		John Cabe
1801	William Shepperd	William F. Strudwick
		James Mebane
1802	William Cain	William F. Strudwick
		Duncan Cameron
1803	William Shepperd	James Mebane
		William F. Strudwick
1804	David Ray	John Thompson
		Michael Holt
1805	Jonathan Lindley	John Thompson
		David Mebane
1806	David Ray	Duncan Cameron
		David Mebane
1807	David Ray	Duncan Cameron
		John Thompson
1808	James Mebane	John Thompson
		David Mebane
1809	James Mebane	John Thompson
		David Mebane
1810	James Mebane	John Thompson
		David Mebane
1811	James Mebane	John Craig
		John Thompson

1812	Archibald D. Murphey	Duncan Cameron
		Isaac Holt
1813	Archibald D. Murphey	Duncan Cameron
		John Craig
1814	Archibald D. Murphey	John Craig
		Frederick Nash
1815	Archibald D. Murphey	Frederick Nash
		John Craig
1816	Archibald D. Murphey	William Holt
		Frederick Nash
1817	Archibald D. Murphey	William Holt
		Frederick Nash
1818	Archibald D. Murphey	James Mebane
		Willie P. Mangum
1819	Duncan Cameron	W. Barbee
		Willie P. Mangum
1820	Michael Holt	Willie Shaw
		James Mebane
1821	Michael Holt	Willie Shaw
		James Mebane
1822	Duncan Cameron	James Mebane
		John McCauley
1823	Duncan Cameron	James Mebane
		John McCauley
1824	William Montgomery	William McCauley
		John Boon
1825	William Montgomery	William McCauley
		John Boon
1826	William Montgomery	John Boon
		John Stockard
1827	William Montgomery	John Boon
		John Stockard
1828	James Mebane	Hugh Waddell
		John Stockard
1829	William Montgomery	Thomas H. Taylor
		John Stockard
1830	William Montgomery	John Stockard
		Joseph Allison
1831	William Montgomery	Joseph Allison
		James Mebane
1832	William Montgomery	Joseph Allison
		Priestly H. Mangum
1833	William Montgomery	Joseph Allison
		John Stockard
1834	William Montgomery	Joseph Allison
		John Stockard

ORANGE COUNTY—1752-1952 351

Year	Senatorial District	Senators	
1835		Joseph Allison	John Stockard
			James Forest
			Hugh Waddell
1836	37th	Hugh Waddell	William A. Graham
			Nathaniel J. King
			John Boon
			John Stockard
1838	37th	Joseph Allison	B. Trollinger
			John Stockard
			H. Sims
			William A. Graham
1840	37th	Willie P. Mangum	William A. Graham
			Nathan J. King
			M. W. Holt
			James Graham
			Cadwallader Jones, Jr.
1842	37th	Joseph Allison	Cadwallader Jones, Jr.
			Julius S. Bracken
			John Stockard
			Henry K. Nash
1844	30th	Hugh Waddell	John B. Leathers
			Loftin K. Pratt
			Giles Mebane
			Chesley F. Faucett
1846	30th	Hugh Waddell	Giles Mebane
			Chesley F. Faucett
			John B. Leathers
			Sidney Smith
1848	30th	John Berry	Cadwallader Jones, Jr.
			Patterson H. McDade
			John Stockard
			Giles Mebane
1850	30th	John Berry	Cadwallader Jones, Jr.
			Daniel A. Montgomery
			Bartlett A. Durham
			George Patterson
1852	30th	John Berry	Samuel F. Phillips
			Josiah Turner, Jr.
			Bartlett A. Durham
			J. T. Lyon
1854	30th	William A. Graham	Samuel F. Phillips
			Josiah Turner, Jr.
1856	30th	P. H. Cameron	William F. Strayhorn

1858	30th	Josiah Turner, Jr.	Pride Jones
			John Norwood
1860	30th	Josiah Turner, Jr.	Hugh B. Guthrie
			William N. Patterson
1862	30th	William A. Graham	John Berry
			William N. Patterson
			J. S. Leathers
1864	30th	John Berry	Samuel F. Phillips
			William N. Patterson
1865	30th	William A. Graham	Samuel F. Phillips
			Robert F. Webb
1866	30th	John Berry	W. W. Guess
			S. D. Umsted [Umstead]
1868	22d	Josiah Turner, Jr.	J. J. Allison
			Thomas M. Argo
			Frederick N. Strudwick
1870	22d	John W. Graham	Frederick N. Strudwick
			Matthew Atwater
1872	20th	John W. Norwood	Pride Jones
			Jones Watson
1874	20th	Calvin E. Parish	Joseph W. Latta
			Matthew Atwater
1876	20th	John W. Graham	J. Knox Hughes
			Calvin E. Parish
1879	20th	(Grouped with Caswell)	
		Giles Mebane	M. E. Angier
		George Williamson	Josiah Turner, Jr.
1881	20th	Calvin E. Parish	W. K. Parish
1883	20th	I. R. Strayhorn	James A. Cheek
1885	20th	Augustus W. Graham	C. W. Johnson
1887	20th	James B. Mason	James A. Cheek
1889	20th	Thomas H. Hughes	Thomas M. Cheek
1891	20th	R. G. Russell	R. N. Hall, Jr.
1893	18th	Thomas M. Cheek	James Norwood
1895	18th	(Grouped with Caswell & Alamance)	
		W. G. Stephens	James A. Cheek
		S. A. White	
1897	18th	(Grouped with Alamance & Durham)	
		E. S. Parker	Albert K. Holmes
		J. E. Lyon	
1899	18th	Thomas M. Cheek	Samuel M. Gattis

ORANGE COUNTY—1752-1952 353

1901	18th	(Grouped with Alamance & Durham)	
		R. W. Scott	Samuel M. Gattis
		Howard A. Foushee	Samuel M. Gattis
1903	19th	W. N. Pritchard	
1905	19th	(Grouped with Durham & Alamance)	
		Howard A. Foushee	Ira E. D. Andrews
		J. A. Turrentine	
1907	19th	John W. Graham	I. W. Pritchard
1909	19th	(Grouped with Alamance & Durham)	
		J. L. Scott, Jr.	Thomas E. Sparrow
		James S. Manning	
1911	19th	John W. Graham	John T. Johnston
1913	18th	(Grouped with Alamance & Durham)	
		J. L. Scott, Jr.	George C. Pickard
		Victor S. Bryant	
1915		E. F. Upchurch &	S. S. Smith
		Frank Nash	
1917		Bennehan Cameron &	Lueco Lloyd
		J. Elmer Long	
1919		Lyndon Patterson &	Lueco Lloyd
		George L. Williamson	
1921		Bennehan Cameron &	A. H. Graham
		J. Elmer Long	
1923	16th	J. Clyde Ray	A. H. Graham
		R. T. Wilson	
1925		W. L. Foushee &	A. H. Graham
		A. M. Carroll	
1927		J. Clyde Ray &	A. H. Graham
		W. B. Horton	
1929	16th	R. W. Scott	A. H. Graham
		S. C. Brawley	
1931	16th	John W. Umstead, Jr.	S. M. Gattis, Jr.
		T. H. Hatchett	
1933		John Sprunt Hill	S. M. Gattis, Jr.
		D. J. Walker	
1935		John Sprunt Hill	B. J. Howard
		Owen S. Robertson	
1937		John Sprunt Hill	B. J. Howard
		E. T. Sanders	
1939		Joseph H. Warren	Roland McClamroch
		John W. Umstead, Jr.	

1941		E. T. Sanders	John W. Umstead, Jr.
		E. C. Brooks, Jr.	
1943		E. T. Sanders	John W. Umstead, Jr.
1945		W. Dennis Madry	John W. Umstead, Jr.
1947	16th	James Webb	John W. Umstead, Jr.
1949		James Webb	John W. Umstead, Jr.
1951		Ralph H. Scott	John W. Umstead, Jr.
1953		Ralph H. Scott	John W. Umstead, Jr.

Members of Constitutional Conventions

Borough Members from Hillsboro

| 1788 | Absolom Tatom |
| 1789 | Samuel Benton |

County Members

1788	Alexander Mebane, William Mebane, William McCauley, Jonathan Lindley
1789	James Christmass, Alexander Mebane, Thomas H. Perkins, William F. Strudwick, Joseph Hodge
1835	James S. Smith, William Montgomery
1861	William A. Graham, John Berry
1865	John Berry, Samuel F. Phillips
1868	Edwin M. Holt, John W. Graham
1875	Josiah Turner, William A. Graham (died before meeting of Convention)

ORANGE COUNTY—1752-1952

SHERIFFS OF ORANGE COUNTY

Alexander Mebane	1752 to 1754
John Gray	1754 to 1756
Lawrence Thompson	1757
Josiah Dixon	1758 to 1760
William Reed	1760 to 1762
Thomas Hart	1763
William Nunn	1765
Thomas Hart	1768
Tyree Harris	1768
John Lea	1769
John Butler	1770
Thomas Donaldson	1772
Alexander Mebane, Jr.	1777 to 1780
John Hawkins	1780
James Mebane	1782 to 1784
James Freeland	1784 to 1786
John Nichols	1787
William McCauley	1789 to 1790
John Sloss	1791 to 1793
John Willis	1793
Joseph Hodge	1794 to 1796
Andrew Murdock	Apt. by Governor June 4, 1796 to 1799
Samuel Turrentine	1799 to 1809
David Ray	1809 to 1810
Josiah Turner	1810 to 1818
Edward Harris	1818
Thomas Clancy	1820 to 1822
Thomas D. Watts	1823 to 1832
James C. Turrentine	1833 to 1852
Richard M. Jones	August 23, 1852 to August 26, 1862
Hugh B. Guthrie	August 26, 1862 to August 22, 1864
Richard M. Jones	August 22, 1864 to July 4, 1865
Hugh B. Guthrie	July 4, 1865 to 1867
E. H. Ray	1867
John Turner	August 15, 1868 to September 5, 1870
Thomas H. Hughes	September 5, 1870 to December 6, 1880
John Knox Hughes	December 6, 1880 to September 5, 1904

S. W. Andrews .... September 5, 1904 to December 8, 1910
R. D. Bain .... December 8, 1910 to December 8, 1916
C. G. Rosemond .... December 9, 1916 to May 3, 1920
Thomas E. Sparrow .... May 3, 1920 to December 6, 1920
L. Bunn Lloyd .... December 6, 1920 to December 1928
W. T. Sloan .... December 1928 to October 1935
S. T. Latta, Jr. .... October 1935 to date

Not all the dates given above can be confirmed.

ORANGE COUNTY—1752-1952

REGISTERS OF DEEDS (first called public registers)

William Churton	1752-1763
Edmund Fanning	1763-1768
James Alston	1780-
James Williams	1783-
John Allison	1793-1794
J. Estes	1795-1799
A. B. Bruce	1800-1811
James Whitted	1812-1813
J. McKerall	1814-1834
A. Mickle	1835-1849
John Laws	1849-1853
Thomas J. Strayhorn	1853-1855
John Laws	1856-1913
H. Myron Durham	1914-1915
A. W. Kenion	1916-1919
J. F. McAdams	1920-1926
Cicero H. Jones	1926-1930
S. W. Andrews	1930-1942
Carolyn H. Hurley	(1 month) 1942-
J. E. Laws	1942-

The years given are those in which the officer's signature appears in the records, and do not in all cases establish the limits of his term.

CLERKS OF THE SUPERIOR COURT
(prior to 1868, the county court)

Richard Caswell	1752-
James Watson	1757-1764
Francis Nash	1764-1777
Nathaniel Rochester	1777-1781
Jesse Benton	1781-1784
Samuel Benton	1784-1791
Abner B. Bruce	1791-
John Taylor	1800-1845
Joseph Allison	1845-1853
George Laws	1853-1883
Pride Jones	1883-1888
Samuel M. Gattis	1888-1894
D. F. Crawford	1894-1898
D. H. Hamilton	1898-1908
Charles Strayhorn	1908-1926
A. W. Kenion	1926-1942
Edwin M. Lynch	1942-

ORANGE COUNTY—1752-1952

COUNTY COMMISSIONERS

Lemuel Lynch	1868-1870
Robert F. Morris	1868-1870
William N. Patterson	1868-1874
John U. Kirkland	1868-1870, 1874-1876
Jones Watson	1868-1872, 1874-1882
J. W. Carr	1870-1872
E. M. Holt	1870-1872
J. T. Hogan	1870-1872
William S. Kirkland	1872-1874
Joseph W. Latta	1872-1874, 1878-1881
John F. Lyon	1872-1886
Nelson P. Hall	1872-1878, 1881-1888
Caleb B. Green	1874-1876
Willie T. Patterson	1876-1878
D. F. Morrow	1876-1886
Nathaniel D. Bain	1878-1882
Merritt Cheek	1884-1886
Henry A. Anderson	1885-1886
E. C. Thompson	1886-1888
Matthew Atwater	1886-1888
H. P. Jones	1888-1889
J. Y. Merritt	1888-1892
W. D. Woods	1888-1892
D. H. Hamilton	1889-1896
N. V. Ray	1892-1894, 1896-1898
W. A. Maddry	1892-1896, 1898-1900
M. W. Moore	1894-1898
Thomas J. Hogan	1896-1898
A. L. Holden	1897-1898
A. J. Gordon	1897-1898
James Monk	1898-1902
James Laws, Jr.	1898-1902
William L. Lloyd	1900-1902, 1908-1910, 1912-1914
Thomas H. Wilson	1902-1904
A. F. Andrews	1902-1904
B. H. McKee	1902-1904
John F. McAdams	1904-1908
Sterling Browning	1904-1908
Joseph W. Pickett	1904-1908
Charles E. Wilson	1908-1912
J. D. Webb	1908-1914, 1922-1926
Thomas A. Atwater	1910-1912
John P. Hughes	1912-1916
W. T. Reynolds	1913-1914

H. J. Walker	1913-1916
A. G. Sykes	1914-1920
P. C. Lloyd	1914-1916
W. D. Neville	1914-1916
Ed. N. Cates	1916-1920
J. P. Dark	1916-1920
John W. Hill	1920-1922
J. D. Woods	1920-1922
R. H. Ward	1920-1926
A. E. Wilson	1922-1924
John E. Hawkins	1924-1926
John A. McCauley	1926-1928
George A. Johnson	1926-1929
John H. Hanner	1926-1928, 1929-1938
W. H. Ray	1928-1930
Jeter C. Lloyd	1928-1932
W. P. Berry	1930-1936
R. A. Eubanks	1932-1934
Carl T. Durham	1934-1938
S. A. Nathan	1936-1938
J. Ed. Laws	1938-1942
Ben F. Wilson	1938-1950
Collier Cobb Jr.	1938-1952
Hubert G. Laws	1942-1951
Sim L. Efland	1950-
Robert O. Forrest	1951-
R. J. M. Hobbs	1952-

REPRESENTATIVES IN CONGRESS OF THE UNITED STATES

	House of Representatives	Senate
Third Congress (Dec. 2, 1793-March 3, 1795)	Alexander Mebane	
Fourth Congress (Dec. 7, 1795-March 3, 1797)	Absalom Tatom (resigned) William Strudwick (succeeded Absalom Tatom, Dec. 13, 1796)	
Fifth-Fourteenth Congress (March 4, 1797-April 9, 1816)	Richard Stanford	
Fifteenth Congress (Dec. 1, 1817-March 3, 1819)	James S. Smith	
Sixteenth Congress (Dec. 6, 1819-March 3, 1821)	James S. Smith	
Eighteenth Congress (Dec. 1, 1823-March 3, 1825)	Willie P. Mangum	
Nineteenth Congress (Dec. 5, 1825-March 3, 1827)	Willie P. Mangum (resigned)	
Twenty-Second Congress (Dec. 5, 1831-March 2, 1833)		Willie P. Mangum
Twenty-Third Congress (Dec. 2, 1833-March 3, 1835)		Willie P. Mangum
Twenty-Fourth Congress (Dec. 7, 1835-March 3, 1837)	William Montgomery	Willie P. Mangum (resigned)
Twenty-Fifth Congress (Sept. 4, 1837-March 3, 1839)	William Montgomery	
Twenty-Sixth Congress (Dec. 2, 1839-March 3, 1841)	William Montgomery	William A. Graham Willie P. Mangum
Twenty-Seventh Congress (May 31, 1841-March 3, 1843)		William A. Graham Willie P. Mangum
Twenty-Eighth Congress (Dec. 4, 1843-March 3, 1845)		Willie P. Mangum
Twenty-Ninth Congress (Dec. 1, 1845-March 3, 1847)		Willie P. Mangum
Thirtieth Congress (Dec. 6, 1847-March 3, 1849)		Willie P. Mangum
Thirty-First Congress (Dec. 3, 1849-March 3, 1851)		Willie P. Mangum
Thirty-Second Congress (Dec. 1, 1851-March 3, 1853)		Willie P. Mangum
Seventy Sixth—Eighty-Third Congress (Jan. 3, 1939 to date)	Carl T. Durham	

ORANGE COUNTY—1752-1952

Members of Congress of the United States Who Were Natives of Orange County

Benton, Thomas Hart .... Mo. House, 1853-1855; Senate, 1821-1851
Harris, George E. .... Miss. House of Rep. 1869-1873
Reade, Edwin G. (Living in Person county when
  elected) .... H.R. 1855-1857
Strowd, William F. (Living in Chatham when elected to
  Congress .... H.R. 1895-99

Members of the Confederate States Congress
(Second Congress (May 2, 1864-March 18, 1865)

Rep.	Senate
Josiah Turner, Jr.	William A. Graham

ORANGE COUNTY VOTE IN ELECTIONS FOR GOVERNOR

W—Whig
D—Democrat
R—Republican
A—American

C—Conservative
P—Populist
Prog.—Progressive

Year	Candidate	Votes	Candidate	Votes
1836	Edward B. Dudley (W)	1,237	Richard D. Spaight (D)	1,132
1838	Edward B. Dudley (W)	1,480	John Branch (D)	1,308
1840	John M. Morehead (W)	1,662	R. M. Saunders (D)	1,549
1842	John M. Morehead (W)	1,576	Louis D. Henry (D)	1,472
1844	William A. Graham (W)	1,756	Michael Hoke (D)	1,555
1846	William A. Graham (W)	1,711	James B. Shepard (D)	1,440
1848	David S. Reid (D)	1,726	Charles Manly (W)	1,714
1850	David S. Reid (D)	1,855	Charles Manly (W)	1,634
1852	David S. Reid (D)	1,796	John Kerr (W)	1,528
1854	Alfred Dockery (W)	1,080	Thomas Bragg (D)	963
1856	Thomas Bragg (D)	1,119	John A. Gilmer (A)	1,045
1858	D. K. McRae (W)	1,037	John W. Ellis (D)	1,012
1860	John Pool (W)	1,238	John W. Ellis (D)	1,109
1862	Zebulon B. Vance	1,451	W. J. Johnston	372
1864	Zebulon B. Vance	1,321	W. W. Holden	227
1865	Jonathan Worth (C)	988	W. W. Holden	264
1866	Jonathan Worth (C)	916	Alfred Dockery (R)	37
1868	Thomas S. Ashe (C)	1,834	W. W. Holden (R)	1,310
1872	A. S. Merrimon (D)	1,945	Tod R. Caldwell (R)	1,321
1876	Zebulon B. Vance (D)	2,410	Thomas Settle (R)	1,675
1880	Thomas J. Jarvis (D)	2,225	R. P. Buxton (R)	1,914
1884	Alfred M. Scales (D)	1,670	Tyre York (R)	1,071
1888	Daniel G. Fowle (D)	1,610	O. H. Dockery (R)	1,288
1892	Elias Carr (D)	1,117	D. M. Furches (R)	875
			W. P. Exum (P)	804
1896	Cyrus B. Watson (D)	1,245	Daniel L. Russell (R)	1,238
			W. A. Guthrie (P)	498
1900	Charles B. Aycock (D)	1,471	Spencer B. Adams (R)	1,469
1904	Robert B. Glenn (D)	952	C. J. Harris (R)	556
1908	William W. Kitchin (D)	1,077	J. E. Cox (R)	1,014
1912	Locke Craige (D)	1,096	Thomas Settle (R)	516
			Iredell Meares (Prog.)	468
1916	Thomas W. Bickett (D)	1,213	Frank A. Linney (R)	1,159
1920	Cameron Morrison (D)	2,081	John J. Parker (R)	1,786
1924	Angus W. McLean (D)	2,015	I. M. Meekins (R)	1,193
1928	O. Max Gardner (D)	2,432	H. F. Seawell (R)	2,045
1932	J. C. B. Ehringhaus (D)	2,999	Clifford Frazier (R)	1,093
1936	Clyde R. Hoey (D)	3,095	Gilliam Grissom (R)	2,086

ORANGE COUNTY—1752-1952

1940—J. Melville Broughton (D)	3,788	Robert H. McNeill (R) 865
1944—R. Gregg Cherry (D)	3,419	Frank C. Patton (R) 1,161
1948—W. Kerr Scott (D)	4,638	George M. Pritchard (R) 959
		Mary Price (Prog.) 114
1952—William B. Umstead (D)	6,369	H. F. Seawell, Jr. (R) 1,975

THE TOWN OF CHAPEL HILL

Chapel Hill was incorporated by act of the General Assembly, January 29, 1851. Manuel Fetter, Jesse Hargrave, Patterson H. McDade, Elisha Mitchell, and Jones Watson were named in the act as "The Commissioners of Chapel Hill." The act provided that:

> The Commissioners shall choose a resident of the Village (not of their own body) a Magistrate of Police to preside at meetings and give the casting vote in case of a tie; a Town Treasurer, constable and Clerk. They shall ascertain and settle the boundaries of Chapel Hill and cause a plot thereof to be recorded in the journal of their proceedings.

The first record extant is of a meeting July 17, 1869, of the Board of Commissioners composed of H. C. Thompson, James F. Craige, and Greene Brewer. James B. Mason served as clerk. W. S. Guthrie, "Censor," reported a "white population 483 and the blacks 454, making all told 937." A month later, August 20, 1869, the Commissioners were Solomon Pool, Thomas Kirby, and Greene Brewer. H. B. Guthrie was Magistrate of Police. An item in the minutes of March 30, 1870, indicates that Thomas Kirby had been succeeded by J. F. Craige, and J. J. Rigsbee is listed as Treasurer. This interesting item appears in the minutes:

> It having come to the knowledge of the Board that certain citizens of the village, viz: J. R. Hutchins, Jno. H. Watson, J. W. Newton, J. F. Freeland and D. McCauley were claiming to be the municipal officers of the village, that they had obtained possession of some of the books and papers and had appointed Mr. A. Mickle as Magistrate of Police; on motion Mr. Pool was appointed to see the aforesaid gentlemen and inform them that they were acting without authority of law; to advise them to at once return such books and papers of the Board as they were holding, and to warn them that their course was subjecting them to the liability of a suit under the laws of the State . . .

The charter of Chapel Hill, as amended in 1879, provided for a Mayor, "clothed with all the powers of the peace in the County of Orange."

Magistrates of Police, 1869-1879

1869-1872	H. B. Guthrie
1872	John H. Watson
1873	J. W. Carr
1874-1875	Andrew Mickle
1876-1878	John H. Watson

Mayors of Chapel Hill since 1879

1879-1881	Merritt Cheek
1882	Jones Watson
1883	John H. Watson
1884	A. J. McDade
1885-1886	J. H. Watson

1887	W. N. Pritchard
1888-1890	A. J. McDade
1891-1894	John H. Watson
1895-1900	A. S. Barbee
1901-1902	J. C. McRae, Jr.
1903-1906	W. S. Roberson
1907-1910	A. S. Barbee
1911-1912	W. S. Roberson
1913	L. P. McLendon
1914-1926	W. S. Roberson
1927-1932	Zeb P. Council
1933-1942	John M. Foushee
1943-1948	R. W. Maddry
1949-1953	E. S. Lanier

Town Managers

1922-1928	E. M. Knox
1928-1932	J. M. Foushee
1932-1944	J. L. Caldwell
1944-1947	T. E. Hinson
1947-1949	G. W. Ray
1949-	Thos. D. Rose

CHAPEL HILL POSTMASTERS, 1795-1953

The exact date of the establishment of the Chapel Hill post office is not recorded. However, Samuel Hopkins, the first postmaster appointed to serve at the office, rendered his first account as of July 1, 1795. Mr. Hopkins served until his successor, John Pucket, was appointed. The date of Mr. Pucket's appointment is not known, but he rendered his first account as of January 1, 1799. Samuel Hopkins succeeded John Pucket as postmaster. The date of his appointment is not given in the records, but he rendered his first account as of July 1, 1802. Mr. Hopkins served until his successor, John Craig, was appointed. Mr. Craig rendered his first account as of April 1, 1805, and he served until Jones Watson was appointed. Mr. Watson rendered his first account as of December 20, 1809. The other postmasters for this office and the dates of their appointments are as follows:

Postmaster	*Date Appointed*
Edward Robson	March 14, 1811
William Barbee	November 8, 1816
Robert M. Galloway	August 31, 1820
Henry Thompson, Jr.	March 22, 1821
Charles Chalmers	March 15, 1827
Isaac C. Partridge	August 1, 1833
John W. McGee	May 31, 1836
James B. McDade	March 12, 1838
John White	July 14, 1865
Hugh B. Guthrie	August 20, 1874
Thomas M. Kirkland	July 7, 1876
Hugh B. Guthrie	July 18, 1876
Andrew Mickle	May 19, 1877
Thomas M. Kirkland	January 31, 1881
W. P. Mallett	November 3, 1885
Thomas M. Kirkland	June 15, 1889
William N. Pritchard	March 3, 1896
Herbert Lloyd	March 31, 1900
William A. Lloyd	August 2, 1904
William E. Lindsay	February 12, 1908
Robert S. McRae	June 18, 1913
Robert L. Strowd (acting)	July 30, 1921
Robert L. Strowd	July 21, 1922
Robert D. Herndon	March 2, 1923
Robert A. Eubanks (acting)	April 5, 1933
Robert A. Eubanks	January 16, 1935
Willie S. Hogan	August 9, 1939

ORANGE COUNTY—1752-1952

HILLSBOROUGH or HILLSBORO

The record of mayors for the Town of Hillsboro prior to 1845 is not available. However, the town was governed by trustees, directors or commissioners. This list of commissioners, etc., acting for the town executed deeds which are of record in the Office of the Register of Deeds of Orange County starting with the date of August 29, 1768 and continuing through November 3, 1838. The names of the commissioners who signed deeds in the chronological order of the deeds with the date the name first appeared are as follows:

James Watson	August 29, 1768
William Nunn	August 29, 1768
Edmund Fanning	August 29, 1768
Francis Nash	August 29, 1768
William Johnston	August 31, 1769
Ralph McNair	March 16, 1772
William Hooper	February 1, 1784
James Hogg	February 1, 1784
John Estis	February 1, 1784
William Courtney	February 1, 1784
John Nichols	February 1, 1784
James Williams	February 1, 1784
John Taylor	February 1, 1784
Josiah Watts	August 15, 1786
William Watters	August 15, 1786
John Allison	August 15, 1786
William Lytle	March 6, 1787
Henry Thompson	March 6, 1787
Francis Child	July 23, 1790
Sterling Harris	July 23, 1790
David Ray	July 23, 1790
William Nash	July 23, 1790
William F. Strudwick	February 2, 1804
Abner Benton Bruce	February 2, 1804
John Taylor, Jr.	February 2, 1804
James Child	February 2, 1804
Catlet Campbell	February 2, 1804
Richard Thompson	February 2, 1804
Thos. N. L. Hargis, M. of P.	October 15, 1821
John Young	October 15, 1821
William Huntington	October 15, 1821
Jonathan P. Sneed	October 15, 1821
William Whitted, Jr.	October 15, 1821
John Scott	October 15, 1821
John U. Kirkland	August, 1831
William E. Anderson	August, 1831

Hugh Waddell .... August, 1831
Samuel Scott .... August, 1831
Ashley Wood .... August, 1831
William Nelson .... August, 1831
Richard Nichols 1835
Stephen Moore 1835
James M. Palmer 1835
Thomas Faucett 1835
Thomas D. Crain .... November 3, 1838
Osborn F. Long .... November 3, 1838
William H. Brown .... November 3, 1838
Isaiah Spencer .... November 3, 1838
James C. Holland .... November 3, 1838
Lemuel Lynch .... November 3, 1838

Magistrates of Police of Hillsboro

Thomas Clancey .... February 1843 to February 3, 1844
Richard Nichols .... February 3, 1844 to February 1, 1845

Mayors of Hillsboro

Lemuel Lynch .... February 1, 1845 to February 1849
Osmond Long .... February 1849 to February 1852
Thomas H. Turner .... February 1852 to February 1853
John J. Freeland .... February 1853 to February 1854
Thomas H. Turner .... February 1854 Resigned May, 1854
A. C. Murdock .... May 1854 to May 1855
Lemuel Lynch .... May 1855 to May 1856
James M. Palmer .... May 1856 to June 2, 1857
Dr. Roscoe Hooker .... June 2, 1857 to February 5, 1859
Calvin E. Parish .... February 5, 1859 to February 4, 1860
A. C. Murdock .... February 4, 1860 to February 7, 1863
C. M. Latimer .... February 7, 1863 to February 5, 1864
A. C. Murdock .... February 5, 1864 to February 3, 1866
D. D. Phillips .... February 3, 1866 to February 1866
E. C. Parrish .... 1866 to February 1869
A. C. Murdock .... February 1869 to February 1870
William F. Strayhorn .... February 1870 to May 1871
James B. McDade .... May 1871 to July 1873
John O. Welbon .... July 1873 to 1873
E. H. Pogue .... 1873 to 1874
A. C. Murdock .... 1874 to 1875
John M. Blackwood .... 1875 to June, 1876
Thomas Webb .... June 1876 to December 28, 1876
A. W. Graham .... December 28, 1876 to 1877
T. J. Wilson .... 1877 to 1877
David Anderson .... 1877 to 1877

Orange County—1752-1952

C. S. Cooley	1877 to 1878
Henry K. Nash	1878 to May 1883
George C. Corbin	May 1883 to May 1885
Joseph A. Harris	May 1885 to May 1892
W. H. Newman	May 1892 to October 1892
James Parks	October 1892 to October 31, 1892
William Strain	October 31, 1892 to May 1893
Joseph A. Harris	May 1893 to May 1894
N. W. Brown	May 1894 to May 1895
Joseph A. Harris	May 1895 to May 1898
J. T. Shaw	May 1898 to May 1899
Joseph A. Harris	May 1899 to May 1901
James Norwood	May 1901 to May 1903
Joseph A. Harris	May 1903 to May 1907
Frank Nash	May 1907 to May 1911
Charles A. Whitaker	May 1911 to October 5, 1911
John Christmas	October 5, 1911 to May 6, 1915
John T. Johnston	May 6, 1915 to May 9, 1917
Jeff Turner	May 9, 1917 to May 1921
T. M. Arrasmith	May 1921 to May 1933
Ben G. Johnston	May 1933 to date

HILLSBORO POSTMASTERS, 1792-1953

Records of the Post Office Department now in the custody of the National Archives for the period 1789-1930 do not contain any information about the post office at Hillsboro (formerly known as Orange, Corbinton, or Childsburg) prior to 1792. Names of postmasters and dates of their appointment were:

Postmaster	Date of Appointment
David Ray	December 18, 1792 (about)
William Hooper	April 12, 1793 (about)
James Christmass	November 20, 1793 (about)
Henry Thompson	January 1, 1794
John Allison	April 1, 1794
John McKenell	July 1, 1799
Barnabus O'Farrell	January 1, 1800
James Hogg, Jr.	April 1, 1804
James Webb	January 1, 1805
William Lockhart	July 1, 1807
William Cain, Jr.	April 1, 1811
Thomas Chaney	September 24, 1811
Richard L. Cook	January 6, 1817
William Cain, Jr.	January 2, 1832
Thomas Clancey	July 10, 1835
James M. Palmer	May 24, 1845
Dennis Heartt	August 22, 1849
James M. Palmer	August 27, 1853
Calvin E. Parish	September 16, 1857
Dennis Heartt	June 24, 1865
Henrietta Heartt	May 1, 1870
Archibald C. Hunter	May 31, 1870
Harriet H. Strayhorn	May 26, 1873
William F. Strayhorn	September 27, 1881
Mary E. Berry	May 22, 1882
Thomas D. Tinnin	August 11, 1885
Harry L. Parish	June 27, 1886
Nathan W. Brown	April 24, 1889
Eugene L. Hassell	August 31, 1893
J. Clyde Cheek	June 28, 1897
Charles G. Rosemond	May 1, 1903
George C. Lynch	May 4, 1914
Thomas E. Sparrow	December 4, 1922
Thomas R. Sparrow	October 4, 1929
Shepperd Strudwick	June 18, 1934
Mrs. Cora L. Lynch (Acting)	February 28, 1946
Thomas E. Bivens	June 18, 1948

MAYORS OF CARRBORO

[Carrboro was settled about 1898 and was first incorporated as Venable, in 1911 named in honor of F. P. Venable, president of the University of North Carolina. The name was changed to Carrboro in 1913 and named for Julian S. Carr. Mayors are chosen for a two-year term and take office in May.]

1917	W. H. Parker
1917-1919	Dr. B. B. Lloyd
1919-1923	H. B. Durham
1925-1927	T. N. Mann
1927-1933	H. B. Durham
1933-1935	C. C. Head
1935-1937	Roy Riggsbee
1937-1941	W. H. Parker
1941-1943	R. B. Studebaker
1943-1949	I. A. West
1949-1951	I. F. Hardee
1951 to date	J. Sullivan Gibson

PRESIDENTS OF THE UNIVERSITY OF NORTH CAROLINA AT CHAPEL HILL

[From 1795 to 1804, the chief administrative officer of the University was the "presiding professor." David Ker (Kerr) was chosen for this position in 1795.]

1804-1812	Joseph Caldwell
1813-1816	Robert Hett Chapman
1817-1835	Joseph Caldwell
1835-1868	David L. Swain
1869-1871	Solomon S. Pool
1871-1875	University was closed
1875-1876	Charles Phillips, Chairman of the Faculty
1876-1891	Kemp Plummer Battle
1891-1896	George Tayloe Winston
1896-1900	Edwin Anderson Alderman
1900-1914	Francis Preston Venable
1914-1918	Edward Kidder Graham
1919-1930	Harry Woodburn Chase
1930-1949	Frank Porter Graham

(In 1932 Graham became President of the Consolidated University of North Carolina and Robert Burton House was appointed Dean of Administration at the Chapel Hill unit. In 1945, House's title was changed to Chancellor.)

1950-	Gordon Gray

Index

Names appearing in the appendices only are not listed in the index.

Abercrombie, Charles, 173, 175
Abernethy, E. A., 320
Academies, 132-137, 319
Adams, William M., 102
Adshusheer Indians, 12
African Methodist Episcopal Churches, 304-305
African Methodist Episcopal Zion Church, 307
Agricultural Conservation Program, 250, 253
Agricultural Extension Work, 213-214, 240, 244, 246, 262
Agricultural statistics, 122, 228, 229, 231-235, 237-239, 248-251, 254
Aid to Dependent Children, 213
Aiken, Sandy, 307
Air R. O. T. C., 153
Alamance, Battle of, 38-39
Alamance Church, 295
Alamance County, 15-19, 21, 45, 83, 115. 118, 120, 181, 226, 292, 344
Alamance Creek, 57, 58, 266-267
Alamance River, 11, 15
Albemarle section, 157, 291
Albright, Alexander, 86
Albright, Jacob, 15, 45
Alderman, Edwin A., 147, 152, 372
Alexander, Eben, 143
Alexander, Elam, 132
Alexander, Joseph, 69
Allen, Captain, 58
Allen, George, 96
Allison, James, 167
Allison, John, 113, 357, 367, 370
Allison, Joseph, 85, 86, 88, 350-351, 357
Allison, Julius F., 110
Allston, James, 110, 357
Alpha Woolen Mills, 270
Alves, Walter, 78, 96, 132, 349
Anderson, R. M., 237
Anderson, W., 136, 293, 367
Anderson's Female Boarding School, 136-137
Andrews and Lloyd Lumber Co., 284
Andrews, James, 125
Andrews, Mark, 301
Andrews, S. W., 321, 356-357
Andrews, T. Wingate, 140-141, 322
Andrews, W. V., 200
Angier, A. M., 190
Anglican clergy, 289
Ansley, William, 178
Anson County, 17, 29, 35-36
Antioch Baptist Church, 301, 315-316, 262

Apparel, Inc., 281
Apprenticeship system, 130-131
Archaeological Society of North Carolina, 12
Argo, Thomas M., 113, 352
Armstrong, William, 174
Arrowood, M. C., 295
Arthur, David E., 283
Asbury, Francis, 297
Ashe, Samuel, 48, 73
Ashe, Thomas S., 113
Assembly, General, 20, 32-33, 37, 150, 175-177, 183-184, 186, 198, 201, 204, 209-210
Astronomy, 153
Atkinson, John, 43, 45, 345
Atkinson, W. M., 137
Atwater, Matthew, 120, 352, 358
Avery, Waightstill, 48, 69
Aycock, Charles B., 128, 140
Aycock School, 141, 262

Back Creek, 15
Bacon, J. G., 132
Badger, George E., 107, 125, 322
Bain, James M., 188
Bain, Nathaniel, 187, 356, 358
Baker-Mebane Hosiery Mill, 281
Baker, Robert, 174
Bald mountain, 2
Bank of Cape Fear, 273-274
Bank of Chapel Hill, 237, 240, 274, 284
Bank of Orange, 274
Banking, 273-275
Bankston, Lawrence, 166, 289
Baptists, 25, 123, 299, 299-301, 315-317
Baptist Church of Chapel Hill, 301, 317
Baptist convention, 300
Barbee, Christopher, 75, 148
Barham, Dave, 78
Barnes, Edwin P., 214
Baron, Thomas, 133
Barringer, Daniel A., 85
Bass, James, 101
Bass, Walter N., 298
Bassett, Professor John S., 37
Bath, 28
Battle, Kemp P., 75, 80, 81, 134, 152, 322, 372
Battle, William H., 99, 322
Beard, L. E., 275
Beasley, C. T., 274
Beef Cattle, 242-243
Bell, John, 107
Bellevue Manufacturing Co., 275

374 INDEX

Bennehan, Richard, 16, 96, 173-174, 323
Bennett House, 112
Benton, Jesse, 323, 348, 357
Benton, Samuel, 67, 347, 349, 354, 357
Benton, Thomas Hart, 278, 323, 361
Berkeley, Sir William, 288
Berry, Harriet M., 323
Berry, John, Captain, 21, 23, 88, 107-109, 324, 351, 352, 354
Berry, Joseph, 304
Berry's Mills, 270
Berryhill, W. Reece, 163-164
Berry's Grove Baptist Church, 301, 315-316
Betheden Baptist Church, 301
Bethel Baptist Church, 301
Bethlehem Presbyterian Church, 295, 315-316
Bethlehem School, 136
Bethsada Baptist Church, 307, 315-316
Bingham, Robert, 110, 324
Bingham School, 133, 160
Bingham Township, 194, 200-201, 204, 207
Bingham, William, 132-133, 324
Bingham, William J., 89, 134, 324
Bird, Harry, 300
Bivens Liner Co., 277
Blackwood mountain, 2
Blackwood, Polly, 187
Blackwood, William, 15
Bladen County, 14, 17, 166, 290
Blake, John C., 310
Blalock, F. Y., 187
Bloodworth, Timothy, 65
Blount, Thomas, 77, 79, 81
Blount, William, 72
Board of Censors, 160
Board of County Commissioners, 188, 192, 195, 197-203, 218, 221-222
Board of Education, 140-141, 200
Board of trustees of UNC., 151
Board of War, North Carolina, 50, 51, 52
Bolling, William, 289
Bond issues, 142, 205, 208, 223-227
Book of Common Prayer, 292
Booker, E. B.,
Booker, John M., 154
Boon, John, 85, 350-351
Booth, H. D., 302
Bowlin's (Bolins) Creek, 76, 148
Bowman, Willie, 309
Boyd, C. T., 309
Boyd, W. K., 124
Bracken, Julius, 88, 351
Brainerd, Lavinia, 136
Brauer, John C., 164
Brecht, E. A., 164
Brevard, Ephraim, 69
 Brewer, Ezekiel, 101

Bridgers, Joe, 301
Bridgers, J. R., 304
Bright, Alfred, 306
British Baptists, 299
Brooks, J. B., 306
Brooks, Judge, 120
Brown, Henry N., 119
Brown, John H., 237
Brown, William H., 181, 185, 368
Bryan, Andrew, 305
Buchanan, Hastie and Company, 24
Buckhorn community, 5
Buckhorn Creek, 15
Buffalo Creek, 15
Buffalo Presbyterian Church, 15, 295
Bulla, Ben, 267-269
Bureau of Vital Statistics, 218
Burke, Andrew, 183
Burke, Thomas, 42, 45, 46, 47, 50, 58, 59, 60, 61, 62, 68, 310, 324-325, 345, 348
Burlington *Daily Times-News*, 266
Burrington, George, Governor, 15, 324-325
Burt, M. C., 214
Burwell's Female School, 137
Business Administration School, 153
Bute county, 32
Butler, James, 33, 35
Butler, John, 43, 44, 45, 46, 49, 56, 58, 59, 60, 62, 64, 68, 173, 175, 178, 325, 345-346, 348, 355
Butler, William, 29
Byars, Miss Woodward, 215

Cabarrus, Stephen, 72
Cadmus, Robert R., 164
Cain (Cane) Creek, 60
Cain, John W., 184
Cain, William, 16, 78, 84, 96, 132, 136-137, 173, 176
Caldwell Community, 260
Caldwell, David, 69, 88, 146, 295
Caldwell, James, 104
Caldwell, Joseph, 65, 98, 150, 318-319, 325, 372
Caldwell Lodge, 320
Caldwell School, 141
Caldwell, Tod R., 120
Caldwell, W. E., 320
Calvander Grange, 249-250, 262
Camden, S. C., Battle of, 50, 54
Cameron Avenue, 148, 311
Cameron, Bennehan, 325, 353
Cameron, Duncan, 83, 84, 91, 93, 104, 125, 132, 325, 350
Cameron, Paul, 16, 88, 96-97, 107, 325, 351
Cameron, William, 110
Camp New Hope, 259, 261

INDEX 375

Campbell Town, 60
Campbell, Orville, 284
Canada, Charles S., 143
Canada, John W., 143
"Canada School," 143
Cane (Cain) Creek, 6, 15-16, 136, 269, 290-291
Cane Creek Baptist Church, 300-301, 315-316
Cane Creek Monthly Meeting, 290-291
Cannady, A. G., 308
Cape Fear River, 6, 17, 24
Capital Act of 1766, 28
Carmichael, William D., Jr., 154
Carolina Inn, 284
Carolina Quarterly, 129
Carr Community, 260
Carr, G. P., 141
Carr, John W., 181, 188, 196
Carr, Julian S., 274
Carr Methodist Church, 299, 315-316
Carraway, Ruby, 215
Carrboro, 6, 148, 207, 246, 248, 260, 282-284, 298, 302, 309, 317, 321
Carrboro Baptist Church, 302, 317
Carrboro Church of God, 309, 317
Carrboro Methodist Church, 298, 317
Carrboro school, 141
Carrboro Woolen Mills, 283
Carrington, James, 183
Carrington, John, 183
Carroll, Charles, 310
Carroll, Daniel, 310
Caswell County, 17, 20, 45-46, 118, 120, 137, 146, 161, 294, 300
Caswell, Richard, 15, 43, 46, 63, 167, 172-173, 326
Catawba Indians, 10
Cates, Neverson P., 196
Cates, Thomas, 300-301
Catholic Church of Chapel Hill, 310, 317
Catholics, 309-310
Cedar Grove, 237, 260, 294
Cedar Grove Methodist Church, 297, 315-316
Cedar Grove Ruritan Club, 262
Cedar Grove School, 141
Cedar Grove Township, 194, 197, 200-201, 207
Certification of teachers, 143
Chamblee, Minerva, 187
Chapel Hill, N. C., 6-7, 10, 76, 77, 79, 80, 81, 98, 99, 103, 104, 105, 111, 117, 128, 137, 140, 143, 145-146, 148-151, 161-165, 190, 237, 242, 262, 272-274, 284-285, 290, 292-293, 301, 317-318, 320-321
Chapel Hill Academy, 136
Chapel Hill and Durhamsville Plankroad Company, 184

Chapel Hill and Morrisville Plankroad Co., 184
Chapel Hill and Raleigh Plankroad Co., 184
Chapel Hill Baptist Church, 143
Chapel Hill Blue Cross Plan, 165
Chapel Hill Masonic Temple, 301
Chapel Hill Monthly Meeting of Friends, 292, 317
Chapel Hill News, 128
Chapel Hill recorder's court, 219
Chapel Hill Rotary Club, 237, 243
Chapel Hill schools, 143-145
Chapel Hill township, 194, 200-201, 204-207, 219
Chapel Hill Weekly, 128, 282, 285
Chapel Hill Weekly Ledger, 127-128
Chapel of the Cross, 293, 317
Chapman, Robert Hett, 372
Charleston, S. C., 49, 61, 62
Charlotte, 52, 74
Chase, Harry W., 152, 372
Chatham County, 15-20, 43, 47, 163, 291-292, 300, 302-303
Chatham District, 175
Chavis, A. A., 306
Chavis, E. U., 307
Cheek, L. C., 301
Cheek, Merritt, 196
Cheek's township, 205, 207
Cheshier, Isaac, 308
Chestnut Ridge Methodist Church, 298, 315-316
Child, Col. Samuel, 295
Child, Thomas, 20, 25, 326
Childsburg, 20, 25
Choplin, T. W., 309
Chowan County, 26
Chrisman, W. G., 243
Christmas, James, 67
Christmas, John, 23
Churches, 24, 123, 167, 288-317
Churches of God, 309
Church of England, 288-290, 292-293, 296
Church of God of Carrboro, 309, 317
Church of God of West Hillsboro, 309, 317
Church of the Holy Family, 293, 317
Churton, William, 19, 23, 169, 217, 326-327
Christian Church, 123, 302
City and Regional Planning, 153
Cincinnati, Society of, 64
Cipritz Bridge (Prince's Bridge), 74, 75
Civil War, 107-123, 148, 178, 188, 190, 293, 304
Clancey, George, 183
Clancy, Thomas, 84, 101
Clapp, Ludwig, 15
Clapp's Mill, 58

Clark, Calvin, 197
Clark, Henry T., 164
Clark, James P., 137, 188
Clarke, A. W., 206
Clay, Henry, 85, 127
Claytor, R. H., 141, 210
Clegg, James, 302
Clements, W. C., 303
Clemmons, Susan, 187
Clerk of court, 180, 220
Clerk of the Pleas, 168
Climate of Orange County, 6-7
Clinton, Sir Henry, 49
Clover Garden Methodist Church, 298, 315-316
Cobb, Collier, Sr., 10
Cole, E. D., 309
Cole, E. H., 309
Cole, W. C., 237
Collins, Paul C., 274
Colonial Press, 284
Colonization Society, 103, 104
Colored Methodist Episcopal Churches, 307
Columbia Street, 148
Columbian Repository, 128
Commerce School, 153
Committee on University Government, 154
Committees of Safety, 41-42, 43
Commons, House of, 20
Commons, town—Hillsboro, 23
Communication Center, 153
Community Activities, 260-262
Compton, James S., 251, 254
Cone House, 143-144
Cone Mills, 276
Confederate Tax Act, 189
Congregational Christian Churches, 302-303
Conservative party, 115
Consolidated schools, 141-142
Consolidation of the UNC., 152
Constitution of 1776, 172
Constitution of 1868, 151, 191-192, 194-195
Constitutional changes of 1835, 181
Constitutional Conventions, 65, 67, 69, 70, 76, 86
Constitutional Union Guards, 116
Continental Army, 310
Conway, W. I., 302
Cooper, E. C., 312
Cooper, Henry, 174
Corbett, James, 306
Corbin, Francis, 19, 25, 327
Corbin Town, 19-20, 25
Cordal, Green, 304
Cornwallis, Lord Charles, 49, 52, 53, 54, 56, 57, 58, 68
Cotton Chapel, 307

Couch mountain, 2
Council of Safety, Provincial, 42-43
Council, Zeb, 321
County Agents, 213-214
County Board of Education, 140
County Board of Public Welfare, 211
County court, 20-23, 111
County Finance Act, 223
County Fiscal Control Act, 221-222
County indebtedness, 222-227
County Line Baptist Church, 300
County Line Creek, 14, 15
County superintendent of schools, 202
County treasurer, 176
Courts, 166, 172, 174-175, 178-179, 180-181, 183, 191, 218-219
Court house, 15, 19-23, 169, 185, 192, 197
Court of Pleas and Quarter Sessions, 192, 218
Court of Wardens, 186-188
Courtney, William, 16, 20, 46, 48, 173, 175
Covenant Presbyterian Church of Chapel Hill, 296, 317
Cowan's Ford, 53
Cowpens, Battle of, 52, 53
Cox, William, 30
Crabtree, Beth, 101
Crabtree, Dolphus, 301
Crabtree, O. L., 211
Craftique, Inc., 281
Craig, James, 52, 60, 61, 101, 136
Craig, John, 84, 85, 295
Craig, William, 15, 148
Craige, Burton, 108
Craven County, 37
Craven, Peter, 35
Crawford mountain, 2
Crawford, William, 85
Crews, Ruby, 215
Crops, 230, 233-239, 240-241, 251
Cross Creek [Fayetteville], 44
Cross Roads Baptist Church, 301, 315-316
Crudup, Josiah, 85
Cumberland County, 26
Curb Market (Chapel Hill), 258
Currie, J. L., 141, 200
Currituck county, 26
Currituck court house, 297
Curtis, Dr., 293
Curtis, Moses Ashley, 293, 327

Dairy Industry, 241-242
Damascus Christian church, 303
Damascus Congregational Christian Church, 303, 315-316
Daniel, George, 78, 148
Daniel, Robert T., 301
Dan River, 14, 53, 57

INDEX

Davidson, Brig. Gen. William Lee, 53
Davie, William R., 61, 65, 70, 71, 72, 73, 74, 76, 77, 78, 79, 80, 148, 150
Davis, C. C., 222
Davis, C. W., 145
Davis, George, 108
Davis, James, 124
Davis, Orrondates, 50
Davis, Thomas, 63
Day, L. E., 306
Decker, S. T., 304
Deems, Charles F., 298
Deep River, 14, 56, 57, 62, 75, 300
Deep River Baptist Church, 300
Deniell, John O., 56
Devinney, Samuel, 34, 35
Dickerson's A.M.E. Church, 292, 304, 317
Dickey, James, 167-168
Dickson, Alex, 187
Dickson and Brown Co., 270
Dickson, Stephen, 110
Diocese of North Carolina, 292
District of St. Mark's, 178
Dixon, Joseph, 72
Dixon, Josiah, 19, 23, 345, 355
Dixon, Robert, 72
Dobbs, Arthur, 28, 289
Dockery, Alfred, 109
Donaldson, Thomas, 355
Drainage of Orange county, 6
Duke, James Buchanan, 327
Duke University, 11
Duke, Washington, 120-121, 271, 327-328
Durham, 12, 18
Durham Bank and Trust Co., 240, 274
Durham, Bartlett, 88
Durham County, 17, 19, 45, 83, 199, 203, 226, 303, 344
Durham Fat Stock Show, 243-244, 259
Durham Hosiery Mills, 283
Durham Morning Herald, quoted, 142
Durham township, 19, 194

Eagle Laundry, 269-270
Eagle Hotel, 125
Eagle Lodge, 318-320
Eastern Star, Order of, 320-321
East-West sectionalism, 25-30
Eastwood lake, 6
Eaton, W. R., 301
Ebenezer Baptist Church, 301, 315-316
Eccles, Gilbert, 174
Eddington, Rev. Mr., 301
Edenton, 23
Edgecombe county, 36
Education in Orange County, 130-146, 319
Edwards, Morgan, 38

Efland, 209, 237, 260, 275, 277-278
Efland Baptist Church, 302, 317
Efland (Ephland), David, 15
Efland, John L., 275, 277, 278
Efland Knitting Co., 278
Efland, Mack P., 278
Efland, Madison L., 278
Efland Methodist Church, 298, 317
Efland Presbyterian Church, 295, 317
Efland school, 141
Elks Club, 321
Ellison, James, 289
Elmore, S. E., 302
Empey, James, 174
Employment statistics, 286
Eno Cotton Mill, 275-276
Eno Indians, 11-12
Eno Meeting, 292
Eno Methodist Church, 299, 317
Eno Presbyterian Church, 294, 295, 315-316
Eno River, 6, 11-12, 14, 17, 19, 22, 49, 166-167, 169, 269-270, 295, 310
Eno Town, 11-12
Eno township, 205, 207
Eno-Will, 12
Enrollment of U. N. C., 151-152
Ensign, John E., 295-296
Episcopal Church, Hillsboro, 22
Episcopal Churches, 123
Epperson, Francis, 100
Estes (Estis), John, 183, 357, 367
Eubanks, Clyde, 274
Evans, C. N. B., 127

Faculty Council, 154
Faddis, John, 101
Faddis, Thomas J., 85, 348
Fairfield, 209
Fairfield Presbyterian Church, 295, 315-316
Fairfield School, 137
Fairview Baptist Church of Hillsboro, 302, 317
Fanning, David, 22, 55, 58, 59, 60, 61, 62, 328
Fanning, Edmund, 22, 27-28, 30-32, 34-38, 171, 217, 328, 345, 357, 367
Farm forestry, 248-249
Farm homes, 256-257
Farmers' Cooperative Dairy, 242
Farmers' Home Administration, 255-256
Farm mechanization, 249
Farmers and Merchants Bank, 274
Farmers' Mutual Exchange, 243-248
Faucett, Chesley, 88
Faucett, Thomas, 182
Faust, Christian, 15
Faust, John, 15
Fayetteville, 64, 66, 83, 147

378 INDEX

Fee system, 171-172
Ferguson, C. V., 254
Ferguson, Robert, 183
Fetter, Manuel, 98, 320
Few, William, 328
Fields, Jeremiah, 36
First African Baptist Church of Savannah, 305
First Baptist Church of Chapel Hill, 305, 317
First Baptist Church of Hillsboro, 301, 317
First Pentecostal Holiness Church of West Hillsboro, 308, 317
Fiscal Control, 221-222
Fitch Lumber Co., 284
Fitch, R. B., 284
Fitzsimmons, Thomas, 310
Flat Rock A.M.E. Church, 304, 315-316
Flinn, Andrew, 132
Fogleman, M. D., 298
Forest Resource Appraisal of N. C., 8-9
Forrest, Nathan Bedford, 117
Four-H Clubs, 215, 243, 258-259
Franklin, Benjamin, 148
Franklin County, 118
Franklin Street, 148
Fraternal Orders, 318-321
Frazier, R. C., 308
Freedman's Bureau, 112
Freeland, John F., 109
Freeland, John J., 181
Freeland, William G., 109
Friends (see Quakers)
Friends of Philadelphia, 292
Frost, J. Milton, 298
Fuller, Henry, 306
Future Farmers of America, 259-260
Fyke, Malachie, 35

Gaines, Robert, 301
Gain's Chapel A.M.E. Church, 304, 315-316
Gardner, O. Max, 208
Garvin, O. D., 216
Gasoline taxes, 208
Gaston, William, 90, 104
Gates, Maj. Gen. Horatio, 49, 50, 51, 52, 55
Gattis, Alexander, 297-298
Gattis, Samuel M., 319, 328, 346, 352-353, 357
General College, 153
General Court of N. C., 169
Geology Museum of University, 10
George III, 22, 42-43, 54, 57
Georgia, 290, 296, 311
German immigrants to Orange, 14-15, 25
G. I. Bill, 155
Gilmer, John A., 87, 89
Gilmore, George, 263
Glass, Lettie, 145

Glen Lennox, 143
Glenn's Grove Baptist Church, 306, 315-316
Gobbel, J. T., 274
Good Health Association, 163
Goodlee, Daniel R., 118
Gordon, Charles Pendleton, 89
Gore, J. W., 274
Goshen, N. C., 74
Gosnell, W. P., Jr., 309
Gospel Baptist Tabernacle, 302, 315-316
Governor's Palace, 29
Graduate School, 152
Graham, A. H., 346, 353
Graham, Edward K., 152, 372
Graham, Frank P., 152-154, 321, 372
Graham, James, 88, 110, 351
Graham, John W., 110, 113, 120, 328, 352-354
Graham, Joseph, 55
Graham, Mary Owen, 214
Graham, Robert D., 110
Graham, William A., 85, 87, 88, 91, 92, 93, 107-109, 119-121, 328-329, 346, 348, 351-352, 354, 360-361
Graham, William A., Jr., 110
Grand Army of the Republic, 117
Grand Lodge of N. C., 318-319
Granville County, 14, 17, 20, 25, 32, 34-46, 43, 60, 166, 171, 344
Granville District, 17, 25
Granville, Earl of, 19-20, 167, 217, 288, 294
Graves, Elijah, 135, 295
Graves' Female School, 135
Graves, Louis, 128, 143, 282, 285
Gray, Gordon, 154, 372
Gray, John, 19, 32, 166, 289, 345, 355
Great Wagon Road from Pennsylvania, 14
Greeley, Horace, 120
Green, Sydney, 276
Green, Thomas, 114
Green, William Mercer, 21, 136, 293, 329
Greene, Maj. Gen. Nathanael, 52, 53, 56, 57, 58, 61, 63, 71
Greensboro Female College, 319
Gregory's Boarding School (Mrs.), 135
Grier's Presbyterian Church, 294
Grimes, William, 174
Gross, Solomon, 35
Guess, W. G., 109
Guess, W. W., 109
Guilford County, 15, 17, 115, 292
Guilford Court House, 53, 58
Gun Factory, 47
Guthrie, George, 268
Guthrie, Hugh B., 88, 107, 190, 355, 364, 366
Gwin, Edwin, 45
Gwynn, J. Minor, 145

INDEX 379

Habel, Samuel Tilden, 301
Hackney, C. D., 306
Hackney, L. C., 307
Hailey, James R., 297-298
Halifax, N. C., 20, 45, 49, 50, 52, 58, 65, 68, 172, 318
Halifax County, 25, 32, 35
Hall, Nelson P., 181, 199, 358
Hamilton, D. H., 110, 202, 357-358
Hamilton, John, 72
Hamilton, Matthew, 35
Hamilton, Ninion, 35
Hamilton, Ninion Bell, 35
Hamlin, E. J., 128
Hammond's Creek, 60
Hampton Roads Conference, 108
Hannah, William, 125
Harbinger (The), 128
Hargett, Frederick, 75, 77, 81
Harmony Primitive Baptist Church, 304, 315-316
Harris, C. P., 306
Harris, Edward, 90, 355
Harris, George E., 329, 361
Harris Grove A.M.E. Church, 305, 315-316
Harris, Isaac Foust, 143
Harris, Joseph A., 127
Harris, Sterling, 183, 367
Harris, T. W., 163
Harris, Tyree, 29, 345, 355
Harriss, Junius Thomas, 143
Harrisse, Henri, 329
Hart, Thomas, 23, 32, 41-42, 173, 278, 329, 345, 355
Hartgrove, Fred, 105
Hart's Mill, 55, 278
Hartzo, John Phillip, 34-35
Harvey, John, 42
Harvey's Chapel C.M.E. Church, 307, 315-316
Haw Fields (Hawfields), 11-12, 14, 49, 64, 278-279, 294
Hawfield Academy, 135
Hawkins, John, 173, 174, 355
Hawkins, William, 197
Hawks, F. L., 329
Haw River, 6, 10-12, 14-15, 19, 56-58, 75, 167, 169, 267, 269, 290, 300-301
Haw River Baptist Church, 300
Haw River Mountain Church, 301
Haywood, John, 77, 80
Health Affairs, 153, 155, 157
Hearn, Bunn, 143
Heartt, Dennis, 22, 85, 86, 87, 99, 124-127, 132, 329-330
Heart, Edwin A., 184
Heathcock, Jesse, 101
Henderson, Richard, 36, 133, 330

Hentz, Caroline, 98
Herty, C. H., 274
Hesslein and Co., 275
Hewes, Joseph, 43, 46
Hickory Grove Baptist Church, 306, 315-316
Hico (Hyco) River, 14, 15, 17
High Towers, 294
Highsmith, E. M., 145
Hill Bakery, 285
Hill, John Sprunt, 246
Hill, George Watts, 242
Hill, William H., 75, 80
Hillsboro, 2, 10, 12, 15-16, 18-19, 20-25, 27, 29, 30-31, 34-38, 41, 42, 44, 45, 46, 49, 50, 51, 52, 53, 54, 55, 57, 58, 59, 60, 61, 62, 63, 64, 65, 66, 67, 74, 78, 83, 84, 86, 89, 90, 91, 96, 100, 101, 102, 119, 124-125, 127-128, 132, 134, 136-137, 140, 141, 146, 148, 160-161, 169, 174, 190, 209, 242, 246, 260, 262-264, 274, 291, 295, 297, 317-321
Hillsboro and Chapel Hill Plankroad Co., 184
Hillsboro and Milton Plankroad Co., 184
Hillsboro Confederate Memorial Library, 215
Hillsboro District, 43, 44, 47, 62, 63, 64, 84, 174-175
Hillsboro Exchange Club, 263
Hillsboro Lions Club, 263
Hillsboro Methodist Church, 297, 317
Hillsboro Military Academy, 319
Hillsboro Presbyterian Church, 295, 317
Hillsboro Township, 194, 200-201, 204-205, 207, 223
Hillsborough Academy, 125, 132, 135
Hillsborough, Earl of, 17, 20, 22
Hillsborough Female Seminary, 136
Hillsborough Recorder, 18, 21-22, 85, 86, 98, 101, 102, 103, 124-127, 184-185, 265, 269-271, 274
Hillsboro Savings Institution, 274
Hincher, John, 174
Hines, E. M., 277
Hines Liner Co., 249, 277
Hinton, John, 43
History of the U. N. C., 152
Hocutt, J. C., 141, 302
Hodge, Joseph, 67, 355
Hogan Creek, 14
Hogan, Henry S., 249, 254
Hogan, John, 42, 47, 48, 75, 96, 120, 174, 176
Hogan, M. E., 274
Hogan, Thomas, 184, 358
Hogan, William J., 181, 187
Hogan's Lake, 6
Hogg and Campbell Co., 24
Hogg, James, 42, 46, 72, 75, 147-149, 174, 330, 367

Holcombe, Grace E., 214-215
Holden, Thomas W., 137, 265, 298
Holden, W. W., 108, 112-115, 119-120, 125-127, 330
Holden's English School, 137
Holleman, Richard, 173
Holman, S. W., 200
Holt, Edwin M., 21, 113, 266, 268, 330, 354
Holt, George, 45
Holt, Jeremiah, 97
Holt, John R., 137
Holt, Michael, 15, 44, 86, 88, 330-331, 349-350
Holt, Thomas, 331
Holt, William, 102, 350
Holy Church of North Carolina and Virginia, 308
Holy Trinity Lutheran Church of Chapel Hill, 312, 317
Home Demonstration Work, 214-215
Honeycutt, A. W., 145
Hooker, A., 194
Hooker, Nathan, 136
Hooker, Octavius, 119, 185
Hooper, Emily, 104
Hooper, William, 43, 46, 69, 96, 101, 104, 128, 348, 367
Hord, A. T., 301
Horse Creek, 17
Horton, George Moses, 98
Hospital Saving Association, 165
House, Robert B., 153, 372
House of Ruth, 321
Howard, W. M., Jr., 298
Howell, Jesse, 301
Howell, Rednap, 28, 34, 38
Howell, Vernon, 274
Howerton, Thomas, 184
Hoyle, C. A., 145
Hubbard, Fordyce M., 72
Hudson, Isaac, 184
Hughes, John K., 120, 200, 355
Hughes, Samuel W., 181
Hunter, Isaac, 66, 67
Hunter, James, 15, 34-35, 44
Hunter's Chapel A.M.E. Church, 305, 315-316
Huntington, Roswell, 332
Huntington, William, 132, 332, 367
Husband, Herman, 20, 25, 30, 33-35, 37-38, 291, 332, 345
Huske, John, 59
Hutchins, John R., 196

Impartial Relation, by Herman Husband, 25
Indians, 10-13
Industrial laborers in county, 123
Industrial statistics, 123
Institute for Research in Social Science, 152

Institute of Government, 152-153
Invisible Empire, 116-118
Iredell, James, 48, 65, 70, 71
Island Ford, 183

Jackson, Andrew, 84, 85, 92
Jackson, Isaac, 35
Jackson, Richard L., 303
Jails, 22-23, 219-220
James, Hinton, 82
Jamison, Milton, 203
Jefferson, Thomas, 83
Jews, 311
Johnson, A. E., 306
Johnson, Charles, 72
Johnson, Charles W., 196
Johnson, George B., 110, 133
Johnson, Tom, 278
Johnston County, 17, 32, 36, 55, 166
Johnston, Gabriel Johnston, 14, 28
Johnston, Joseph E., 112
Johnston Riot Act, 37
Johnston, Samuel, 37, 65, 70
Johnston, William, 43, 45, 46, 47, 108, 332, 345, 367
Jones, A., Jr., 301
Jones, Allen, 69, 70
Jones, Atlas, 75
Jones, Cadwallader, 21, 86
Jones, Cadwallader, Jr., 88
Jones, C. D., 215, 351
Jones County, 118
Jones, Edmund, 75
Jones, Col. H. B., 271
Jones, J. B., 161
Jones, J. H., 306
Jones, J. William, 302
Jones, Nathaniel, 75
Jones, Pride, 88, 107, 109, 119-120, 136, 186, 333, 352, 357
Jones, Sarah, 70
Jones, Thomas, 43
Jones, Tignal, 75
Jones, Troy E., 302
Jones, Willie, 65, 69, 70, 74, 75, 78
Jordan, B. Everett, 267
Journalism School, 153
Junior Order of United American Mechanics, 321
Junto Academy, 137

Kalb, Baron de, 49
Kale Knitting Mill, 281
Kelly, John, 104
Kemble, Elizabeth L., 164
Kennedy, G. C., 276
Ker (Kerr), David, 82, 372

INDEX

Kerr, Daniel W., 137
Kernodle, J. F., 308
Kidder, Maurice Arthur, 293
Kilpatrick, Samuel, 101
Kimbrough, Marmaduke, 15, 19, 22, 167
Kinchen, John, 42, 43, 45, 345, 346, 348
King, Nathan J., 88
King's Mountain, Battle of, 52
Kinston, 28
Kirk, Jack, 245
Kirkland, John, 132
Kirkland, John M., 21
Kirkland, John U., 181, 187, 193, 274, 346, 358, 367
Kirkland, William W., 110, 125, 132, 196, 272, 358
Kirkland-Webb and Co., 272
Knights of King David, 321
Knights of King Solomon, 321
Knights of Pythias, 321
Ku Klux Klan, 116-119
Kyser, Kay, 148

Lacy, D., 137
Ladies Aid Societies, 111
Lady Mary, 148
Lady Rose, 148
Lambeth, J. H., 301
Land, classified by slope, 8
Land valuations, 188-190, 201-202
Lane, Joel, 43, 67
Lark, John, 43
Latta Cooperative Dairy, 242
Latta Grove Baptist Church, 306, 315-316
Latta, Joseph W., 120
Latta, Lantham, 245
Latta, Milton, 261
Laughlin, Hugh, 269
Lawrence, George H., 210-211, 249
Laws, George, 119, 193, 333, 357
Laws, John, 193, 217, 333, 357
Lawson, John, 11-13
League of Good Templars, 321
Leathers, James S., 108
Leathers, John B., 88
Lebanon township, 19, 194
Lebanon Methodist Church, 297, 315-316
Lederer, John, 10-12
Lee County, 17
Lee, Lt. Col. Henry "Light Horse Harry," 56, 57
Lee's Chapel Baptist Church, 306, 315-316
Leigh, John, 74
Lenoir county, 118
Lenoir, William, 72
Lewis, George, 102
Lewis, Henry B., 297-299

Library service, 215
Lincoln, Abraham, 107
Lincoln, Maj. Gen. Benjamin, 49
Lindley, Jonathon, 16, 65, 66, 348-349, 354
Lindley, Thomas, 33, 269
Lindley's Mill, 60
Link, Silas M., 194
Lipscombe Grove Baptist Church, 307, 315-316
Literary Fund of state, 138, 146
Little River, 6, 15, 48-49, 269, 295, 315-316
Little River Presbyterian Church, 295, 315-316
Little River township, 1, 49, 200-201, 203-205, 207
Littlefield, Milton S., 115
Livestock, 231-232, 236, 241-247
Livestock Auction Market, 246-247
Lloyd, Braxton B., 333
Lloyd, Lueca, 283
Lloyd, Thomas, 15, 30, 32, 282, 333, 345
Lockhart, John P., 109
Lockhart, J. L., 222
Lockhart, S. P., 141
Lockhart, William, 347
Log College, 146
Long, J. W., 161-162
Long Meadow, 135, 160
Long Meadow Dairies, 242
Long, O. F., 21
Lovelatty (Loveletter), 167, 289
Lowrie, H. B., 109
Lucas farm, 6
Lutherans, 311-312
Lynch, Lemuel, 22, 188, 193, 333, 368
Lynch, Thomas, 181
Lyon, John, 88
Lytle, Archibald, 64, 347

Macay, Spruce, 69, 79, 81
MacDonald, Brig. Gen. Donald, 44
Maclaine, Archibald, 43, 50, 65
MacNider, W. de B., 163
McAden, Hugh, 294-295
McCabe, John, 45, 46, 68, 350
McCauley, George, 110
McCauley, Matthew, 76, 96, 303
McCauley, William, 65, 76, 85, 148, 173, 175-176, 178, 306, 348-350, 354-355
McClellan, John, 174
McCorkle, Samuel Eusebius, 69, 80, 81, 82
McCoy, S. G., 308
McDade, Charlie, 211
McDade, Patterson, 88, 184
McDaniel, Eli, 173
McDonald, John, 33
McDowell, Joseph, 65

McDuffie, J. F., 302
McDuffie Memorial Baptist Church, 302, 315-316
McGavran, E. G., 164
McGee, John, 168
McMannen, John A., 270
McMillan, Alexander, 48
McMullen, Robert J., 295
McNair, Ralph, 42, 271, 345
McNeil, Col. Hector, 22, 59, 60
McQueen, Hugh, 129
McVey, John, 33
Mack, George, 174
Maddock, Joseph, 23
Maddock's Mill, 30
Maddry, Abel, 196
Maddry, Charles E., 141, 143, 301
Maddry, W. A., 200, 202
Mallet, Sally, 104
Mangum, A. W., 320
Mangum, Charles S., 163
Mangum, Priestly, 85, 136, 333, 350
Mangum township, 19, 194
Mangum, Willie P., 84, 85, 87, 88, 91, 92, 100, 137, 191, 333, 347, 350-351, 360
Manley J. R., 305-306
Manning, Isaac H., 163-165
Manumission Society, 104
Marcom, Chadles, 184
Marion, Brig. Gen. Francis, 62
Mark Creek, 16
Marrow, H. B., 145
Mars Hill Baptist Church, 292, 301, 315-316
Marshal, John, 91
Marshall, Abraham, 305
Martin, Alexander, 50, 60, 61, 62, 63, 68, 69
Martin, Charles, 308
Martin, Josiah, 24, 37-38, 42, 44, 54, 289
Martin, William J., 110, 167, 334
Mason, A., 125, 273
Mason Farm, 10
Mason Hall, 137
Mason Hall Eagle Hotel, 273
Mason, J. P., 301
Mason, Randall C., Jr., 303
Masonic Lodge, Eagle of Hillsboro, 21; University Lodge of Chapel Hill, 21, 301, 318-320.
Masset, William, 30
Masterton, R. C., 293
Matheson, Don S., 213-214, 249
Mattox, W. T., 212
Maxwell, Henry, 174
Meade, William, 104
Mebane, 10, 209, 278-281
Mebane, Alexander, 14, 23, 46, 60, 63, 65, 66, 67, 68, 72, 75, 77, 79, 81, 83, 84, 96, 168, 173, 280, 289, 334, 345, 348-349, 354-355, 360
Mebane, Benjamin F., 187
Mebane Chapel of Hillsboro, 308, 317
Mebane Congregational Christian Church, 303, 315-316
Mebane, Frank, 279
Mebane, Giles, 88, 351-352
Mebane, James, 84, 85, 86, 90, 93, 102, 334, 346, 349-350, 355
Mebane Lumber Co., 281
Mebane-Royal Co., 280
Mebane School District, 209
Mebaneville Depot, 134
Mecklenburg county, 29, 32, 34
Medical Care Study Commission, 163
Medical Examiners, 159-160
Medicine, 153-155, 157
Mendenhall, Mary, 135
Merrimon, A. S., 120
Methodist Churches, 296-299, 302, 307
Methodist Episcopal Church of Philadelphia, 304
Methodists, 123, 300
Mickle, Andrew, 184, 196, 357, 364-366
Micklejohn, George, 44, 290, 293, 334
Miers, William, 19
Militia, Orange County, 44, 49, 52, 53, 58-59, 60, 62, 66
Miller, Jesse, 110
Milton, 184
Minute Men, 42
Misenheimer, K. M., 295
Mitchell, Andrew, 166, 289
Mitchell, Elisha, 98, 128, 148, 295, 334-335
Mize, Edd, 309
Moffitt, William, 35
Mohler, R. L., 254
Monogram Club, 284
Monro, James, 174
Montgomery, William, 335
Moore, Alfred, 61, 70, 74, 77, 78, 79, 80
Moore, David, 105
Moore, James (Col.), 43
Moore, Joseph, 183
Moore, M. W., 202
Moore, Maurice, 35, 37
Moore, Stephen, 136, 181, 185, 335
Moore, William, 44, 45, 63
Moore, William H., 161
Montgomery, Daniel A., 88
Montgomery, William, 15, 85, 86, 87, 88, 89, 90, 350, 354, 360
Morehead, James T., 89
Morehead, John M., 89
Morehead Planetarium, 153
Morgan Creek, 6, 10, 15-16, 76, 148

INDEX 383

Morgan, Brig. Gen. Daniel, 52
Morgan, Hardy, 76, 96
Morgan, Henry A., 301
Morgan, J. L., 312
Morgan, John, 16
Morgan, Mark, 15-16, 76, 95, 148, 167, 289, 345
Morris, Robert F., 193
Morrissey, Francis J., 310
Morrison, Fred W., 145
Morphis, Sam, 99, 105
Morrow, E. Graham, 110
Morrow, George W., 136
Mosby, T. M., 307
Moser, E. R., 145
Motes Creek, 268
Mounair, John, 174
Mount Adar Baptist Church, 301, 315-316
Mount Bright Baptist Church of Hillsboro, 306, 317
Mount Carmel Baptist Church, 300, 315-316
Mount Carmel Home Demonstration Club, 257
Mount Collier, 2
Mount Gilead Baptist Church, 307, 315-316
Mount Hermon Baptist Church, 301, 315-316
Mount Moriah Baptist Church, col., 307, 315-316
Mount Moriah Baptist Church, w., 301, 315-316
Mount Olive Baptist Church of Efland, 306, 317
Mount Pleasant Academy, 137
Mount Repose, 134
Mount Sinai Baptist Church, 305, 315-316
Mount Zion Association, 300
Mount Zion Congregational Christian Church, 303, 315-316
Munch, H. F., 145
Murphey, Archibald De Bow, 70, 73, 80, 84, 85, 88, 90, 91, 102, 125, 146, 335, 347, 350
Murphey School, 141, 146
Murray, William, 21, 45

Nash, Abner, 49, 50, 52
Nash, Francis, 23, 27, 32-33, 42-43, 47, 125, 137, 169, 335, 345, 357, 367
Nash, Frederick, 84, 85, 86, 88, 90, 91, 335-336, 346-347
Nash, Henry K., 88, 107
Nash, William, 84, 347, 367
Nash-Kollock Boarding School, 137
National Grange Community Service Contest, 260
Nation, Christopher, 35
Naval R.O.T.C., 153
Navy Pre-Flight School, 153

Navy V-12, 153
Neal, William B., 285
Negro churches, 304-307
Negro schools, 139-143
Nelson, William, 181
Neuse River Soil Conservation District, 253-254
Neville, Jesse, 78, 303
New Bern, 20, 28-29, 36-37, 41-42, 47, 64, 90, 147, 169, 174
New Bethel Methodist Church, 298, 315-316
New Hanover County, 318
New Hope (Chapel Hill), 48, 49, 58, 74, 75, 147-148, 167
New Hope Chapel, 174, 190
New Hope Community, 260
New Hope Creek, 6, 14-15
New Hope Grange, 260
New Hope Presbyterian Church, 294-295, 315-316
Newlin, James, 268
Newlin, Jonathan, 268
Newlin, John, 267-269
New Sharon Methodist Church, 245, 297, 315-316
Newman, William, 183
News of Orange County, 128, 142
Newspapers in Orange County, 124-129
Nichols, John, 173, 355, 368
Nichols, Richeson, 21
Noble, M. C. S., 274
Norfolk Herald, quoted, 126
North Carolina B'nai B'rith Hillel Foundation, 311, 317
North Carolina Board of Public Charities, 209
North Carolina *Democrat*, (Hillsboro), 127
North Carolina Department of Agriculture, 2
North Carolina Experiment Station, 237
North Carolina Gazette, 20, 47
North Carolina Gazette of Hillsboro, 124
North Carolina Journal, 78, 79
North Carolina Memorial Hospital, 157, 164
North Carolina Railroad, 134, 278
North Carolina State College of Agriculture and Engineering, 152, 259
North Carolina Yearly Meeting of Friends, 291
Norwood, John W., 119-120, 132, 137, 229-230, 335-336
Norwood, Walter A., 161
Norwood, William, 125, 132, 293, 336, 347
Nunn, William, 33, 306, 355
Nunn's Chapel Baptist Church, 306, 315-316
Nursing, 153-155

Oak Grove Baptist Church, 302, 315-316

Oak Grove Holiness Church of Hillsboro, 309, 317
Oakley, Ernest, 304
Oaks, 134
O'Bryant's A.M.E. Zion Church, 307, 317
Occoneechee Farm, 247
Occoneechee (Occaneechee) Indians, 12, 17, 19
Occoneechee Lodge, 321
Occoneechee mountain, 2
Odd Fellows, order of, 321
Odum, Howard, 242
O'Kelly, James, 302-303
Old East, 318
"old field" schools, 130-131
Oldham, S. W., 302
Oldham, Thomas D., 181, 188
Olmsted, Denison, 336
Oneal, John, 35
O'Neal, Peter, 45
O'Neil, Col. William, 56, 96
Orange Chapel Methodist Church, 298, 315-316
Orange County Conservation Committees, 251
Orange County losses in Civil War, 110
Orange County Observer, 127
Orange County, organized, 17, 162, 166, 318, 341-343
Orange County Recorder's Court, 219
Orange County Training School, 143-144
Orange Cross Roads Baptist Church, 306, 315-316
Orange District, 175
Orange Factory, 200
Orange Furniture Craftsmen, 277, 279
Orange Grove Community, 245, 250, 260
Orange Hosiery Mill, 278
Orange Methodist Church, 297, 315-316
Orange Presbytery, 48, 294
Orange Printshop, 285
Orange Rural Fire Department, 263
Oxford, 3, 19

Pacific Mills, 283
Paine, John, 45
Paisley, Samuel, 295
Paisley, William, 135
Palmer Grove Methodist Church, 299, 315-316
Paper Mill, 47, 124
Parent Teachers Associations, 262
Parham, K. W., 222
Parish, Calvin E., 120
Parish of St. Matthew, 17, 289
Parker, D. S., 200
Parker, Harrison, 21, 181
Parker, J. Roy, 128
Parks, David C., 193, 197

Parrish, D. C., 186, 215
Parrish (Parish), William K., 109
Partridge, Isaac C., 128
Pasquotank county, 26
Pasturage, 240-241
Patent, B. C., 200
Patillo, Henry, 294-295, 336
Patridge, I. C., 273
Patterson, David, 104
Patterson, George, 88
Patterson, I. N., 16, 96, 97
Patterson, James, 78, 79
Patterson, John, 167, 174, 289
Patterson, Mark, 348
Patterson, Quentin, 254
Patterson, R. A.
Patterson township, 19, 194
Patterson, W. N., 107-108, 121, 193, 196
Payne, William, 35
Paynes Chapel A.M.E. Church, 305, 315-316
Peace, A. W., 274
Peabody Fund, 195
Pell, R. P., 128
Penn, John, 19, 50
Pennsylvania, 14, 290-291, 294, 299
Pentecostal Holiness Church, 308
Peoples Bank (Chapel Hill), 274
Perkins, Thomas H., 67, 96, 354
Perquimans county, 26
Perquimans river, 299
Person county, 17-19, 45
Person, Thomas, 43, 72, 183
Peter, Jesse, 305
Peters, Lucy, 105
Pharmacy, School of, 153, 157
Phelps, J. L., 237
Philadelphia Charity Hospital, 160
Phillips, Charles, 151, 184, 295, 336
Phillip's Female School, 137
Phillips, James, 137, 295, 336
Phillips, Samuel F., 88, 108-109, 120, 337, 346, 354
Phipps, L. J., 288
Physical characteristics of county, 1-9
Pickard, John H., 135
Pickens, Brig. Gen, Andrew, 56, 57
Piedmont Packing Co., 244, 276-277
Pilgrim Holiness Churches, 307
Pilgrim Holiness Church of West Hillsboro, 308, 315-316
Pilmore, Joseph, 297
Piney Ford, 19, 22, 167, 169
Piney Grove Baptist Church, 306, 315-316
Pirtle, George, 301
Pitman, John, 289
Pittman, John, 167
Pittsboro, N. C., 59, 74

Pittsborough Academy, 134
Plank Roads, 183-184
Pleasant Green Methodist Church, 298, 315-316
Plumer, William S., 137
Pogue, E. J., 271
Pole Cat Creek, 15
Polk, James K., 98
Polk, Thomas, 50, 69
Poll taxes, 21, 29, 171-172
Poly, Max, 295
Pool, John, 107
Pool, Solomon, 104, 320, 327, 372
Poor relief, 185-189, 195-196
Population Statistics, 24, 26, 122, 344
Porter, William, 72
Poultry and eggs, 236, 244-245
Powell, E. M., 303
Powell, Elias, 45
Pratt, Alfred, 306
Pratt, Joseph Hyde, 207
Pratt, Loftin K., 88
Presbyterian Church of Chapel Hill, 295, 317
Presbyterians, 25, 123, 294-295, 317
Presidents of UNC., 152
Prestwood Creek, 15
Price, David, 125
Primitive Baptists, 303
Prince Hall Masons, 321
Pritchard, Birdie, 143
Pritchard, Isaac, 283
Pritchard, W. N., 320
Pritchard's mill, 300
Pritchett, William, 265
Privy Council, 28, 37
Production and Marketing Administration, 250-252
Professional schools at UNC., 152-153
Proffit, G. T., 141
Progressive education, 135
Progressive Education Association, 135
Property valuations, 122, 226
Prospect Hill, 137
Protestant Episcoapl Churches, 292-293
Providence Meeting House, 18
Provincial Congress, North Carolina, 41, 42, 45, 46, 47
Pryor, John, 20, 35, 345
Public education during Civil War and Reconstruction, 138-139
Public Health, 153-155, 157, 215-217
Public school statistics, 139
Public school system established, 137-138
Public Welfare Work, 209-213
Public Works Administration, 224
Pugh, William, 285
Purefoy, George W., 301

Pyle, Dr. John, 44, 56

Quakers, 16, 25, 291-292, 294, 317

Radio, 153
Rainey, William, 173, 175
Rains, William, 174
Raleigh, 81, 152, 158, 162
Raleigh *Register*, quoted, 132-134, 136
Ramsay, Ambrose, 43, 47
Randolph county, 16-18, 300
Rankin, S. M., 295
Ray, David, 84, 347, 349, 355, 367
Ray, Frank, 277
Ray, Gilbert W., 222
Ray, John, 173
Ray, W. M., 306
Reckard, Charles H., 295
Reconstruction, 140, 192-198
Reed, James, 174
Reeves, Thomas, 303
Register of Deeds, 217-218, 357
Regulators, 17-18, 20, 24-40, 171, 217, 291, 295
Reid, Capt., 59
Reid, David S., 87
Reinhardt, R. A., 285
Reitzel, Walter, 237
Religion, 153
Reorganization Act of 1877, 199
Republican Methodists, 297, 302
Republican party, 113-115, 117
Revolution, American, 176-178, 290-292, 294, 297, 310
Rhodes, W. H., 145
Rice, Thomas, 174
Richardson, Charles, 173
Richardson, W. P., 216
Richmond, Virginia, 64
Roads, 24, 182-185, 200-201, 203-205, 209
Road overseers, 182
Roberson, Foy, 143
Roberson, Nellie, 143
Roberts, Clyde, 237
Roberts, James, 203
Roberts, Oliver, 259
Robinson, David, 174
Rochester, Nathaniel, 20, 44, 45, 46, 47, 48, 68, 173-175, 271, 337, 345, 357
Rockfish-Mebane Yarn Mills, 281
Rock Hill Baptist Church, 305
Rock Spring Baptist Church, 300
Rockingham county, 17-18
Rocky River Baptist Church, 300
Rogers, John, 133
Rogers, Michael, 43
Rolston, David W., 307
Roman Catholic Church, 309-310, 312

386 INDEX

Rosemary Street, 148
Rosenzweig, Efraim M., 311
Ross, William, 174
Rougemont, 237
Roundtree, J. M., 307
Rourk, Dr. M. H., 216
Rowan County, 17, 29, 32, 36-37, 291
Rowan, Matthew, 168
Roxboro, 184
Royal-Borden Manufacturing Co., 280
Royster, Hubert A., 159
Rudisill, D. P., 312
Ruffin, Allen J., 275
Ruffin, R. B., 187
Ruffin, Thomas, 84, 86, 88, 89, 90, 91, 92, 97, 102, 112, 119, 125, 191, 293, 337, 346-348
Rural Electrification, 249, 256
Rural Progress Program, 257, 263
Russell, Elizabeth, 133
Rutherford, Gen. Griffith, 44
Rutledge, John, 52

St. Aloph's District, 175
St. John's College (Oxford), 319
St. Joseph C.M.E. Church of Chapel Hill, 307, 317
St. Mark's District, 175
St. Mary's Chapel, 290, 293, 315-316
St. Mary's District, 175
St. Mary's Community, 260
St. Mary's Grange, 26
St. Mary's Home Demonstration Club, 257
St. Mathew's Church, 49, 51, 63, 170, 289, 293
St. Paul A.M.E. Church, 304, 317
St. Thomas District, 175
Salisbury, 20, 50, 52, 174
Sanders, Wiley B., 210
Sandy Creek, 15, 300
Sandy Creek Association, 300
Saunders, James, 45
Saunders, Joseph H., 110
Saunders, Romulus M., 84, 90
Saunders, William L., 110, 117
Saxapahaw Community, 266-267, 269
Saxapahaw (Shackery, Shakeri, Sheccoree, Sissipihaw) Indians, 11-12
Scarlett, R. E., 302
Schley Community, 260
Schley Grange, 260
Schools, 24, 181-182, 189, 194, 200, 202, 209, 223-227
School bus transportation, 142-143
School of Dentistry, 157, 164
School of Education, 153
School of Library Science, 153
School of Medicine, 155, 157, 162-165, 216

School of Nursing, 164, 216
School of Public Health, 153, 164, 216
School statistics, 140, 145, 194, 223-227
School superintendents, 140-141
Schoolfield, L. D., 161
Scofield, S. D., 104
Scotch Highlanders, 15
Scotch-Irish, 14-15, 25, 294
Scott, Edward M., 109
Scott, John, 84, 85, 132, 346-348, 367
Scott, W. Kerr, 154
Scurlock, Mial, 43
Sears-Roebuck Foundation, 243
Secession movement, 107-108
Secession ordinance repudiated, 109
Second Baptist Church of Chapel Hill, 306, 317
Sellars, Charles V., 267
Sellars Manufacturing Co., 267
Sentinel, 121
Settle, Thomas, 120
Seymour, Horatio, 120
Sexton, K. B., 298
Sharp, Peter, 15
Sharpe, William, 69
Shaw, Lemuel, 91
Shaw, Robert C., 274
Shearer, John B., 295
Sheaf, Clifford, 298
Shields, John, 46, 269
Shields, Robert, 269
Shelburne, Earl of, 20, 32
Sheppard, William, 65, 84, 96, 349
Sheriffs, 26-28, 170-172, 174-178, 180, 219-220, 355-356
Sherman, William T., 112
Sides, L. R., 145
Sidwell, John, 19
Sims, Herbert, 86
Sitgreaves, John, 73
Slaves, 95, 96, 97, 98, 99, 100, 101, 102, 103, 104, 105, 106, 109, 172, 177, 179-181, 297, 300, 305
Smith, Benjamin, 72, 73
Smith, Capt. Fred, 282
Smith, J. H., 306
Smith, James S., 21, 84, 85, 86, 90, 136, 337, 354, 360
Smith, Peter, 174
Smith, Samuel, 43
Smith, Sidney, 88
Smith, Ted H., 277
Smithfield, N. C., 64, 74
Snotherly, Philip, 15
Social Work, 153
Soil Conservation Service, 228, 251, 253-254
Soil erosion in Orange County, 7

INDEX 387

Soil Survey of Orange County, 1-2
Soil Types of Orange County, 2-3, 228, 251, 253-254
Sorrel, Timothy, 167
South Building (UNC), 318
South Carolina, 29, 290, 299
South Carolina, *Plan of Regulation*, 39
"South Ireland," 15
South Lowell, 270
Southerland Dyeing and Finishing Mills, 281
Southern Baptist Convention, 300
Spaight, Richard Dobbs, 65, 73, 78
Spanhour, William, 102
Sparrow, Thomas E., 356
Spear, Maria L., 136
Spencer, Cornelia Phillips, 77, 106, 111, 127, 337-338
Spencer, Samuel, 65
Spurgeon, J. S., 274
Stanbury, W. A., 298
Standfield, William H., 306
Stanford, C. W., 254
Stanford, Richard, 83, 84, 338, 360
State Board of Charities and Public Welfare, 209
State Board of Health, 215-216
State Comptroller, 180
State Constitution of 1863, 113
State conventions of 1865 and 1866, 112
State Literary Fund, 185
State Medical Society, 157-159, 161-162, 164-165
Stearns, Shubael, 300
Steel, John, 64, 173
Stevens, B. A., 145
Stewart, James A., 306
Stinking Quarter Creek, 15-16
Stockard, James, 15
Stockard, John, 85, 88
Stokes, John, 72
Stone, David, 75
Stoney Creek, 15
Strayhorn, Gilbert, 15, 295
Streams of Orange county, 6
Strowd, Annie, 212
Strowd, Bruce, 211, 282
Strowd, H. M., 190
Strowd, Ned, 305-306
Strowd, T. W., 303
Strowd, William F., 338, 361
Strudwick, Edmund, 120, 159-161, 165, 184, 338
Strudwick, Frederick N., 113, 116
Strudwick, James, 319
Strudwick, Samuel, 14
Strudwick, Shepherd, 275, 320

Strudwick, William F., 16, 67, 84, 338, 349, 354, 360, 367
Stubbins, Joseph, 183
Sunday Schools, 130-131
Sumner, Dr. G. H., 216
Superintendents of schools, 181
Superior Court, 192, 196, 357
Supreme Court and education, 195
Sutherland, Ransom, 29
Sutphin Mill (Lindley's Mill), 269
Sutton, Thomas D., 303
Swain, David L., 99, 148, 150, 295, 338-339, 372
Swepsonville, 11
Swine, 243-244

Tarboro, 64, 66, 318
Tar Heel (The), 129
Tar Heel Hosiery Mill, 278
Tarleton, Banastre, 49, 52, 56, 57, 58
Tate, Joseph, 167, 289
Tate, Mark, 188
Tatom (Tatum), Absalom, 65, 66, 83, 84, 339, 347, 354, 360
Taxes, 176-183, 185-186, 188-190, 197-202, 204-205, 209
Taylor, James C., 274
Taylor, John, 20, 51, 96, 347, 357, 367
Taylor, Joseph, 43
Taylor, Thomas, 173-175
Temple of Truth, 309, 315-316
Terrell Creek Baptist Church, 305, 315-316
Tew, Charles C., 110, 339
Textiles, 275-276, 281
Thackston, James, 29, 32, 43, 339
Thompson, Enoch, 186
Thompson, Henry, 183, 348
Thompson, John, 43, 84, 141, 200, 202, 349
Thompson, Joseph, 45
Thompson, L. S., 303
Thompson, Lawrence, 19, 168, 355
Thompson, Theophilus, 183
Thompson, Thomas B., 279
Thompson, W. B., 128
Thompson, W. E., 274
Thurman, William R., 296
Tilden, Samuel J., 120
Tillman, Roger, 84
Tinnin, Hugh, 45
Tobacco industry, 18, 234, 235-236, 271
Tompkins, S. G., 304, 307
Tories, 22, 39
Tourgée, Albion W., 115
Tower Hill, 28
Townships, 192-194, 202-203
Trading Path, 10, 19
Trinity College Historical Society Papers, 124

388 INDEX

Trollinger, Adam, 15
Trollinger, Benjamin, 88
Trotter's Creek, 104
Trustees of UNC., 148
Tryon District, 175
Tryon, William, 17, 20, 22, 29, 31-38, 289
Turner, John, 193, 355
Turner, Josiah, Jr., 88, 107-109, 113, 120-121, 354, 361
Turner, R. C., 309
Turner, Thomas H., 161
Turrentine, J. A., 190
Tyrrell county, 26
Tyson, M. D., 299
Tyson, M. E., 298
Twining, Hugh, 173

Umstead, John, 93, 346
Umstead, John W., 353-354
Umstead, S. D., 109, 352
Union Academy, 137
Union Grove Methodist Church, 298, 315-316
Union League, 112-115, 117
Union School, 135
Unitarian Fellowship of Chapel Hill, 312, 317
United Congregational Christian Church of Chapel Hill, 303, 317
United Holy Church of America, 308-309
University Hospital, 153, 216
University Hotel, 273
University Lake, 6
University *Magazine* (The), 129
University Methodist Church of Chapel Hill, 298, 317
University of North Carolina, 6, 10-11, 69-82, 88, 98, 99, 104, 133, 140, 143, 146-156, 209, 284, 310, 318
University of North Carolina Library, 125
University of North Carolina Press, 152
University of Penna., 159-160
U. S. Department of Agriculture, 2
Upshaw, R. L., 304

Vanatta, E. S., quoted, 1-5, 213
Van Buren, Martin, 85
Vance, Zebulon B., 108, 120, 268
Venable, Francis P., 140, 152, 283, 339, 372
Venable, John Manning, 143
Venable, Louise Manning, 143
Vestry Acts, 289

Waddell, Alfred Moore, 339-340
Waddell, Hugh, 85, 88, 340, 346, 350-351, 368
Waddell, Jobe, 304
Wade, George, 308
Wade's Temple, of Efland, 308, 317
Wake county, 17, 19-20, 43, 67, 75, 344
Wake Court House, 58, 66

Walker, H. G., 306
Walker Brothers Grist Mill, 271
Wall, Henry, 101
Walnut Grove, school at, 135
Walnut Grove Methodist Church, 298, 315-316
Walters, Carl, 259
Walton Lumber Co., 281
Ward, Ira A., 222
Wardens of the poor, 185-186
Washington, Gen. George, 52
Watkins, V. G., 248
Watson, Eli F., 319
Watson, James, 19-20, 30, 46, 120, 167, 169, 289, 340, 357, 367
Watson, John H., 364
Watson, Jones, 193, 196, 297, 364
Watts, Josiah, 367
Watts, Thomas D., 180, 183, 355
Wayne county, 118
Webb and Douglas Cotton Factory, 270
Webb, Henry Y., 89
Webb, James, 86, 102, 119, 132, 137, 158-159, 275-276, 319, 354
Webb, J. D., 274
Webb, Joseph C., 110, 116
Webb, O. K., Jr., 302
Webb, Robert F., 109-110, 270
Webb, T. Norfleet, 275
Webb, William, 161
Weidinger, John A., 310
Welsh settlers, 16, 25
Wesley Chapel, 296
West Hill Baptist Church of West Hillsboro, 302, 317
West Hillsboro school, 141
West, John, 168
Whigs, 89
White Brotherhood, 116
White and Blue (The), 129
White, Charles, 15
White Cross, 207, 260-262
White Cross A.M.E. Church, 304, 315-316
White Cross School, 141
White, Dave, 279
White Furniture Co. (Hillsboro Branch), 277
White Furniture Co. (Mebane), 279-280
White, Hugh L., 85
White, James W., 267
White, J. Sam, 279
White Oak Grove Baptist Church, 306, 315-316
White Rock Church, 309, 315-316
White, Stephen A., 279
White, W. N., 306
White, Will, 279
White-Williamson and Co., 267

Whitehead, John, 183
Whitehead, Richard H., 163
Whitehead, William, 183
Whitfield, J. R., 241
Whitted, Henry, 16, 96
Whitted, Jehu, 97
Whitted Tobacco Company, 271
Whitted, William, 132, 367
Wiggers, C. C., 298
Wildman, W. D., 274
Wiley, Calvin H., 138
Wiley, P. H., 308-309
Wilhelm, S. M., 296
Wilkerson, Harris, 181
Wilkinson, Lemuel, 271
William III (of Orange), 17
William, W. H., 306
Williams, A. Morris, 297
Williams-Borough, N. C., 74, 81
Williams, James, 16, 357
Williams, John, 17, 36, 45, 60, 73, 77, 81, 167
Williams, Richard, 183
Williams, William, 45

Williamson, Hugh, 69, 72
Williamson, J. E., 161
Williamson, John L., 267
Williamson, J. W., 109
Williamson, John G. A., 85
Wilmington, 20, 24, 28, 52, 58, 60-61, 318
Wilson, Logan, 154
Wilson, Miss Sallie, 143
Winston, Francis D., 128
Winston, George T., 152
Witherspoon, J., 125, 132-133, 295
Witherspoon, John, Private Boarding School, 136
Woody's Ferry, 135
World War II, 153, 155
Worth, Jonathan, 89, 109

Yancey, Bartlett, 89
Yanceyville, 120, 184
Yarbrough, D., 273
Yates Association, 300
Yates, David W., 293
York, Robinson, 44

www.ingramcontent.com/pod-product-compliance
Lightning Source LLC
Chambersburg PA
CBHW051416290426
44109CB00016B/1316